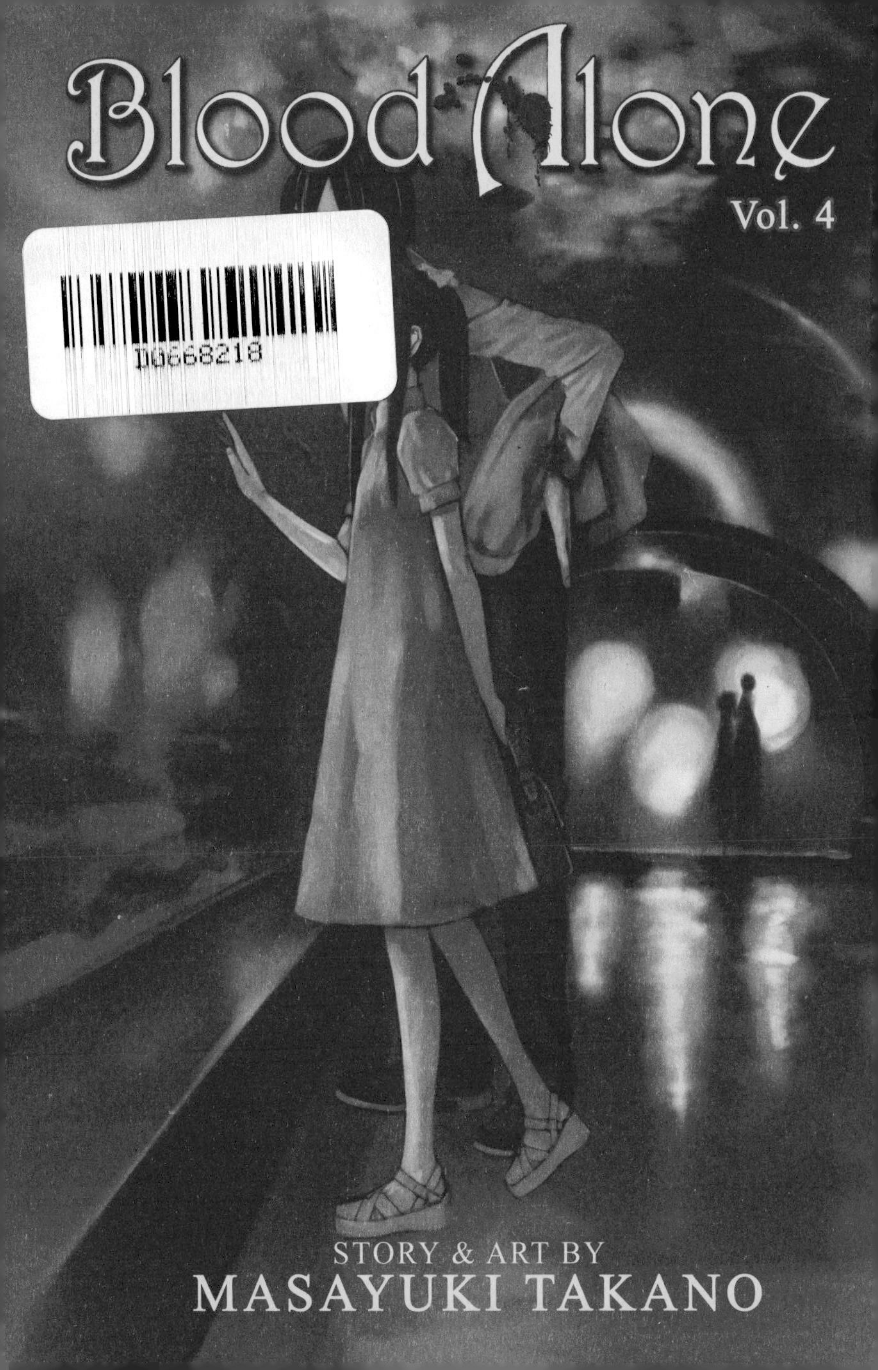
Blood Alone
Vol. 4
STORY & ART BY
MASAYUKI TAKANO

Blood Alone

VOLUME 4

story & art by Masayuki Takano

STAFF CREDITS

translation	Nan Rymer
adaptation	Shannon Fay
lettering	Roland Amago
layout	Bambi Eloriaga-Amago
cover design	Nicky Lim
copy editor	Shanti Whitesides
editor	Adam Arnold
publisher	Jason DeAngelis
	Seven Seas Entertainment

ISBN: 978-1-934876-86-2

Printed in Canada

First Printing: September 2011

10 9 8 7 6 5 4 3 2 1

FOLLOW US ONLINE: www.gomanga.com

READING DIRECTIONS

This book reads from *right to left*, Japanese style. If this is your first time reading manga, you start reading from the top right panel on each page and take it from there. If you get lost, just follow the numbered diagram here. It may seem backwards at first, but you□ll get the hang of it! Have fun!!

Contents

Episode 20
LONDON WALTZ
The Princess in the Mist

GLOSSARY

Absorbire Vampire cannibalism, absorption

Aruhiek An elder vampire

Aruta Special powers possessed by an Aruhiek.

Adevaraht Kurai The Eyes That See the Truth

Blood Clan A clan of vampires that share the
same bloodline

Farumek Glamour, a hypnotic trance used to bend
a person to a vampire's will

Insegrod Sparuda The Crimson Blade

Noursarit To be reborn as a vampire

Orphan A vampire with no clan

Renfield Vampire servant or thrall

Straruda The element in a vampire's blood that
gives them their powers

Sinacolda A Renfield's master, a vampire who has
shared its blood with a Renfield

Vanatoare A vampire hunter or slayer

Blood Alone

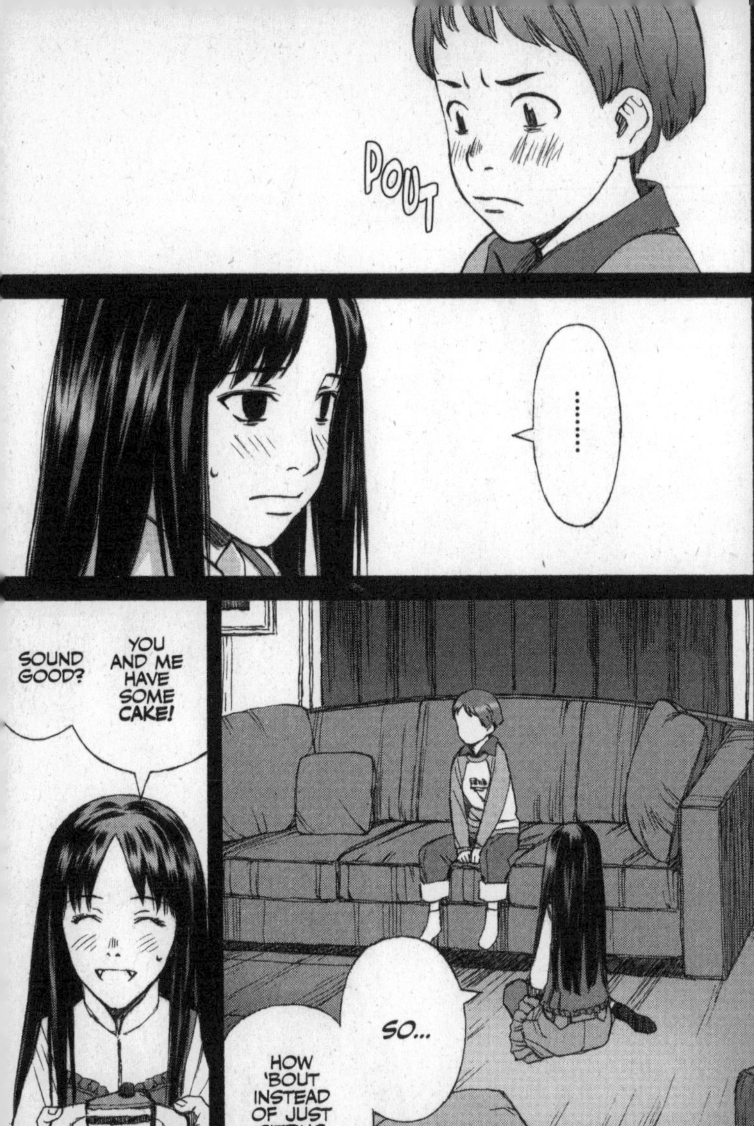
POUT
......
SO...
HOW 'BOUT INSTEAD OF JUST SITTING THERE...
YOU AND ME HAVE SOME CAKE!
SOUND GOOD?

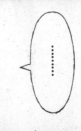

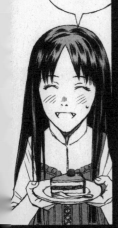

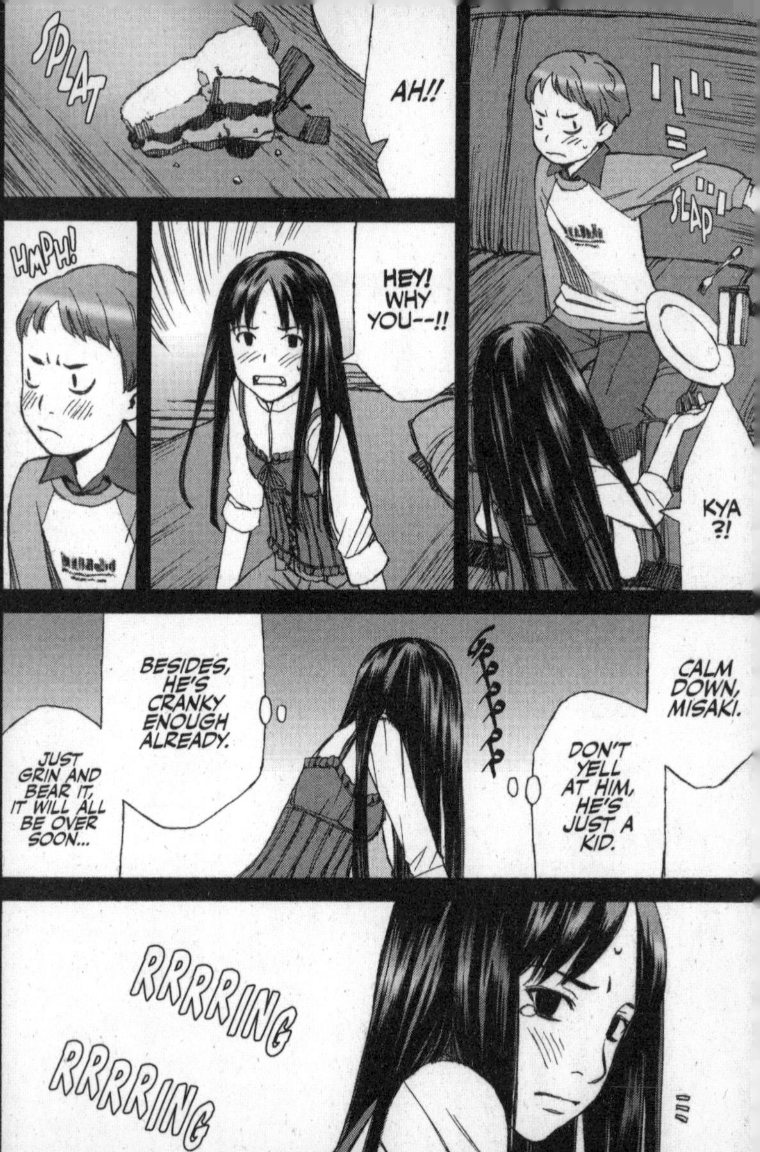
SLAP
KYA ?!
SPLAT
AH!!
HEY! WHY YOU--!!
HMPH!
CALM DOWN, MISAKI.
DON'T YELL AT HIM, HE'S JUST A KID.
BESIDES, HE'S CRANKY ENOUGH ALREADY.
JUST GRIN AND BEAR IT, IT WILL ALL BE OVER SOON...
RRRRING
RRRRING

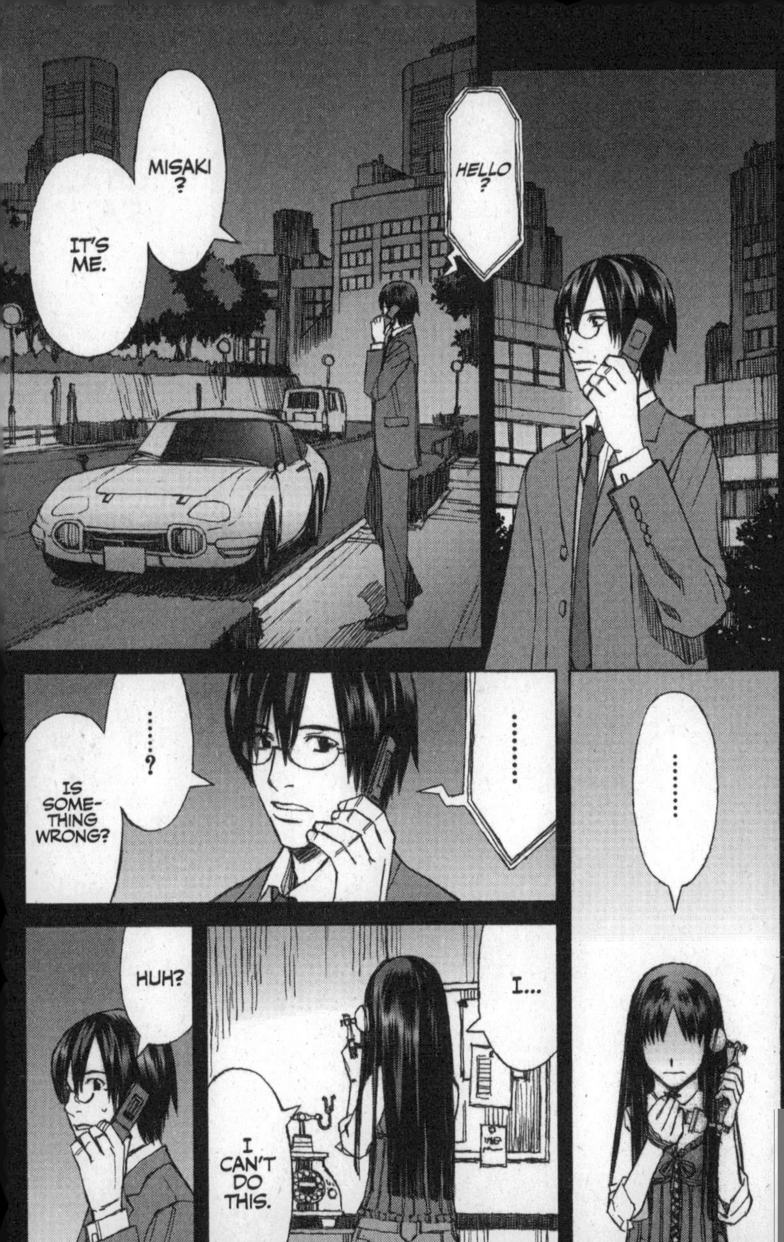
HELLO?
MISAKI?
IT'S ME.
....
....
....?
IS SOMETHING WRONG?
I...
I CAN'T DO THIS.
HUH?

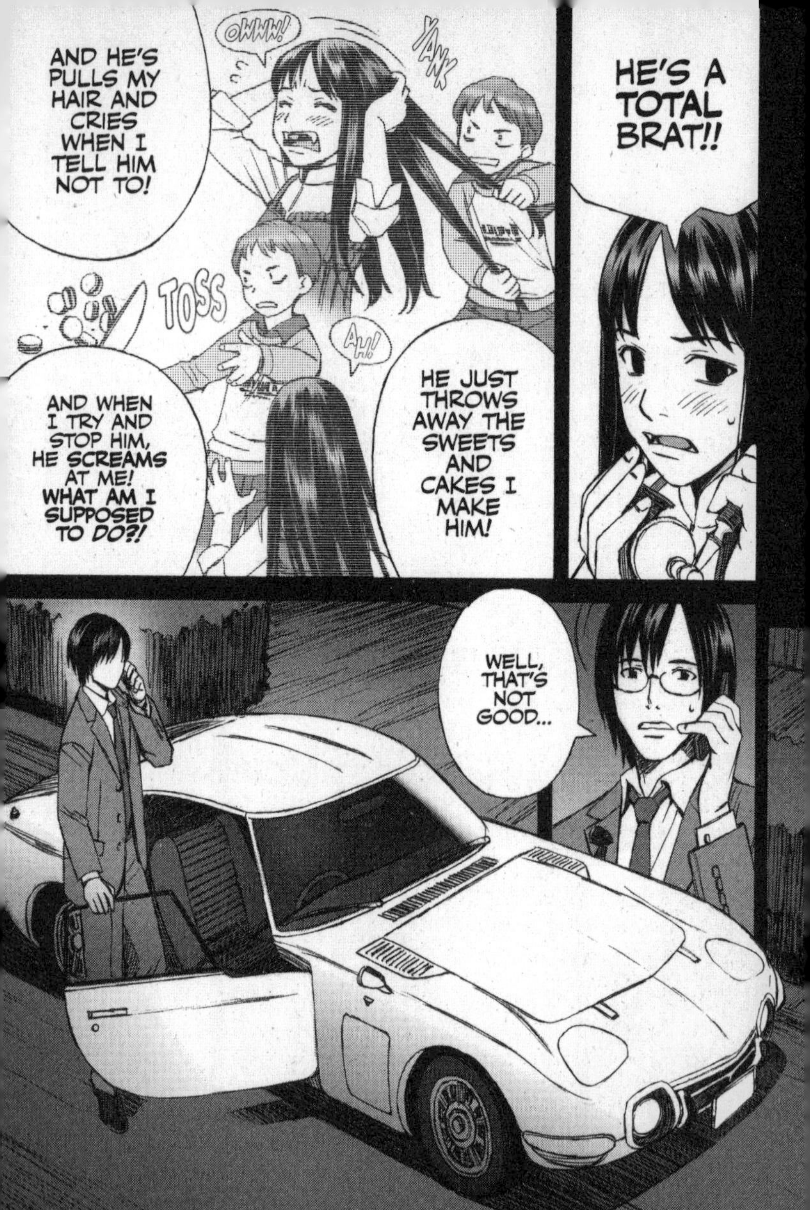
HE'S A TOTAL BRAT!!
YANK
OWWW!
AND HE'S PULLS MY HAIR AND CRIES WHEN I TELL HIM NOT TO!
AH!
TOSS
HE JUST THROWS AWAY THE SWEETS AND CAKES I MAKE HIM!
AND WHEN I TRY AND STOP HIM, HE SCREAMS AT ME! WHAT AM I SUPPOSED TO DO?!
WELL, THAT'S NOT GOOD...

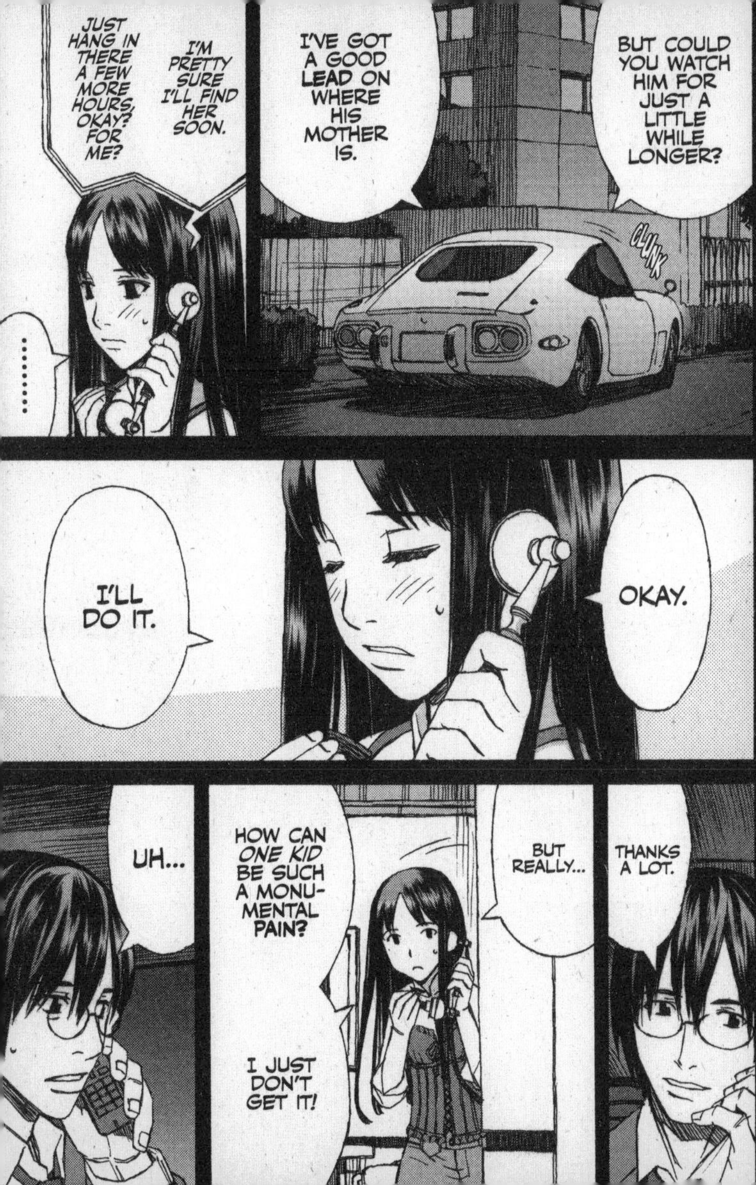
BUT COULD YOU WATCH HIM FOR JUST A LITTLE WHILE LONGER?
I'VE GOT A GOOD LEAD ON WHERE HIS MOTHER IS.
CLUNK
I'M PRETTY SURE I'LL FIND HER SOON.
JUST HANG IN THERE A FEW MORE HOURS, OKAY? FOR ME?
....
OKAY.
I'LL DO IT.
THANKS A LOT.
BUT REALLY...
HOW CAN *ONE KID* BE SUCH A MONUMENTAL PAIN?
I JUST DON'T GET IT!
UH...

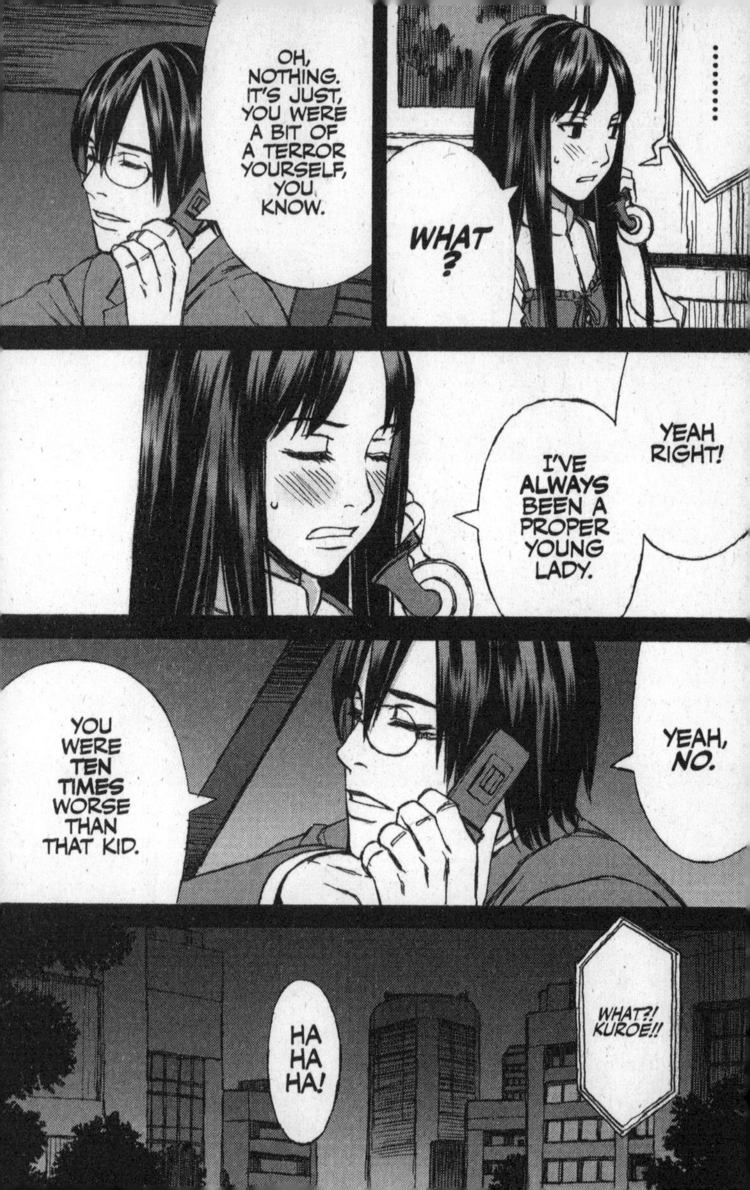
....
WHAT?
OH, NOTHING. IT'S JUST, YOU WERE A BIT OF A TERROR YOURSELF, YOU KNOW.
YEAH RIGHT!
I'VE ALWAYS BEEN A PROPER YOUNG LADY.
YEAH, NO.
YOU WERE TEN TIMES WORSE THAN THAT KID.
WHAT?! KUROE!!
HA HA HA!

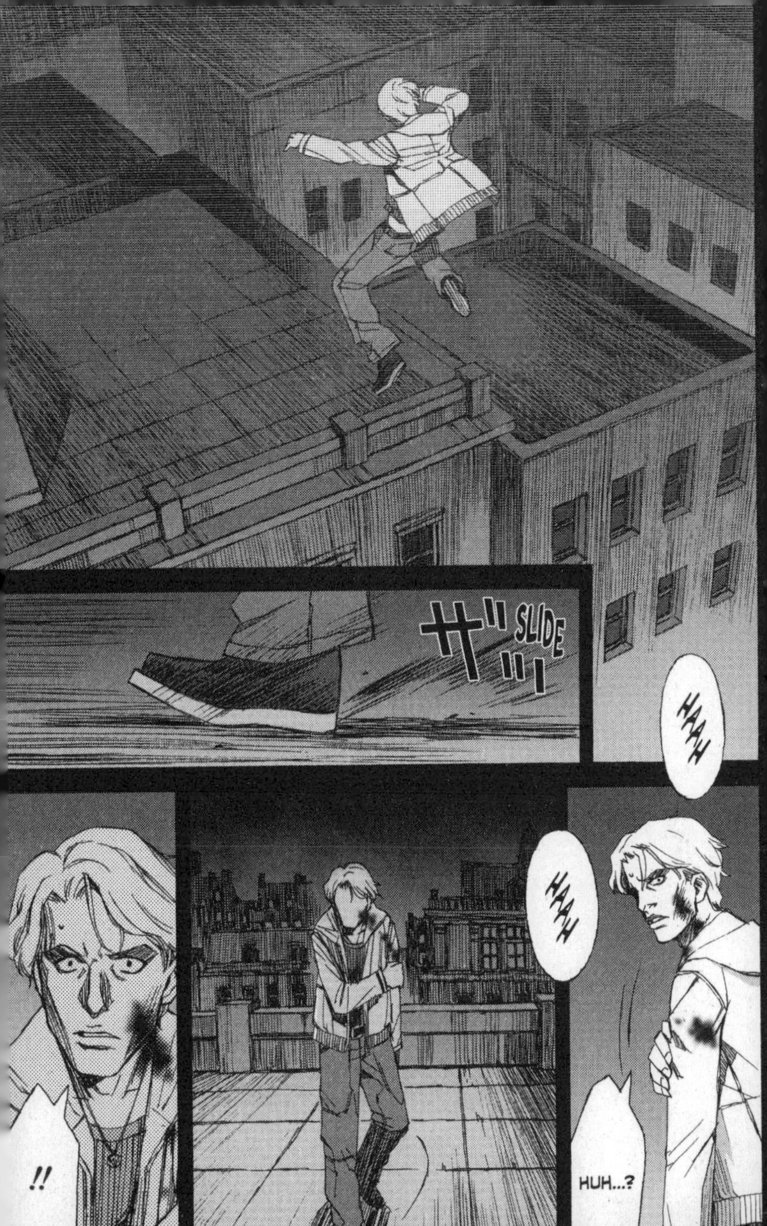
HAAH
SLIDE
HAAH
HUH...?
!!

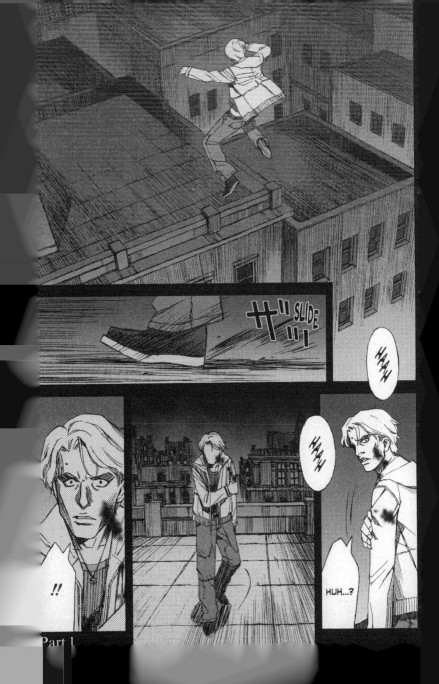

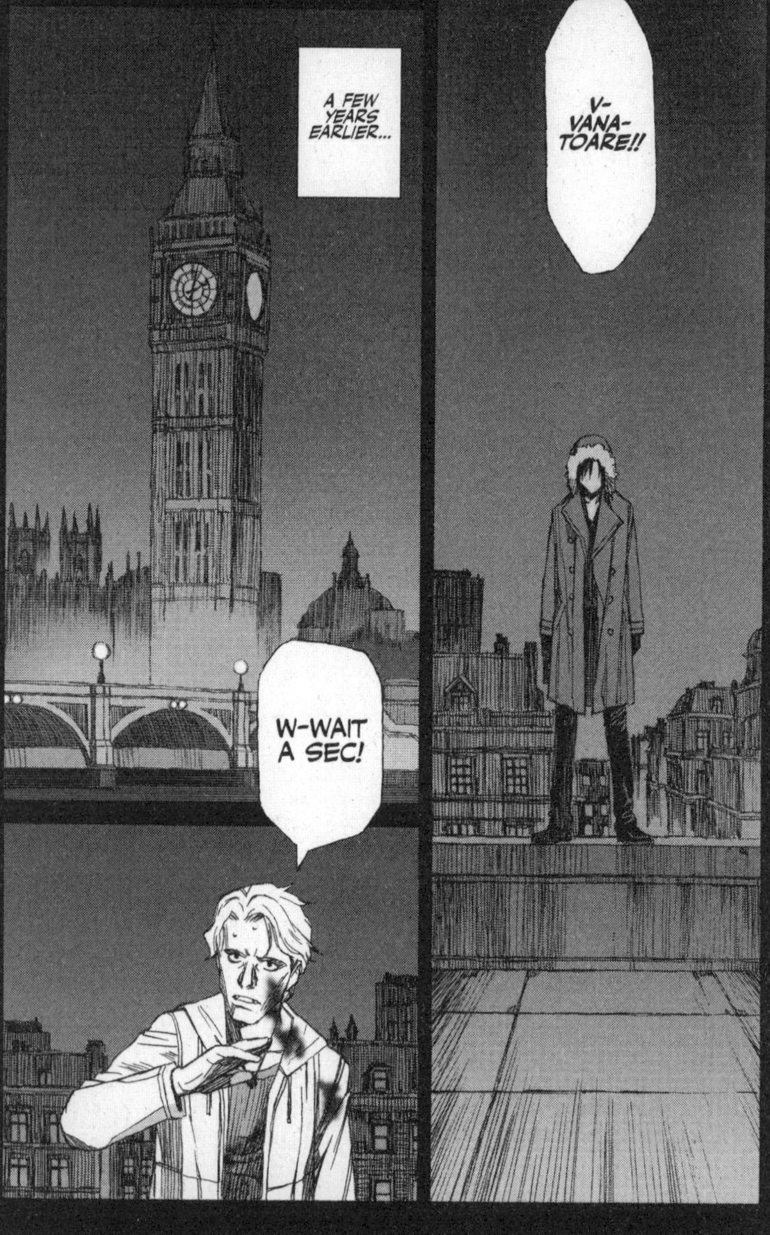
V-
VANA-
TOARE!!
A FEW YEARS EARLIER...
W-WAIT A SEC!

Episode 20

LONDON WALTZ

The Princess in the Mist

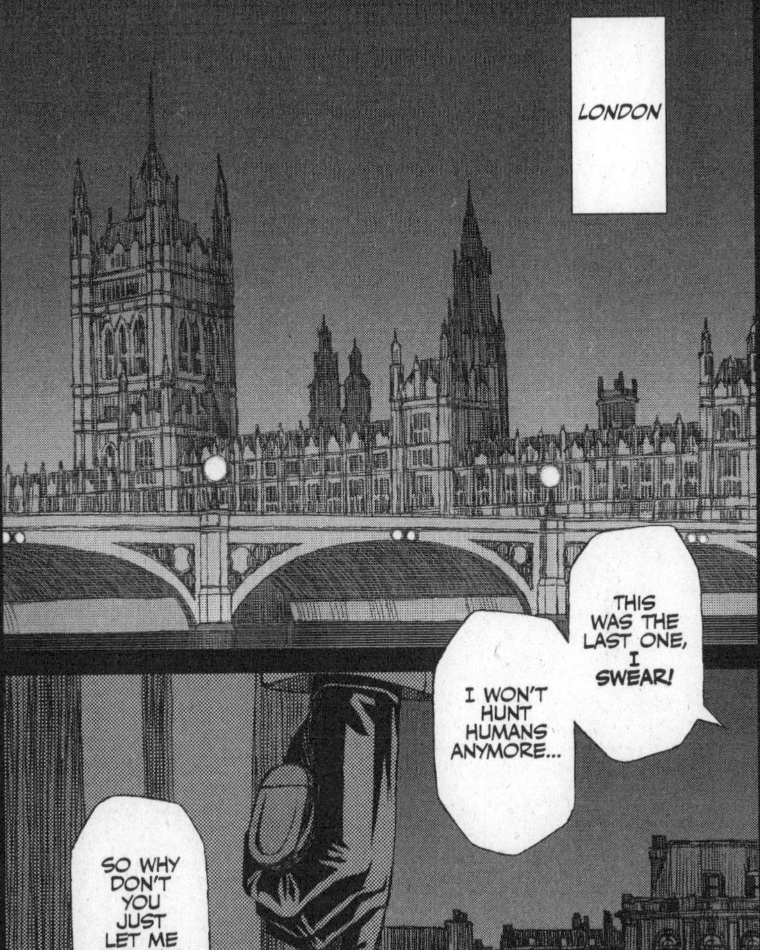
LONDON
THIS WAS THE LAST ONE, I SWEAR!
I WON'T HUNT HUMANS ANYMORE...
SO WHY DON'T YOU JUST LET ME GO THIS ONE TIME?

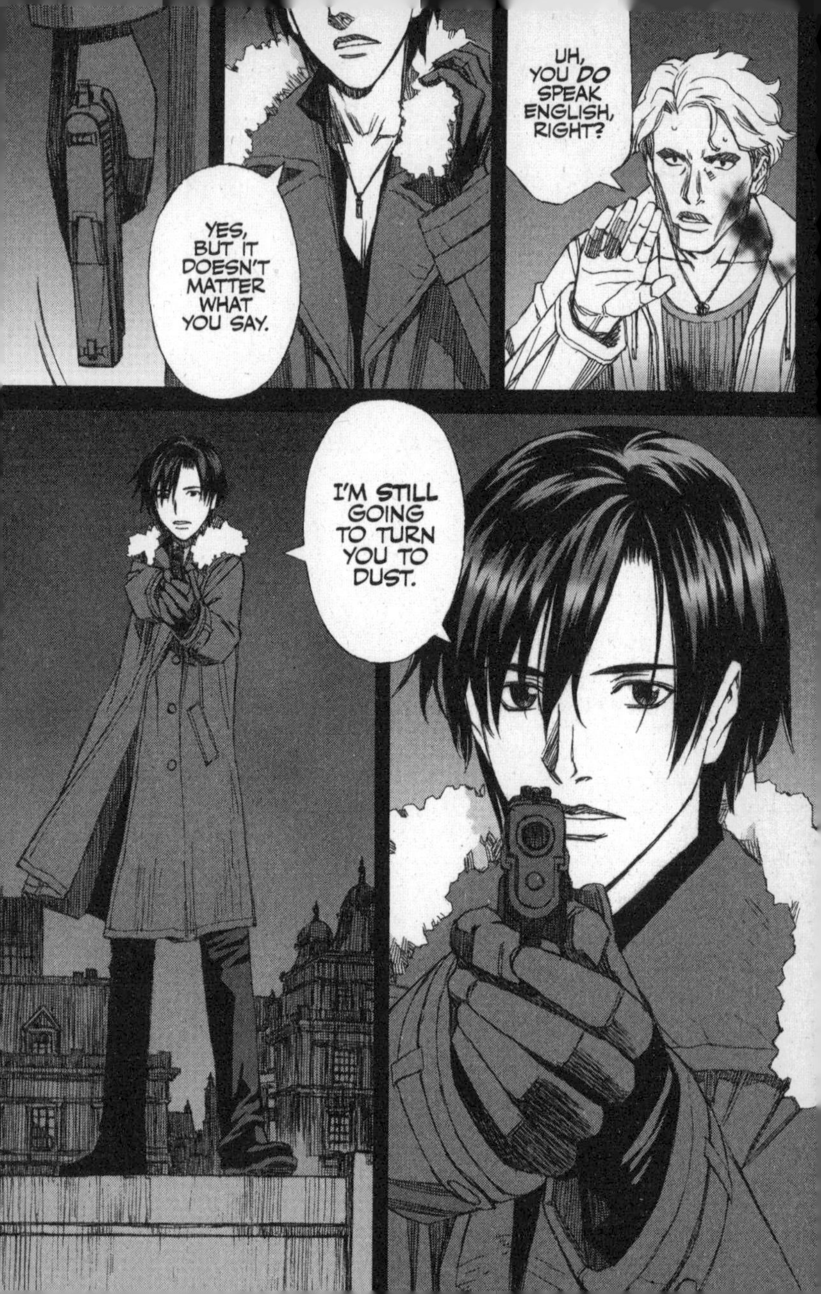
UH, YOU *DO* SPEAK ENGLISH, RIGHT?
YES, BUT IT DOESN'T MATTER WHAT YOU SAY.
I'M STILL GOING TO TURN YOU TO DUST.

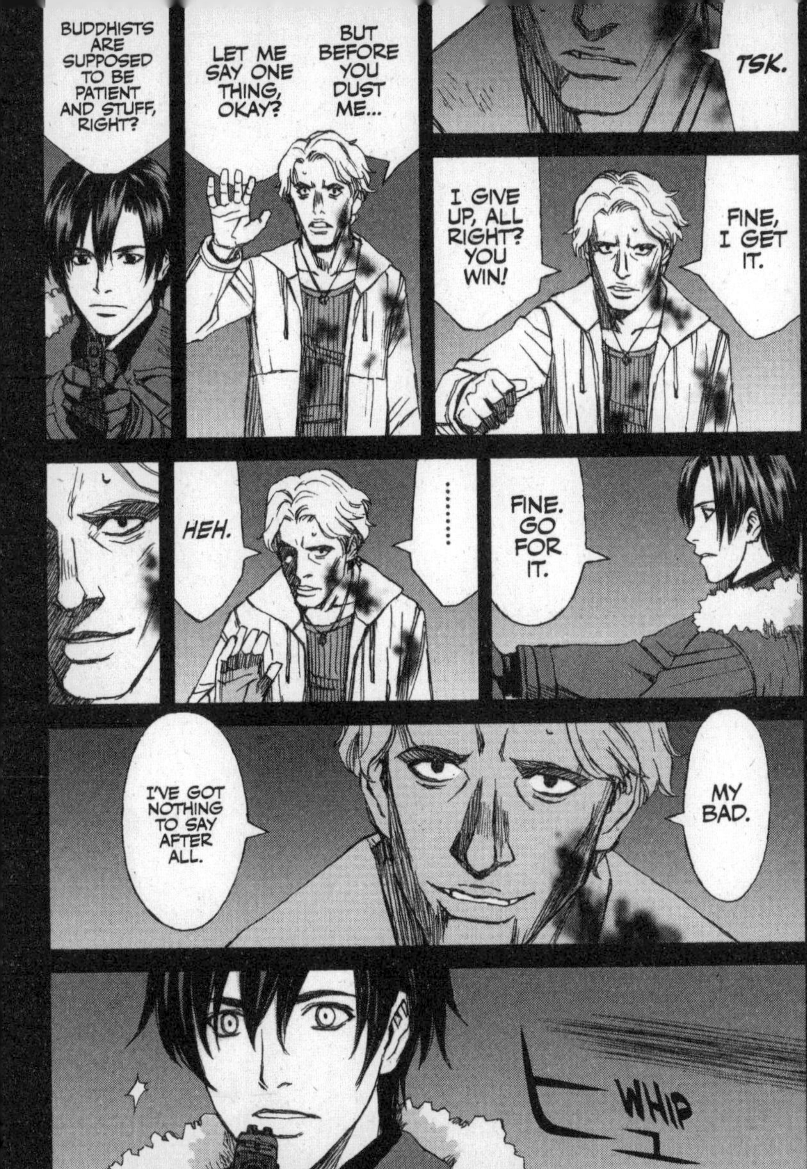
TSK.
FINE, I GET IT.
I GIVE UP, ALL RIGHT? YOU WIN!
BUT BEFORE YOU DUST ME...
LET ME SAY ONE THING, OKAY?
BUDDHISTS ARE SUPPOSED TO BE PATIENT AND STUFF, RIGHT?
FINE. GO FOR IT.
......
HEH.
MY BAD.
I'VE GOT NOTHING TO SAY AFTER ALL.
WHIP

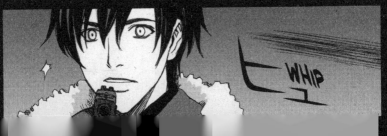

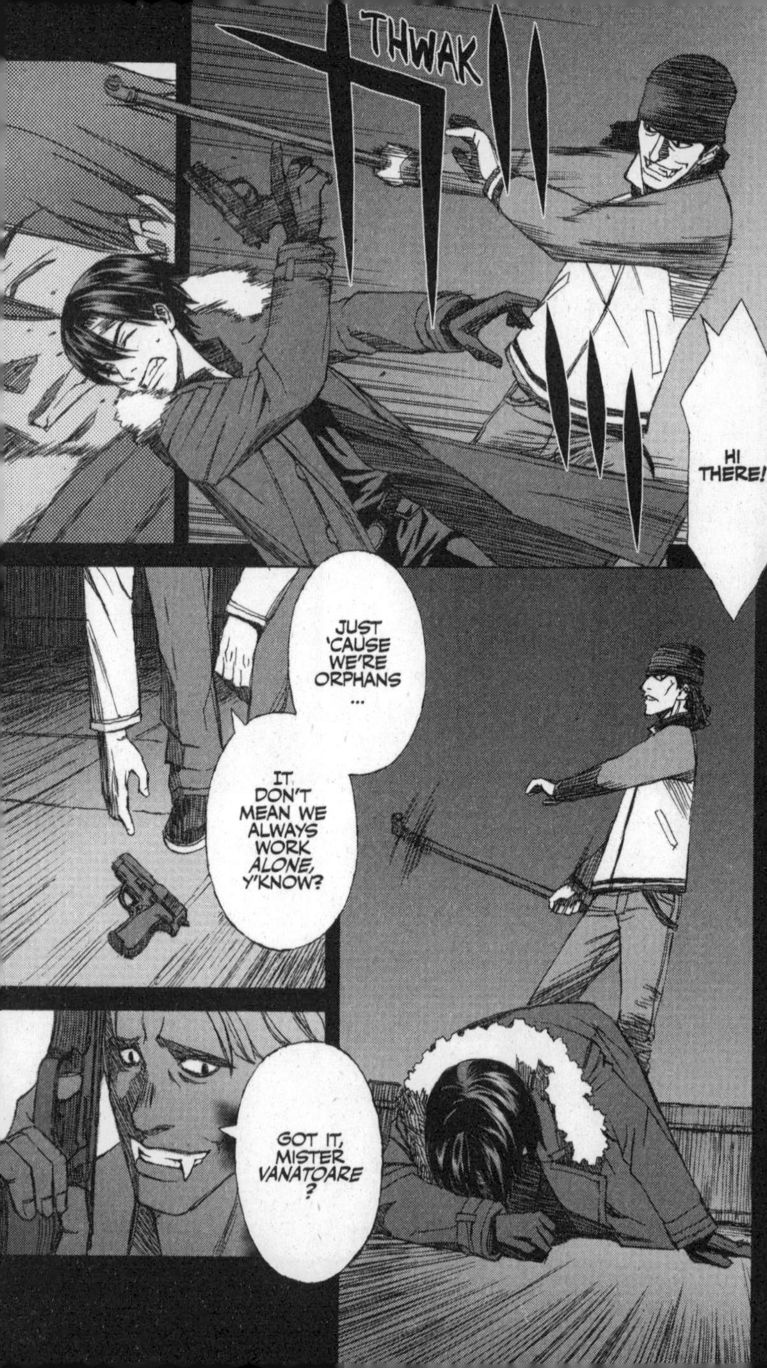
THWAK
HI THERE!
JUST 'CAUSE WE'RE ORPHANS ...
IT DON'T MEAN WE ALWAYS WORK *ALONE*, Y'KNOW?
GOT IT, MISTER VANATOARE ?

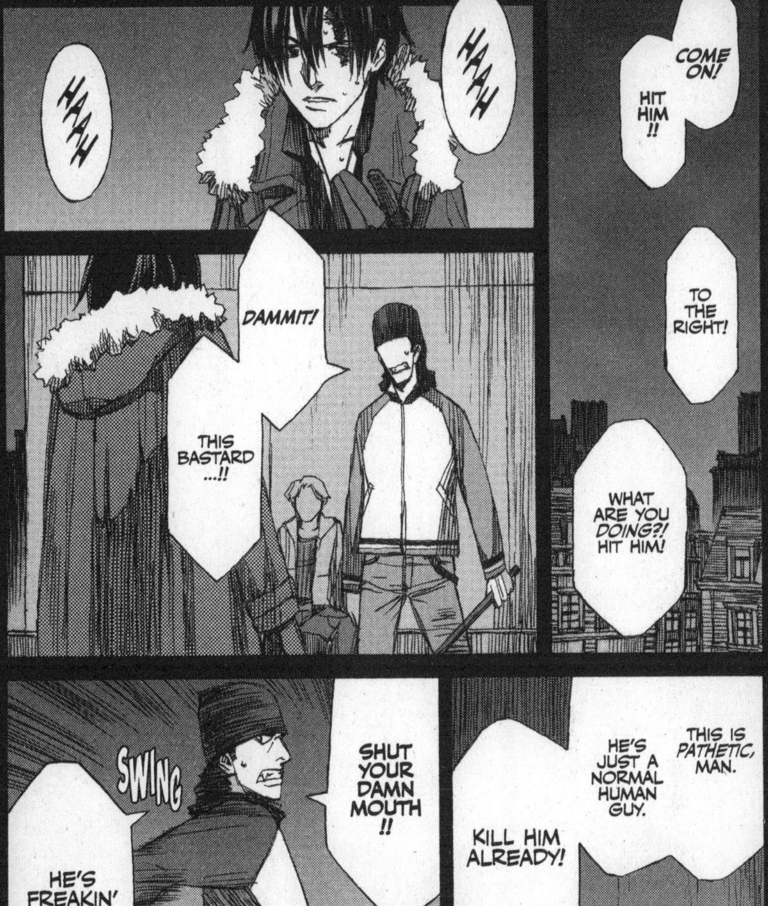
COME ON!
HIT HIM!!
TO THE RIGHT!
WHAT ARE YOU DOING?! HIT HIM!
HAAH
HAAH
DAMMIT!
THIS BASTARD ...!!
THIS IS PATHETIC, MAN.
HE'S JUST A NORMAL HUMAN GUY.
KILL HIM ALREADY!
SWING
SHUT YOUR DAMN MOUTH!!
HE'S FREAKIN' QUICK, DUDE!!
HUH?

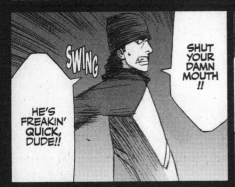

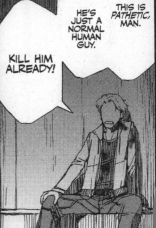

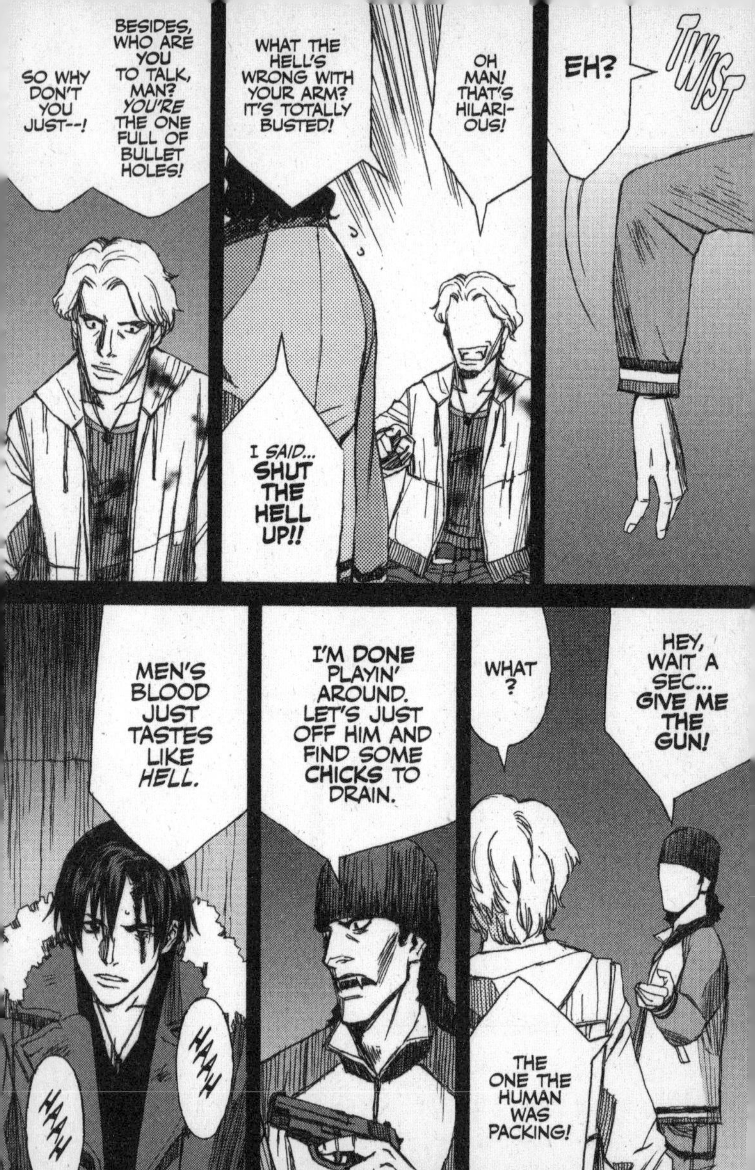
EH?
TWIST
OH MAN! THAT'S HILARI-OUS!
WHAT THE HELL'S WRONG WITH YOUR ARM? IT'S TOTALLY BUSTED!
I SAID... SHUT THE HELL UP!!
BESIDES, WHO ARE YOU TO TALK, MAN? YOU'RE THE ONE FULL OF BULLET HOLES!
SO WHY DON'T YOU JUST--!
HEY, WAIT A SEC... GIVE ME THE GUN!
WHAT?
THE ONE THE HUMAN WAS PACKING!
I'M DONE PLAYIN' AROUND. LET'S JUST OFF HIM AND FIND SOME CHICKS TO DRAIN.
MEN'S BLOOD JUST TASTES LIKE HELL.
HAAH
HAAH

 VANA-
TOARE.

 I'LL TRY TO MAKE THIS QUICK BUT *PAINFUL* ...

THUNK

WHA ....?

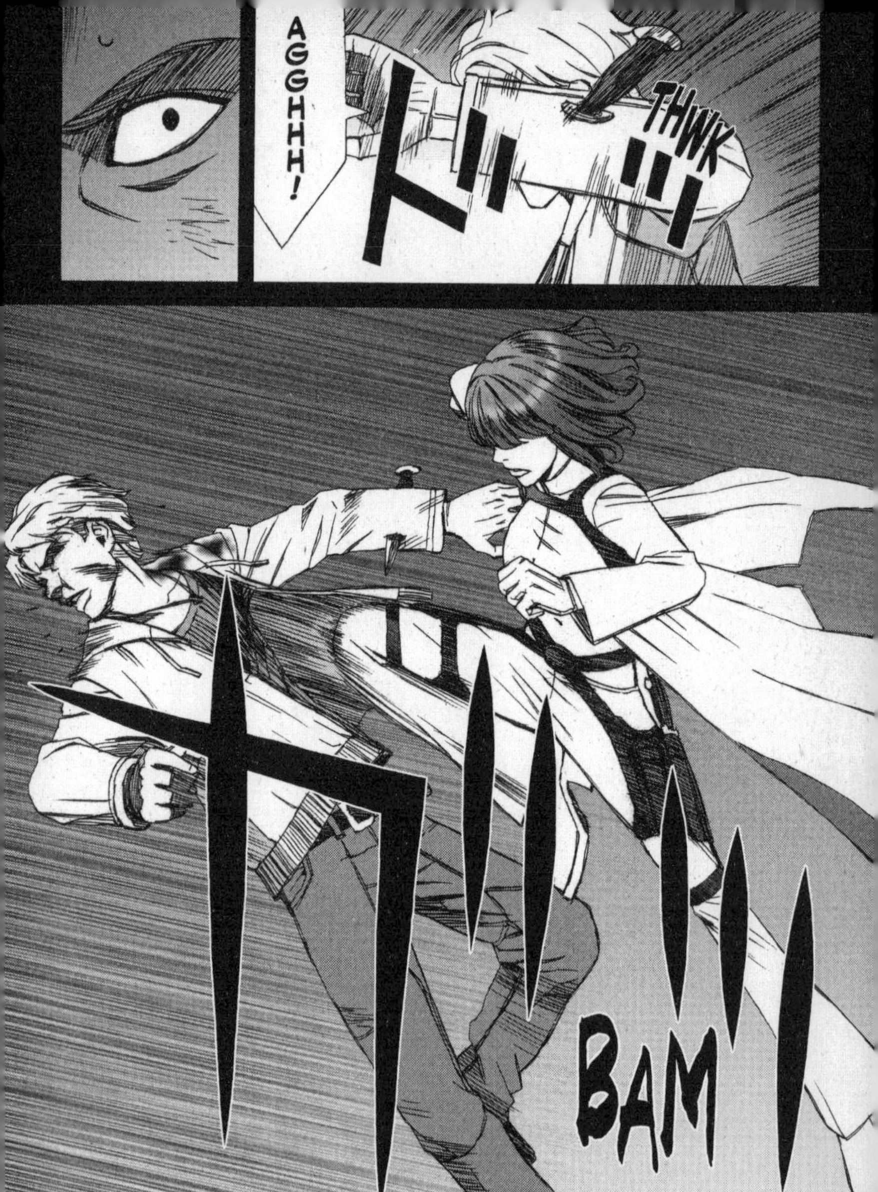
AGGHHH!
THWK
BAM

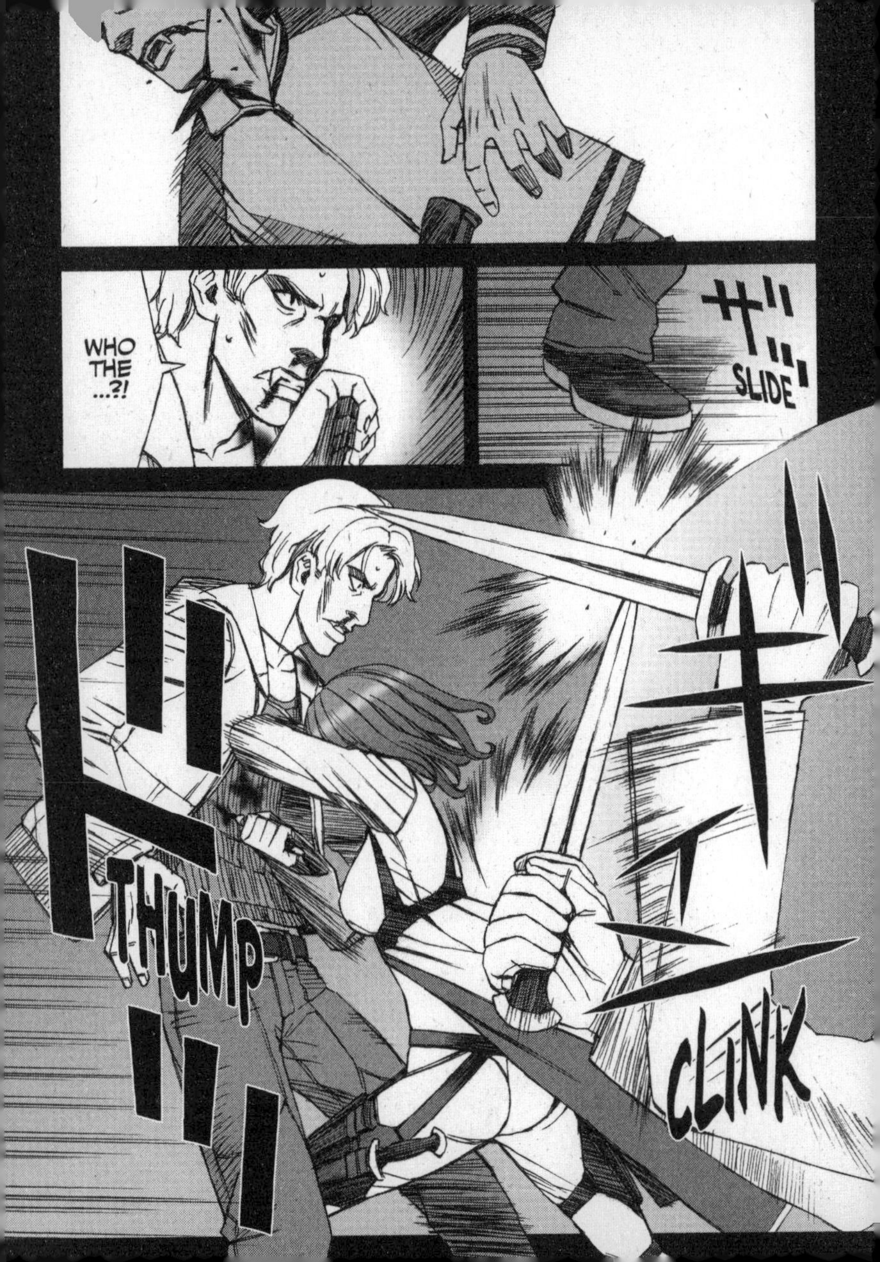
SLIDE
WHO THE ...?!
CLINK
THUMP

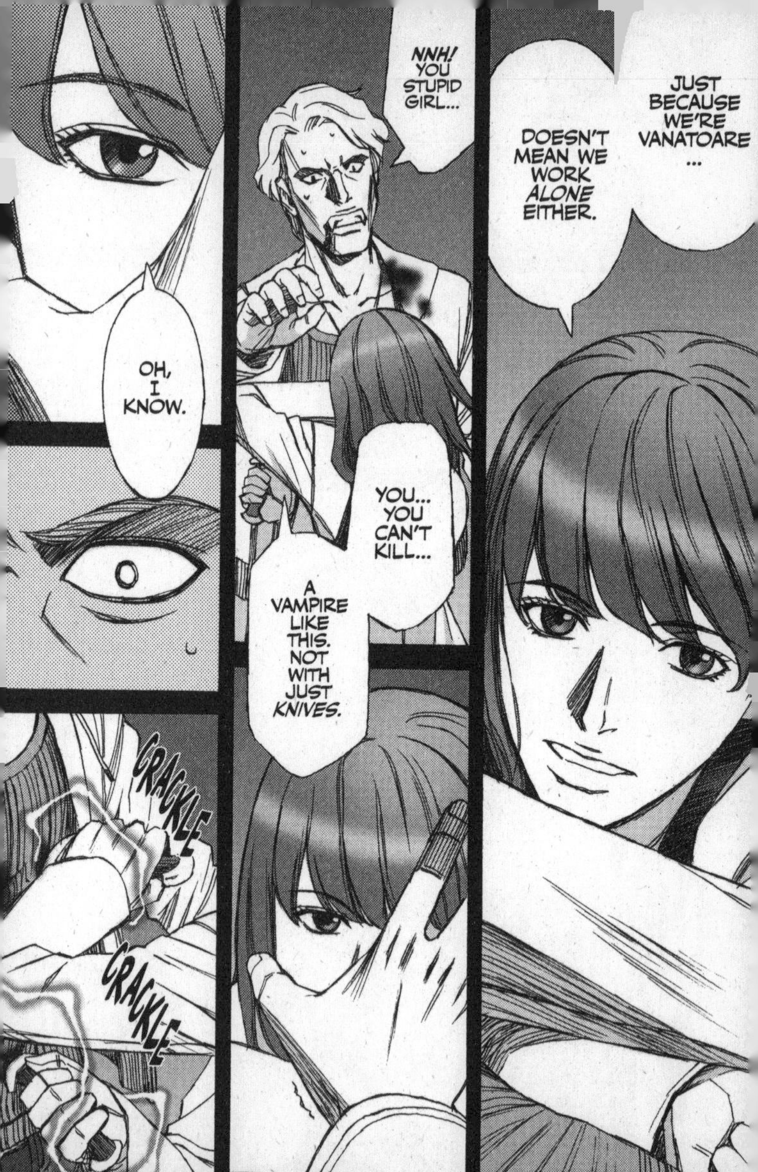
JUST BECAUSE WE'RE VANATOARE ...
DOESN'T MEAN WE WORK ALONE EITHER.
NNH! YOU STUPID GIRL...
YOU... YOU CAN'T KILL...
A VAMPIRE LIKE THIS. NOT WITH JUST KNIVES.
OH, I KNOW.
CRACKLE
CRACKLE

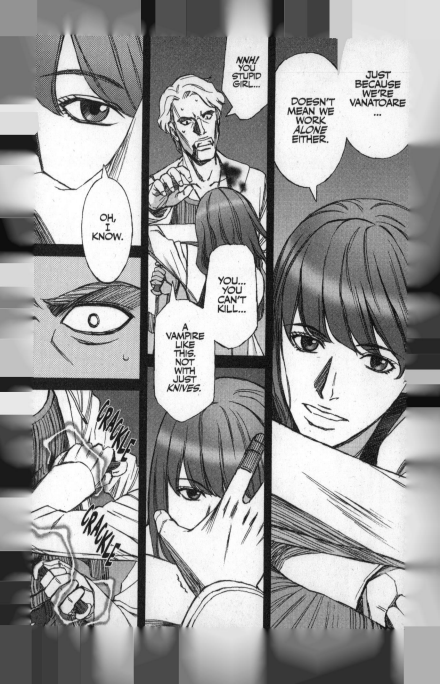

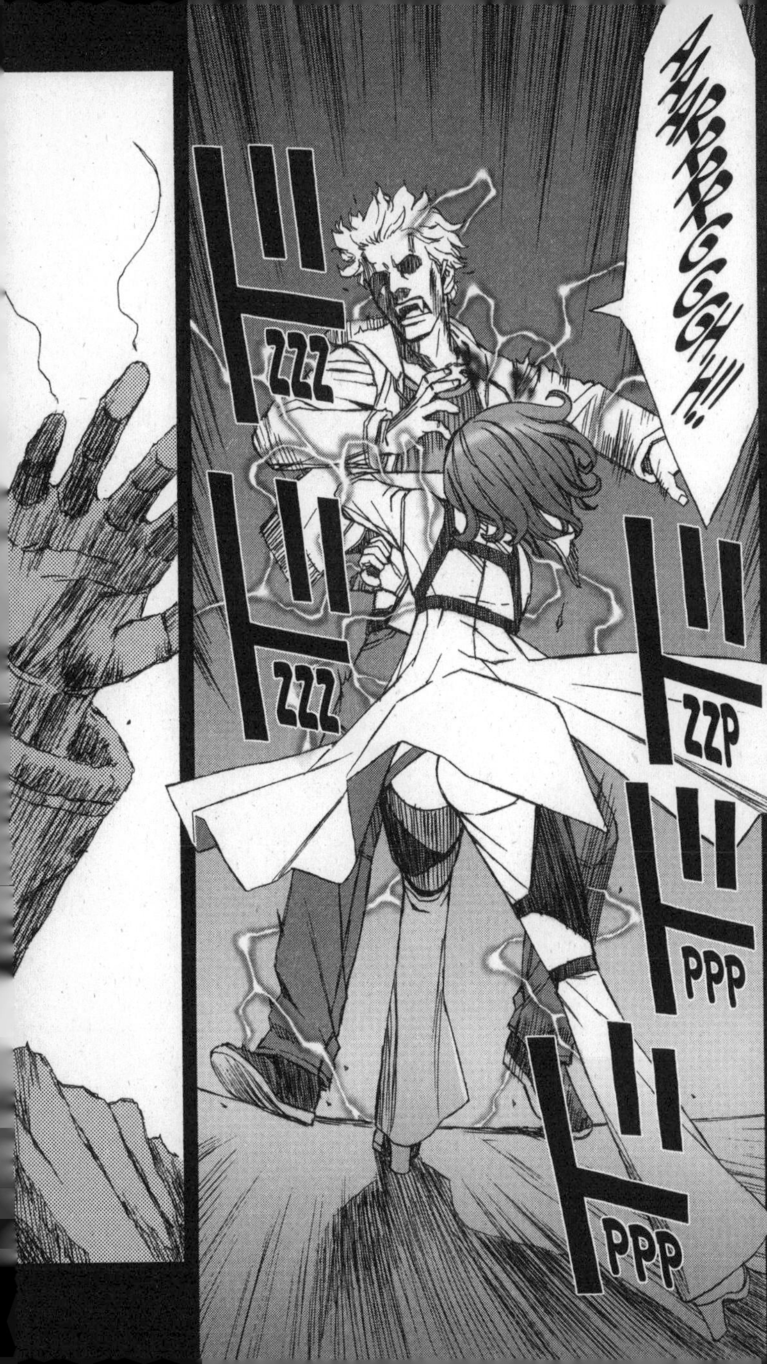
AAARRRRGGGGH!!
ZZZ
ZZP
ZZZ
PPP
PPP

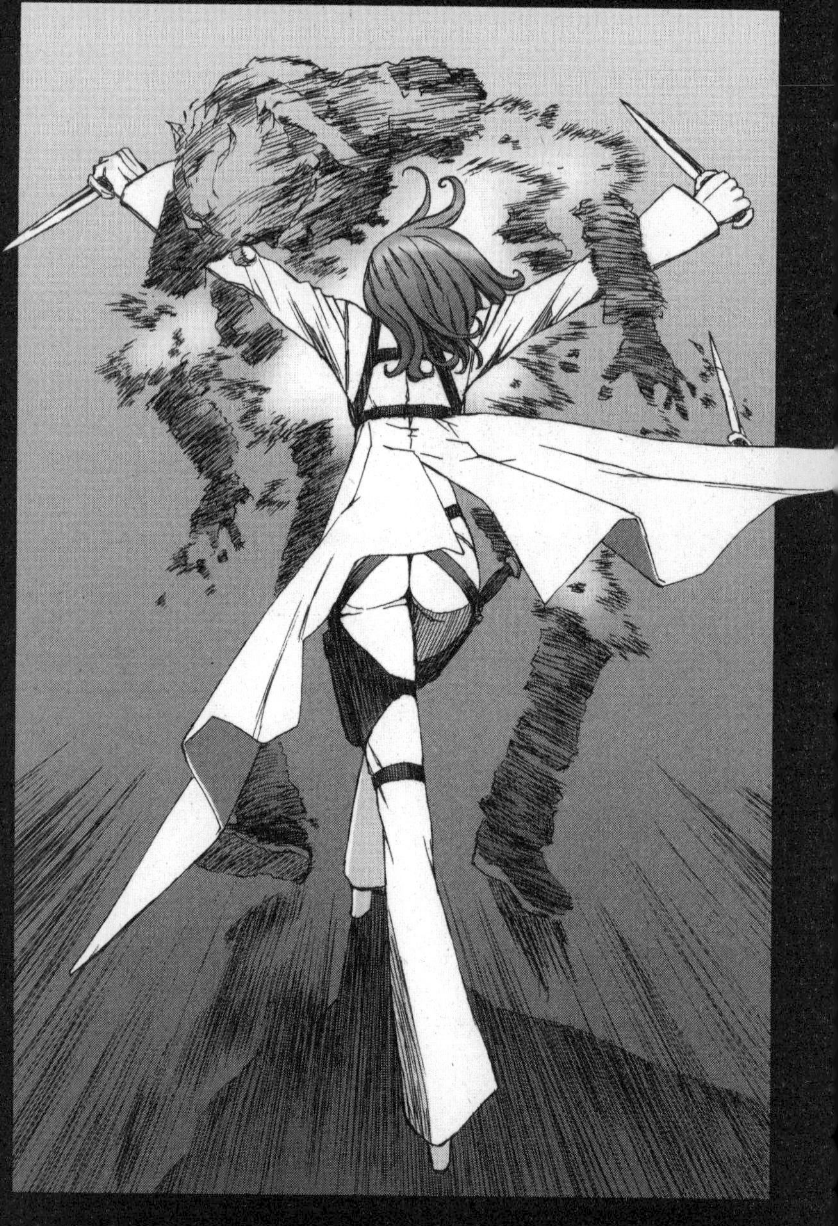

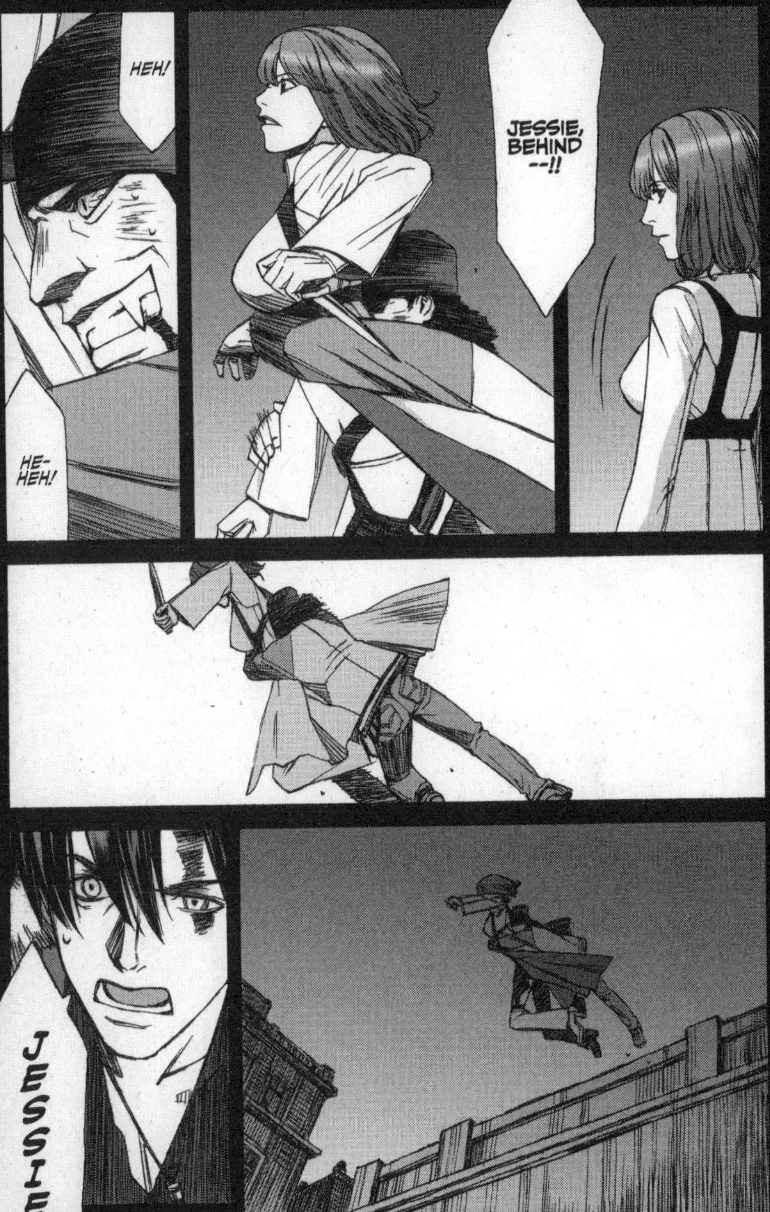
JESSIE, BEHIND--!!
HEH!
HE-HEH!
JESSIE!!

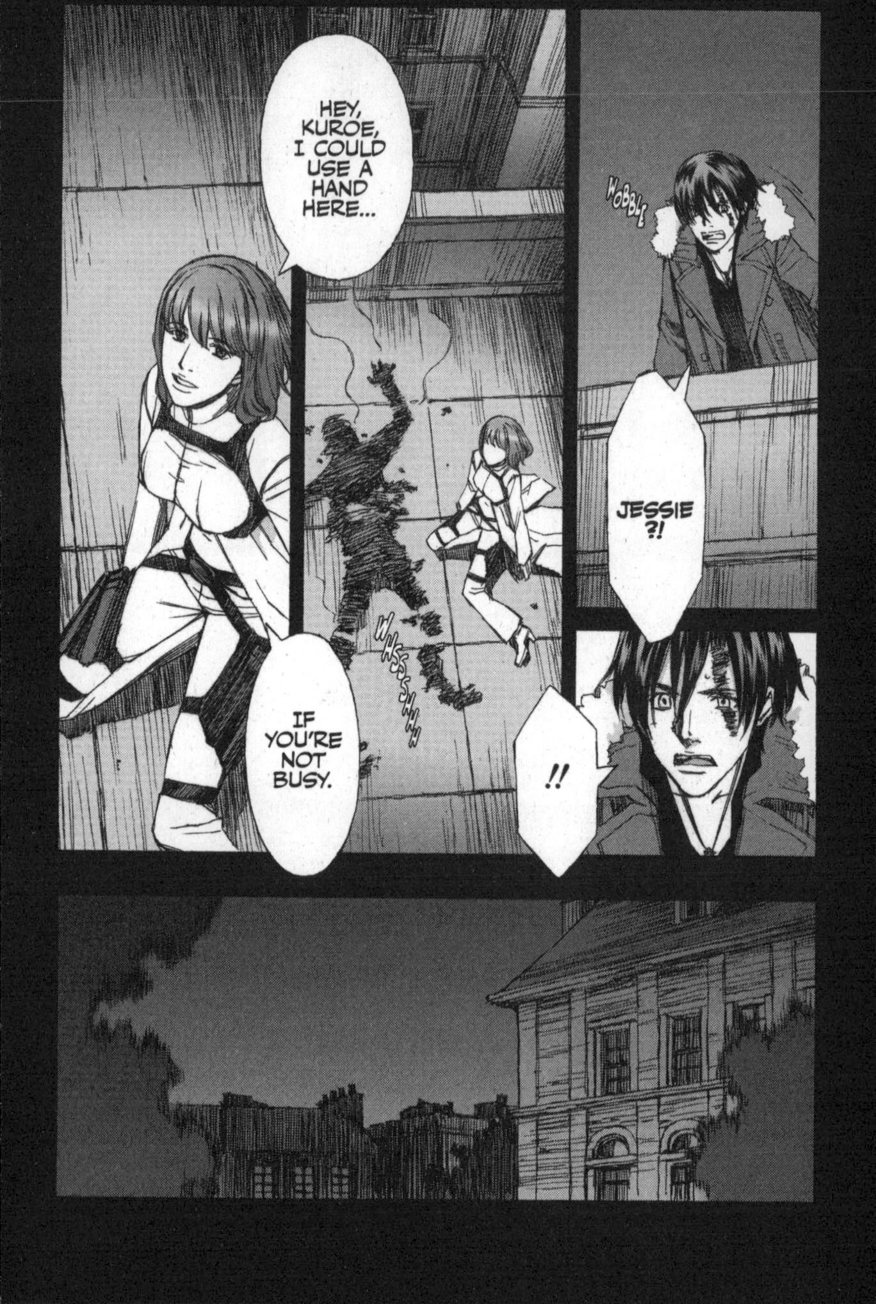
WOBBLE
JESSIE ?!
!!
WHSSSHHH
HEY, KUROE, I COULD USE A HAND HERE...
IF YOU'RE NOT BUSY.

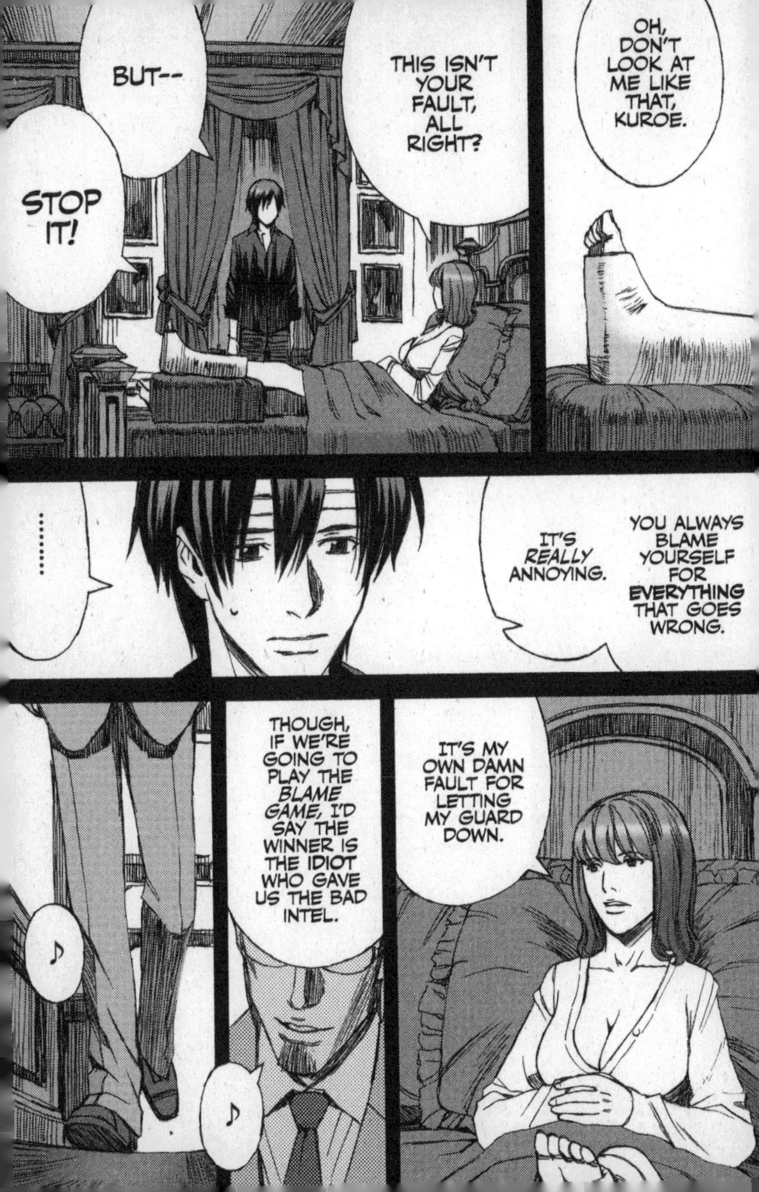
OH, DON'T LOOK AT ME LIKE THAT, KUROE.
THIS ISN'T YOUR FAULT, ALL RIGHT?
BUT--
STOP IT!
YOU ALWAYS BLAME YOURSELF FOR **EVERYTHING** THAT GOES WRONG.
IT'S *REALLY* ANNOYING.
....
IT'S MY OWN DAMN FAULT FOR LETTING MY GUARD DOWN.
THOUGH, IF WE'RE GOING TO PLAY THE *BLAME GAME,* I'D SAY THE WINNER IS THE IDIOT WHO GAVE US THE BAD INTEL.
♪
♪

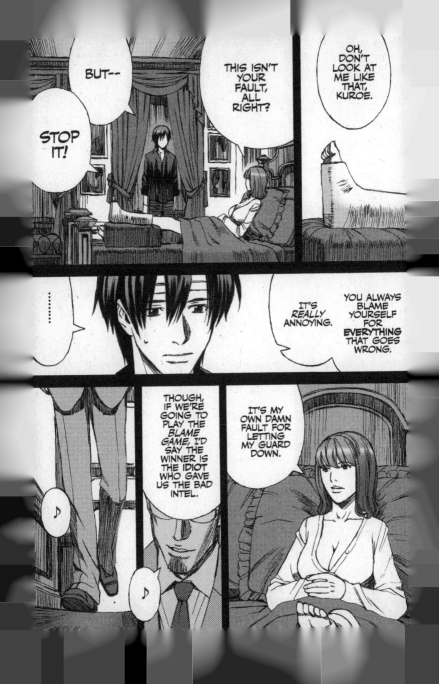

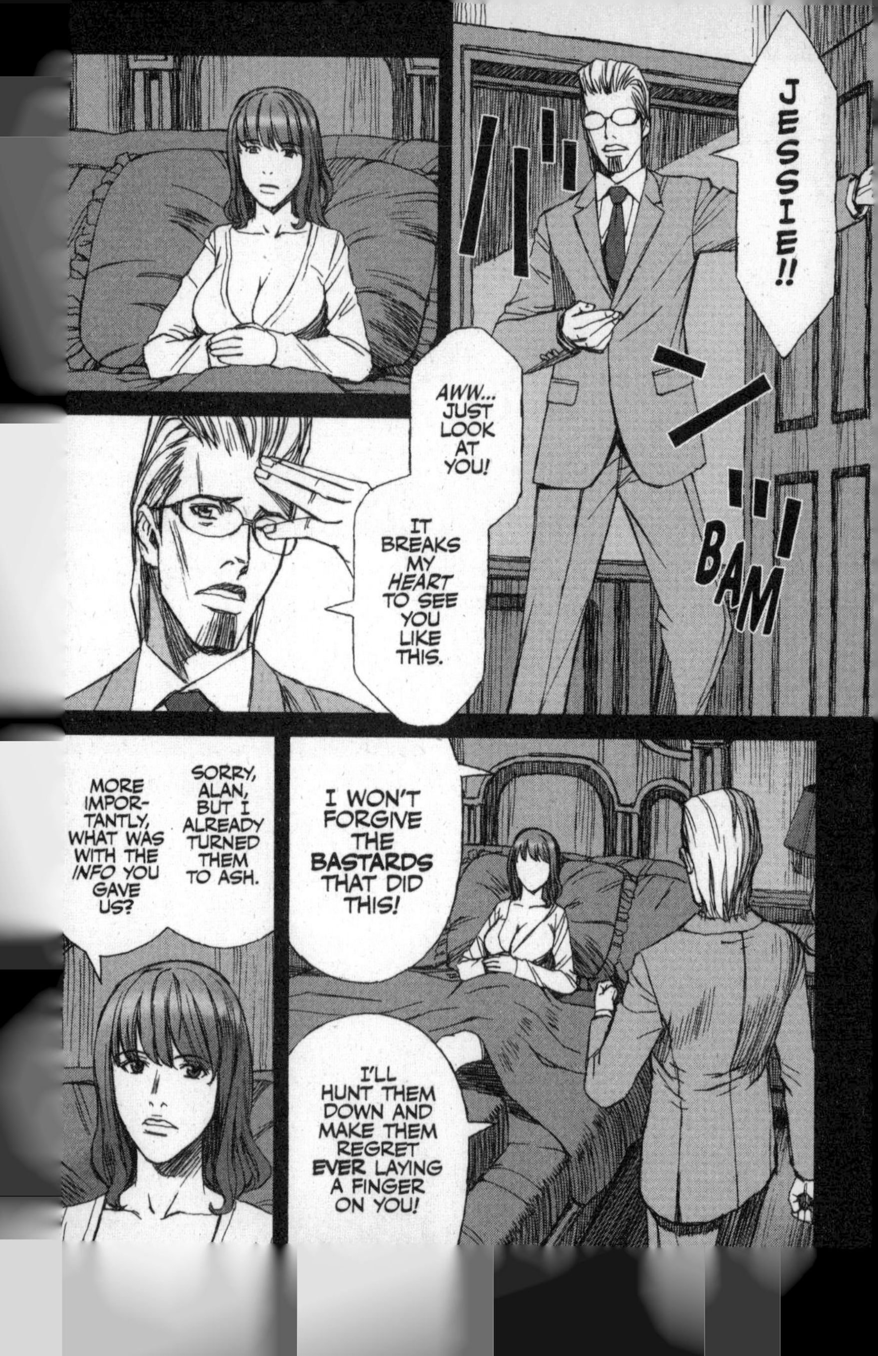
JESSIE!!
BAM
AWW... JUST LOOK AT YOU!
IT BREAKS MY HEART TO SEE YOU LIKE THIS.
I WON'T FORGIVE THE BASTARDS THAT DID THIS!
I'LL HUNT THEM DOWN AND MAKE THEM REGRET EVER LAYING A FINGER ON YOU!
SORRY, ALAN, BUT I ALREADY TURNED THEM TO ASH.
MORE IMPORTANTLY, WHAT WAS WITH THE INFO YOU GAVE US?

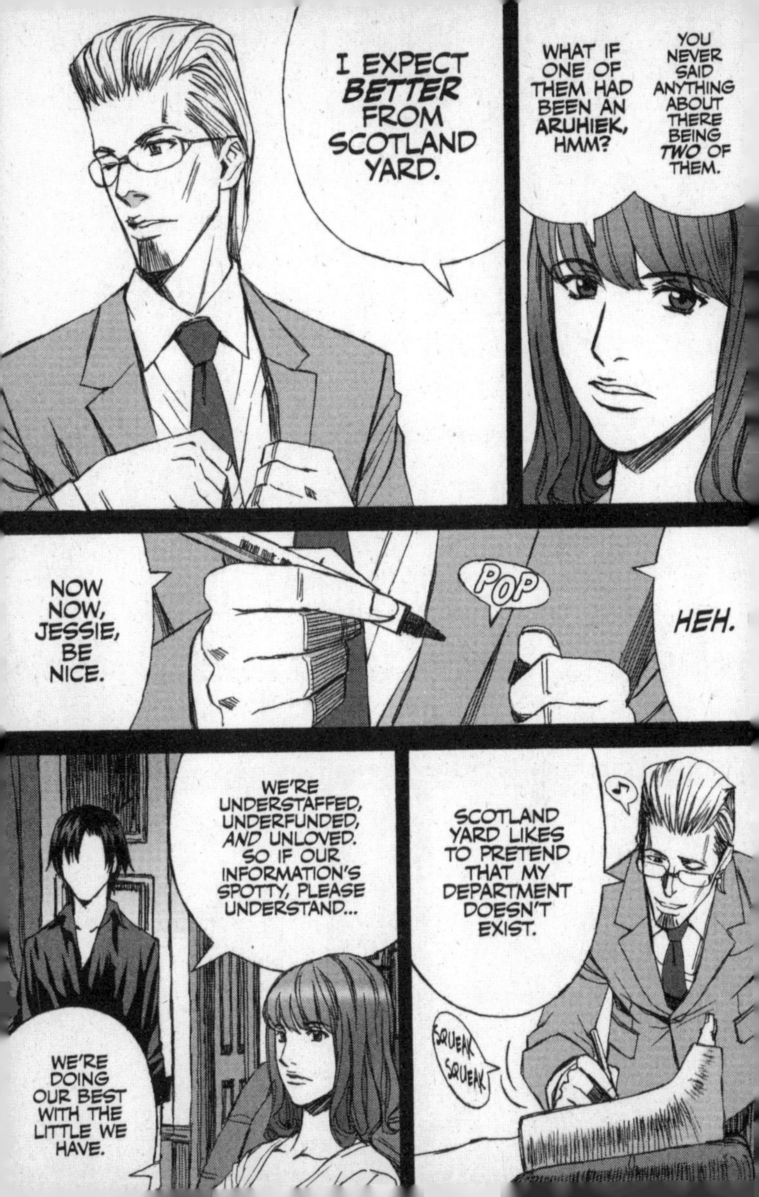
YOU NEVER SAID ANYTHING ABOUT THERE BEING *TWO* OF THEM.
WHAT IF ONE OF THEM HAD BEEN AN **ARUHIEK**, HMM?
I EXPECT ***BETTER*** FROM SCOTLAND YARD.
HEH.
POP
NOW NOW, JESSIE, BE NICE.
♪
SCOTLAND YARD LIKES TO PRETEND THAT MY DEPARTMENT DOESN'T EXIST.
SQUEAK SQUEAK
WE'RE UNDERSTAFFED, UNDERFUNDED, *AND* UNLOVED. SO IF OUR INFORMATION'S SPOTTY, PLEASE UNDERSTAND...
WE'RE DOING OUR BEST WITH THE LITTLE WE HAVE.

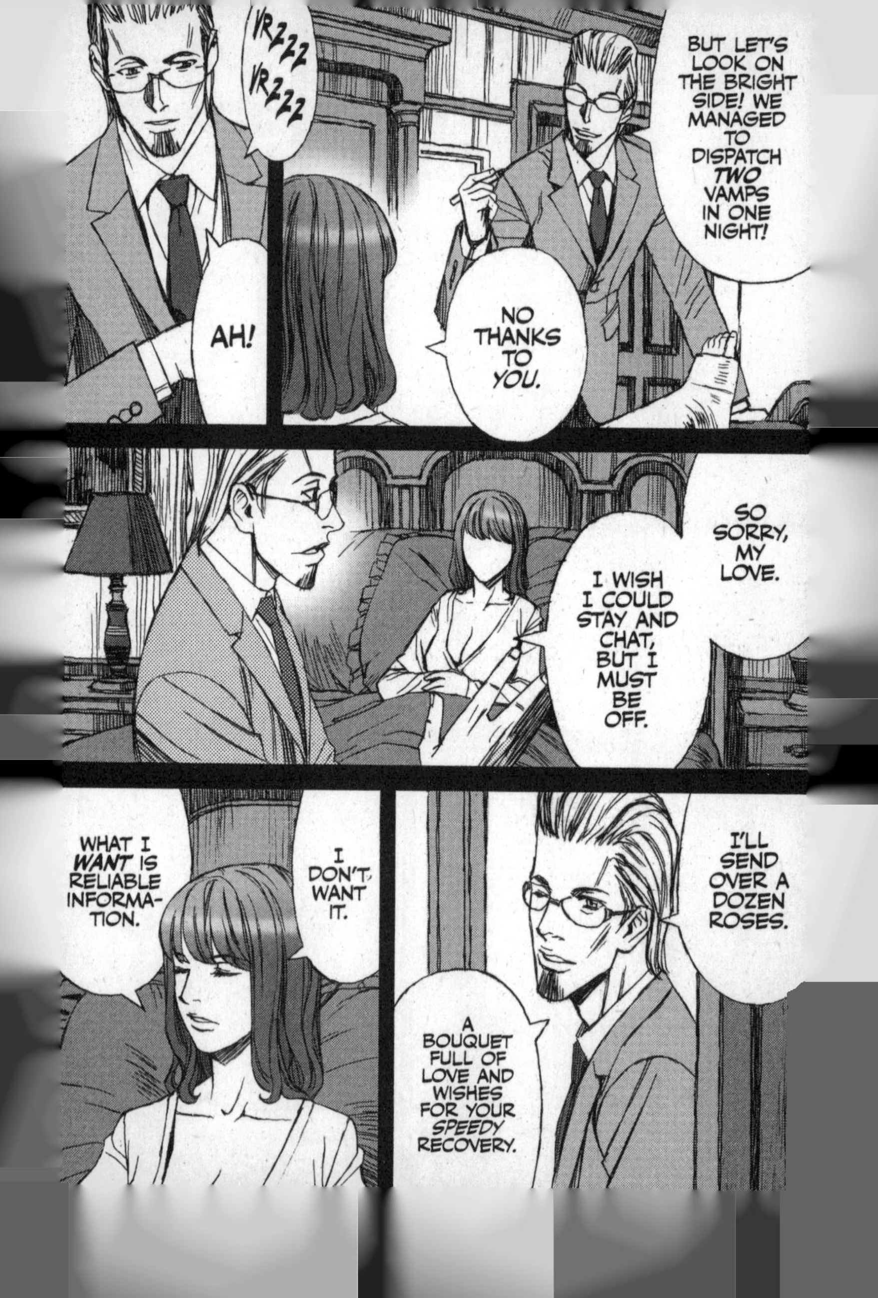
BUT LET'S LOOK ON THE BRIGHT SIDE! WE MANAGED TO DISPATCH TWO VAMPS IN ONE NIGHT!
NO THANKS TO YOU.
VRZZZ VRZZZ
AH!
SO SORRY, MY LOVE.
I WISH I COULD STAY AND CHAT, BUT I MUST BE OFF.
I'LL SEND OVER A DOZEN ROSES.
A BOUQUET FULL OF LOVE AND WISHES FOR YOUR SPEEDY RECOVERY.
I DON'T WANT IT.
WHAT I WANT IS RELIABLE INFORMATION.

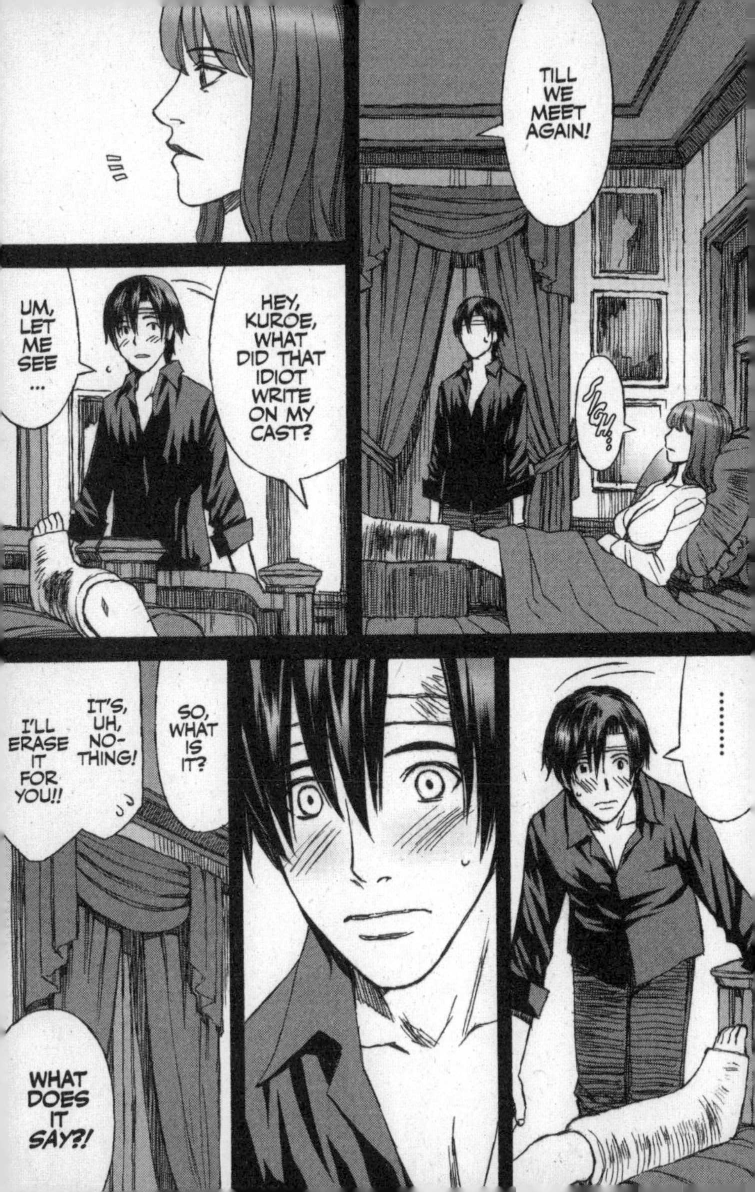
TILL WE MEET AGAIN!
SIGH...
HEY, KUROE, WHAT DID THAT IDIOT WRITE ON MY CAST?
UM, LET ME SEE ...
......
SO, WHAT IS IT?
IT'S, UH, NO-THING!
I'LL ERASE IT FOR YOU!!
WHAT DOES IT *SAY*?!

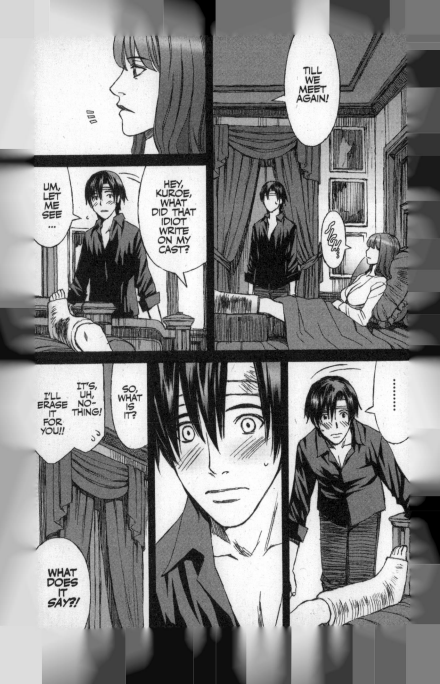

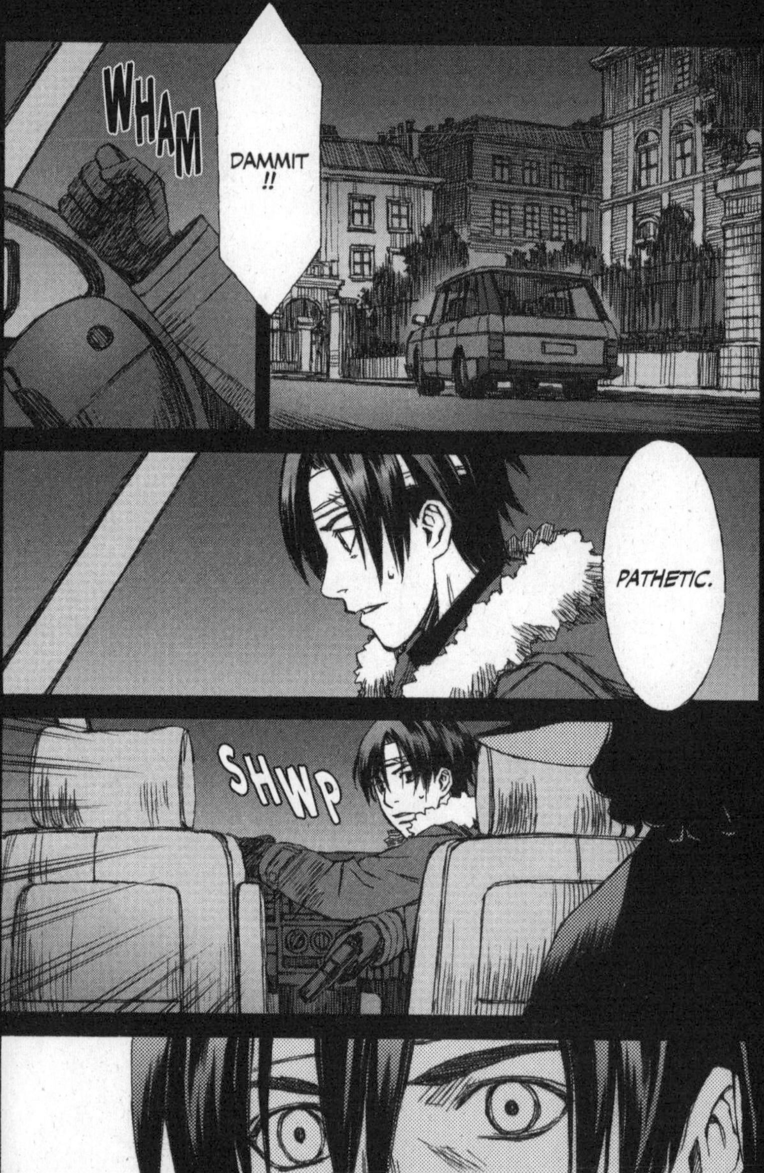
DAMMIT !!
WHAM
PATHETIC.
SHWP

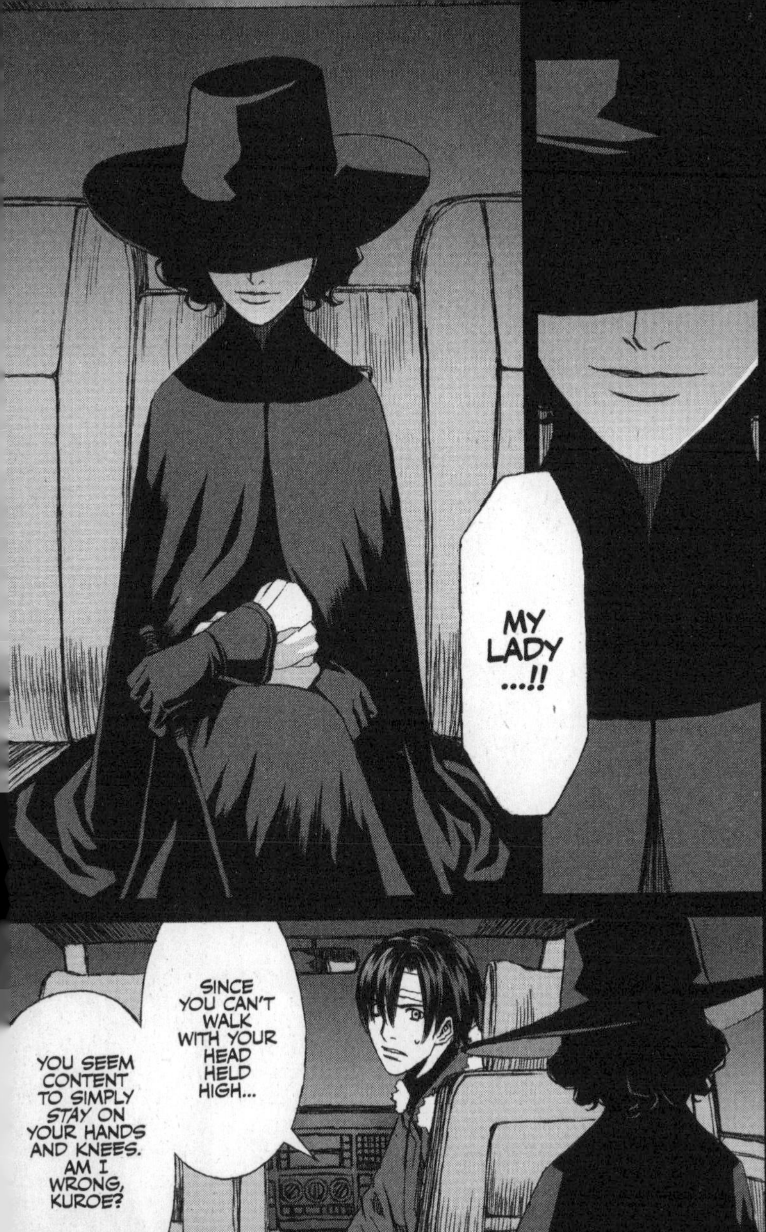
MY LADY ...!!
SINCE YOU CAN'T WALK WITH YOUR HEAD HELD HIGH...
YOU SEEM CONTENT TO SIMPLY STAY ON YOUR HANDS AND KNEES. AM I WRONG, KUROE?

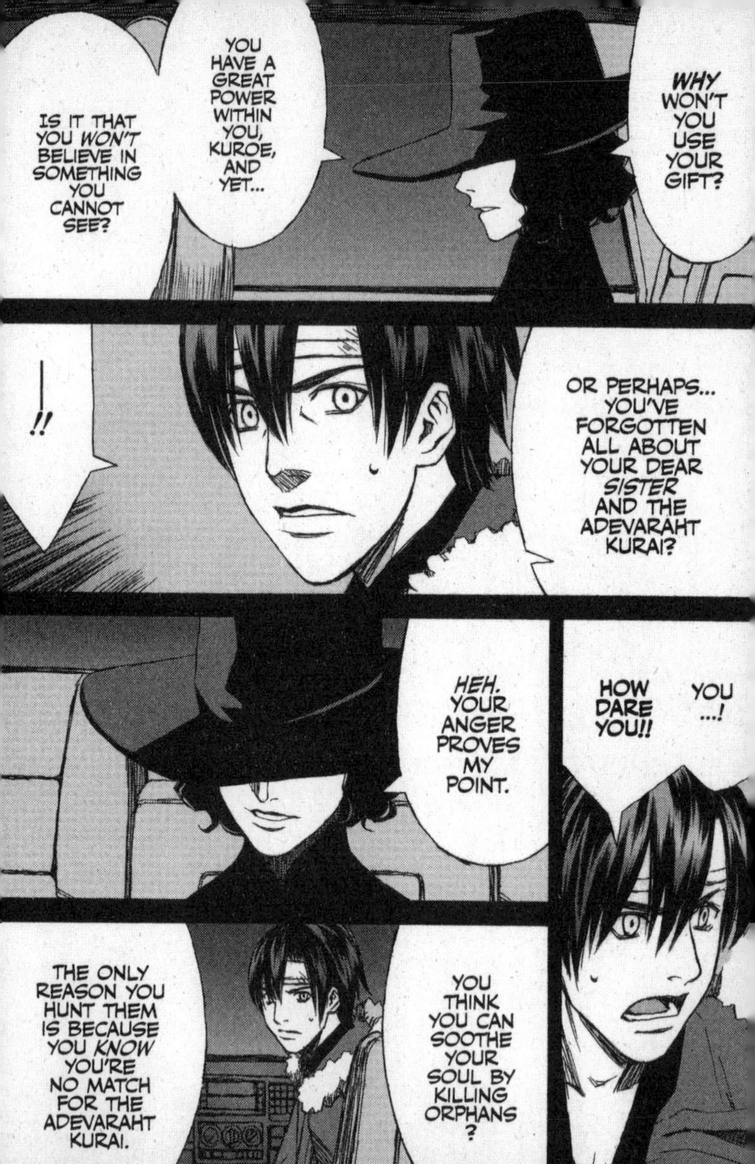
WHY WON'T YOU USE YOUR GIFT?
YOU HAVE A GREAT POWER WITHIN YOU, KUROE, AND YET...
IS IT THAT YOU WON'T BELIEVE IN SOMETHING YOU CANNOT SEE?
OR PERHAPS... YOU'VE FORGOTTEN ALL ABOUT YOUR DEAR SISTER AND THE ADEVARAHT KURAI?
—!!
YOU ...!
HOW DARE YOU!!
HEH. YOUR ANGER PROVES MY POINT.
YOU THINK YOU CAN SOOTHE YOUR SOUL BY KILLING ORPHANS?
THE ONLY REASON YOU HUNT THEM IS BECAUSE YOU KNOW YOU'RE NO MATCH FOR THE ADEVARAHT KURAI.

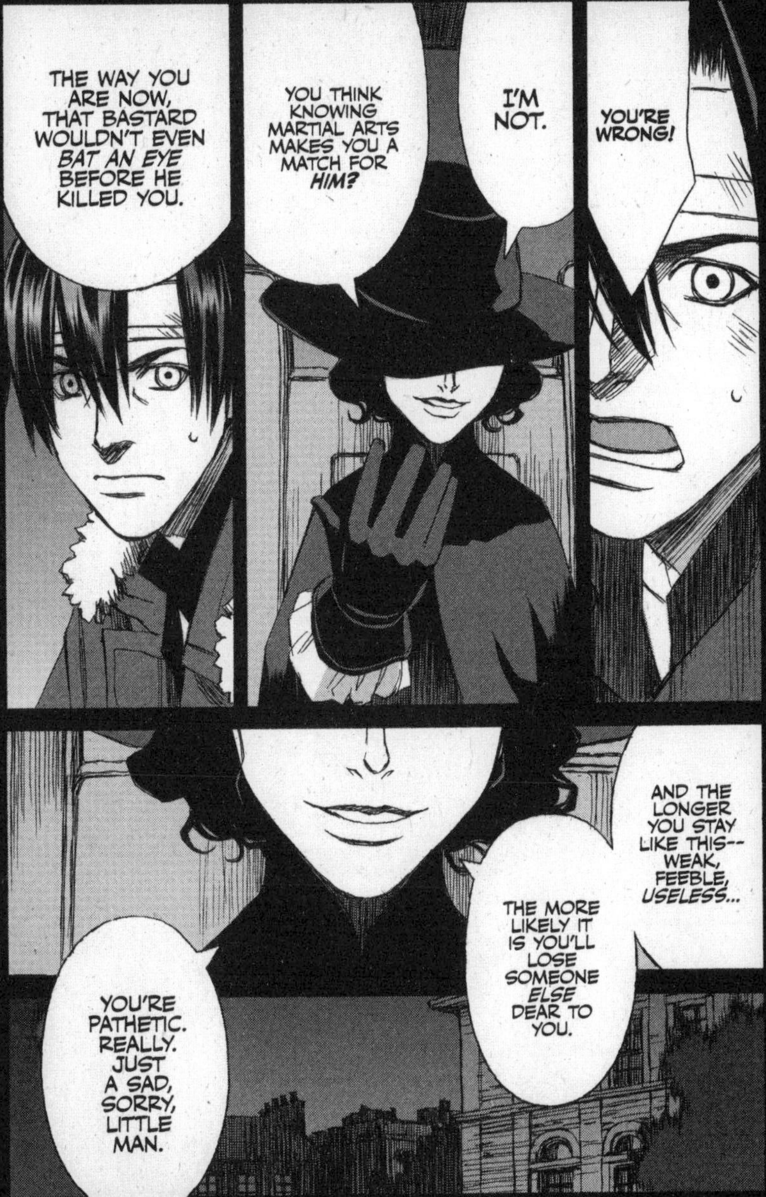
YOU'RE WRONG!
I'M NOT.
YOU THINK KNOWING MARTIAL ARTS MAKES YOU A MATCH FOR *HIM?*
THE WAY YOU ARE NOW, THAT BASTARD WOULDN'T EVEN *BAT AN EYE* BEFORE HE KILLED YOU.
AND THE LONGER YOU STAY LIKE THIS-- WEAK, FEEBLE, *USELESS...*
THE MORE LIKELY IT IS YOU'LL LOSE SOMEONE *ELSE* DEAR TO YOU.
YOU'RE PATHETIC. REALLY. JUST A SAD, SORRY, LITTLE MAN.

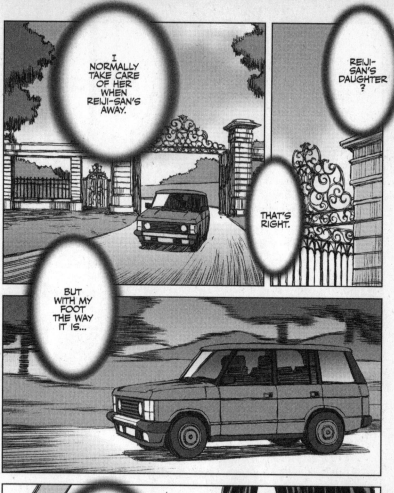

REIJI-SAN'S DAUGHTER?
THAT'S RIGHT.
I NORMALLY TAKE CARE OF HER WHEN REIJI-SAN'S AWAY.
BUT WITH MY FOOT THE WAY IT IS...
I REALLY APPRECIATE YOU HELPING ME OUT, KUROE.

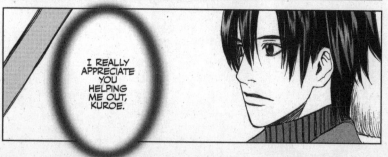

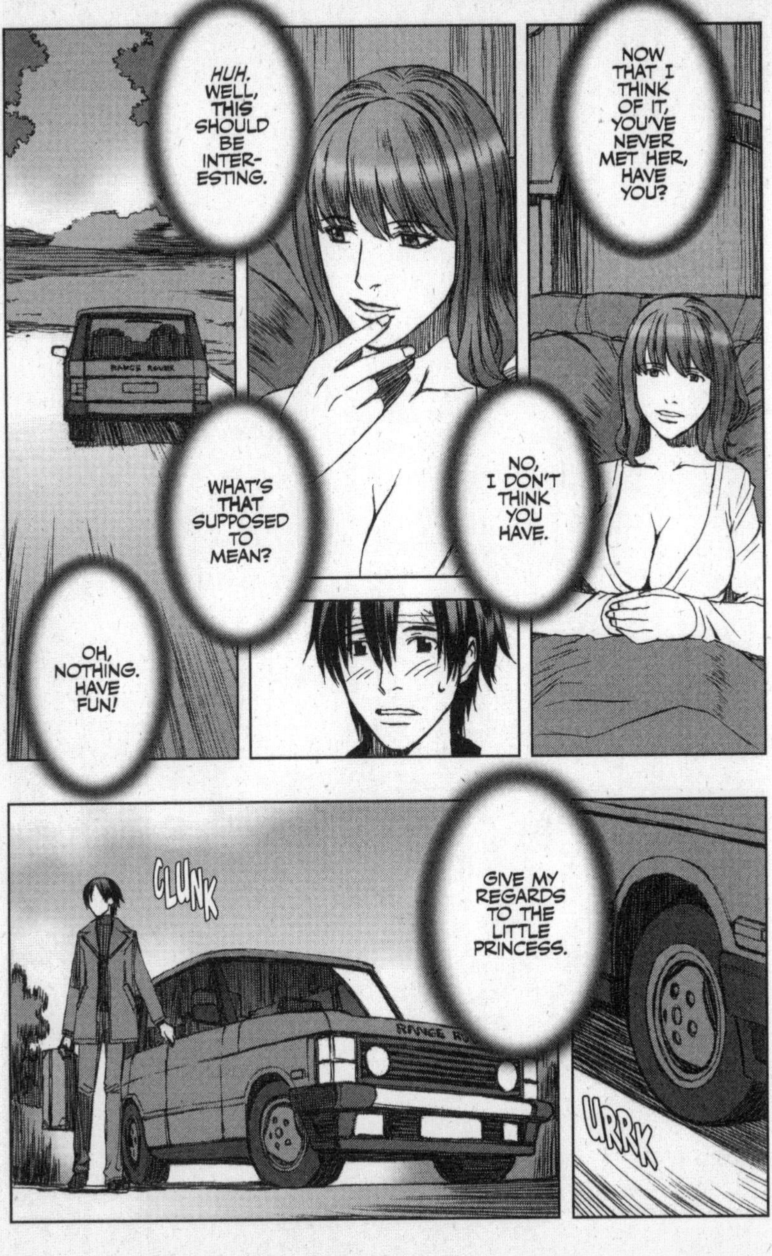
NOW THAT I THINK OF IT, YOU'VE NEVER MET HER, HAVE YOU?
NO, I DON'T THINK YOU HAVE.
HUH. WELL, THIS SHOULD BE INTER-ESTING.
WHAT'S THAT SUPPOSED TO MEAN?
OH, NOTHING. HAVE FUN!
GIVE MY REGARDS TO THE LITTLE PRINCESS.
URRRK
CLUNK

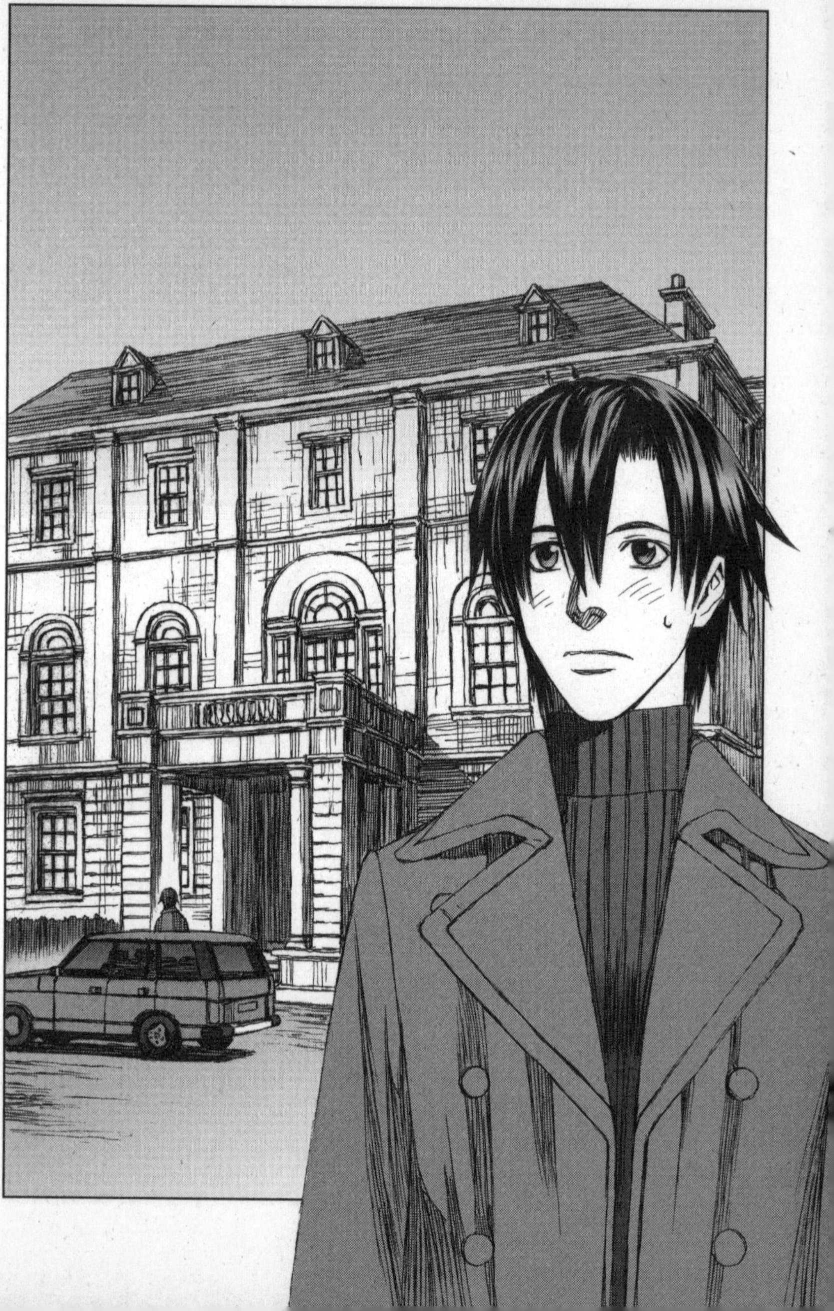

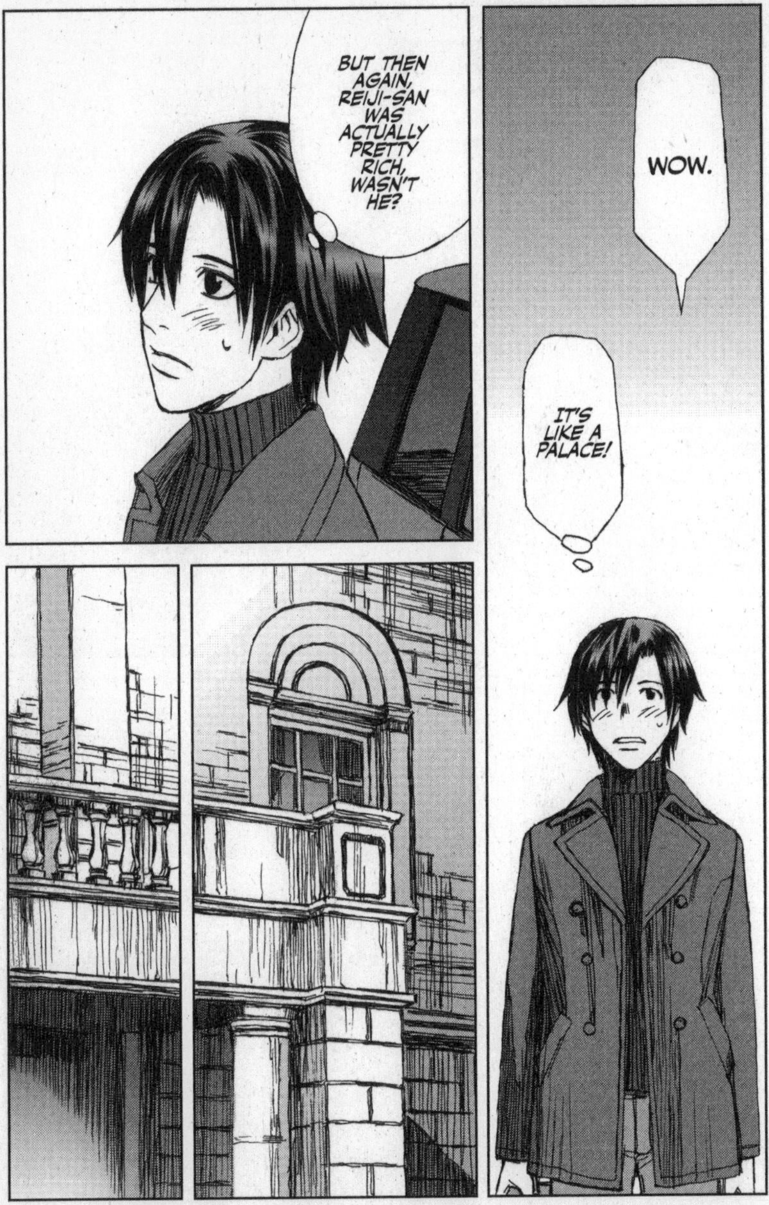
WOW.
IT'S LIKE A PALACE!
BUT THEN AGAIN, REIJI-SAN WAS ACTUALLY PRETTY RICH, WASN'T HE?

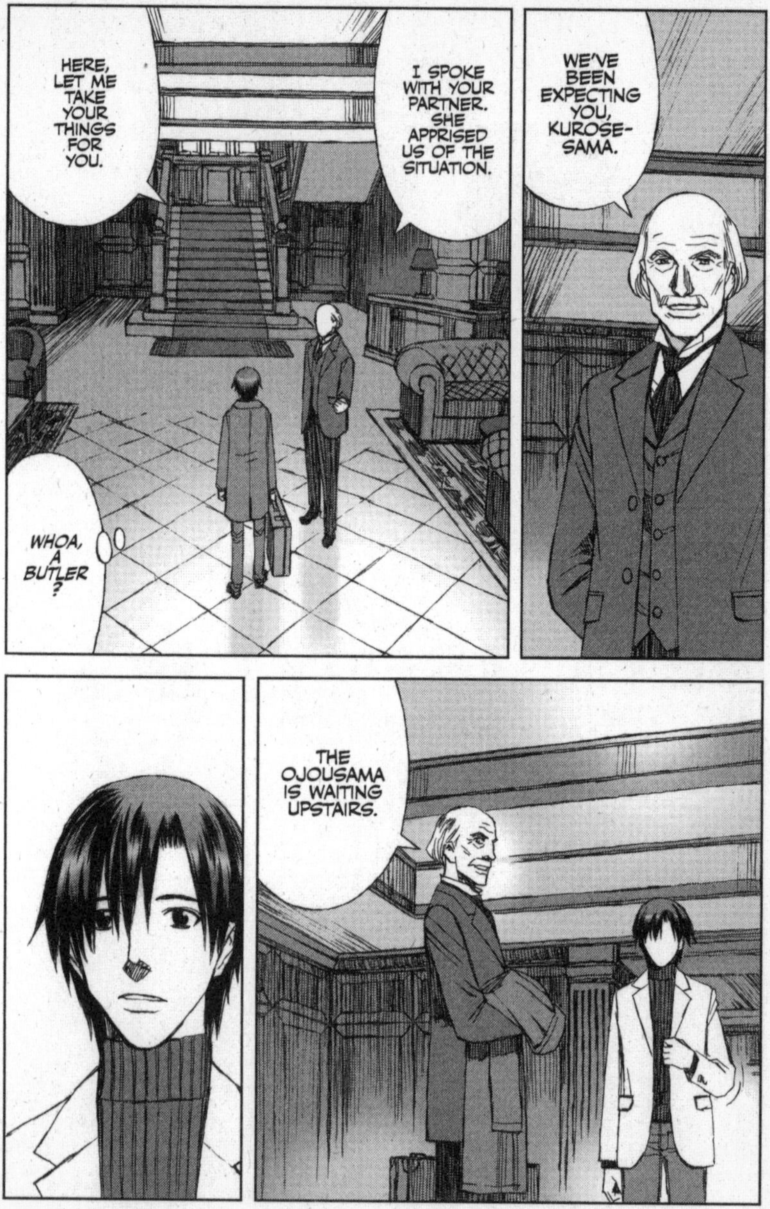
WE'VE BEEN EXPECTING YOU, KUROSE-SAMA.
I SPOKE WITH YOUR PARTNER. SHE APPRISED US OF THE SITUATION.
HERE, LET ME TAKE YOUR THINGS FOR YOU.
WHOA, A BUTLER?
THE OJOUSAMA IS WAITING UPSTAIRS.

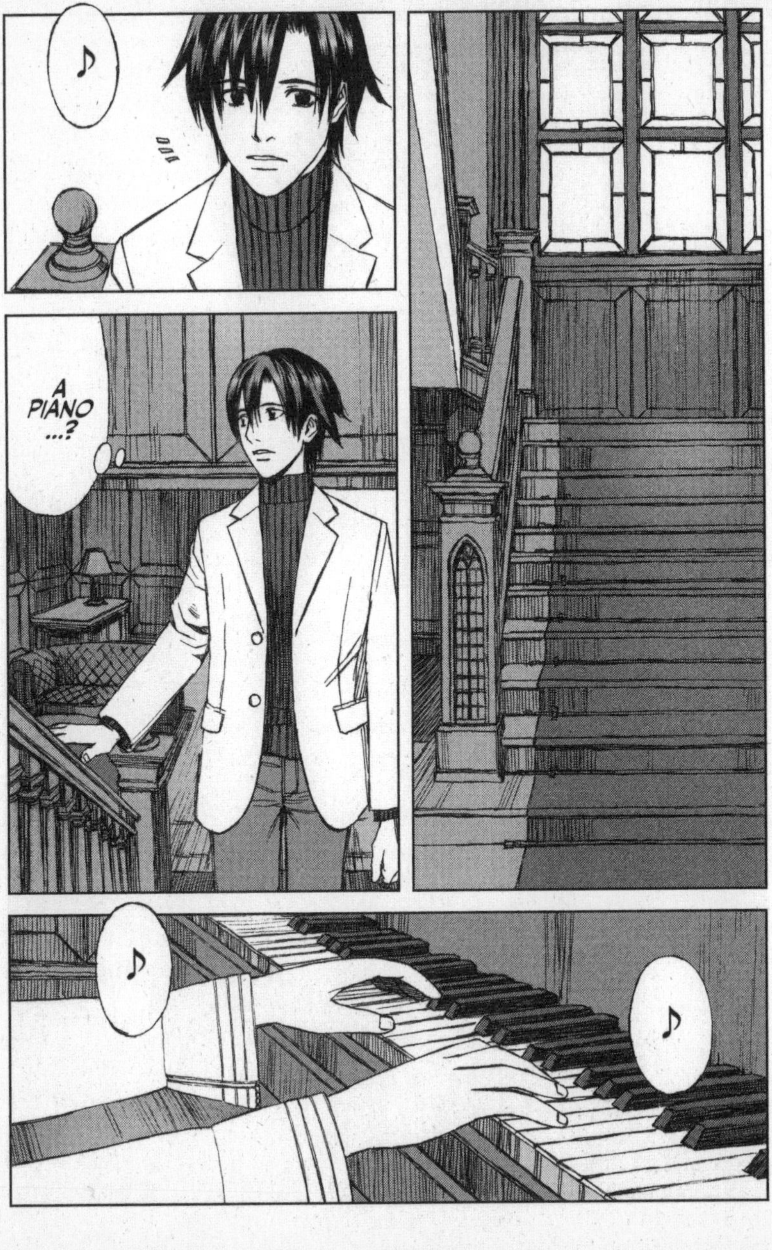
♪
A PIANO ...?
♪
♪

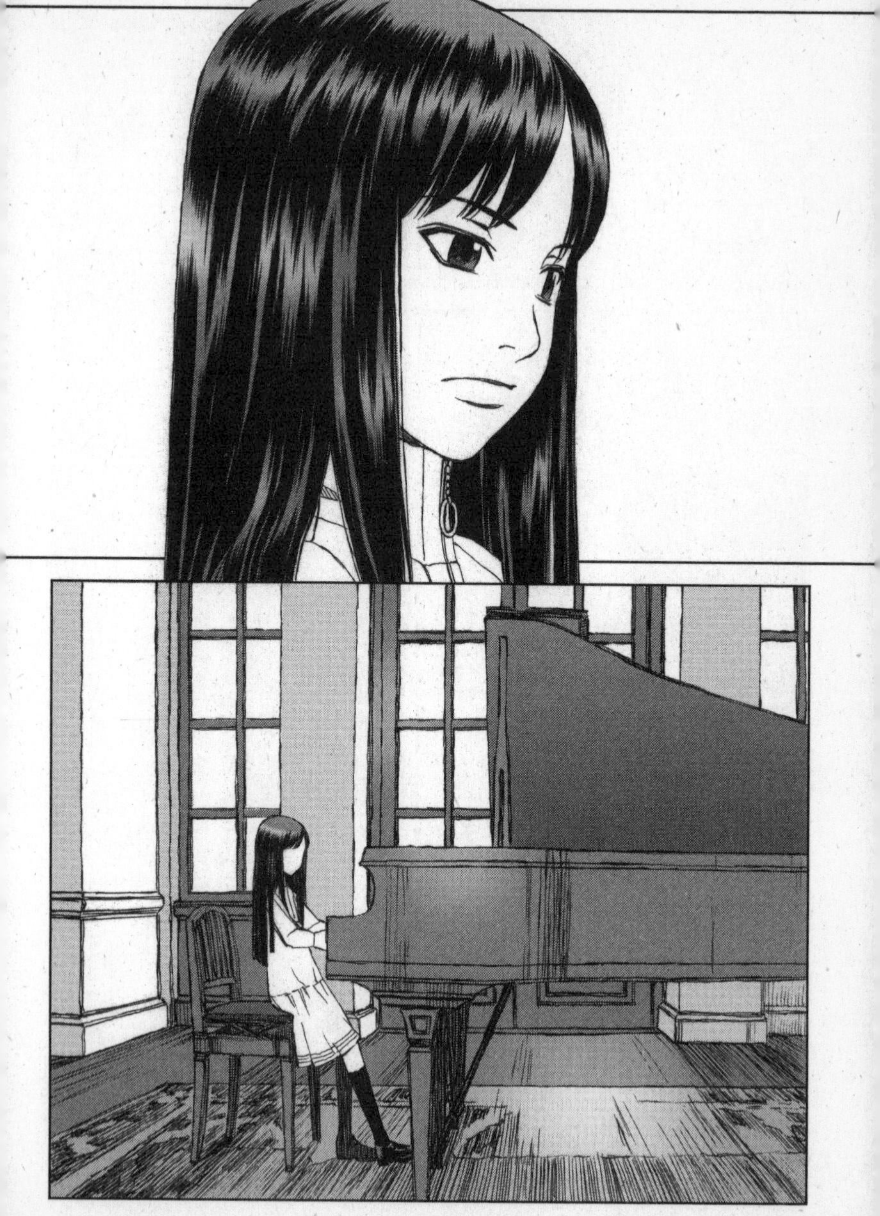

Part 2

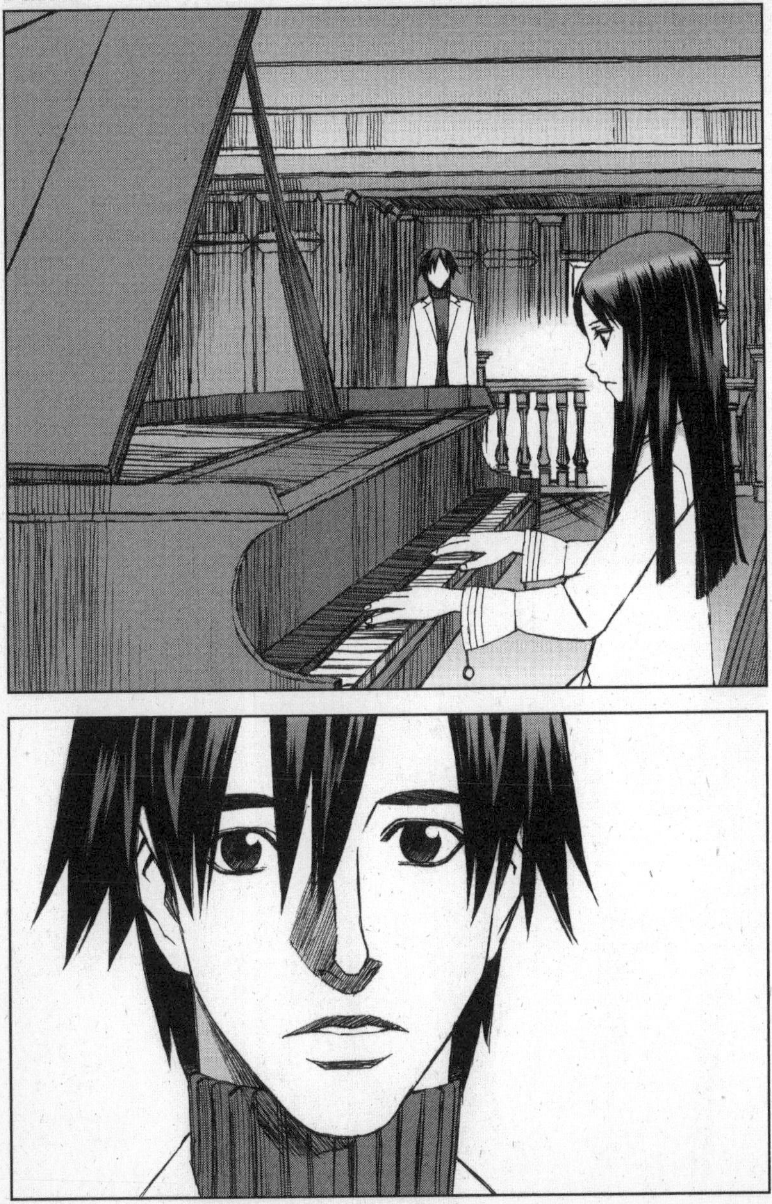

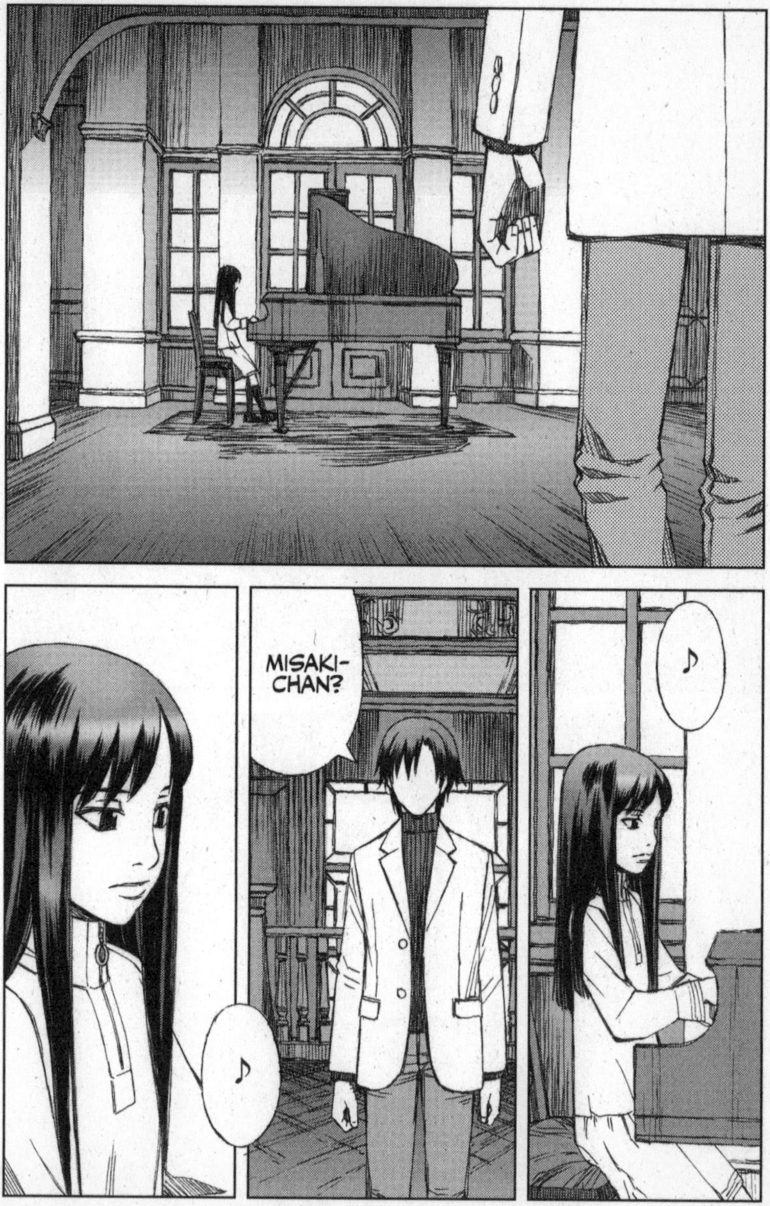
♪
MISAKI-CHAN?
♪

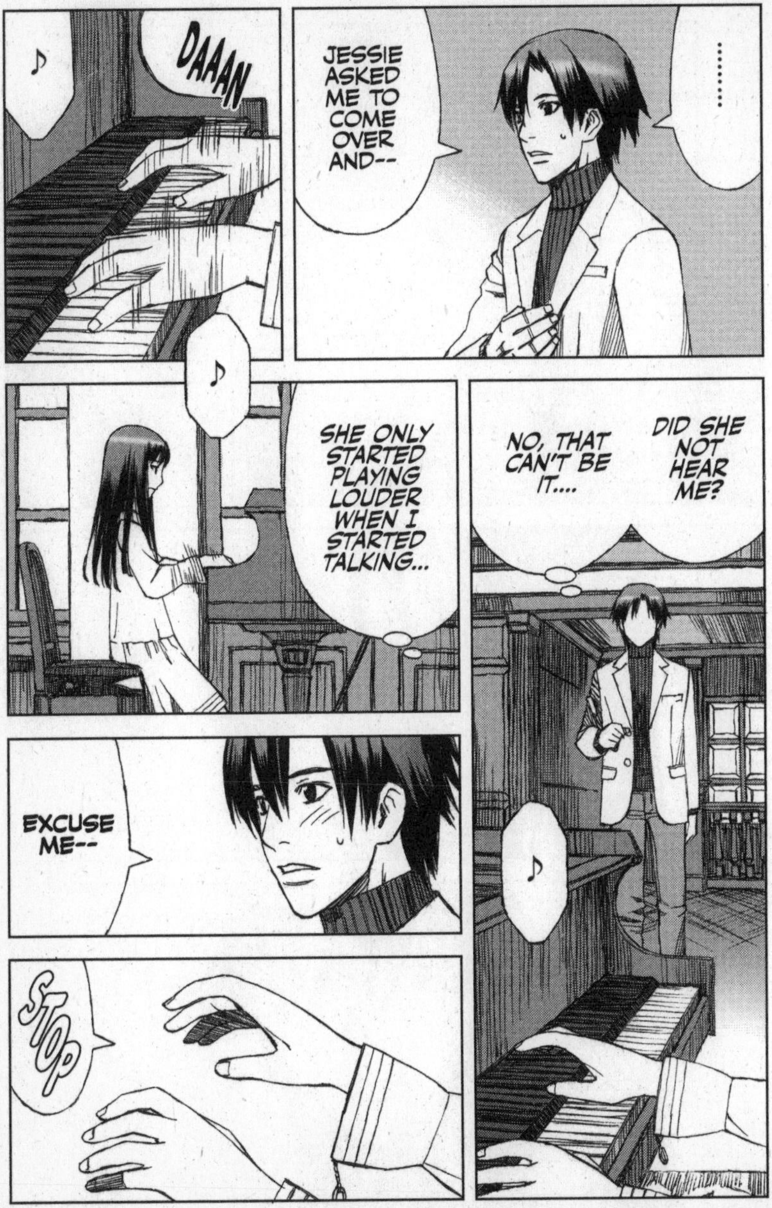
......
JESSIE ASKED ME TO COME OVER AND--
DAAAN
♪
♪
DID SHE NOT HEAR ME?
NO, THAT CAN'T BE IT....
♪
♪
SHE ONLY STARTED PLAYING LOUDER WHEN I STARTED TALKING...
EXCUSE ME--
STOP

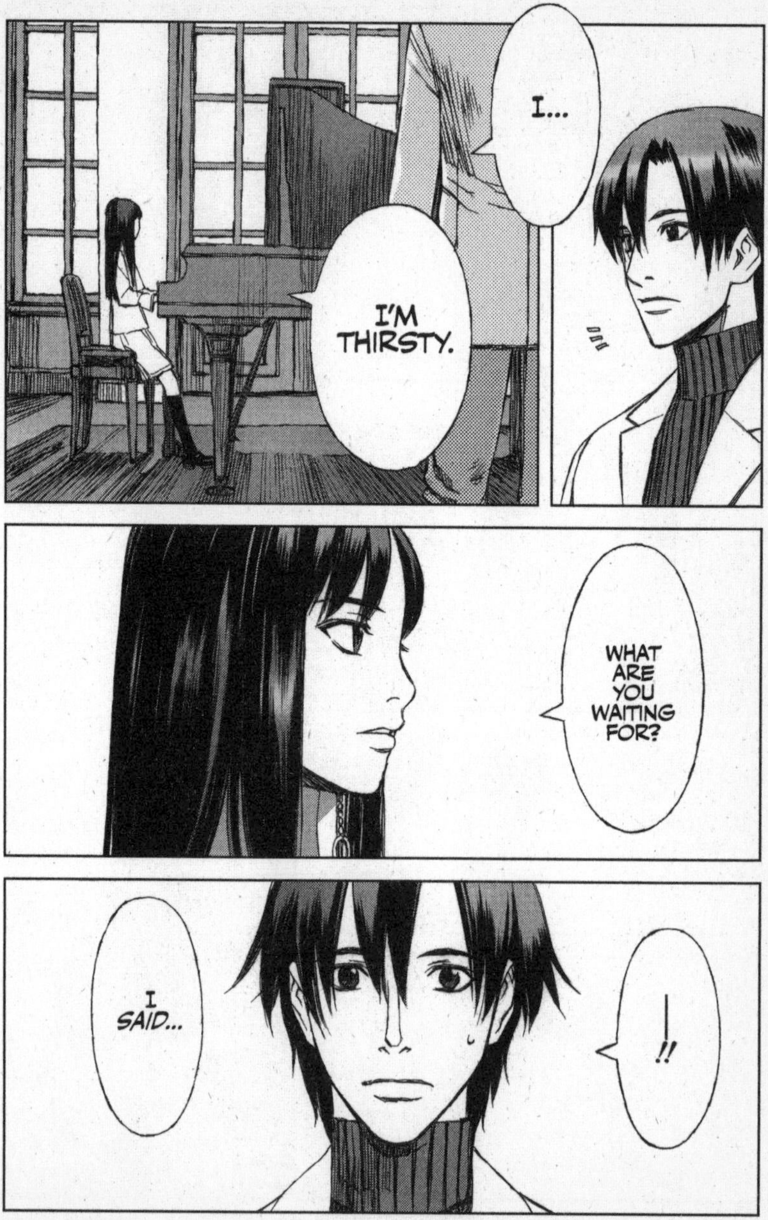
I...
I'M THIRSTY.
WHAT ARE YOU WAITING FOR?
—!!
I SAID...

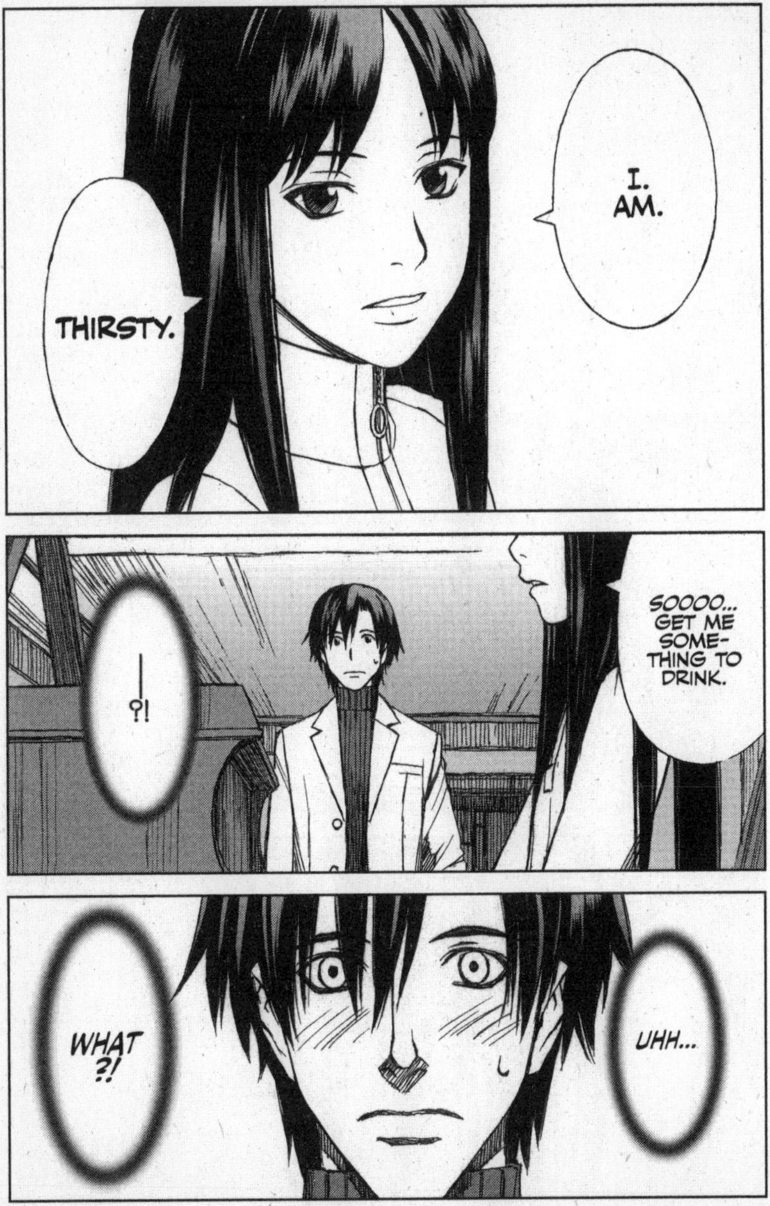
I. AM.
THIRSTY.
SOOOO... GET ME SOME-THING TO DRINK.
—?!
UHH...
WHAT?!

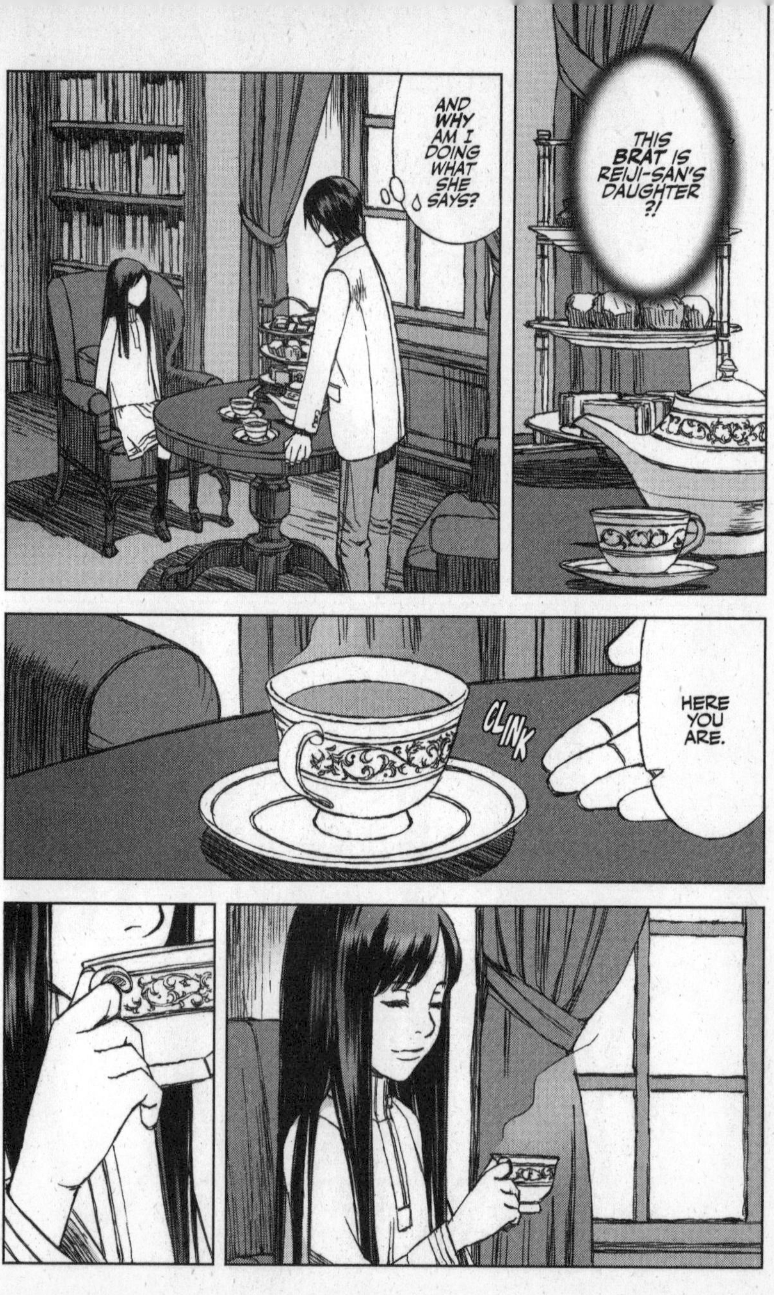
THIS BRAT IS REIJI-SAN'S DAUGHTER ?!
AND WHY AM I DOING WHAT SHE SAYS?
HERE YOU ARE.
CLINK

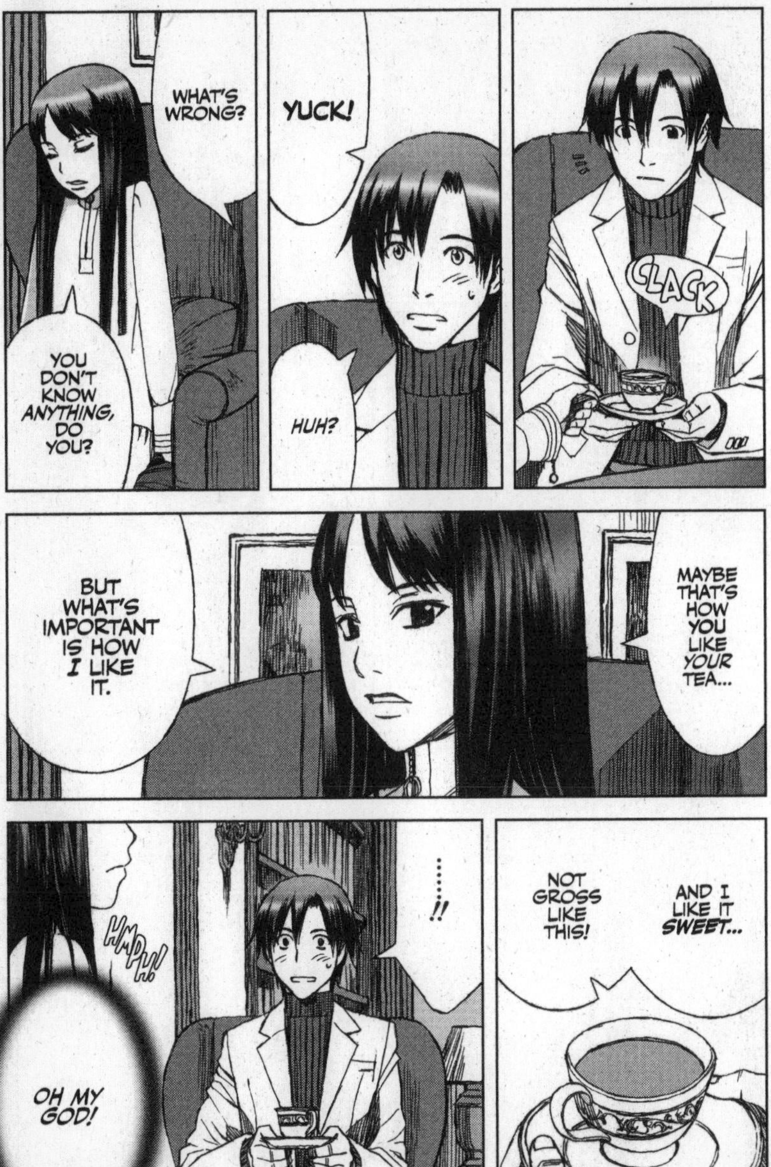
CLACK
YUCK!
HUH?
WHAT'S WRONG?
YOU DON'T KNOW *ANYTHING*, DO YOU?
MAYBE THAT'S HOW YOU LIKE *YOUR* TEA...
BUT WHAT'S IMPORTANT IS HOW *I* LIKE IT.
AND I LIKE IT ***SWEET***...
NOT GROSS LIKE THIS!
......!!
HMPH!
OH MY GOD!

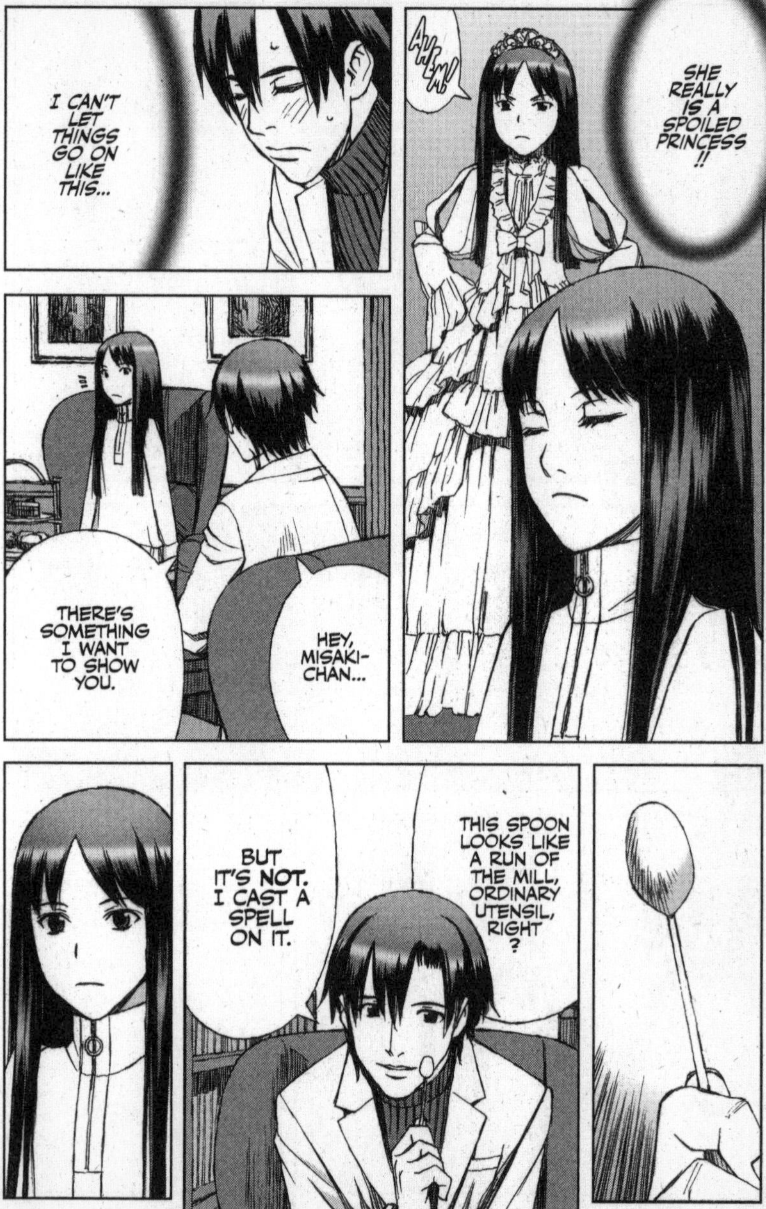
AHEM!
SHE REALLY IS A SPOILED PRINCESS!!
I CAN'T LET THINGS GO ON LIKE THIS...
HEY, MISAKI-CHAN...
THERE'S SOMETHING I WANT TO SHOW YOU.
THIS SPOON LOOKS LIKE A RUN OF THE MILL, ORDINARY UTENSIL, RIGHT?
BUT IT'S **NOT**. I CAST A SPELL ON IT.

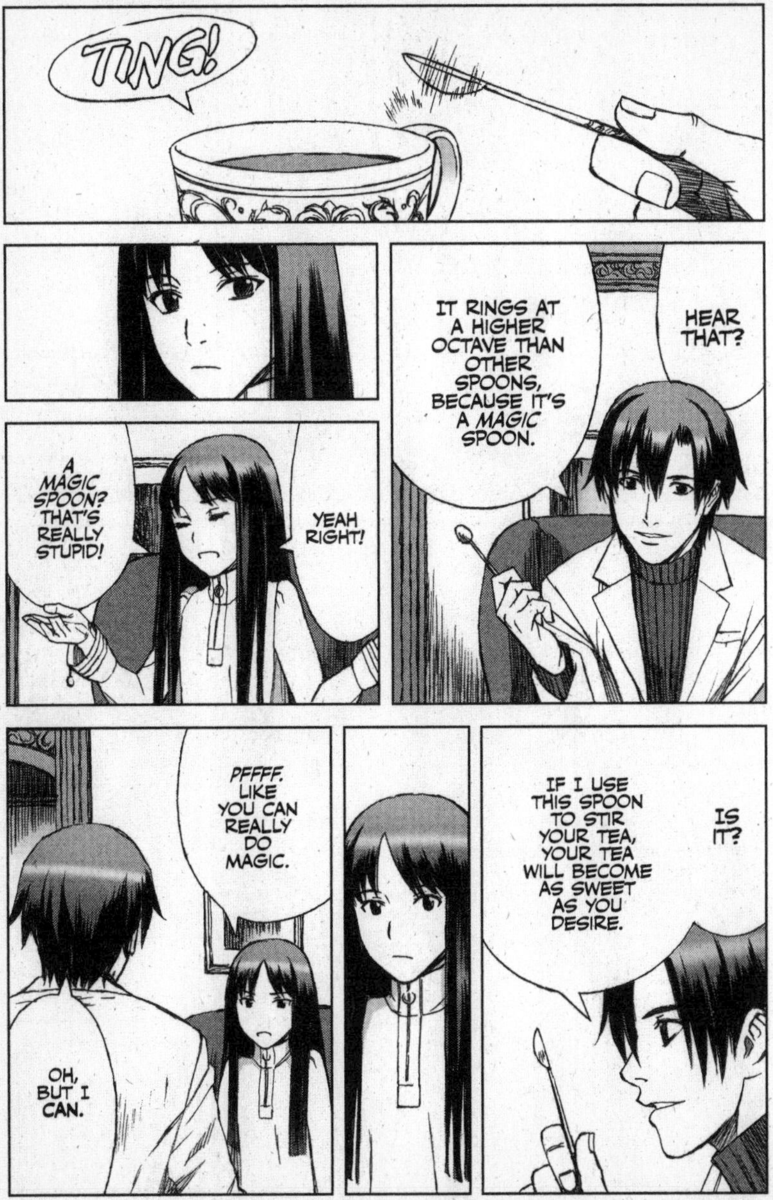
TING!
HEAR THAT?
IT RINGS AT A HIGHER OCTAVE THAN OTHER SPOONS, BECAUSE IT'S A *MAGIC* SPOON.
YEAH RIGHT!
A *MAGIC SPOON?* THAT'S REALLY STUPID!
IS IT?
IF I USE THIS SPOON TO STIR YOUR TEA, YOUR TEA WILL BECOME AS SWEET AS YOU DESIRE.
PFFFF. LIKE YOU CAN REALLY DO MAGIC.
OH, BUT I CAN.

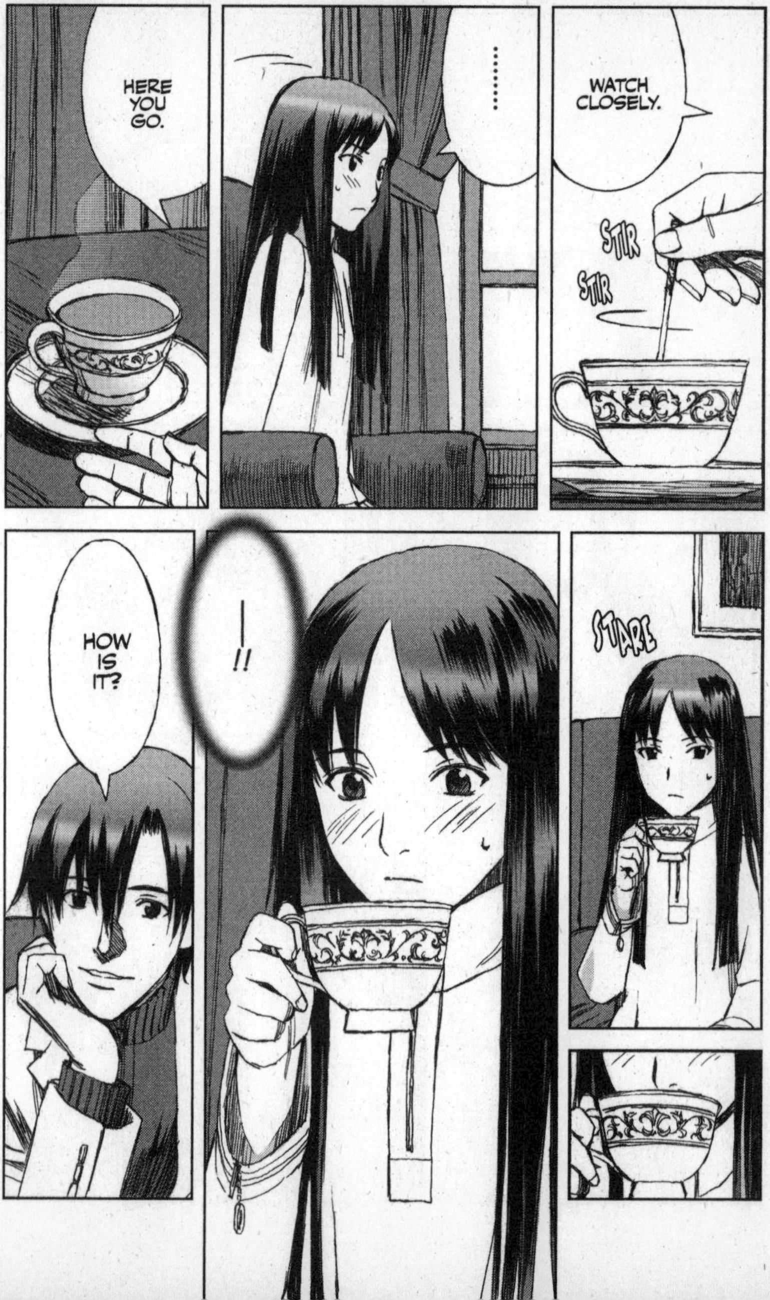
WATCH CLOSELY.
STIR
STIR
....
HERE YOU GO.
STARE
—!!
HOW IS IT?

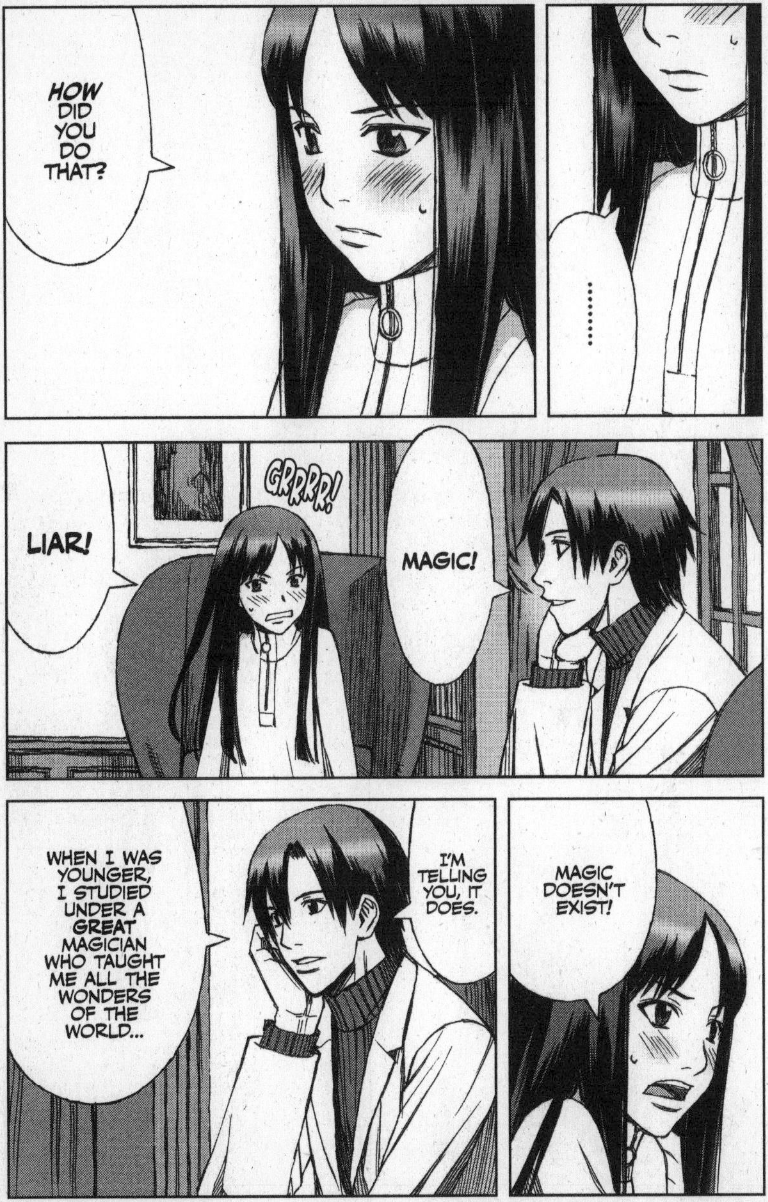

……
HOW DID YOU DO THAT?
MAGIC!
GRRRR!
LIAR!
MAGIC DOESN'T EXIST!
I'M TELLING YOU, IT DOES.
WHEN I WAS YOUNGER, I STUDIED UNDER A **GREAT** MAGICIAN WHO TAUGHT ME ALL THE WONDERS OF THE WORLD...

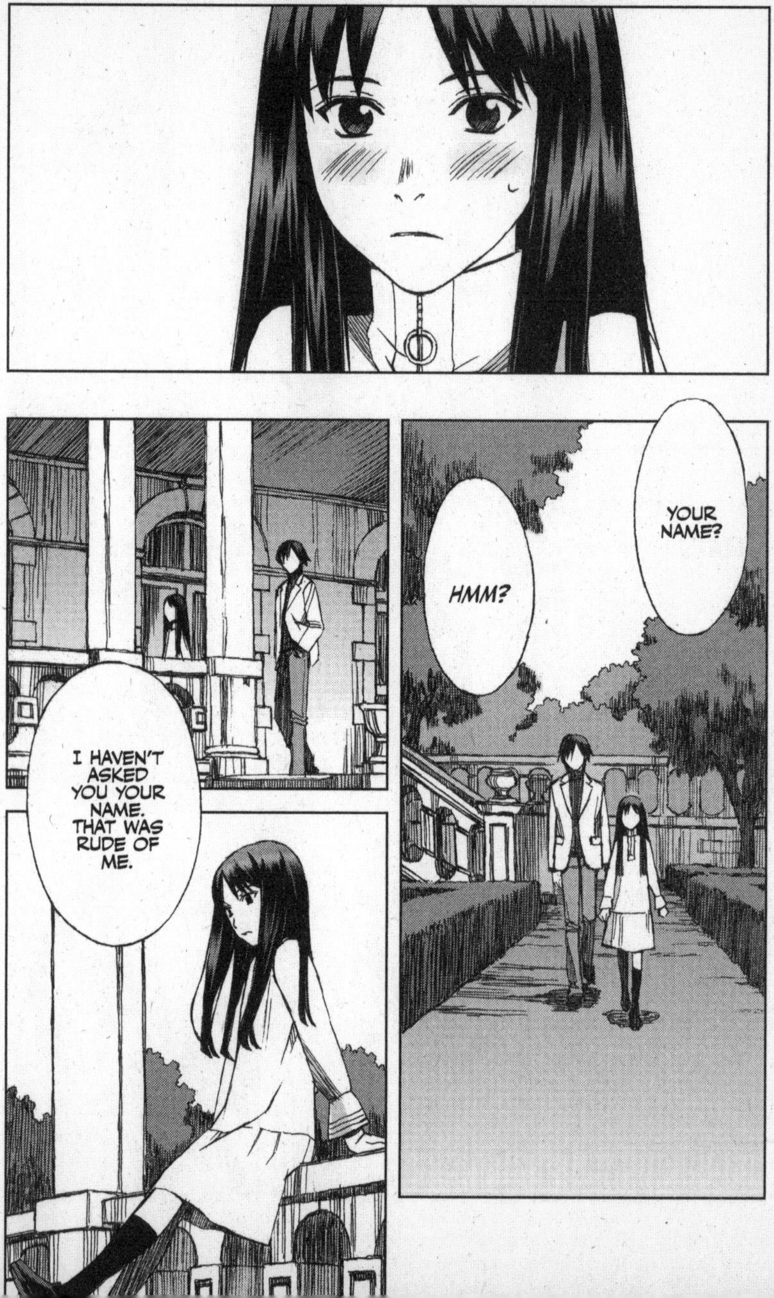
YOUR NAME?
HMM?
I HAVEN'T ASKED YOU YOUR NAME. THAT WAS RUDE OF ME.

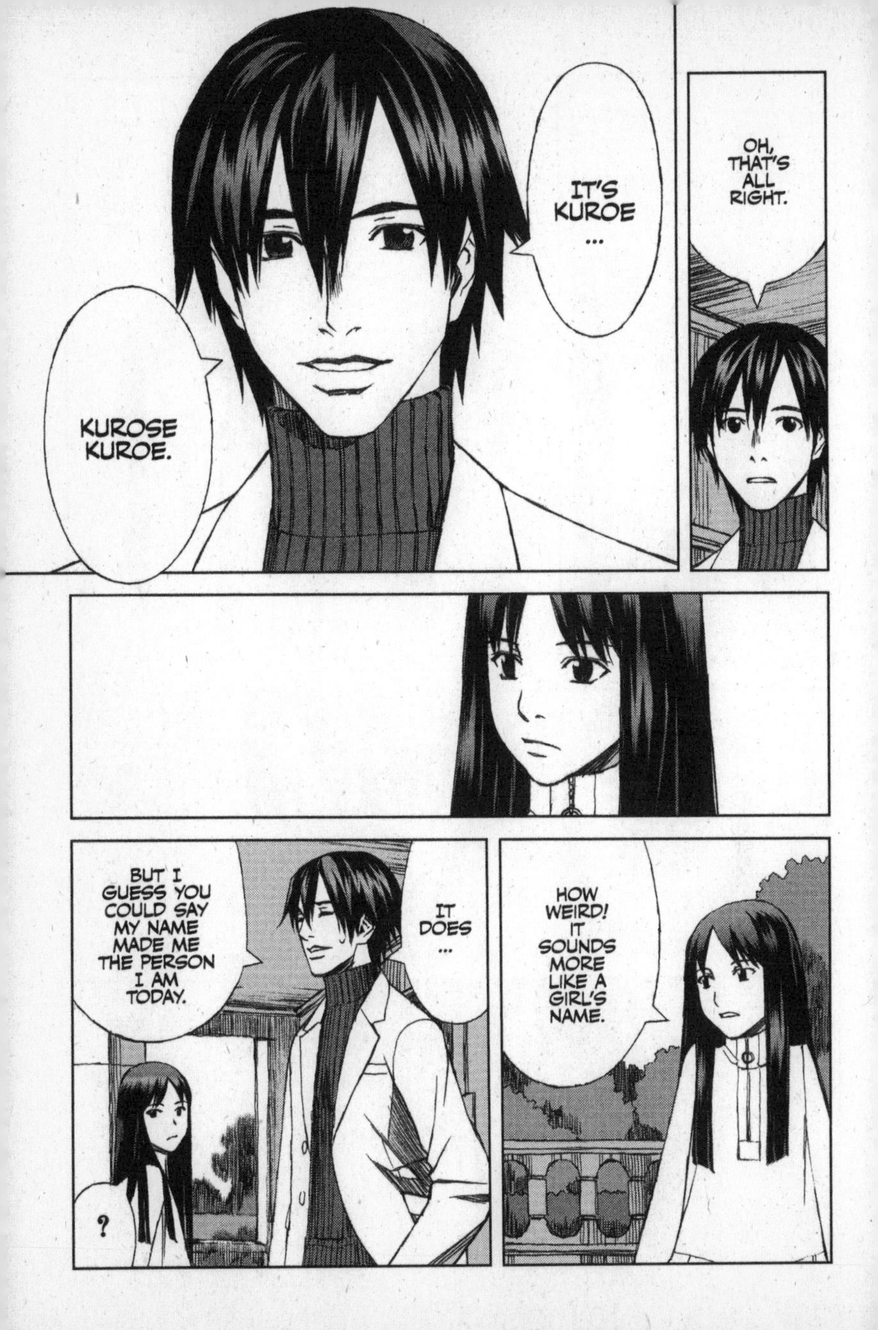
OH, THAT'S ALL RIGHT.
IT'S KUROE ...
KUROSE KUROE.
HOW WEIRD! IT SOUNDS MORE LIKE A GIRL'S NAME.
IT DOES ...
BUT I GUESS YOU COULD SAY MY NAME MADE ME THE PERSON I AM TODAY.
?

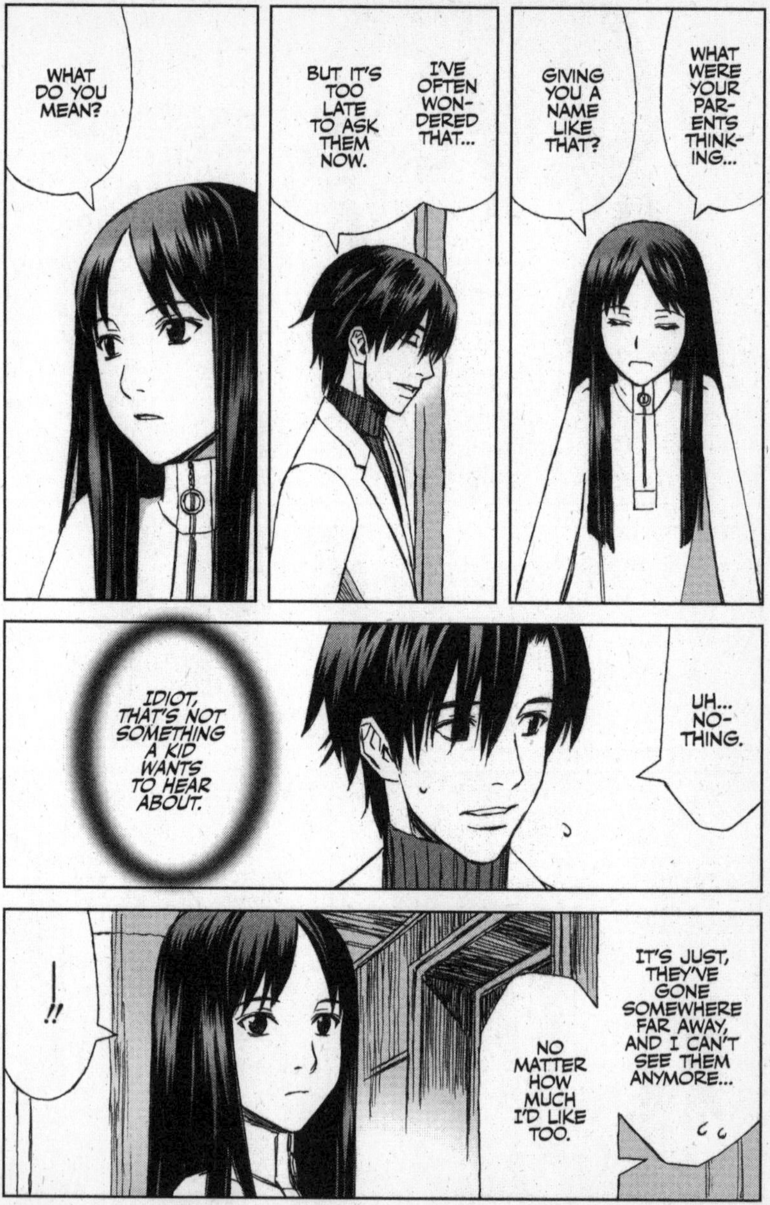
WHAT WERE YOUR PARENTS THINKING...
GIVING YOU A NAME LIKE THAT?
I'VE OFTEN WONDERED THAT...
BUT IT'S TOO LATE TO ASK THEM NOW.
WHAT DO YOU MEAN?
UH... NOTHING.
IDIOT, THAT'S NOT SOMETHING A KID WANTS TO HEAR ABOUT.
IT'S JUST, THEY'VE GONE SOMEWHERE FAR AWAY, AND I CAN'T SEE THEM ANYMORE...
NO MATTER HOW MUCH I'D LIKE TOO.
—!!

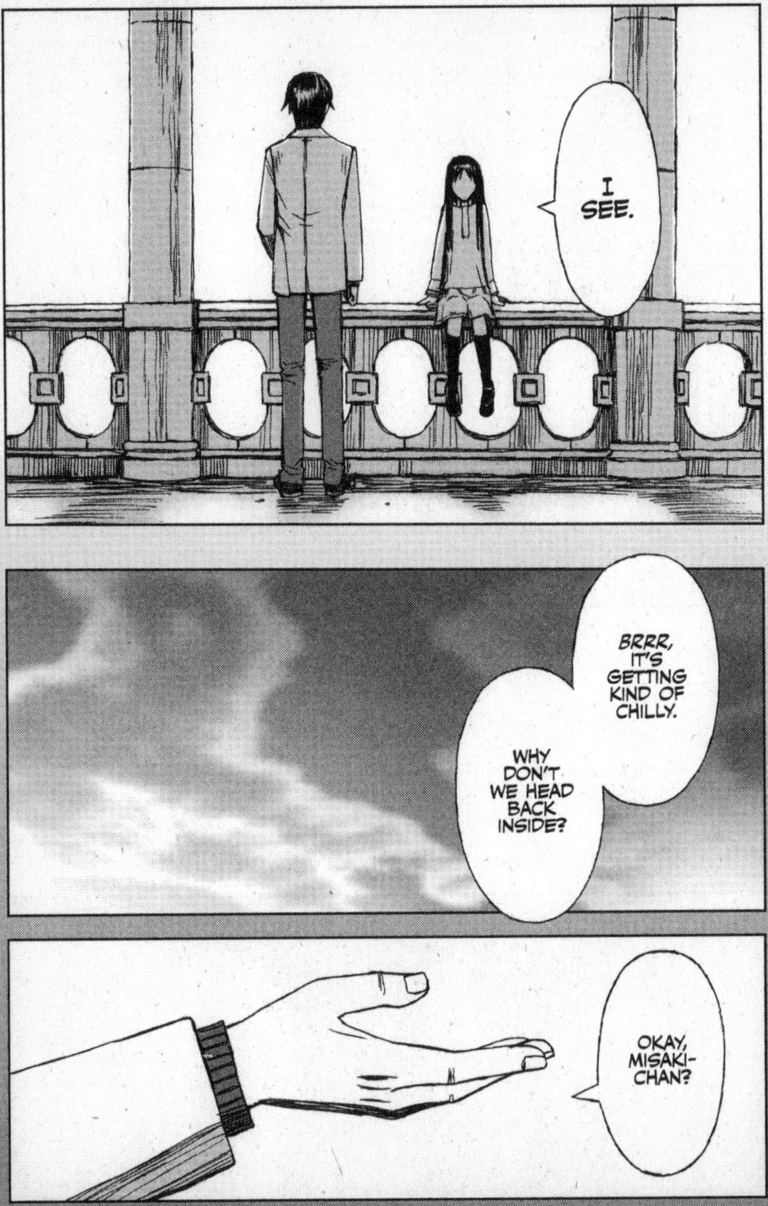
I SEE.
BRRR, IT'S GETTING KIND OF CHILLY.
WHY DON'T WE HEAD BACK INSIDE?
OKAY, MISAKI-CHAN?

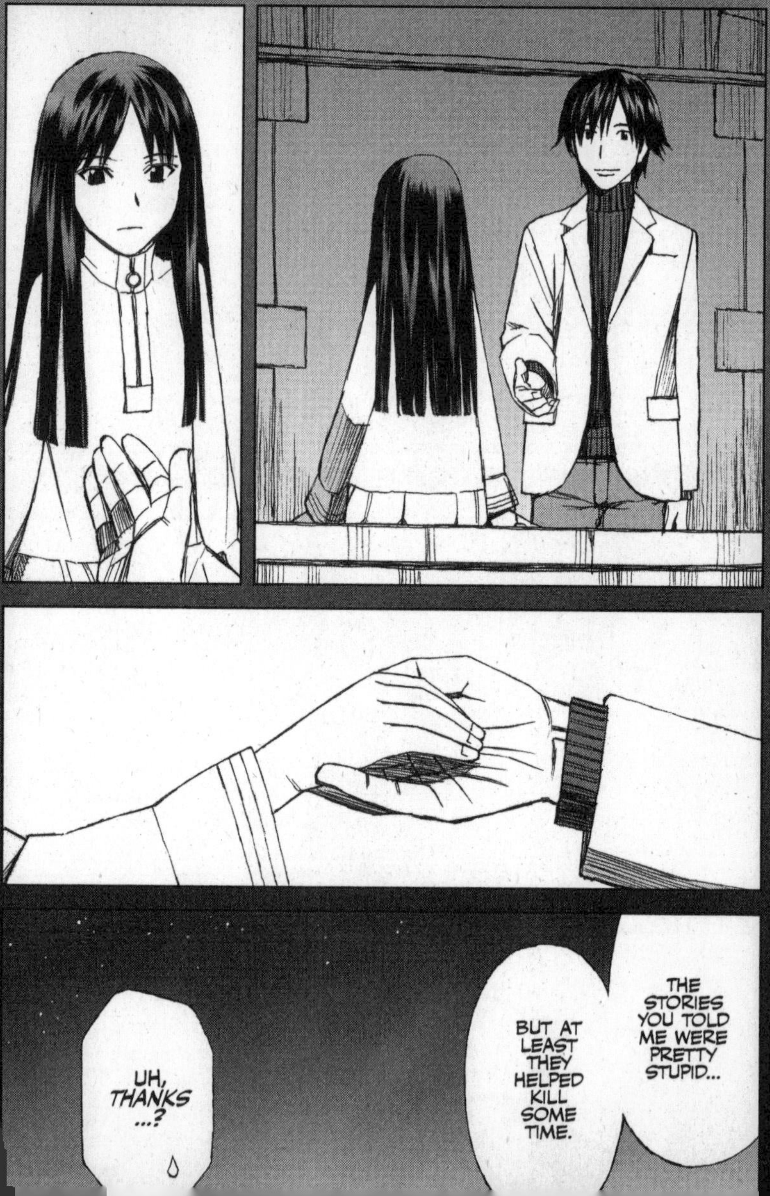
THE STORIES YOU TOLD ME WERE PRETTY STUPID...
BUT AT LEAST THEY HELPED KILL SOME TIME.
UH, THANKS ...?

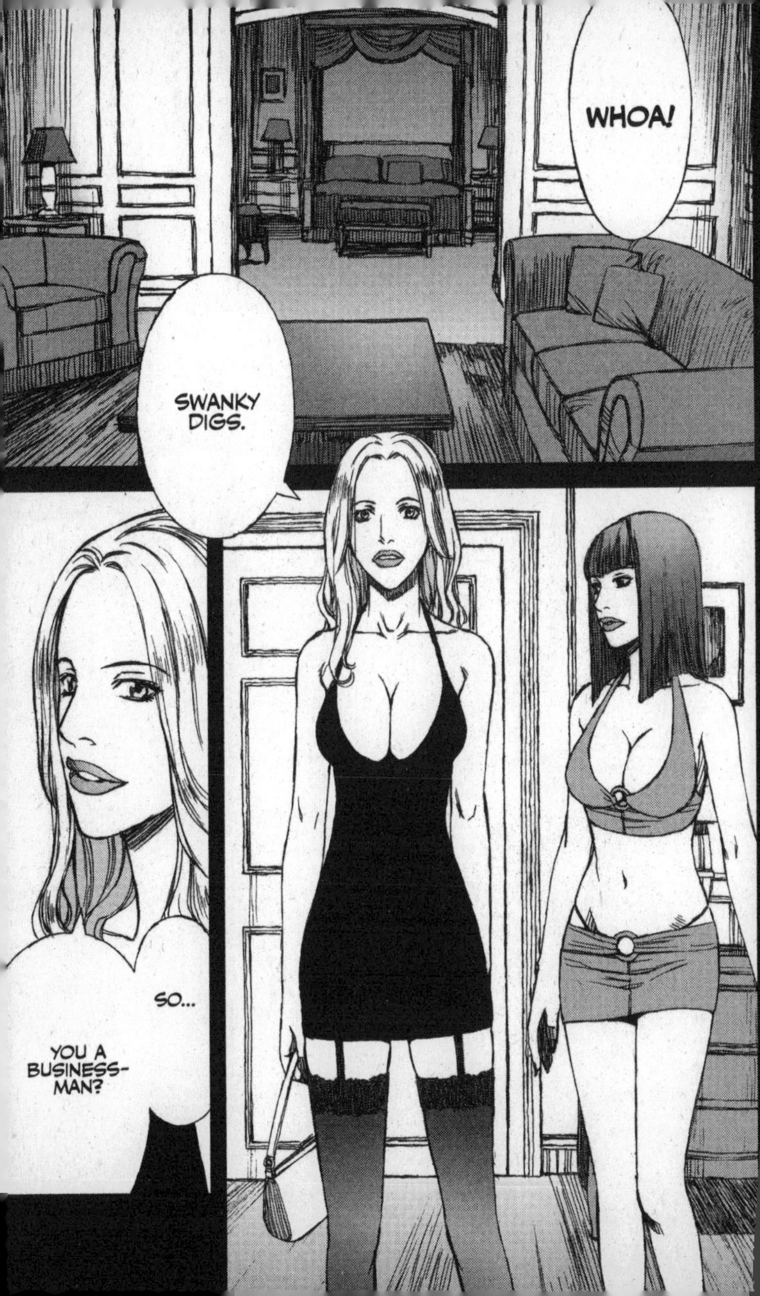
WHOA!
SWANKY DIGS.
SO...
YOU A BUSINESS-MAN?

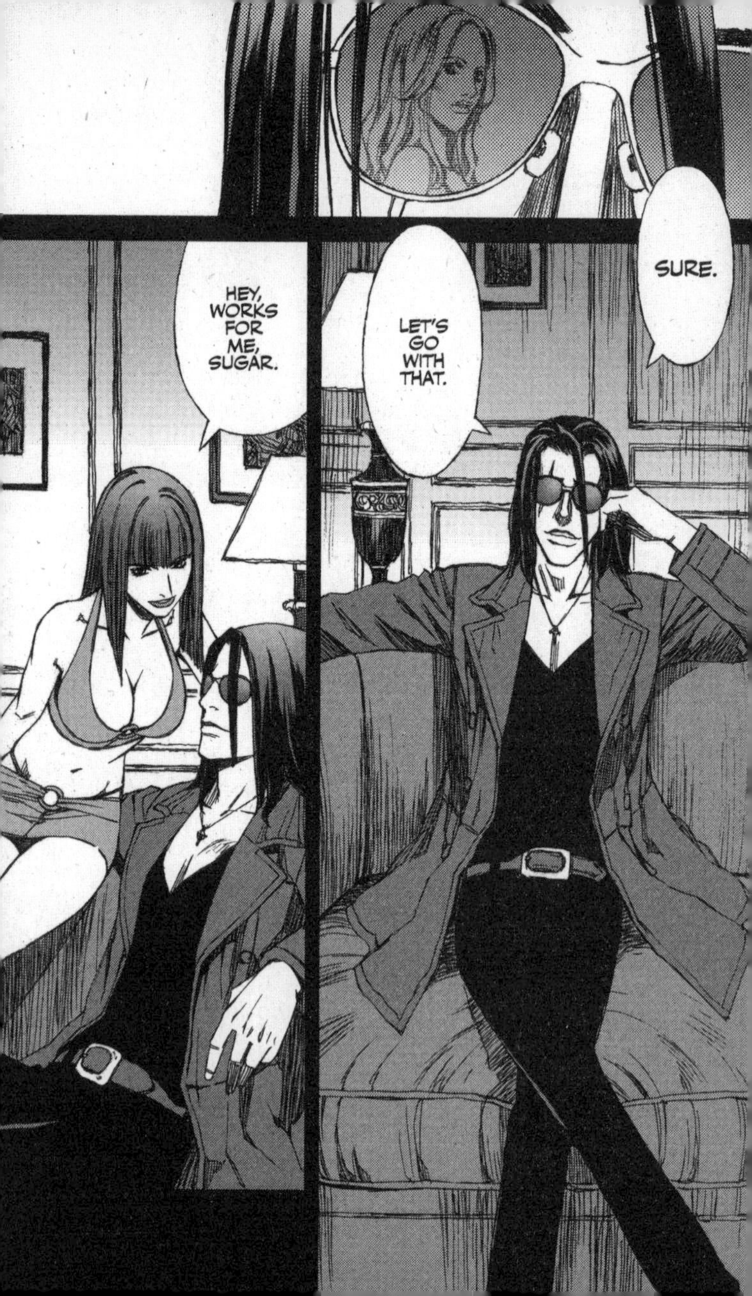
SURE.
LET'S GO WITH THAT.
HEY, WORKS FOR ME, SUGAR.

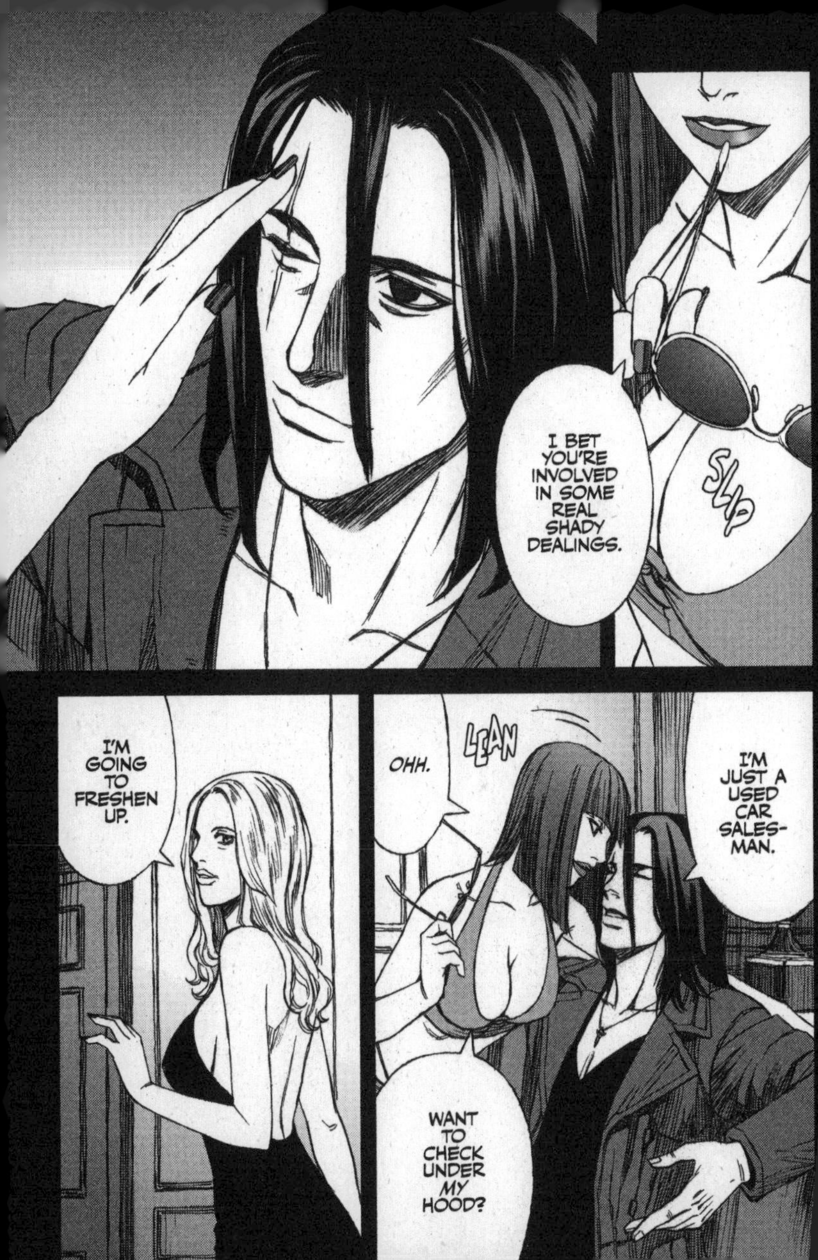
I BET YOU'RE INVOLVED IN SOME REAL SHADY DEALINGS.
SLIP
I'M JUST A USED CAR SALES-MAN.
LEAN
OHH.
WANT TO CHECK UNDER MY HOOD?
I'M GOING TO FRESHEN UP.

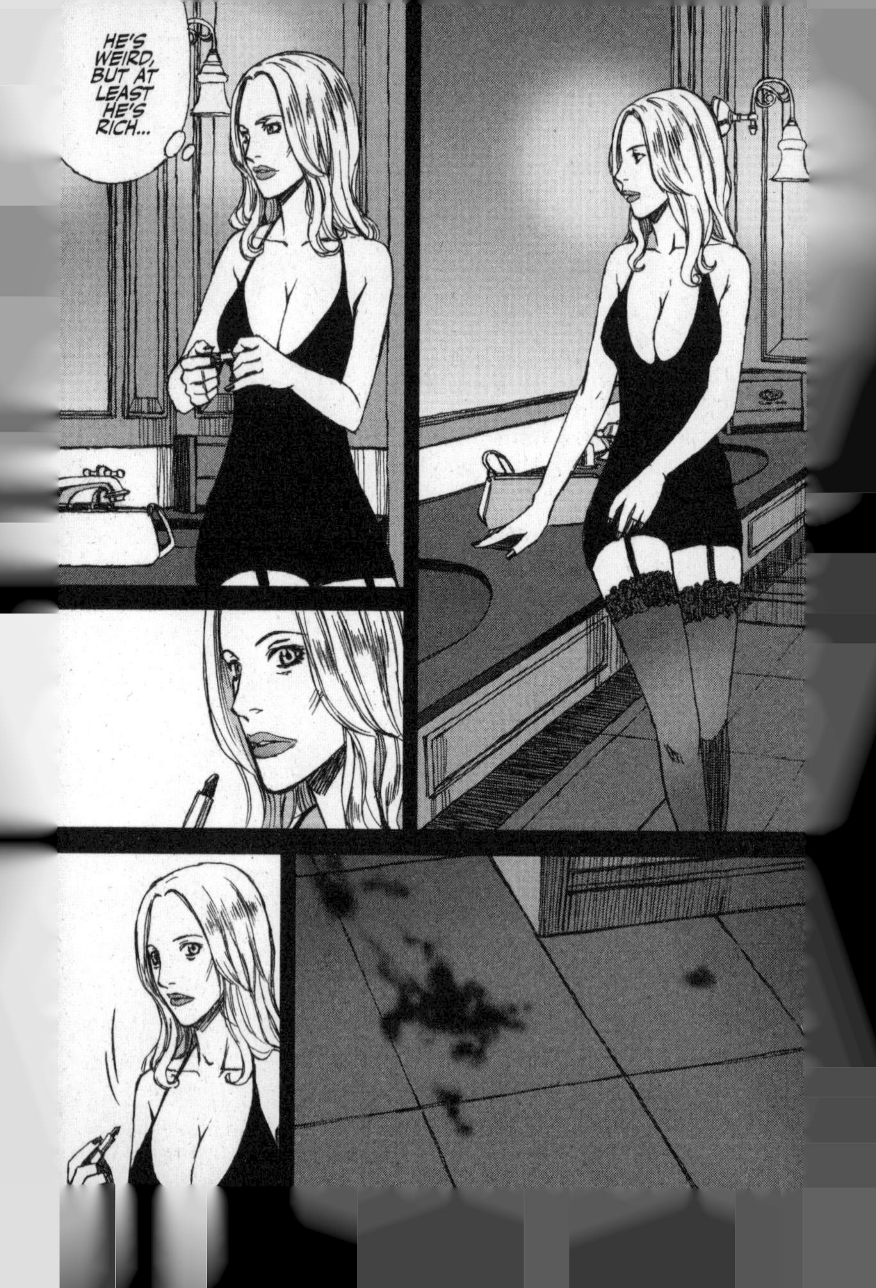
HE'S WEIRD, BUT AT LEAST HE'S RICH...

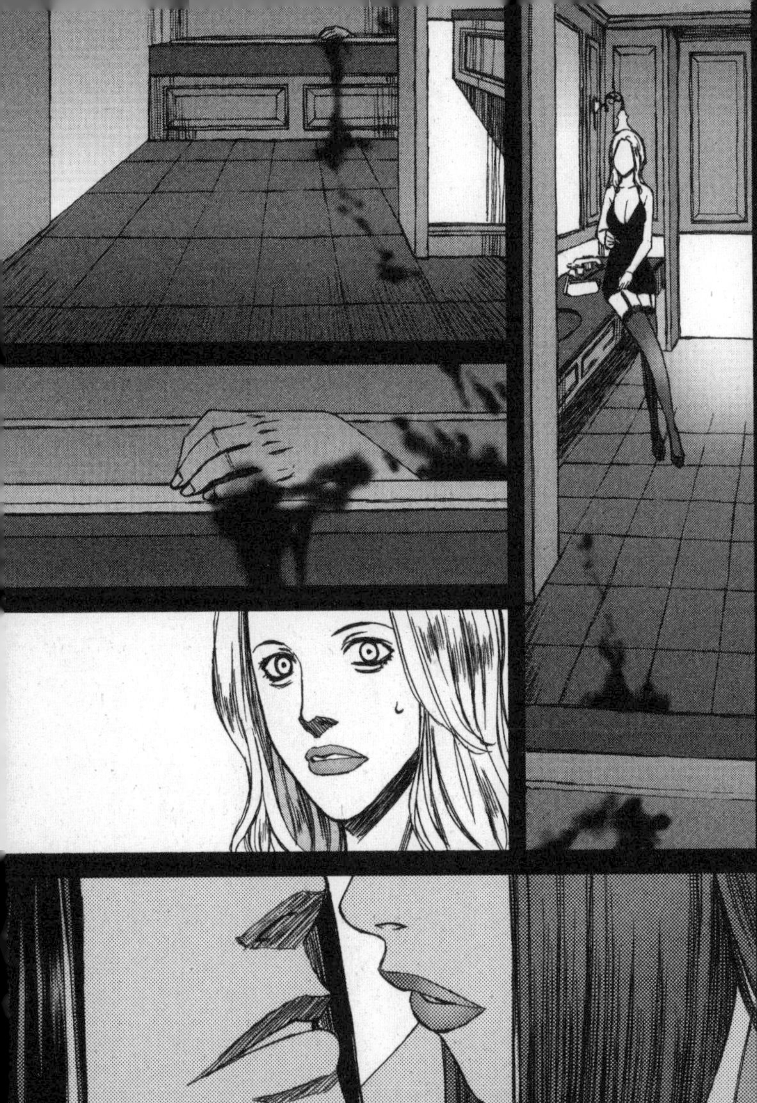

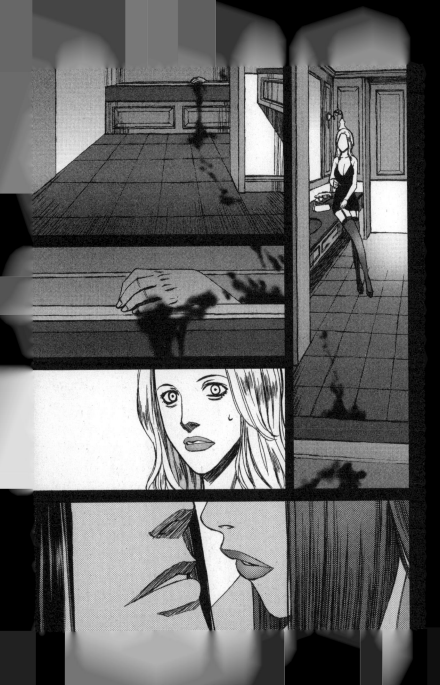

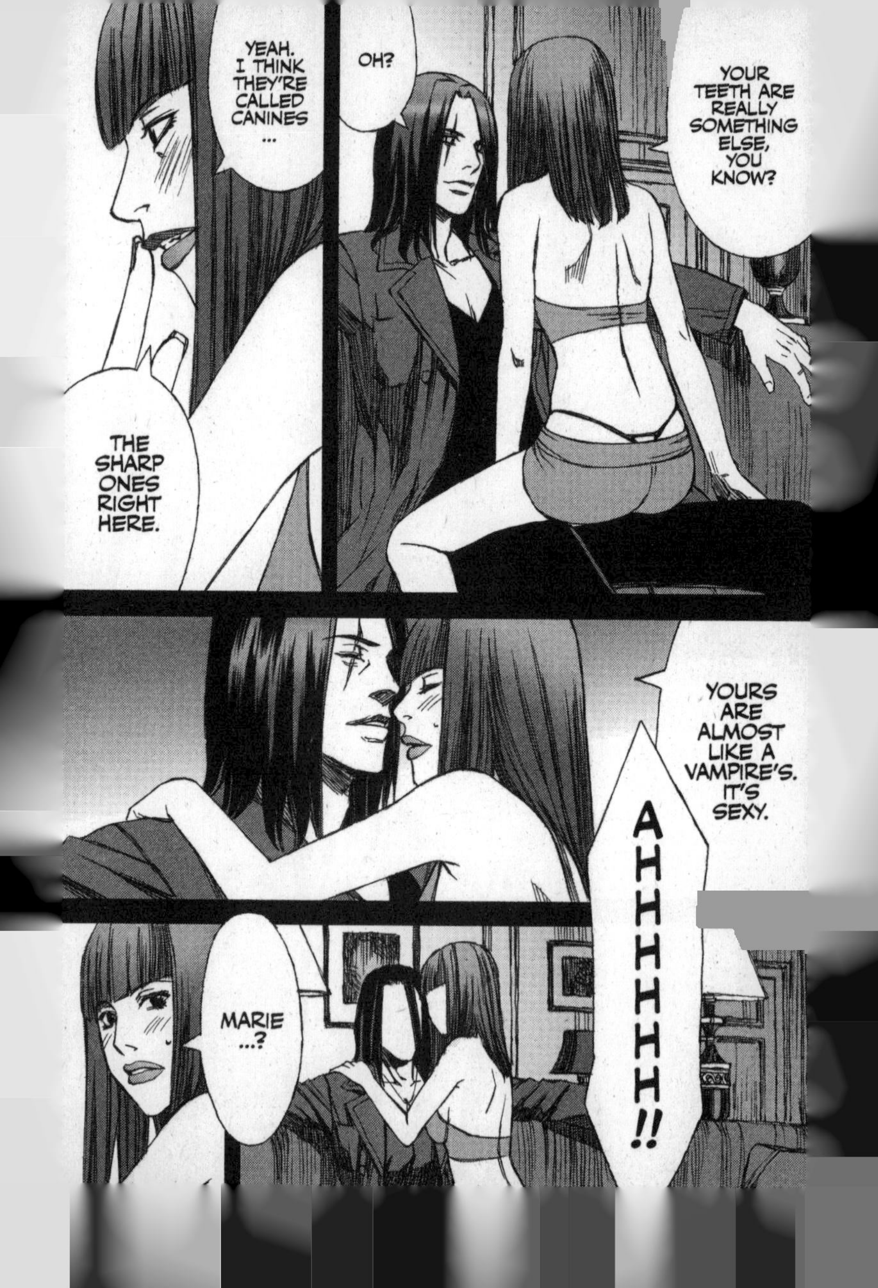
YOUR TEETH ARE REALLY SOMETHING ELSE, YOU KNOW?
OH?
YEAH. I THINK THEY'RE CALLED CANINES ...
THE SHARP ONES RIGHT HERE.
YOURS ARE ALMOST LIKE A VAMPIRE'S. IT'S SEXY.
AHHHHHH!!
MARIE ...?

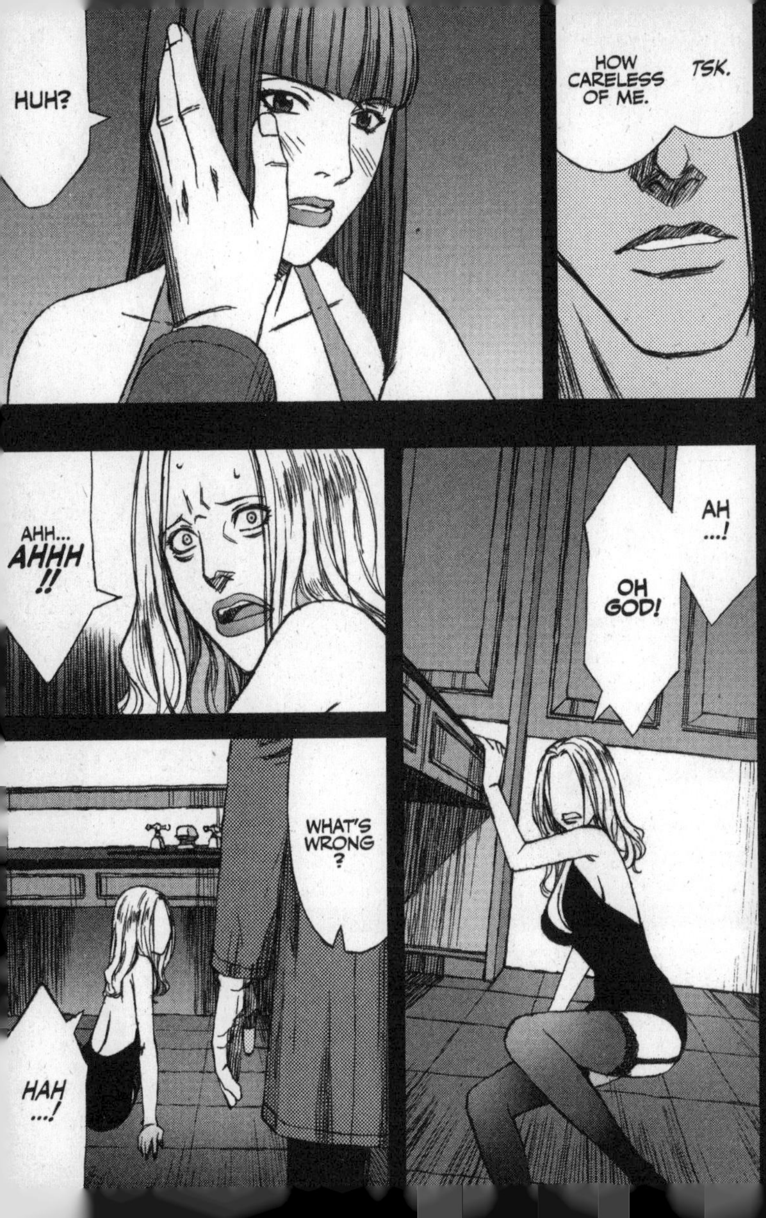
TSK.
HOW CARELESS OF ME.
HUH?
AH ...!
OH GOD!
AHH... AHHH !!
WHAT'S WRONG ?
HAH ...!

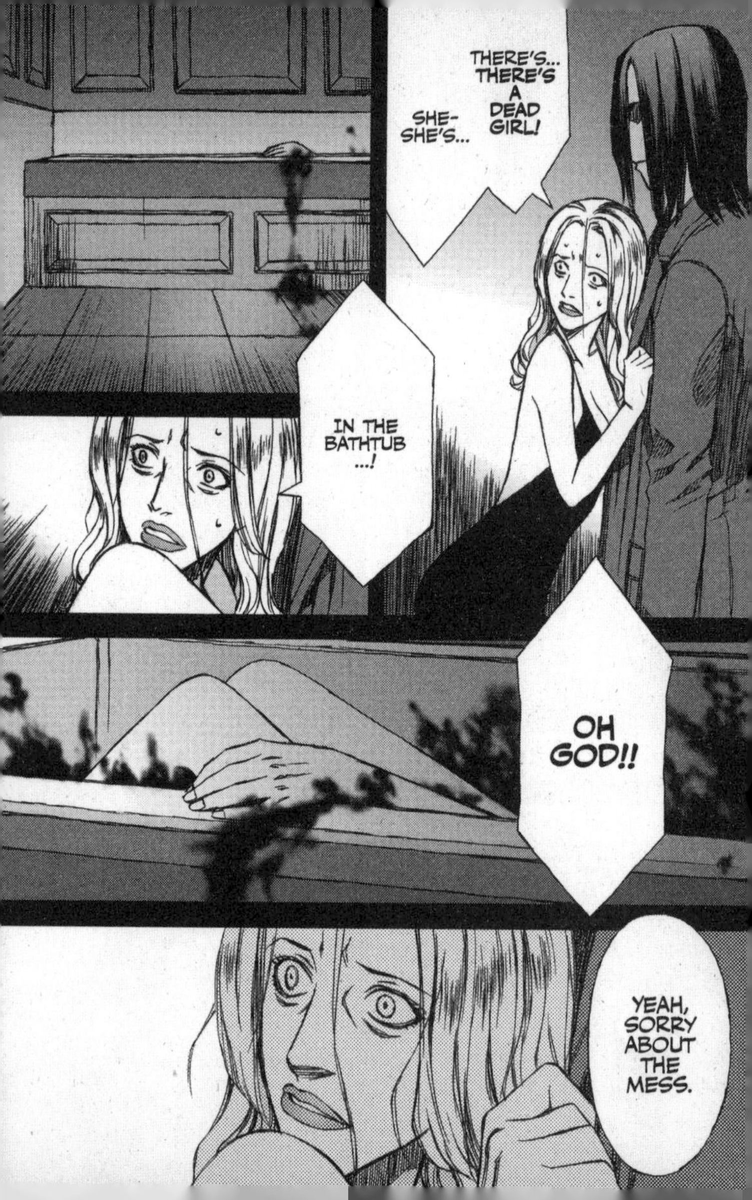
SHE- SHE'S... THERE'S... THERE'S A DEAD GIRL!
IN THE BATHTUB ...!
OH GOD!!
YEAH, SORRY ABOUT THE MESS.

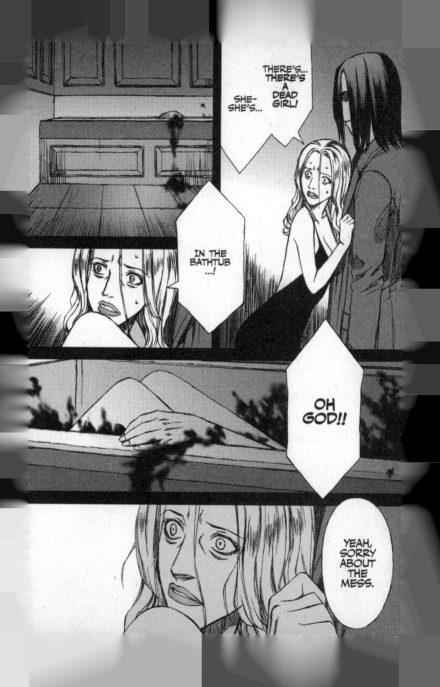

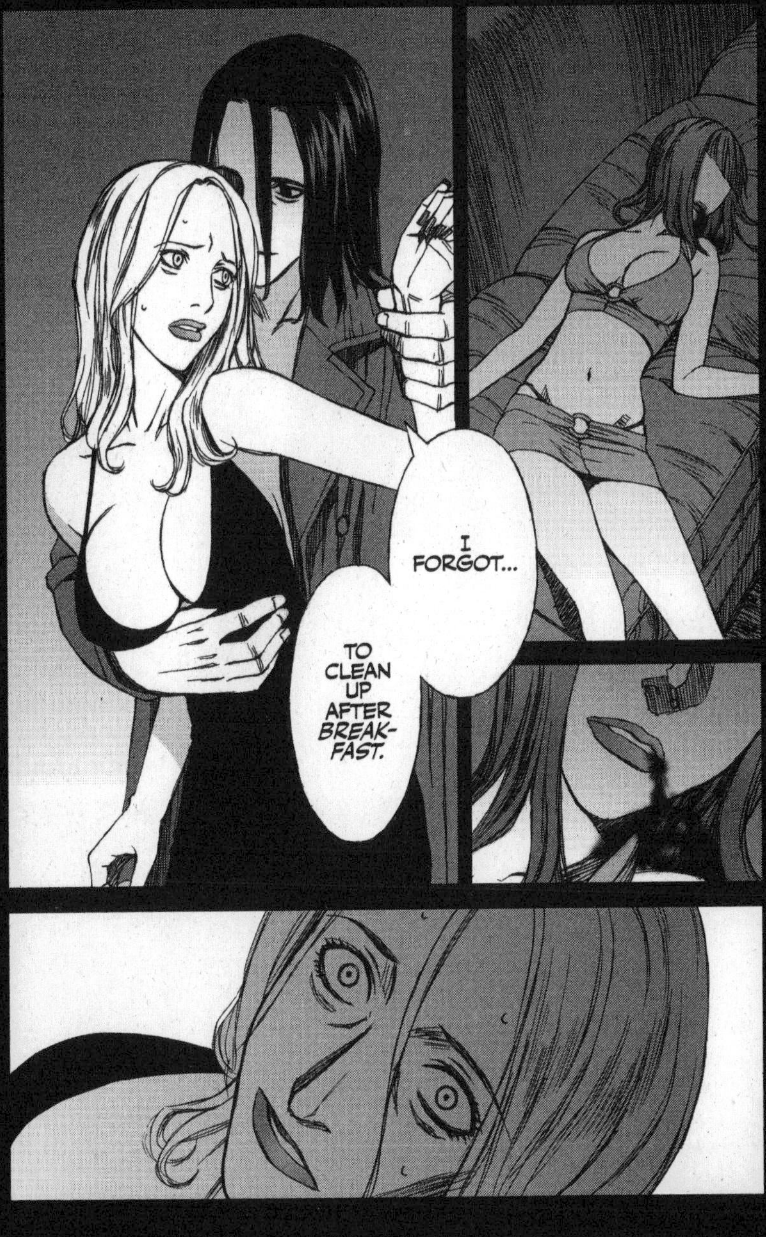
I FORGOT...
TO CLEAN UP AFTER BREAK-FAST.

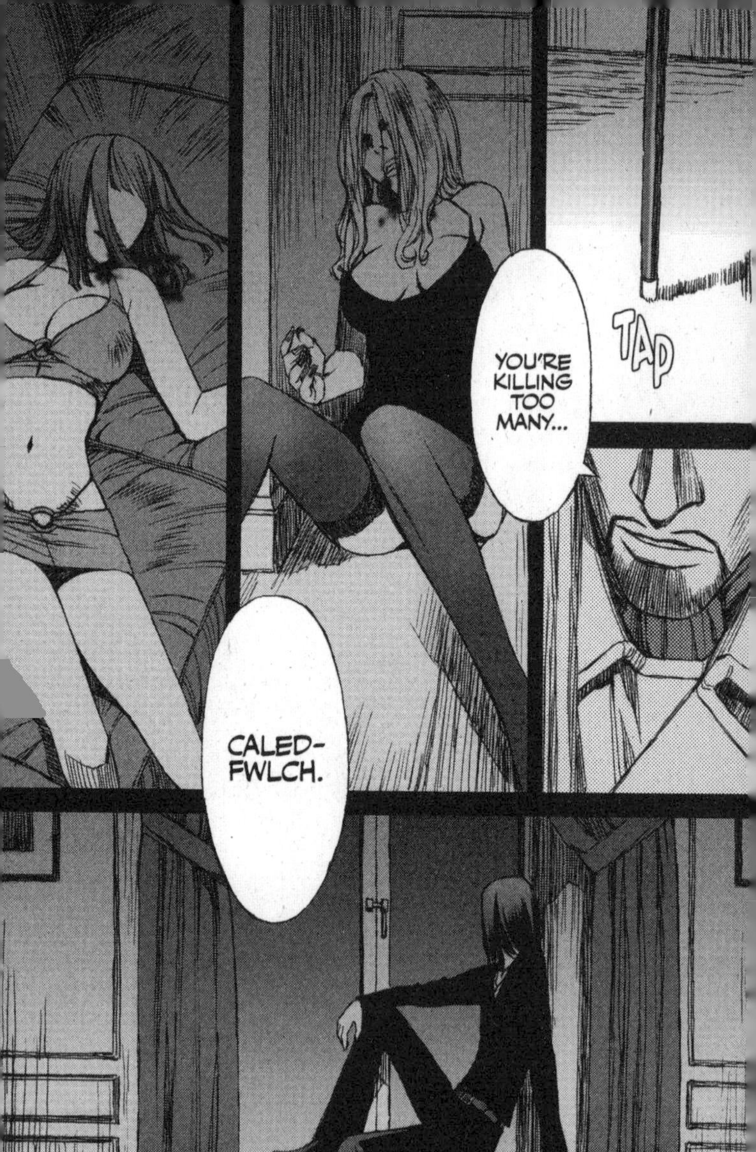
TAP
YOU'RE KILLING TOO MANY...
CALED-FWLCH.

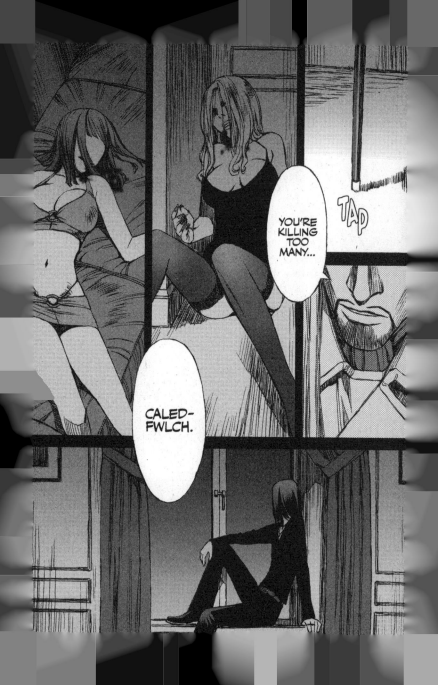

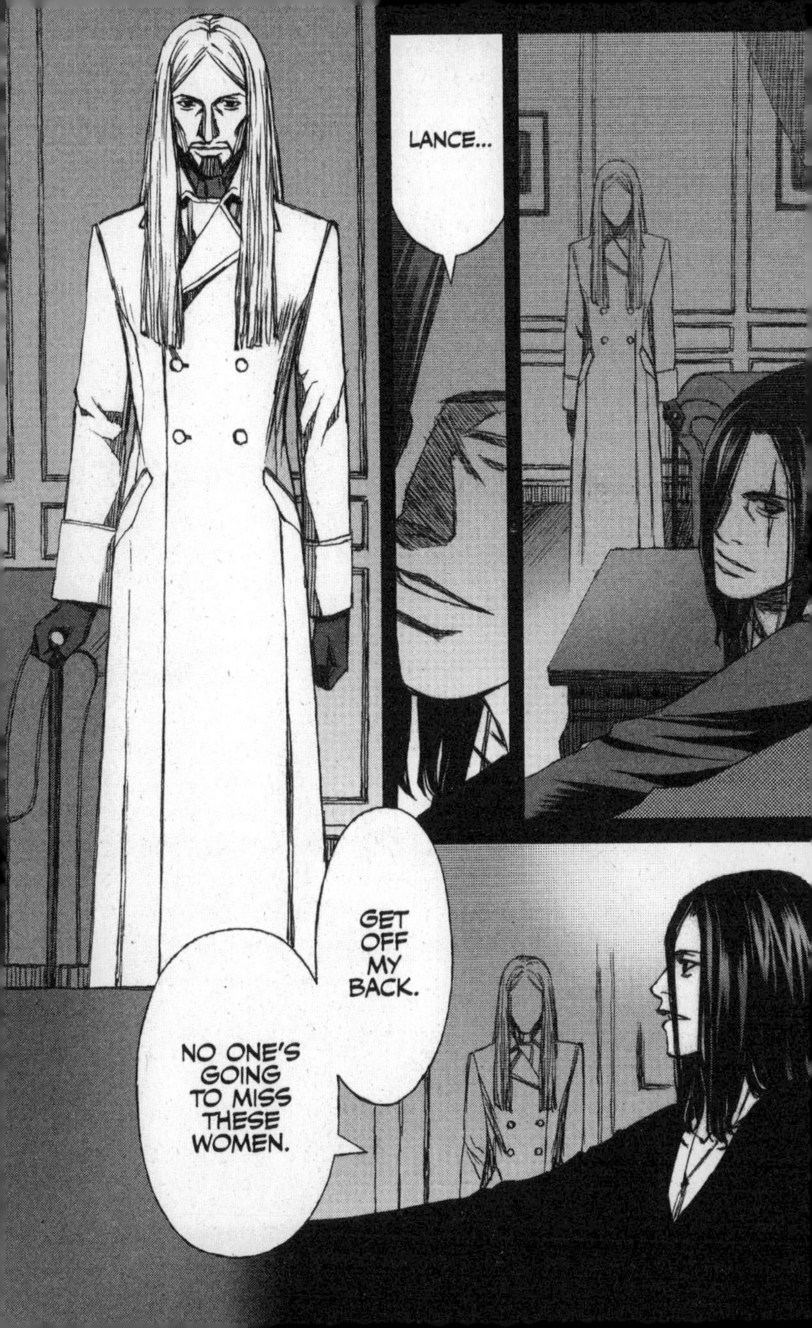
LANCE...
GET OFF MY BACK.
NO ONE'S GOING TO MISS THESE WOMEN.

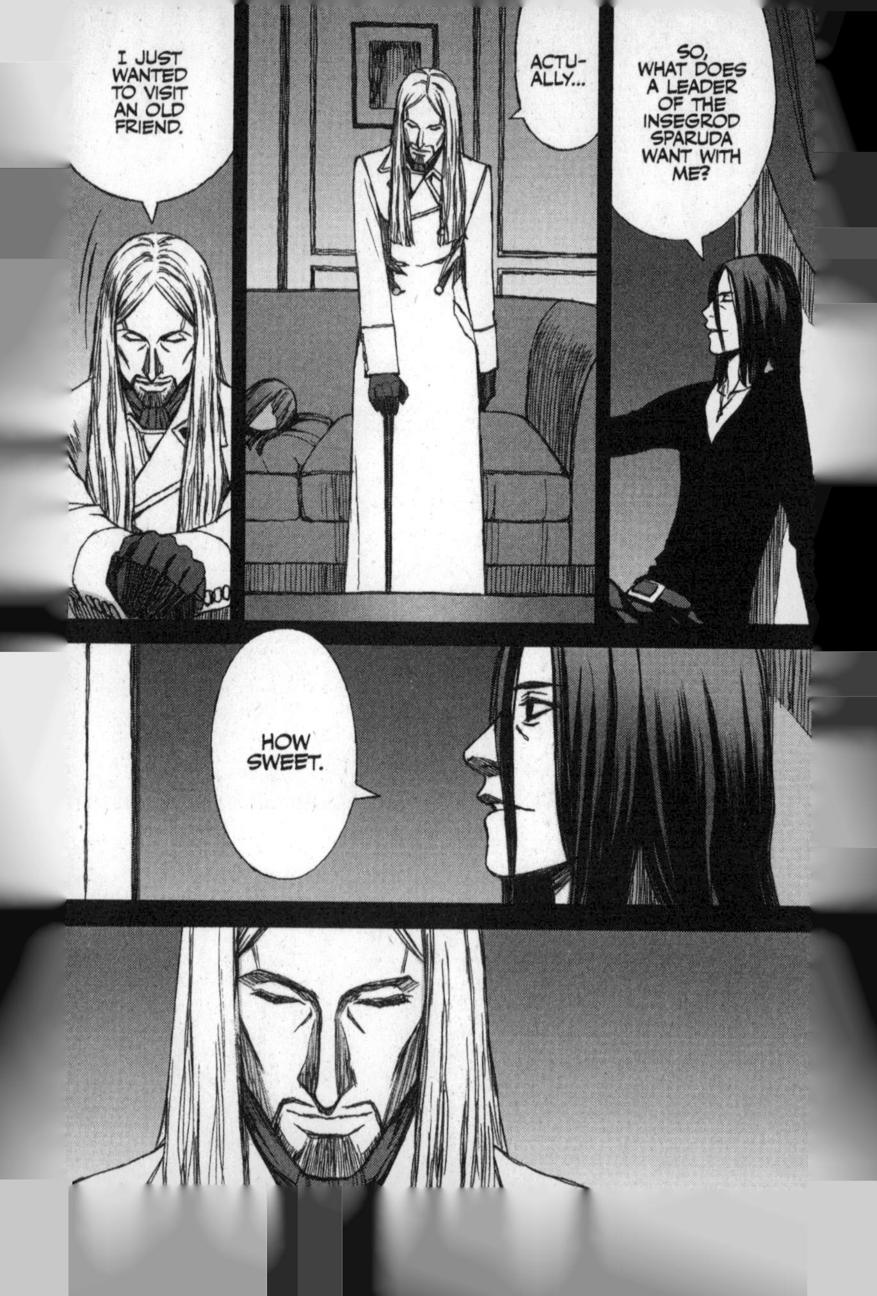
SO, WHAT DOES A LEADER OF THE INSEGROD SPARUDA WANT WITH ME?
ACTU-ALLY...
I JUST WANTED TO VISIT AN OLD FRIEND.
HOW SWEET.

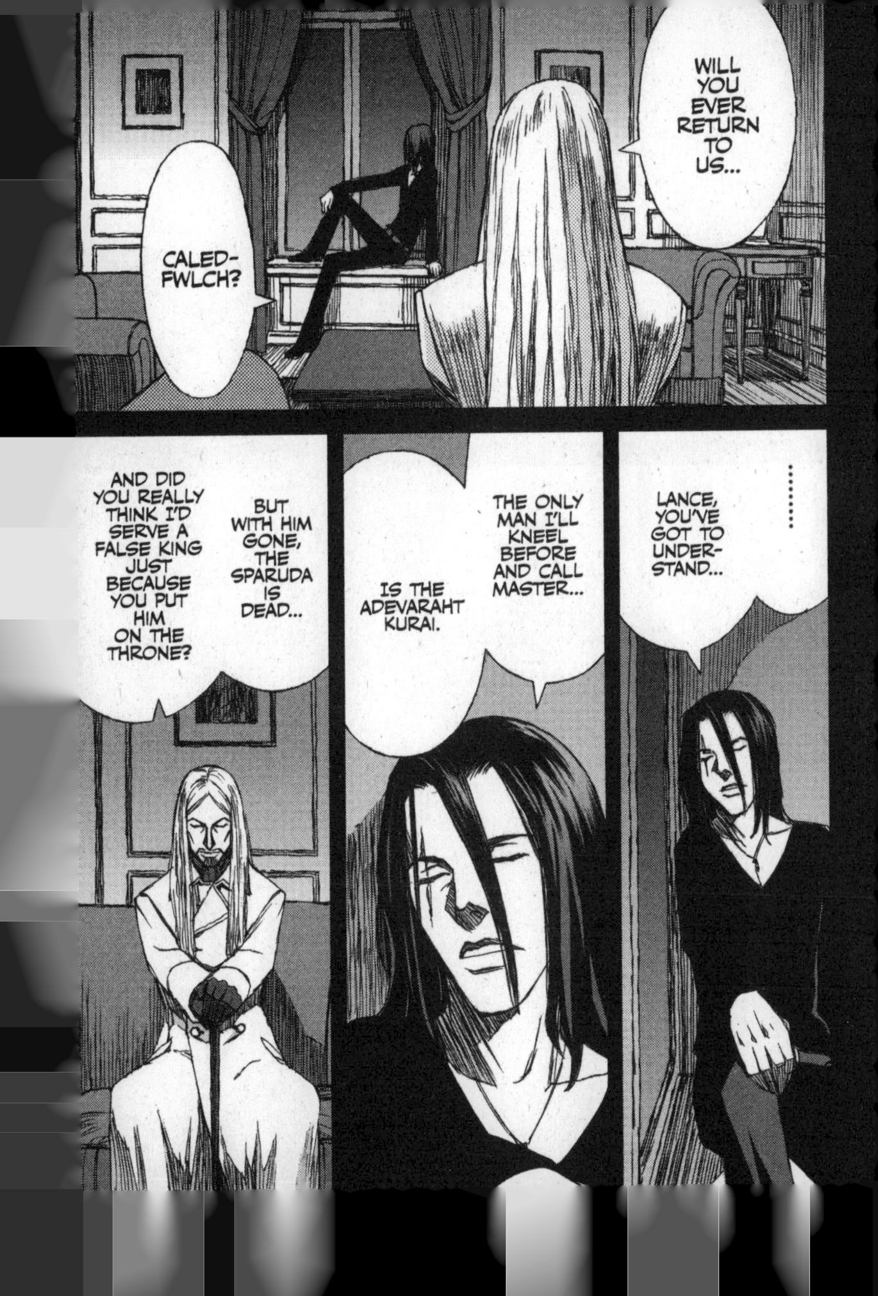
WILL YOU EVER RETURN TO US...
CALED-FWLCH?
....
LANCE, YOU'VE GOT TO UNDER-STAND...
THE ONLY MAN I'LL KNEEL BEFORE AND CALL MASTER...
IS THE ADEVARAHT KURAI.
BUT WITH HIM GONE, THE SPARUDA IS DEAD...
AND DID YOU REALLY THINK I'D SERVE A FALSE KING JUST BECAUSE YOU PUT HIM ON THE THRONE?

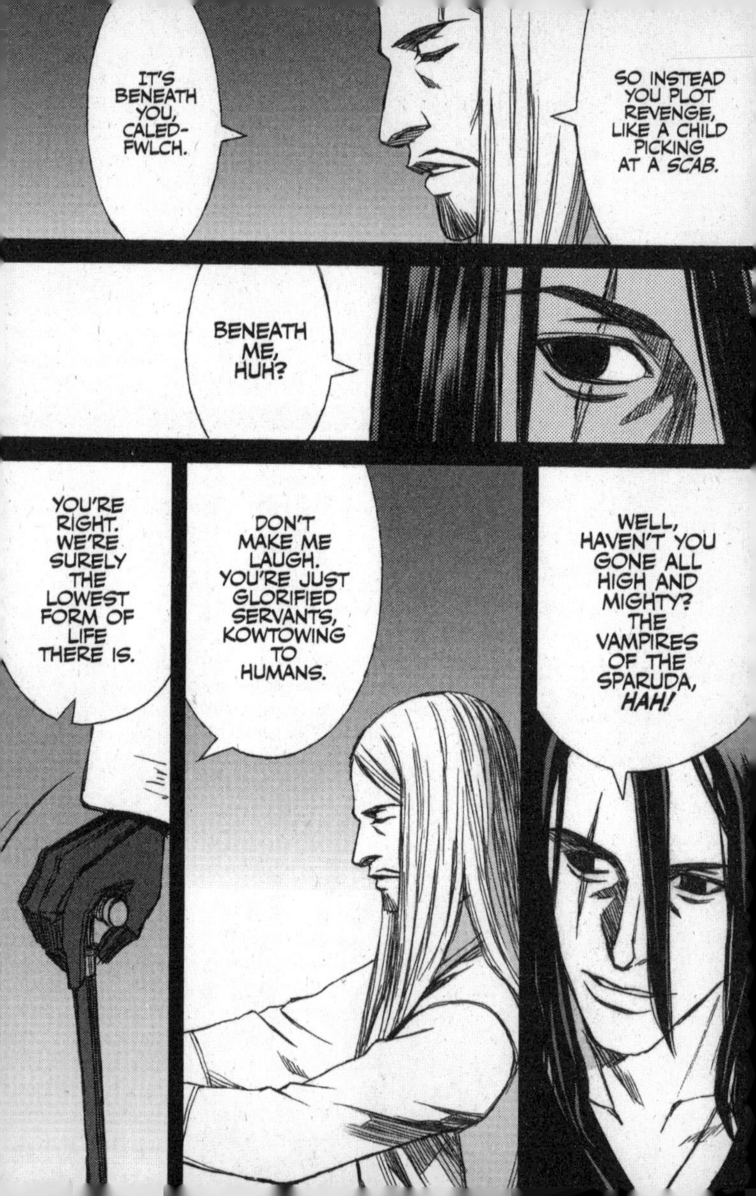
SO INSTEAD YOU PLOT REVENGE, LIKE A CHILD PICKING AT A *SCAB.*
IT'S BENEATH YOU, CALED-FWLCH.
BENEATH ME, HUH?
WELL, HAVEN'T YOU GONE ALL HIGH AND MIGHTY? THE VAMPIRES OF THE SPARUDA, *HAH!*
DON'T MAKE ME LAUGH. YOU'RE JUST GLORIFIED SERVANTS, KOWTOWING TO HUMANS.
YOU'RE RIGHT. WE'RE SURELY THE LOWEST FORM OF LIFE THERE IS.

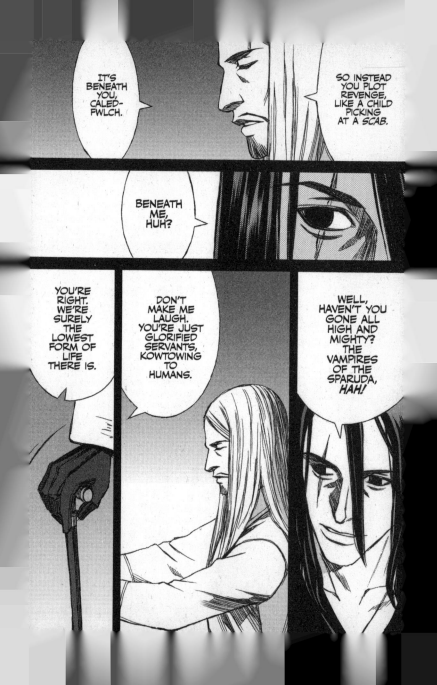

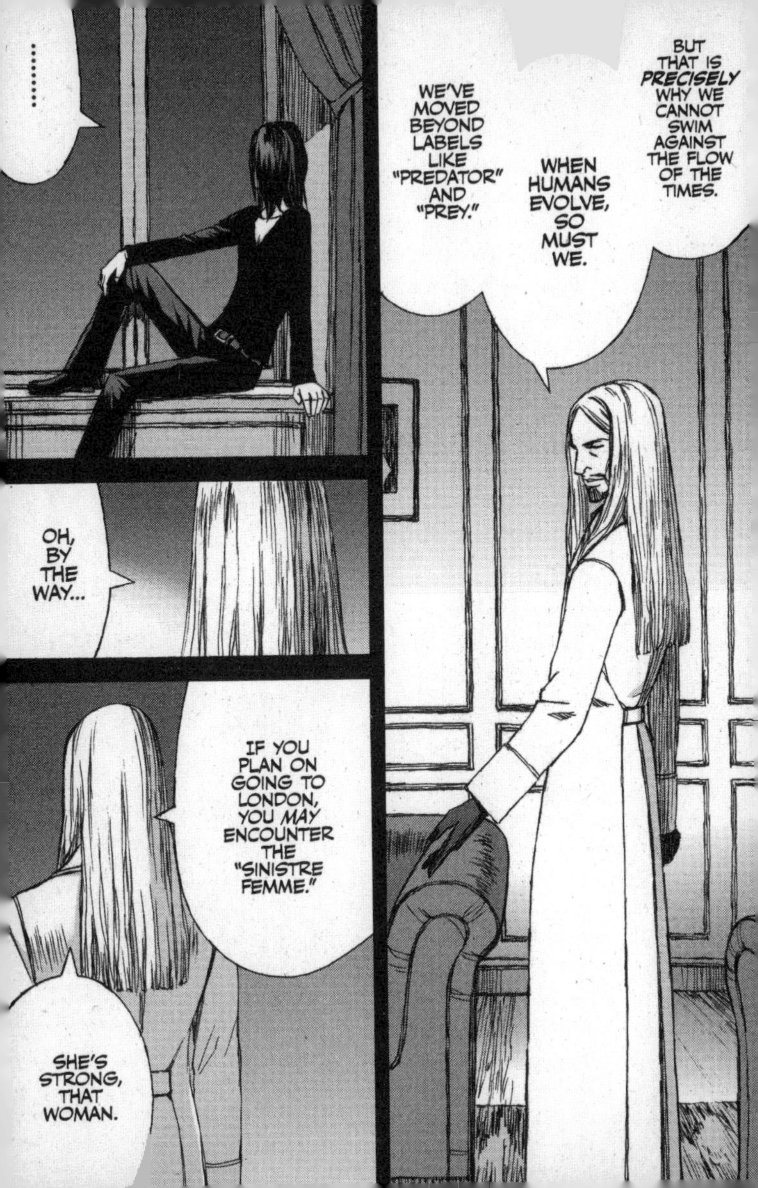
BUT THAT IS *PRECISELY* WHY WE CANNOT SWIM AGAINST THE FLOW OF THE TIMES.
WHEN HUMANS EVOLVE, SO MUST WE.
WE'VE MOVED BEYOND LABELS LIKE "PREDATOR" AND "PREY."
......
OH, BY THE WAY...
IF YOU PLAN ON GOING TO LONDON, YOU *MAY* ENCOUNTER THE "SINISTRE FEMME."
SHE'S STRONG, THAT WOMAN.

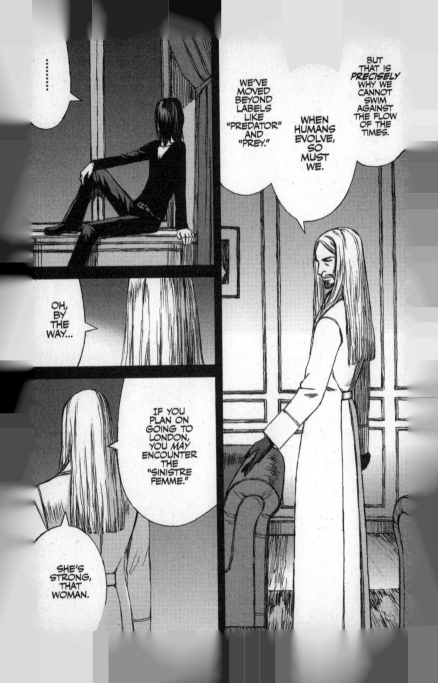

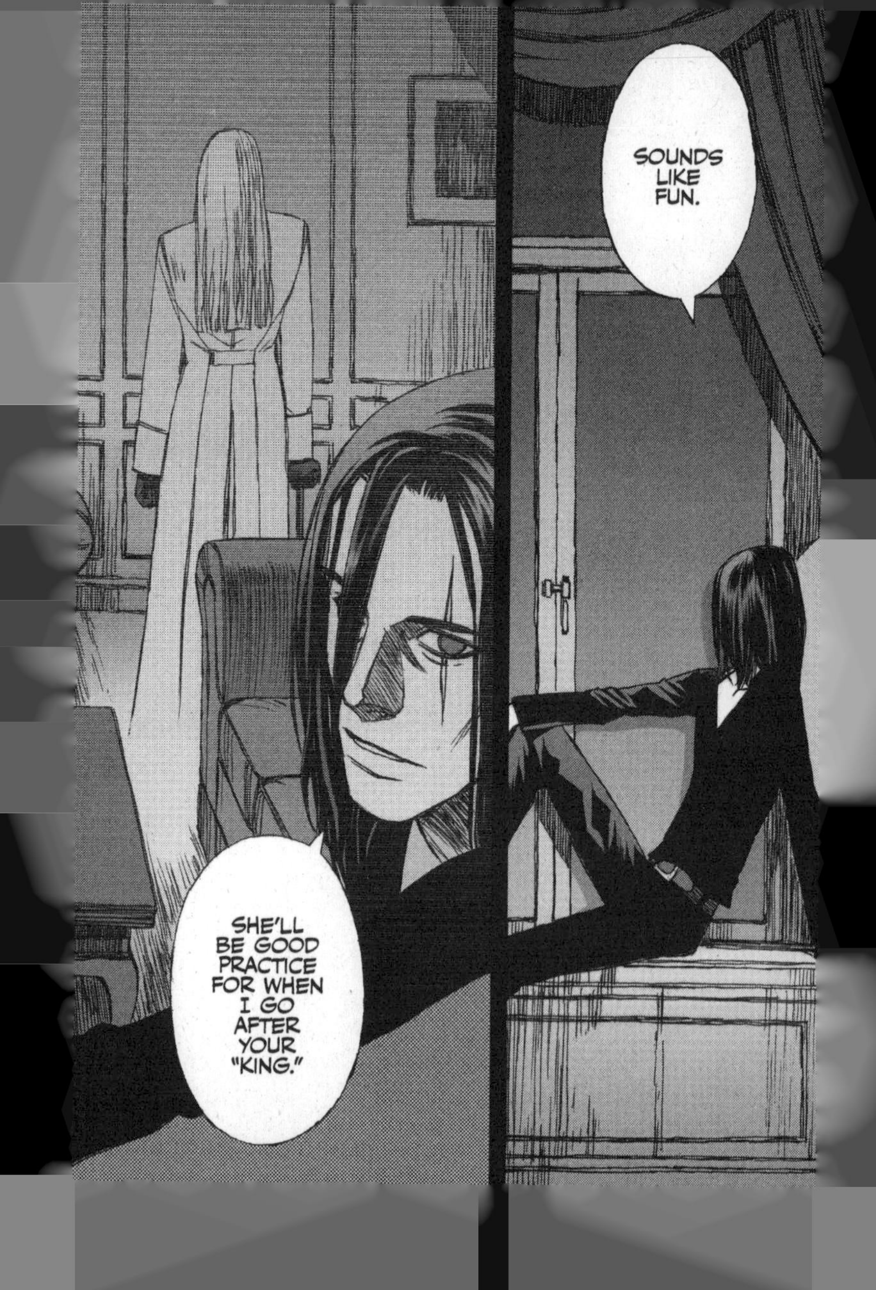
SOUNDS LIKE FUN.
SHE'LL BE GOOD PRACTICE FOR WHEN I GO AFTER YOUR "KING."

Part 3

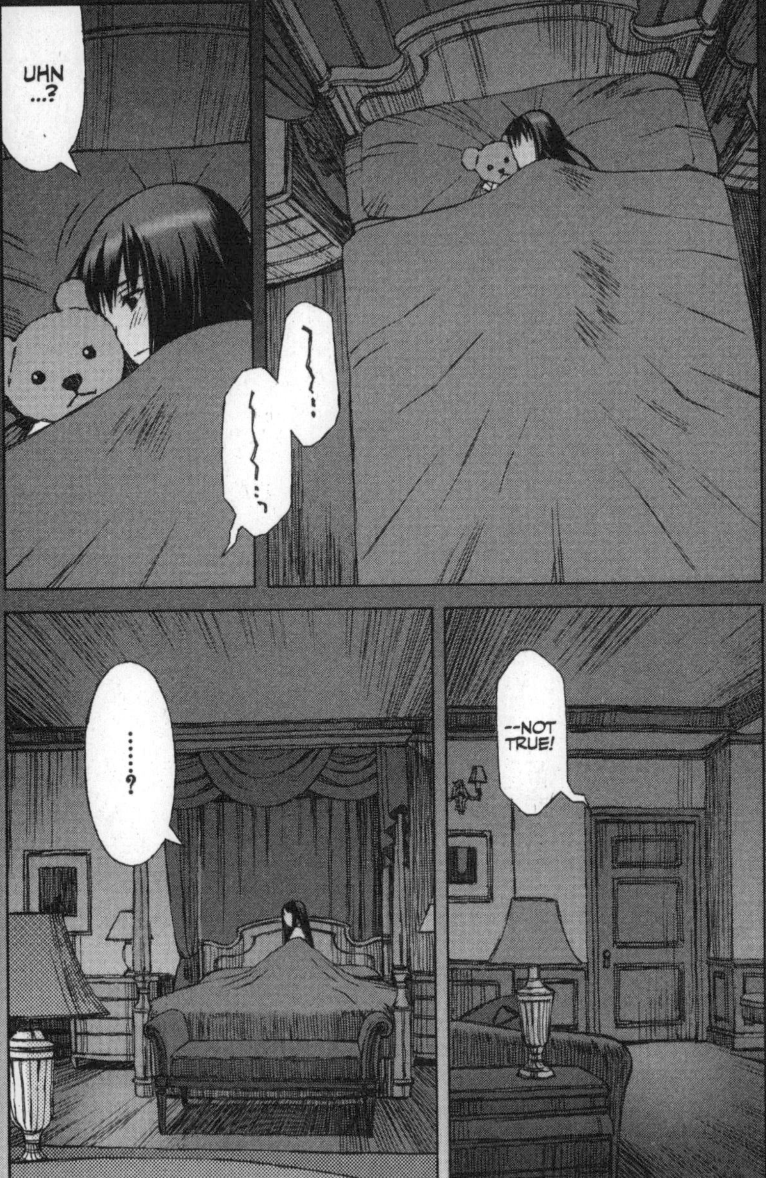
UHN ...?
~~...
~~...
--NOT TRUE!
......?

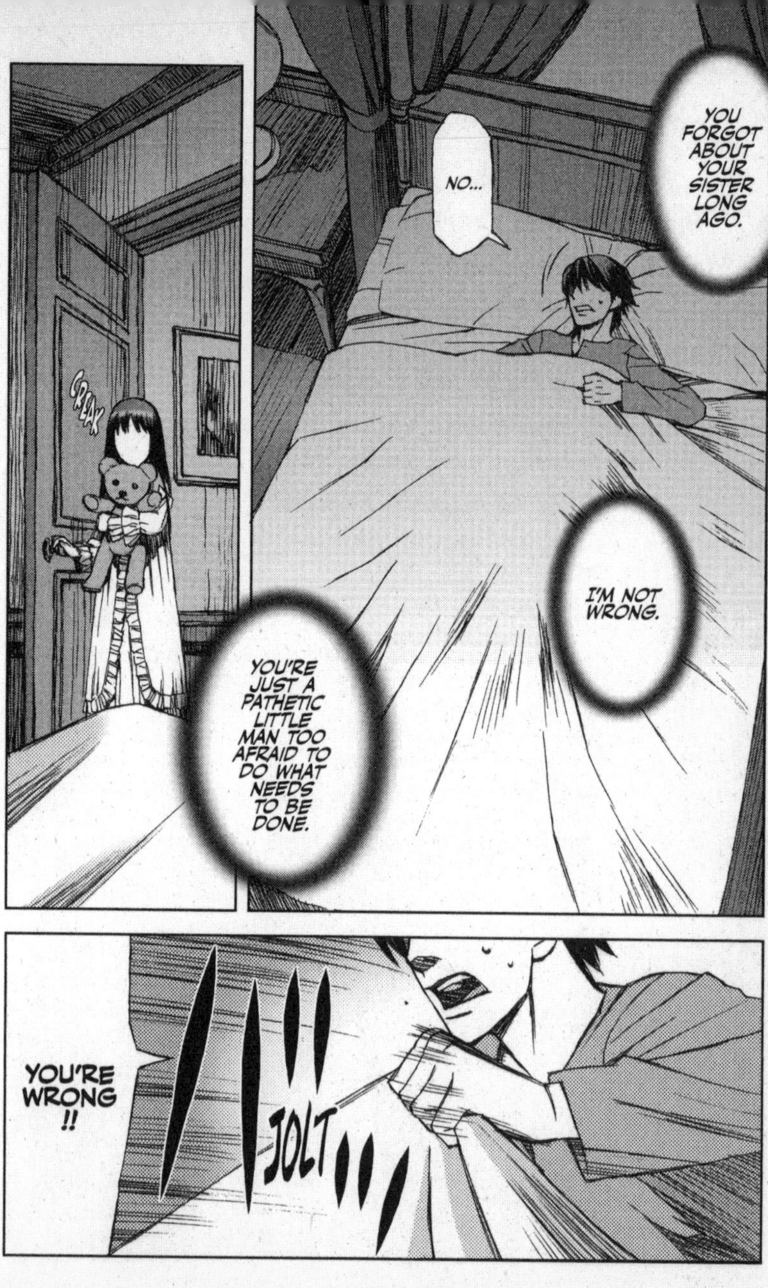
YOU FORGOT ABOUT YOUR SISTER LONG AGO.
NO...
I'M NOT WRONG.
YOU'RE JUST A PATHETIC LITTLE MAN TOO AFRAID TO DO WHAT NEEDS TO BE DONE.
CREAK
YOU'RE WRONG !!
JOLT

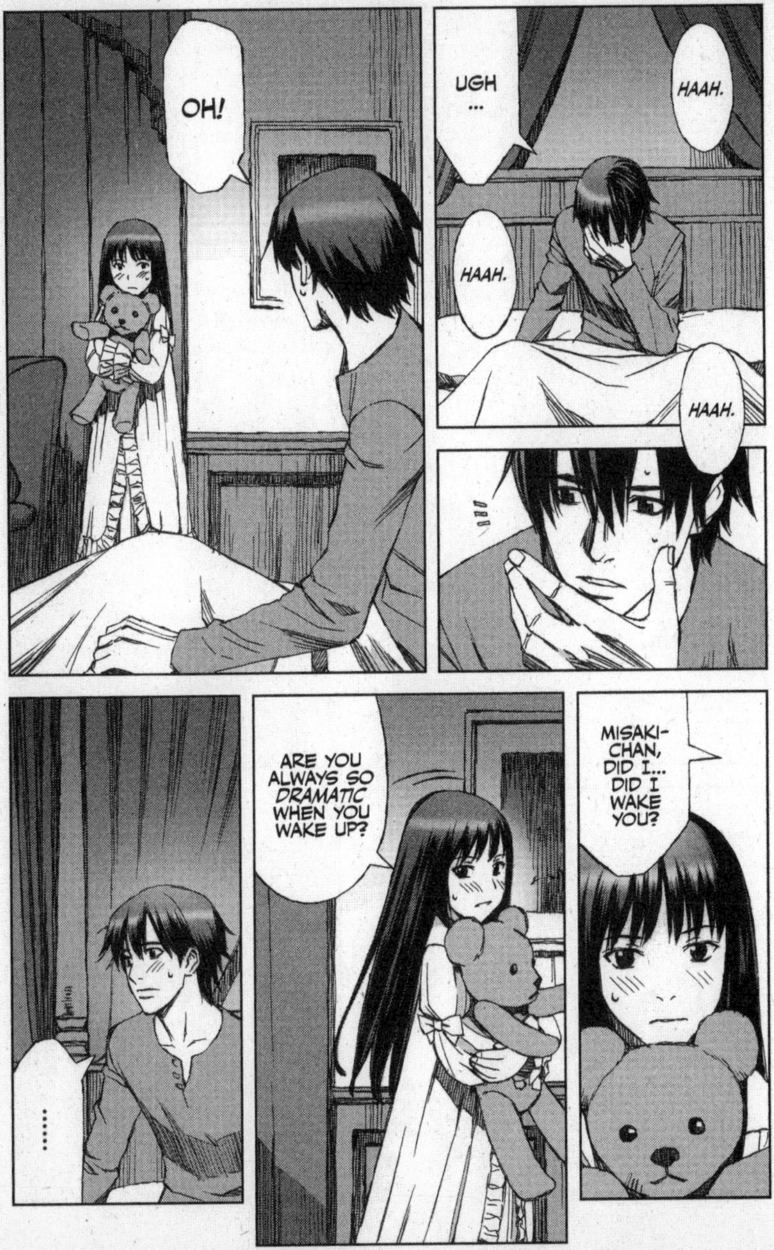
HAAH.
UGH ...
HAAH.
HAAH.
OH!
MISAKI-CHAN, DID I... DID I WAKE YOU?
ARE YOU ALWAYS SO *DRAMATIC* WHEN YOU WAKE UP?
......

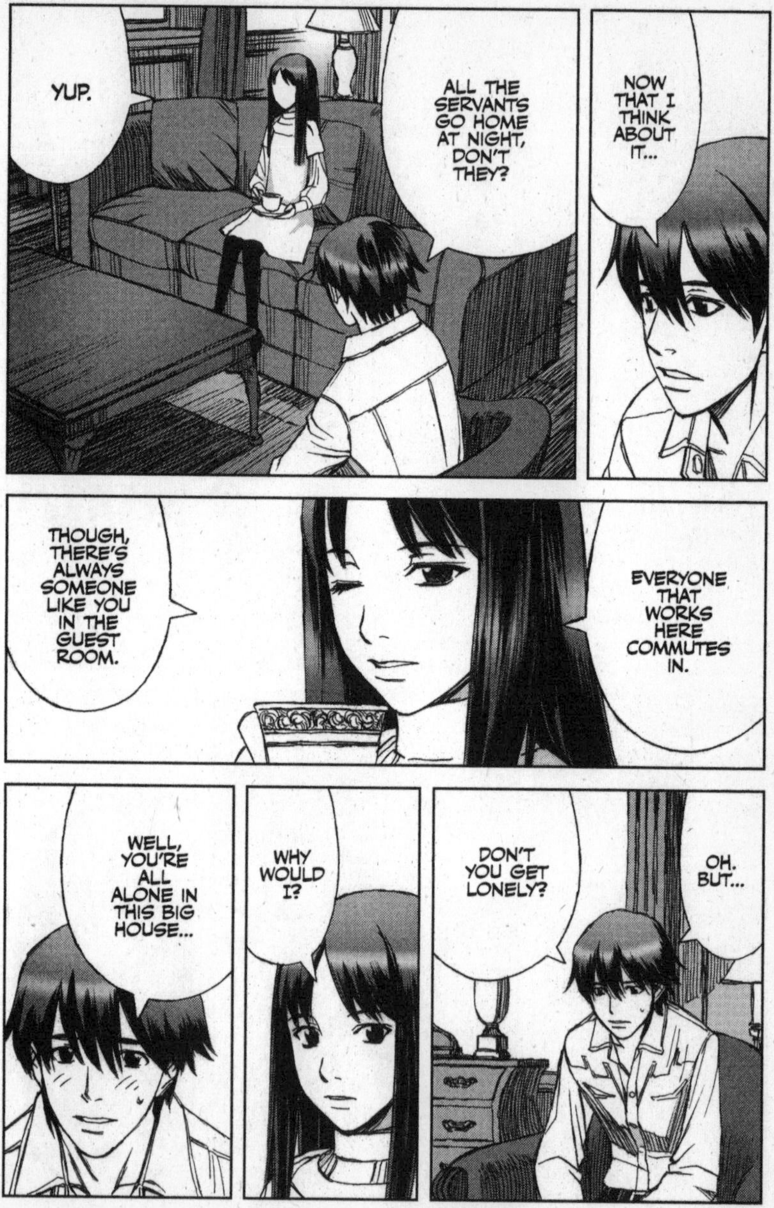
NOW THAT I THINK ABOUT IT...
ALL THE SERVANTS GO HOME AT NIGHT, DON'T THEY?
YUP.
EVERYONE THAT WORKS HERE COMMUTES IN.
THOUGH, THERE'S ALWAYS SOMEONE LIKE YOU IN THE GUEST ROOM.
OH. BUT...
DON'T YOU GET LONELY?
WHY WOULD I?
WELL, YOU'RE ALL ALONE IN THIS BIG HOUSE...

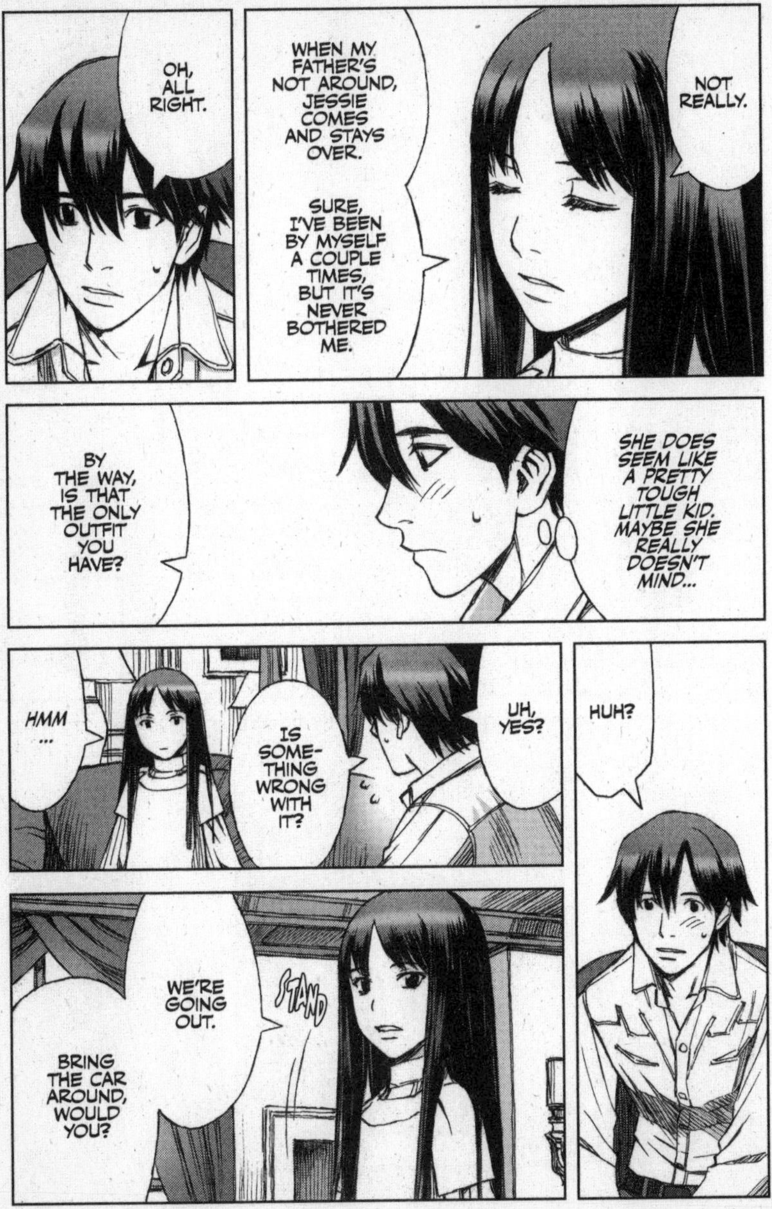
NOT REALLY.
WHEN MY FATHER'S NOT AROUND, JESSIE COMES AND STAYS OVER.
SURE, I'VE BEEN BY MYSELF A COUPLE TIMES, BUT IT'S NEVER BOTHERED ME.
OH, ALL RIGHT.
SHE DOES SEEM LIKE A PRETTY TOUGH LITTLE KID. MAYBE SHE REALLY DOESN'T MIND...
BY THE WAY, IS THAT THE ONLY OUTFIT YOU HAVE?
HUH?
UH, YES?
IS SOMETHING WRONG WITH IT?
HMM...
WE'RE GOING OUT.
STAND
BRING THE CAR AROUND, WOULD YOU?

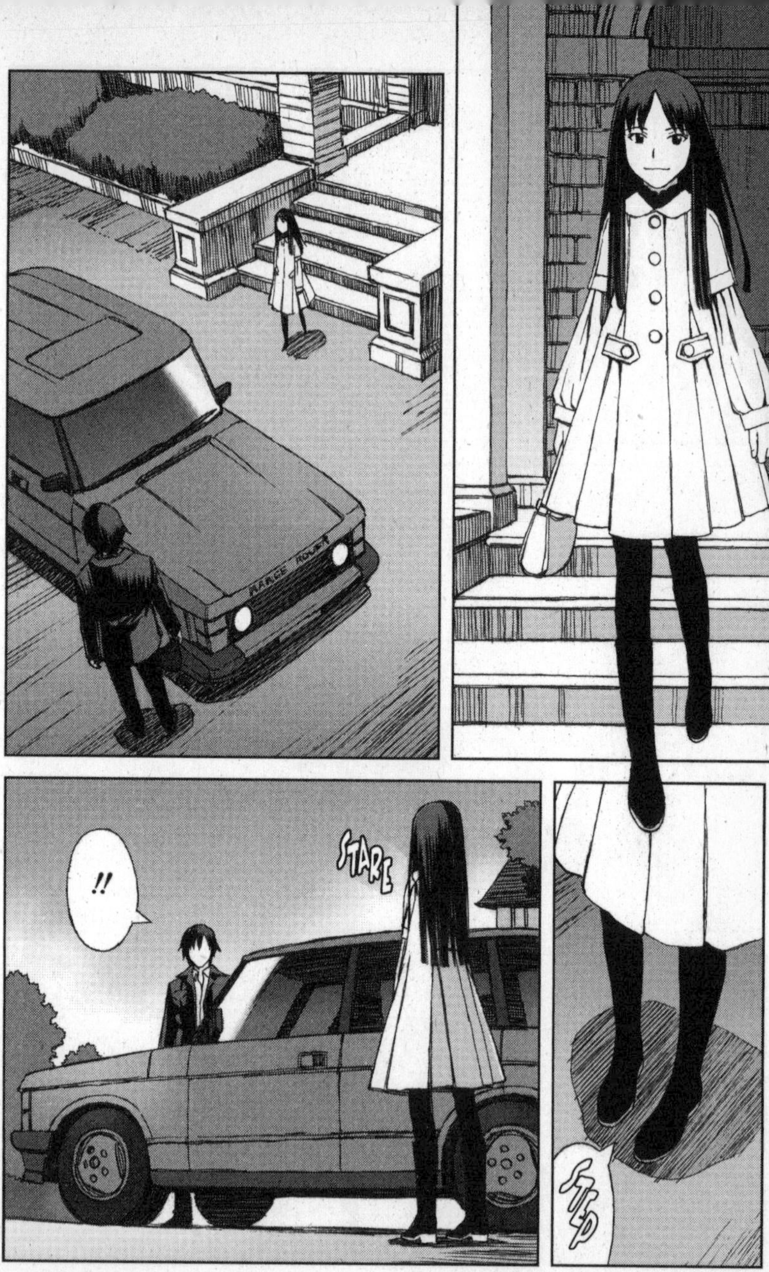
RANGE ROVER
STEP
STARE
!!

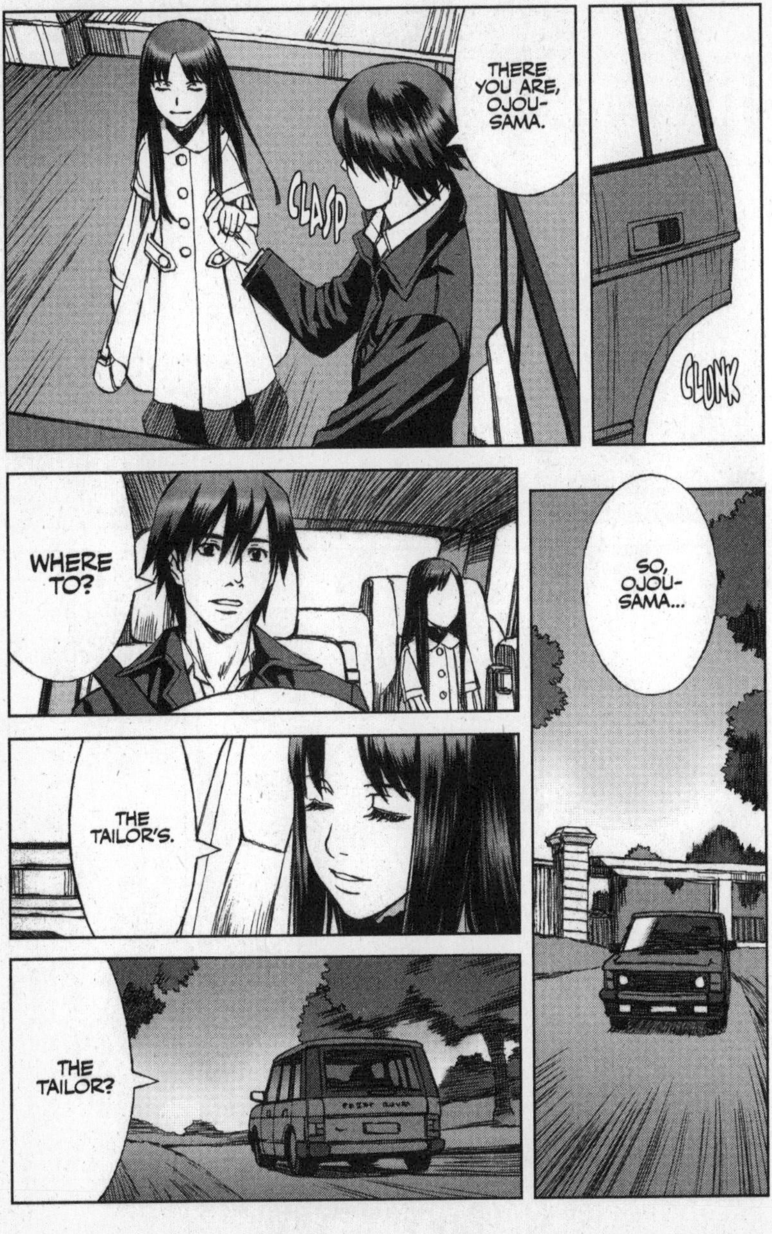
CLUNK
THERE YOU ARE, OJOU-SAMA.
CLASP
SO, OJOU-SAMA...
WHERE TO?
THE TAILOR'S.
THE TAILOR?

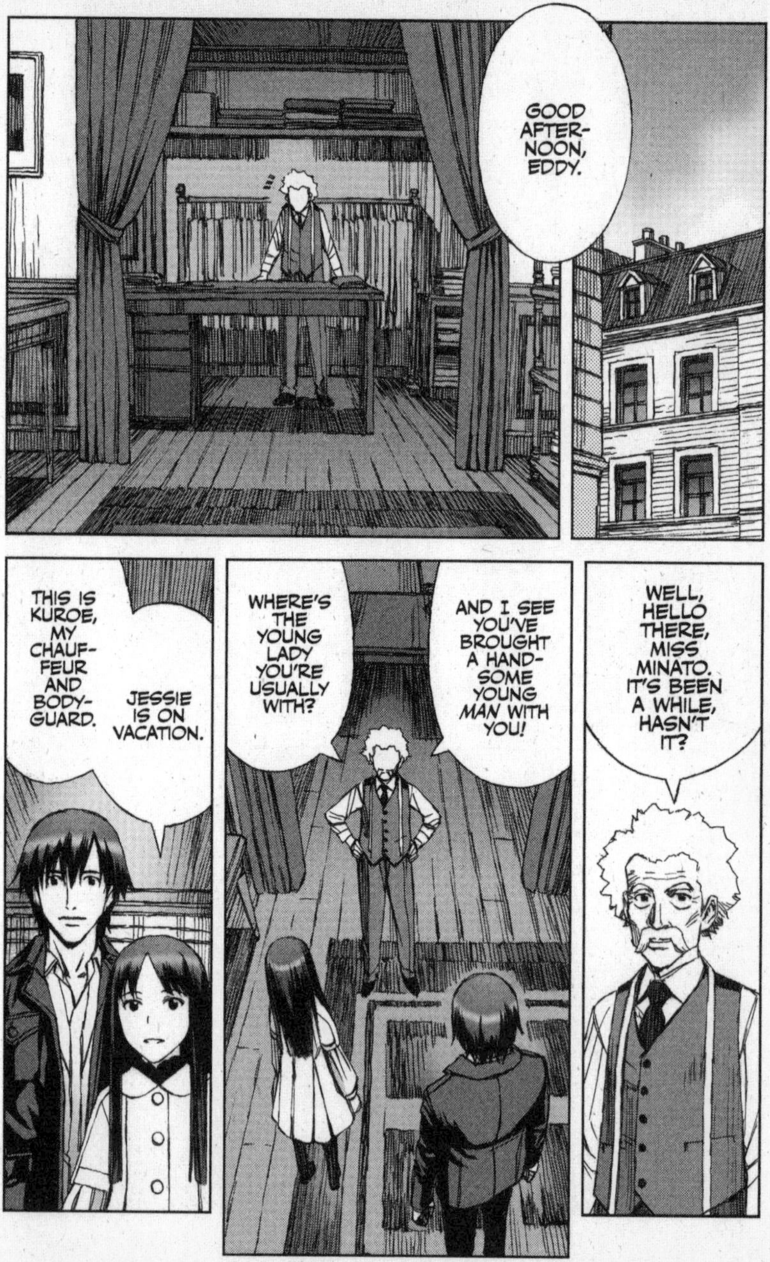
GOOD AFTERNOON, EDDY.
WELL, HELLO THERE, MISS MINATO. IT'S BEEN A WHILE, HASN'T IT?
AND I SEE YOU'VE BROUGHT A HANDSOME YOUNG *MAN* WITH YOU!
WHERE'S THE YOUNG LADY YOU'RE USUALLY WITH?
JESSIE IS ON VACATION.
THIS IS KUROE, MY CHAUFFEUR AND BODYGUARD.

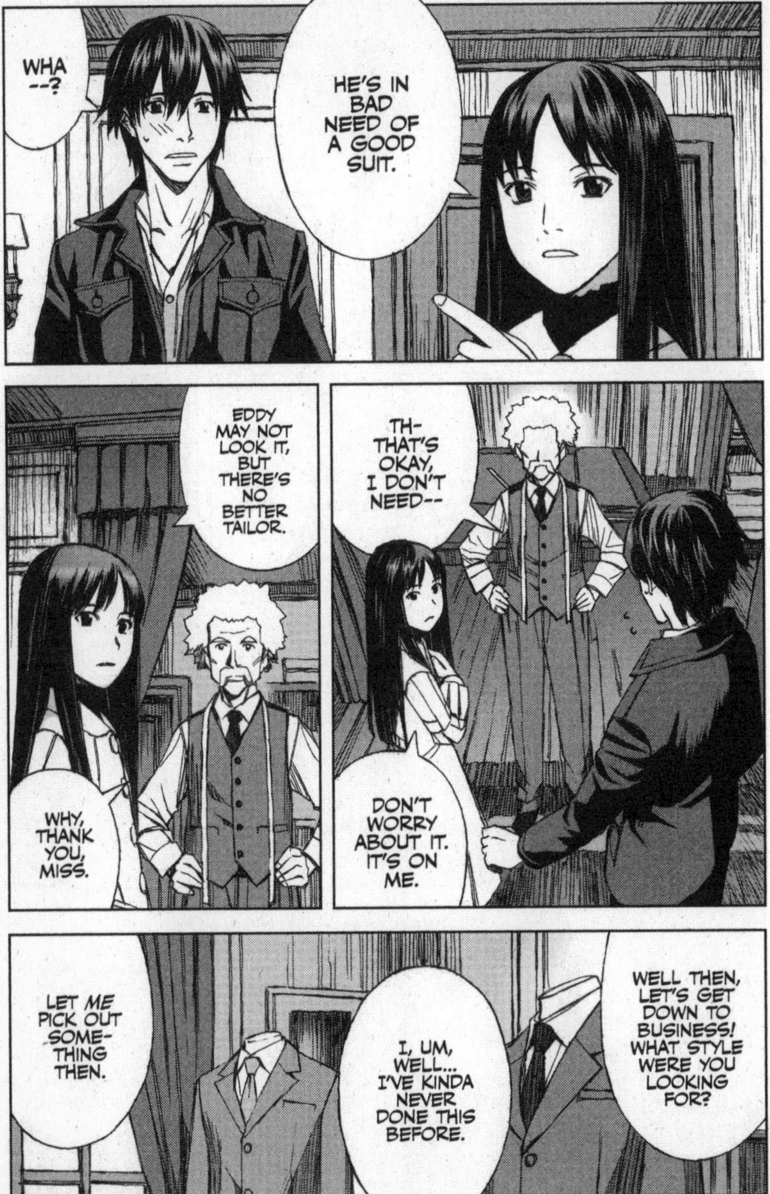
HE'S IN BAD NEED OF A GOOD SUIT.
WHA--?
TH-THAT'S OKAY, I DON'T NEED--
DON'T WORRY ABOUT IT. IT'S ON ME.
EDDY MAY NOT LOOK IT, BUT THERE'S NO BETTER TAILOR.
WHY, THANK YOU, MISS.
WELL THEN, LET'S GET DOWN TO BUSINESS! WHAT STYLE WERE YOU LOOKING FOR?
I, UM, WELL... I'VE KINDA NEVER DONE THIS BEFORE.
LET ME PICK OUT SOMETHING THEN.

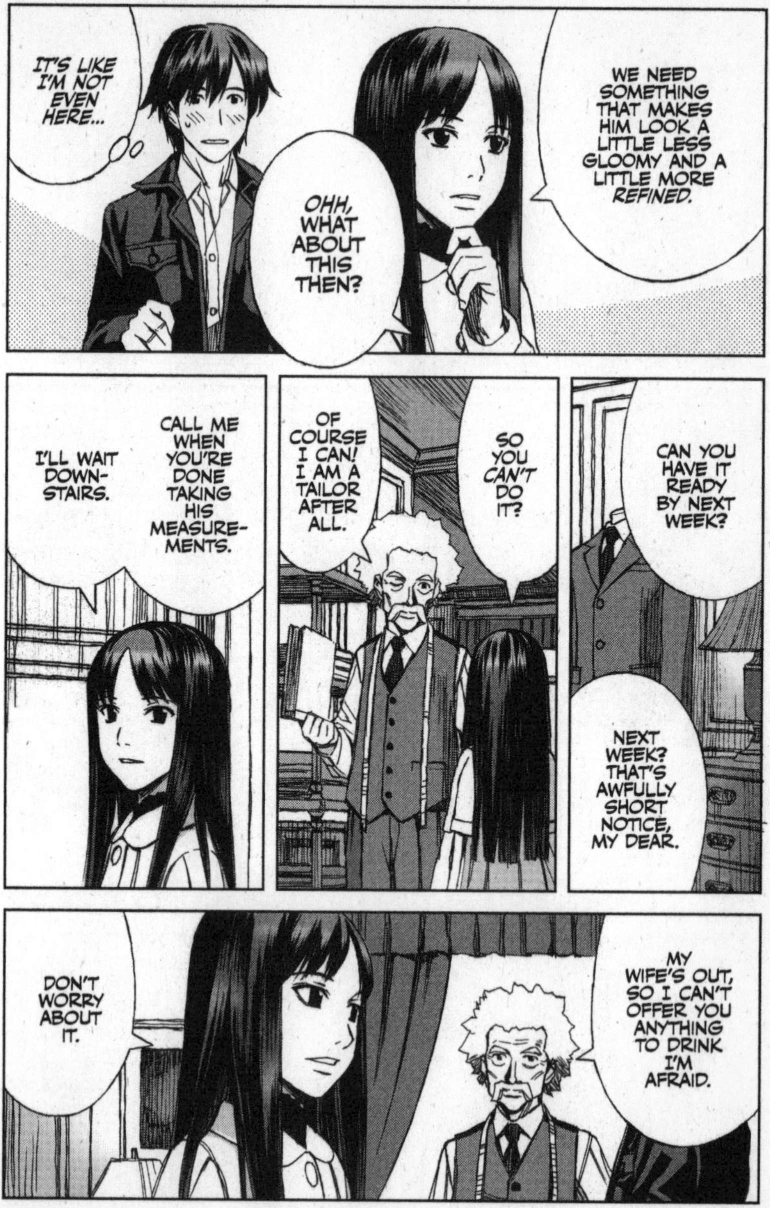
WE NEED SOMETHING THAT MAKES HIM LOOK A LITTLE LESS GLOOMY AND A LITTLE MORE *REFINED.*
OHH, WHAT ABOUT THIS THEN?
IT'S LIKE I'M NOT EVEN HERE...
CAN YOU HAVE IT READY BY NEXT WEEK?
NEXT WEEK? THAT'S AWFULLY SHORT NOTICE, MY DEAR.
SO YOU *CAN'T* DO IT?
OF COURSE I CAN! I AM A TAILOR AFTER ALL.
CALL ME WHEN YOU'RE DONE TAKING HIS MEASUREMENTS.
I'LL WAIT DOWNSTAIRS.
MY WIFE'S OUT, SO I CAN'T OFFER YOU ANYTHING TO DRINK I'M AFRAID.
DON'T WORRY ABOUT IT.

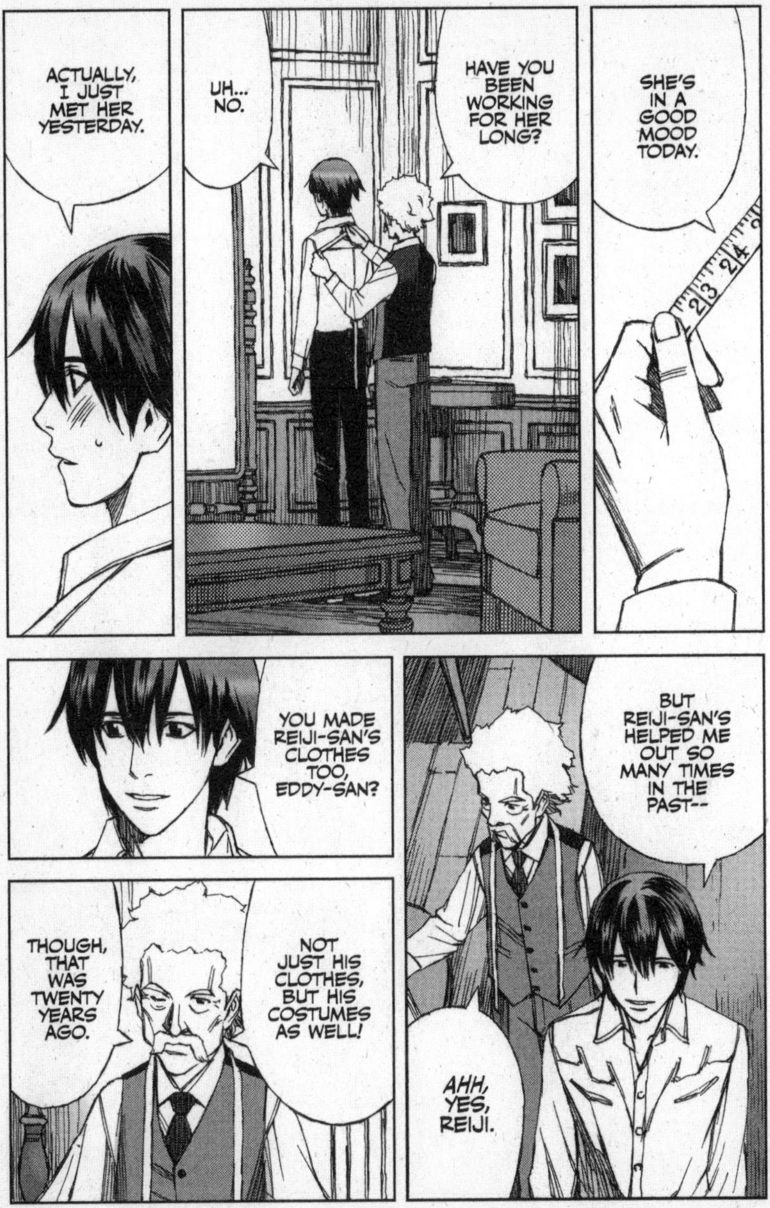
SHE'S IN A GOOD MOOD TODAY.
HAVE YOU BEEN WORKING FOR HER LONG?
UH... NO.
ACTUALLY, I JUST MET HER YESTERDAY.
BUT REIJI-SAN'S HELPED ME OUT SO MANY TIMES IN THE PAST--
AHH, YES, REIJI.
YOU MADE REIJI-SAN'S CLOTHES TOO, EDDY-SAN?
NOT JUST HIS CLOTHES, BUT HIS COSTUMES AS WELL!
THOUGH, THAT WAS TWENTY YEARS AGO.

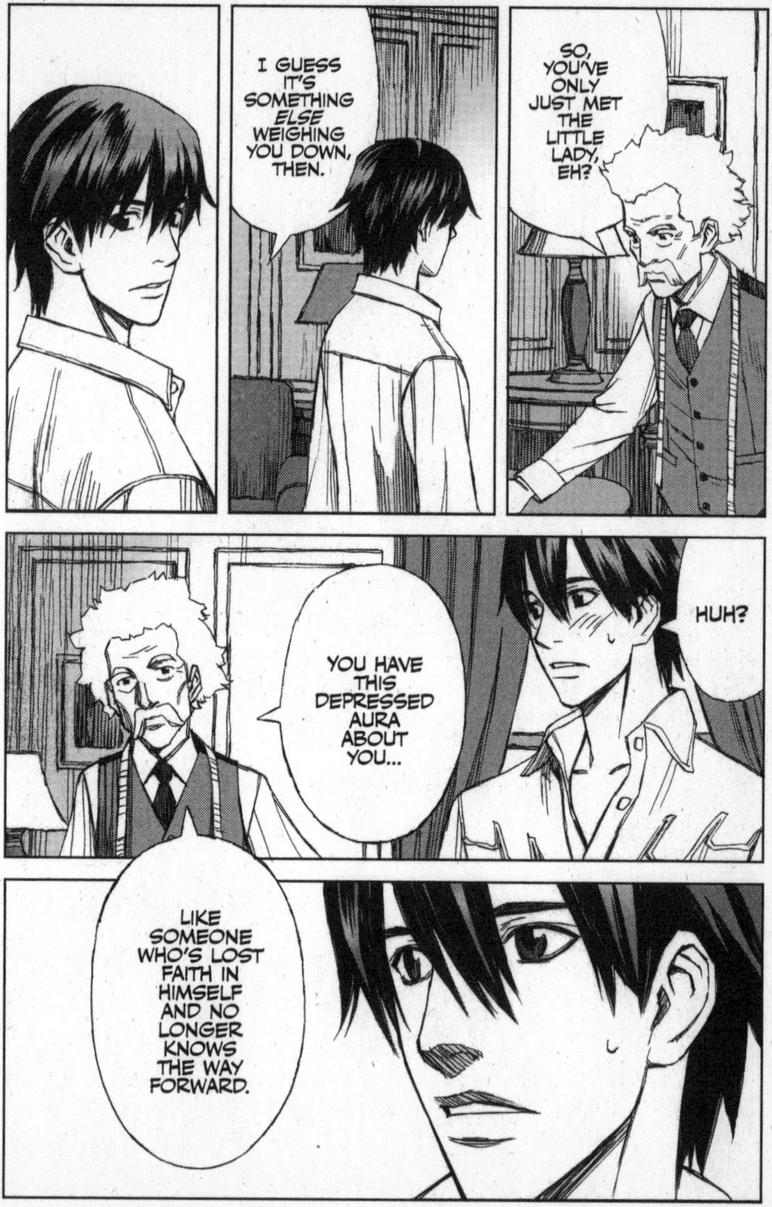
SO, YOU'VE ONLY JUST MET THE LITTLE LADY, EH?
I GUESS IT'S SOMETHING *ELSE* WEIGHING YOU DOWN, THEN.
HUH?
YOU HAVE THIS DEPRESSED AURA ABOUT YOU...
LIKE SOMEONE WHO'S LOST FAITH IN HIMSELF AND NO LONGER KNOWS THE WAY FORWARD.

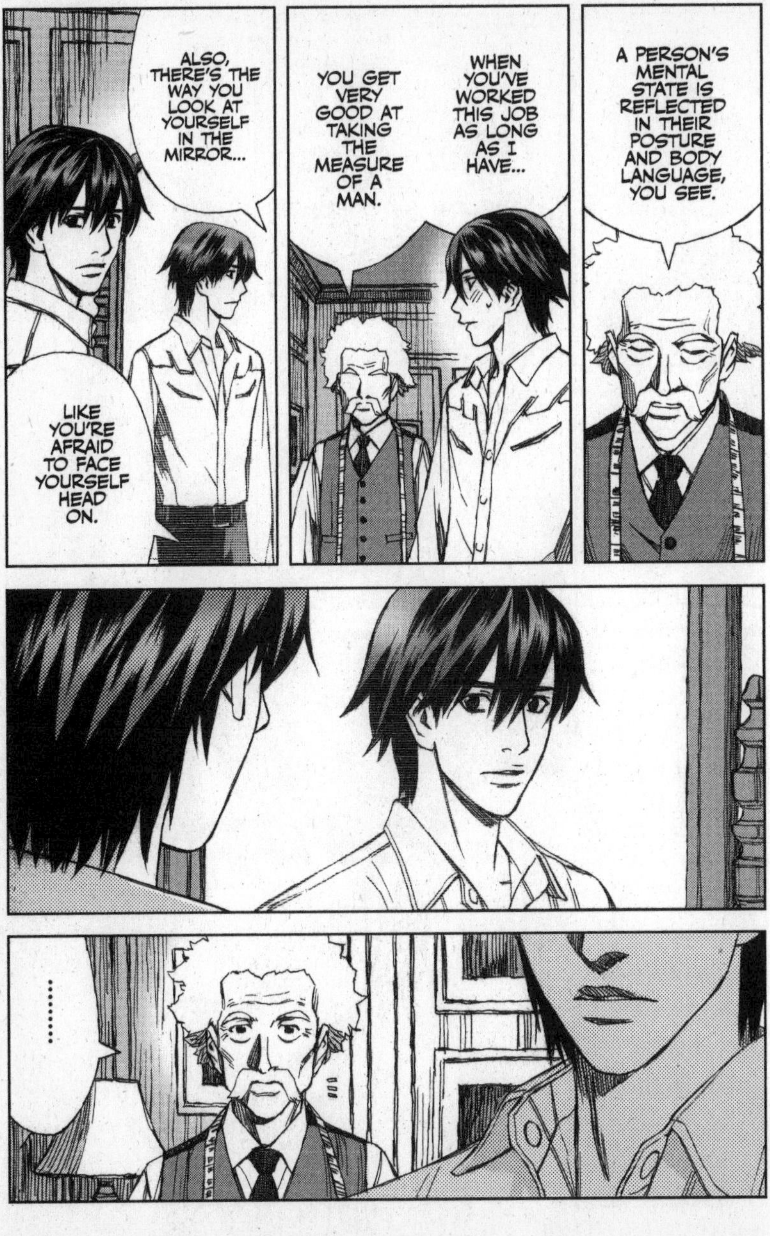
A PERSON'S MENTAL STATE IS REFLECTED IN THEIR POSTURE AND BODY LANGUAGE, YOU SEE.
WHEN YOU'VE WORKED THIS JOB AS LONG AS I HAVE...
YOU GET VERY GOOD AT TAKING THE MEASURE OF A MAN.
ALSO, THERE'S THE WAY YOU LOOK AT YOURSELF IN THE MIRROR...
LIKE YOU'RE AFRAID TO FACE YOURSELF HEAD ON.
......

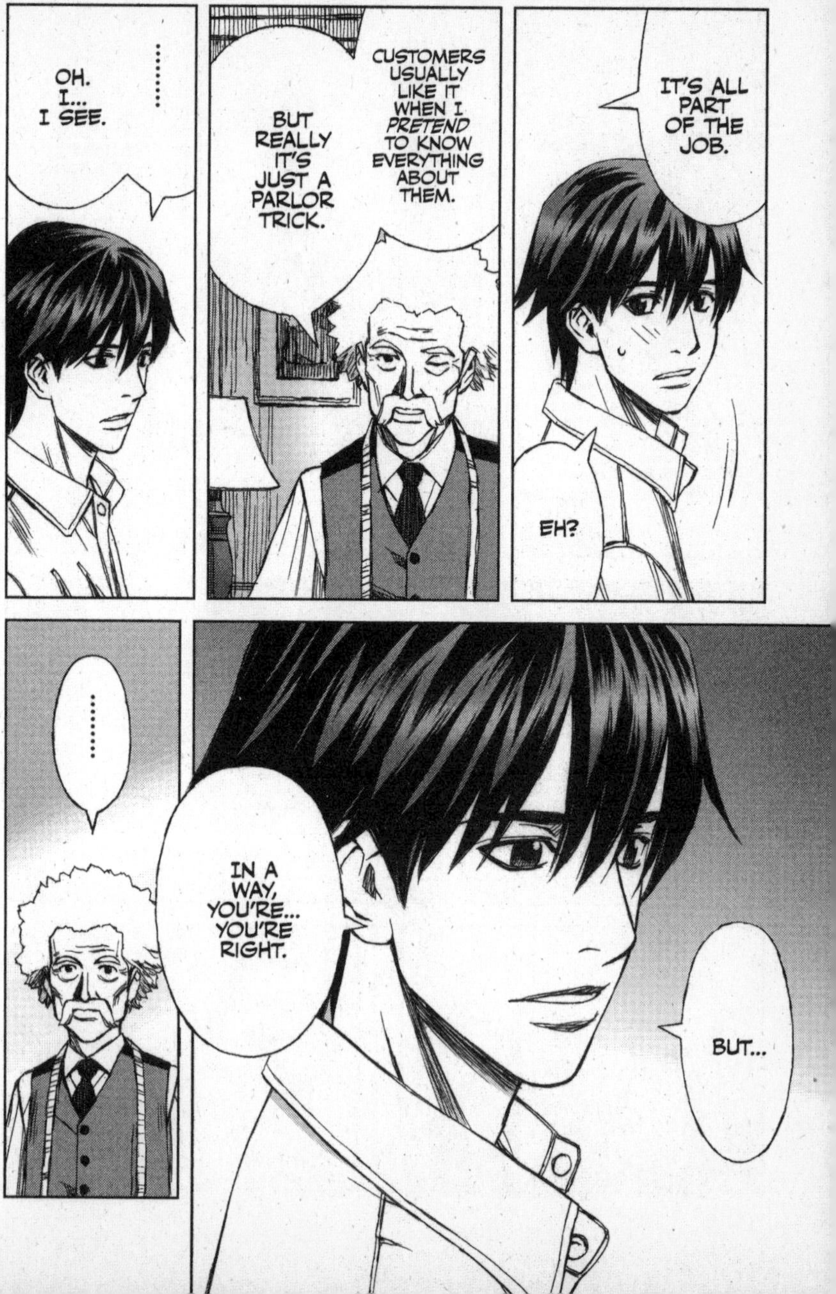
IT'S ALL PART OF THE JOB.
EH?
CUSTOMERS USUALLY LIKE IT WHEN I *PRETEND* TO KNOW EVERYTHING ABOUT THEM.
BUT REALLY IT'S JUST A PARLOR TRICK.
....
OH. I... I SEE.
IN A WAY, YOU'RE... YOU'RE RIGHT.
BUT...
....

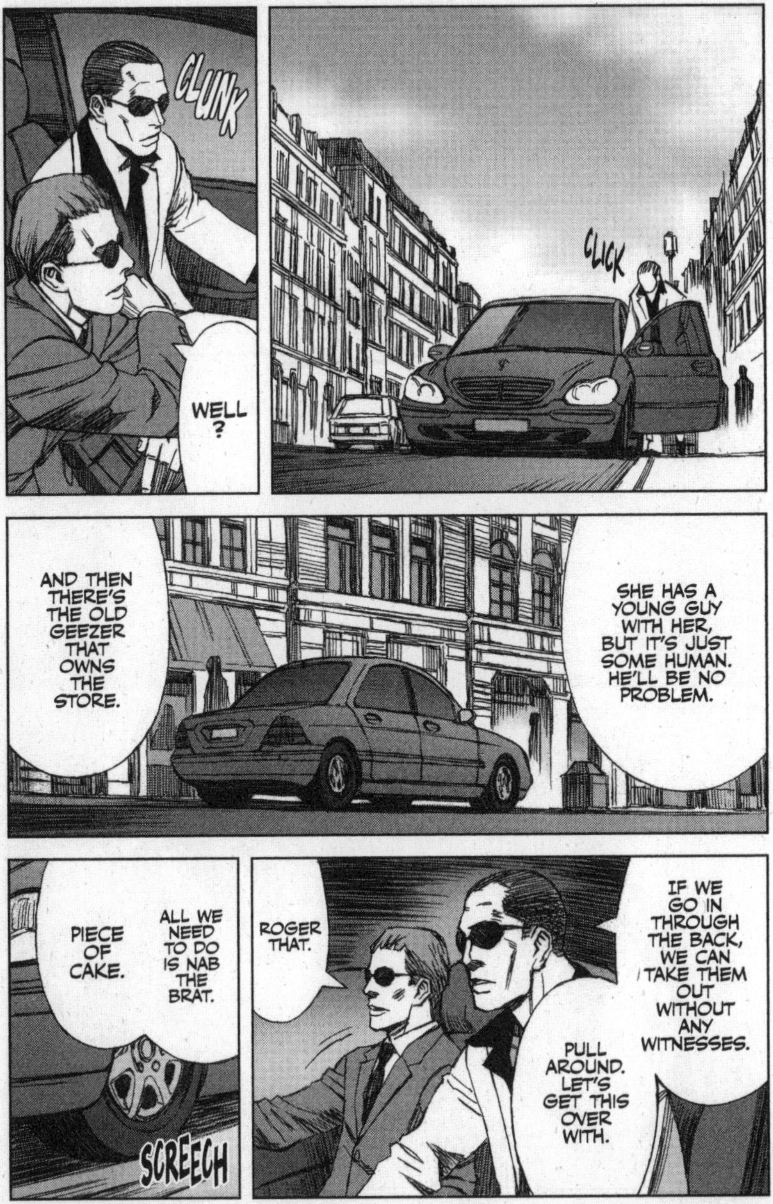
CLICK
CLUNK
WELL?
SHE HAS A YOUNG GUY WITH HER, BUT IT'S JUST SOME HUMAN. HE'LL BE NO PROBLEM.
AND THEN THERE'S THE OLD GEEZER THAT OWNS THE STORE.
IF WE GO IN THROUGH THE BACK, WE CAN TAKE THEM OUT WITHOUT ANY WITNESSES.
PULL AROUND. LET'S GET THIS OVER WITH.
ROGER THAT.
ALL WE NEED TO DO IS NAB THE BRAT.
PIECE OF CAKE.
SCREECH

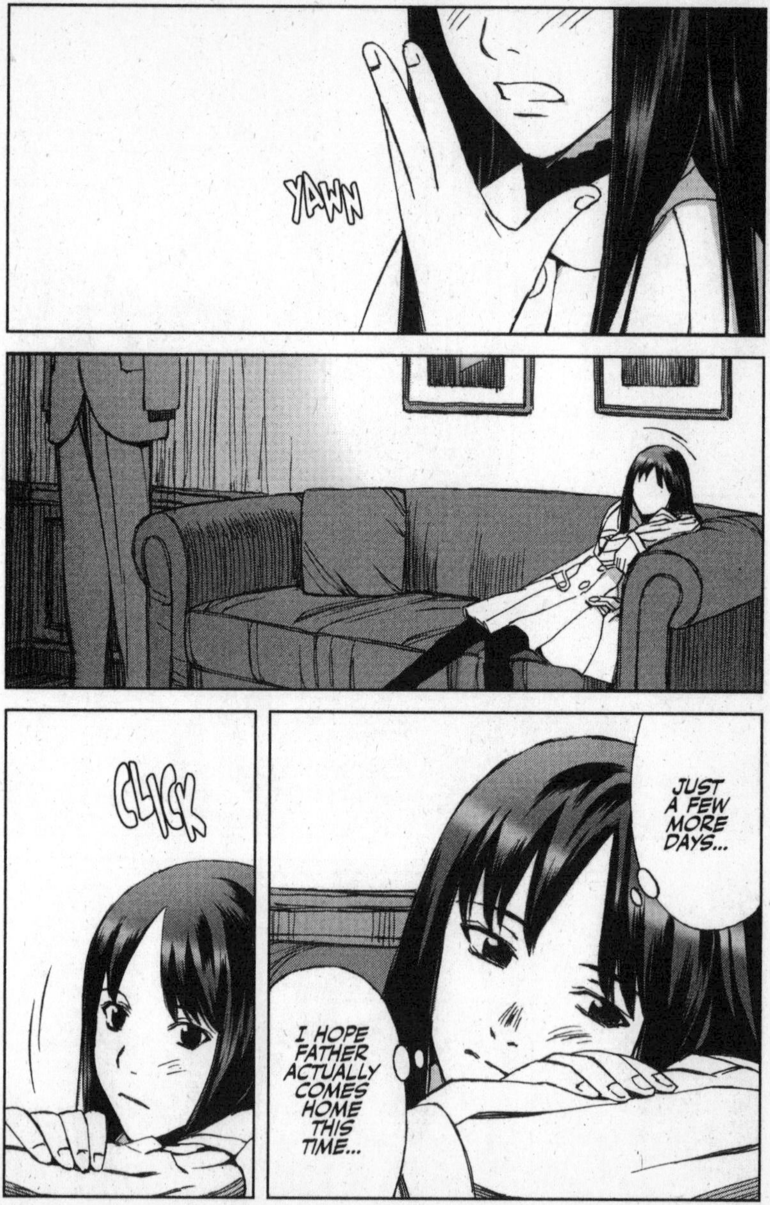
YAWN
JUST A FEW MORE DAYS...
I HOPE FATHER ACTUALLY COMES HOME THIS TIME...
CLICK

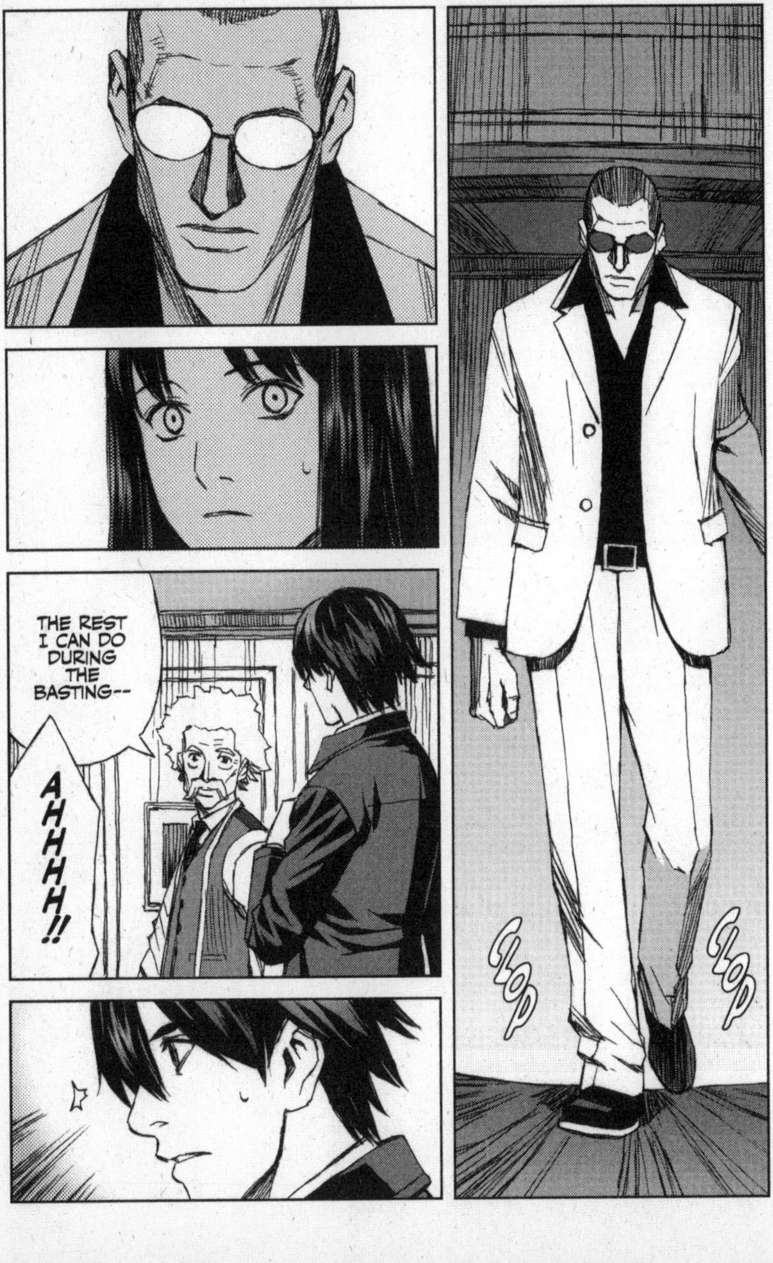
CLOP
CLOP
THE REST I CAN DO DURING THE BASTING--
AHHHHH!!

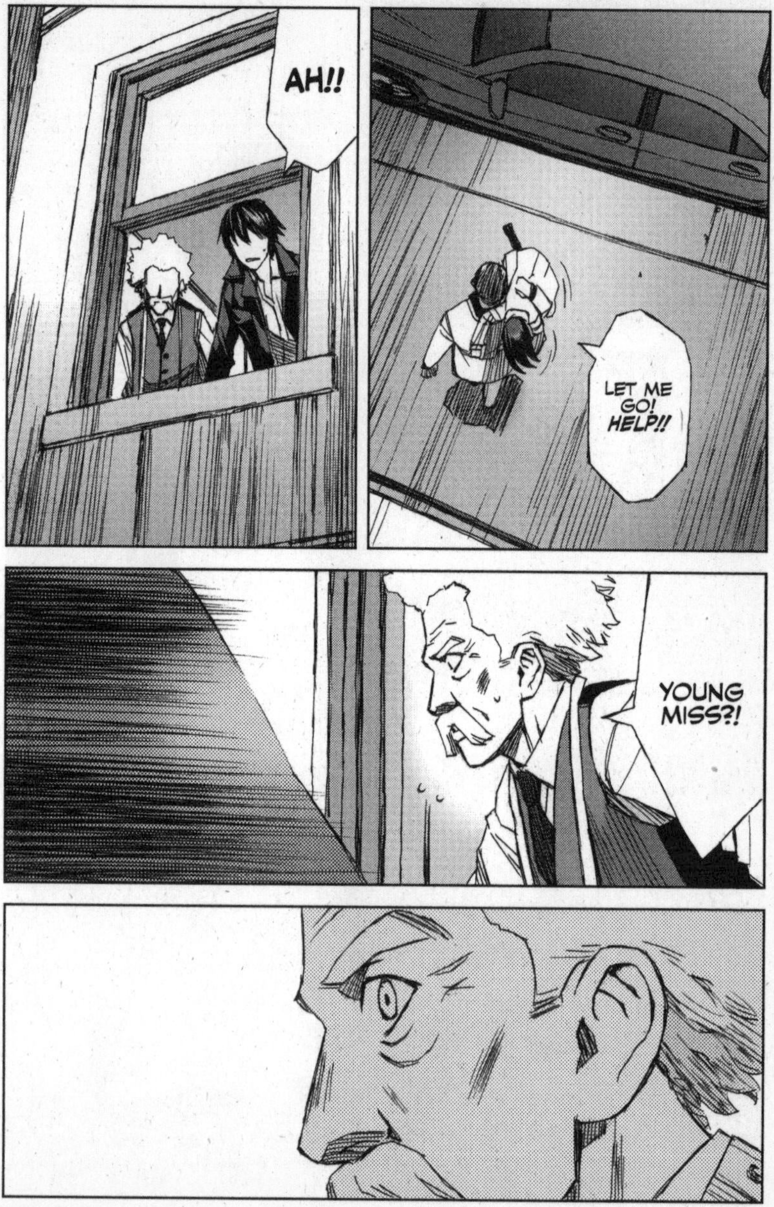
LET ME GO! HELP!!
AH!!
YOUNG MISS?!

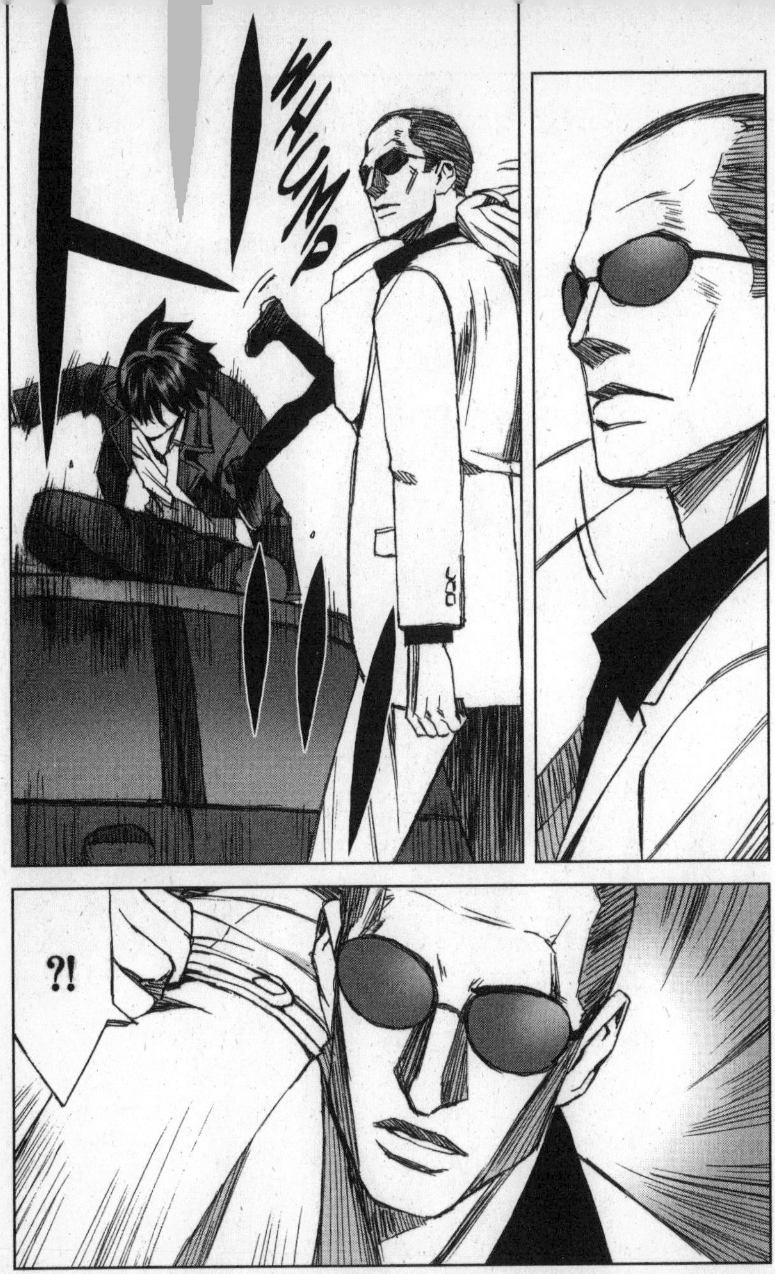
WHUMP
?!

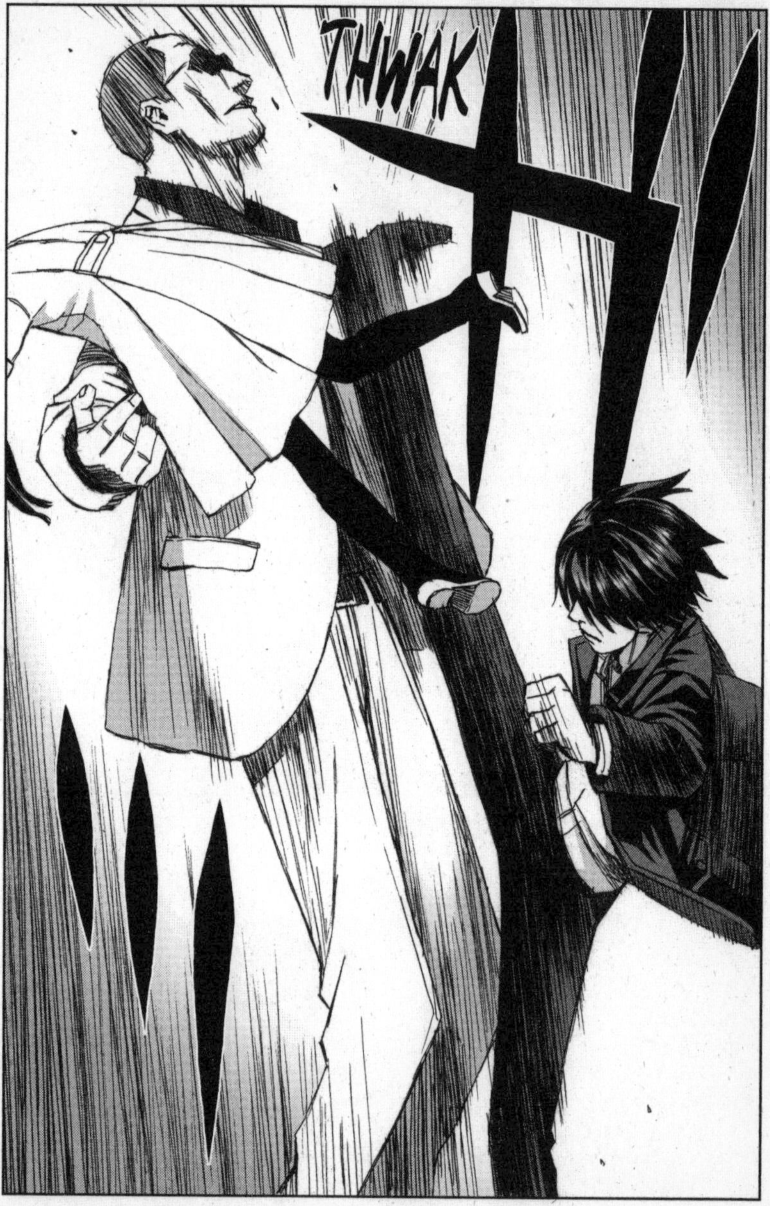
THWAK

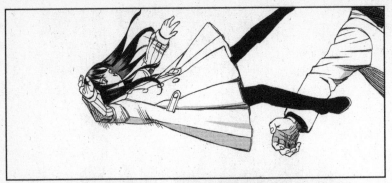

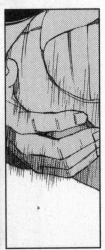

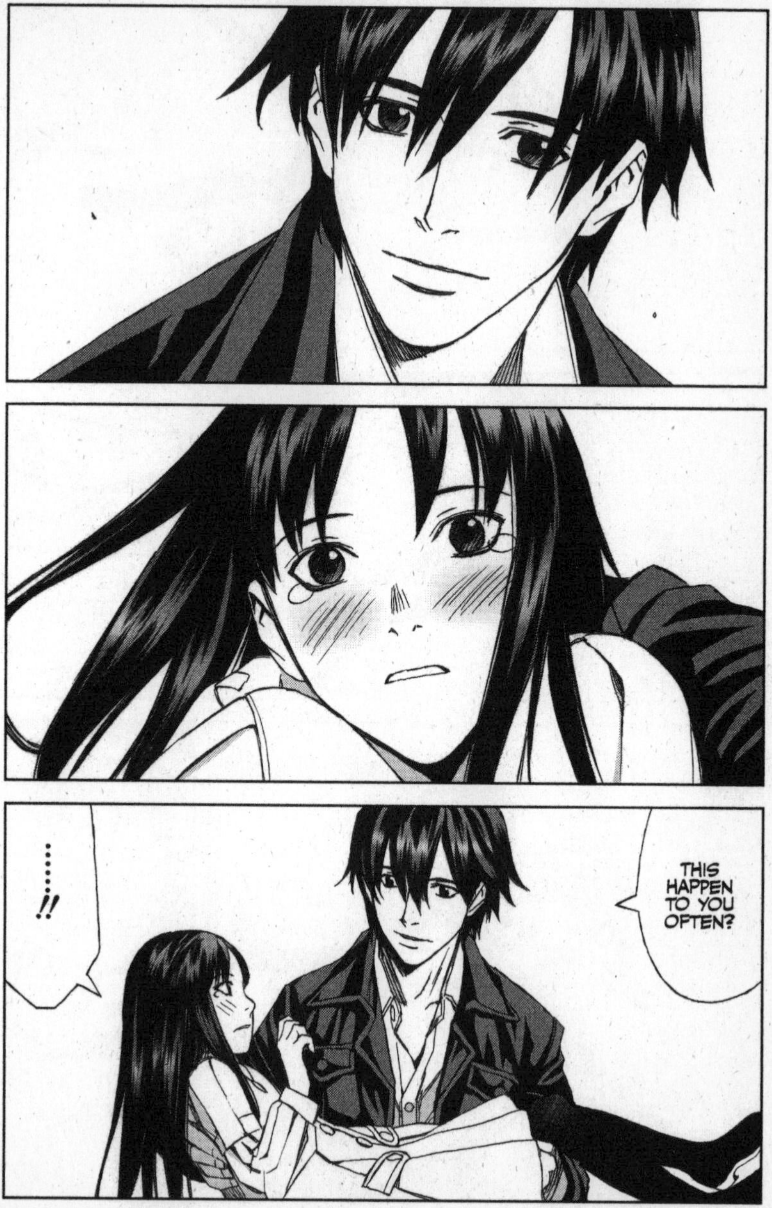
THIS HAPPEN TO YOU OFTEN?
......!!

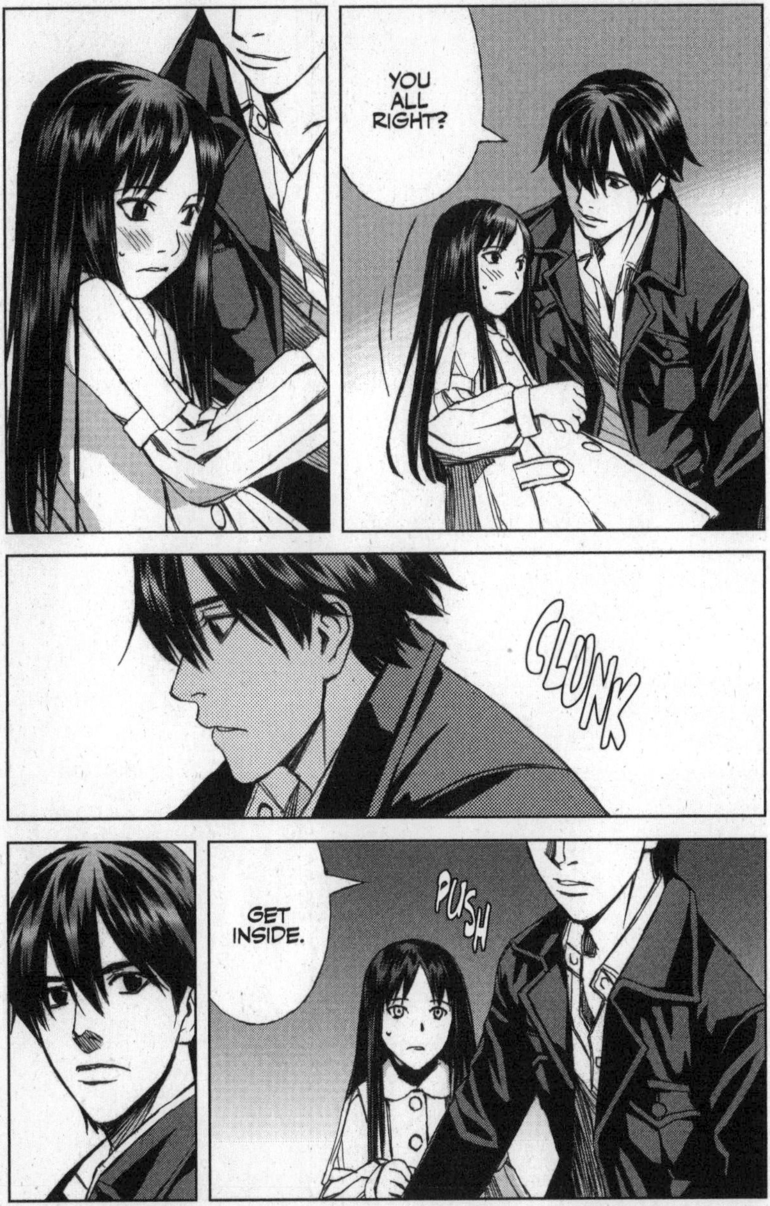
YOU ALL RIGHT?
CLONK
GET INSIDE.
PUSH

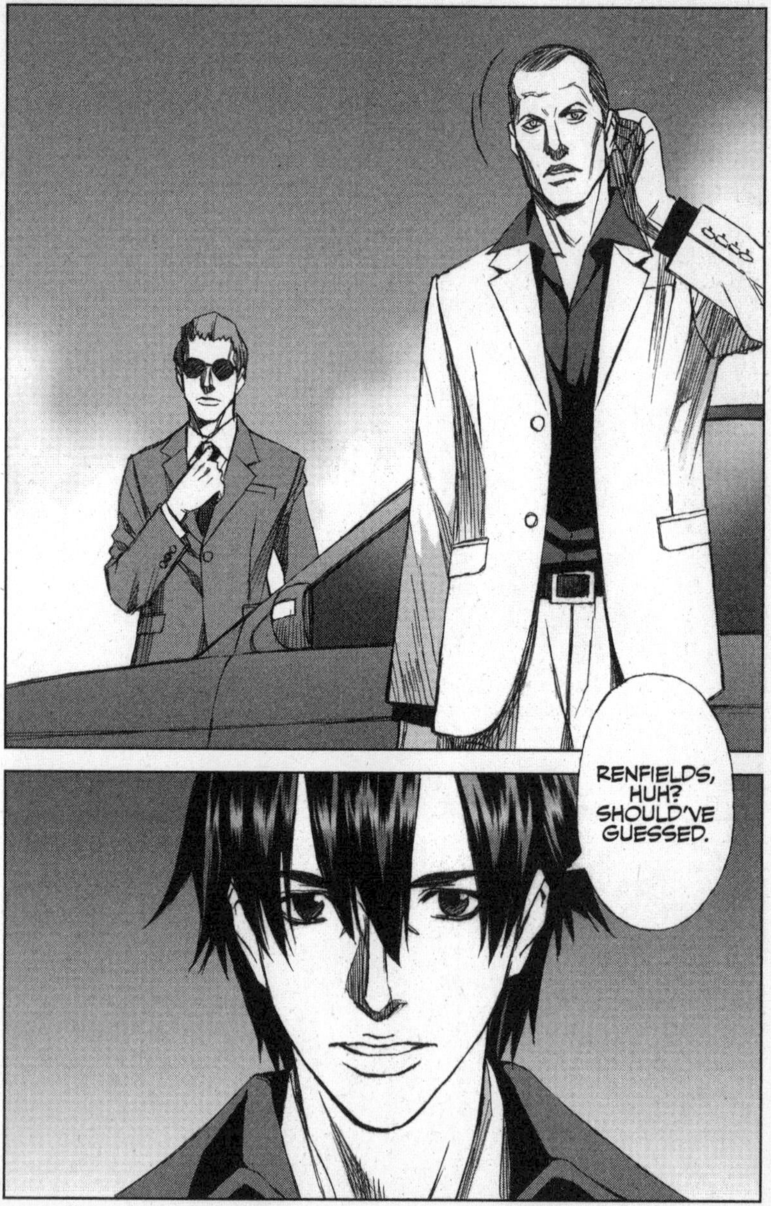
RENFIELDS, HUH? SHOULD'VE GUESSED.

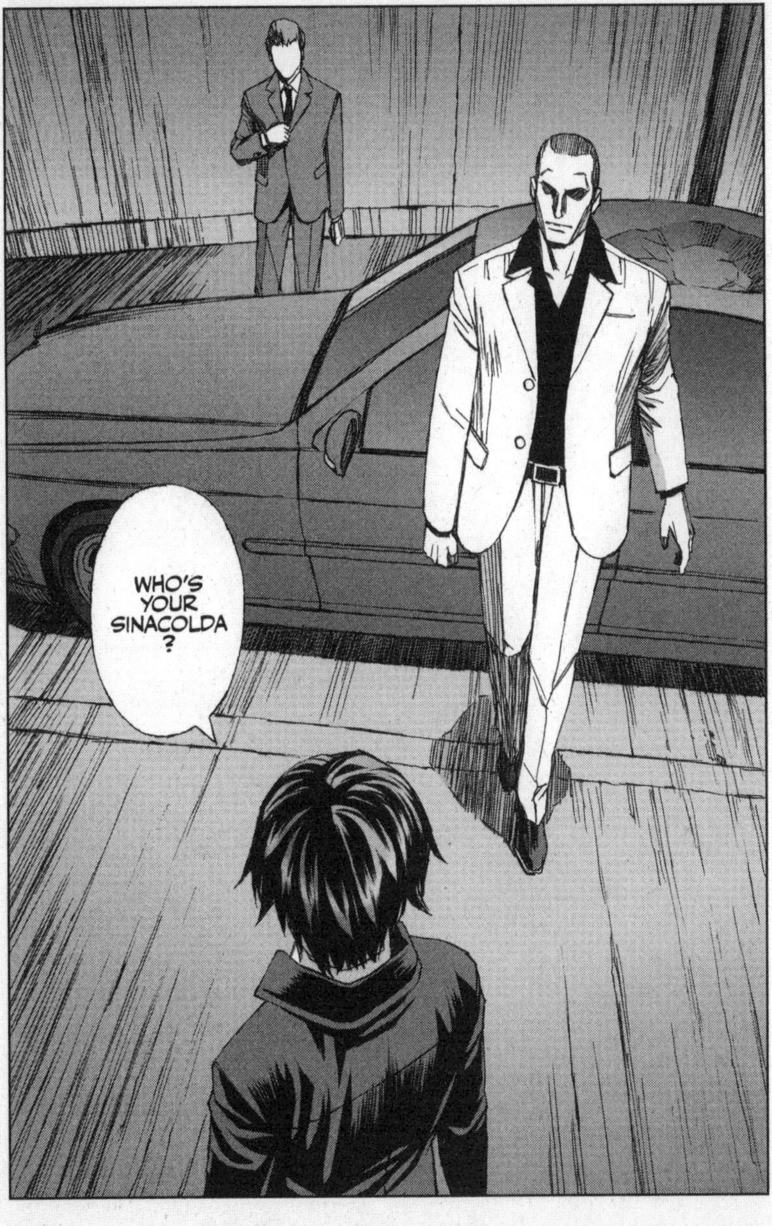
WHO'S YOUR SINACOLDA ?

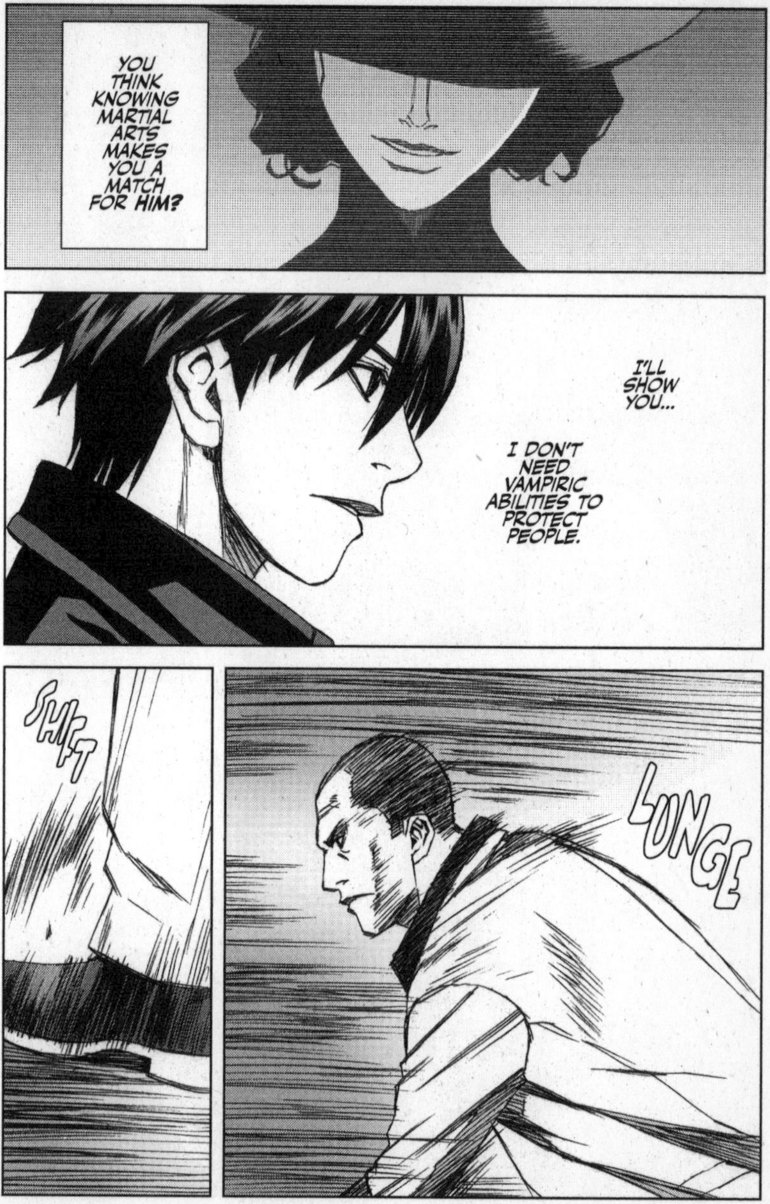
YOU THINK KNOWING MARTIAL ARTS MAKES YOU A MATCH FOR HIM?
I'LL SHOW YOU...
I DON'T NEED VAMPIRIC ABILITIES TO PROTECT PEOPLE.
LUNGE
SHIFT

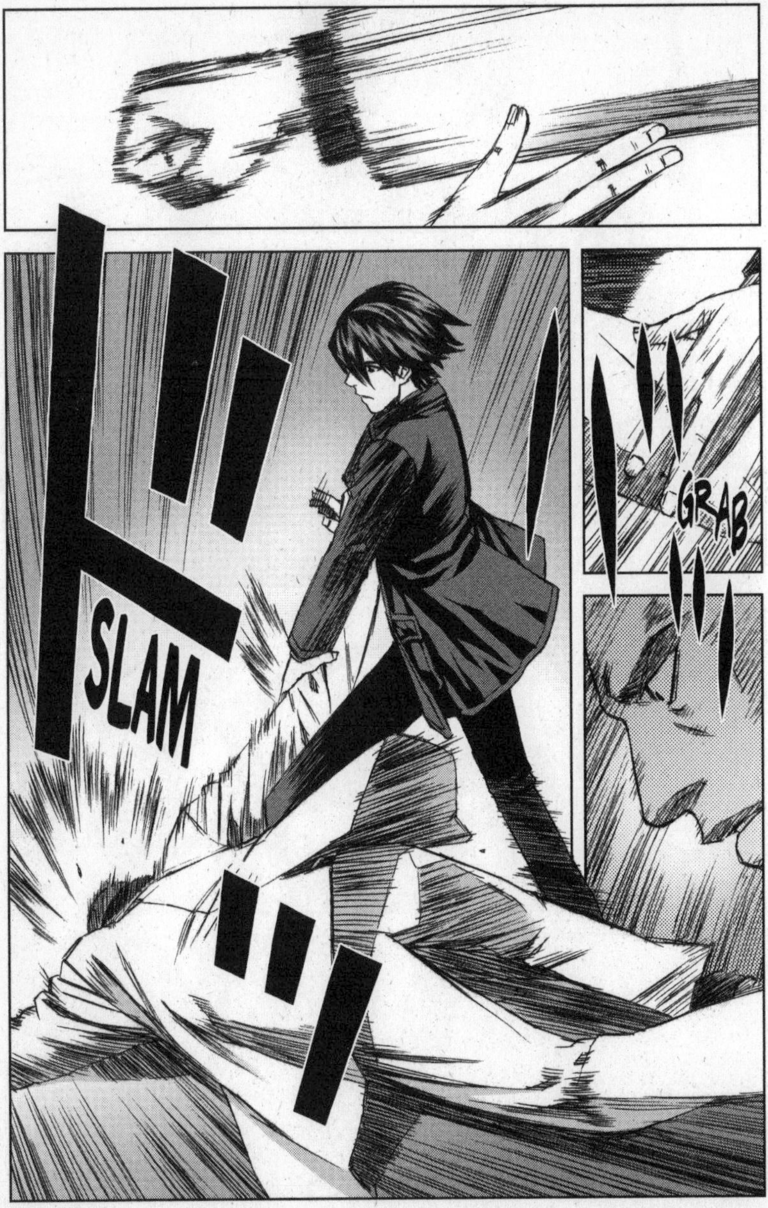
GRAB
SLAM

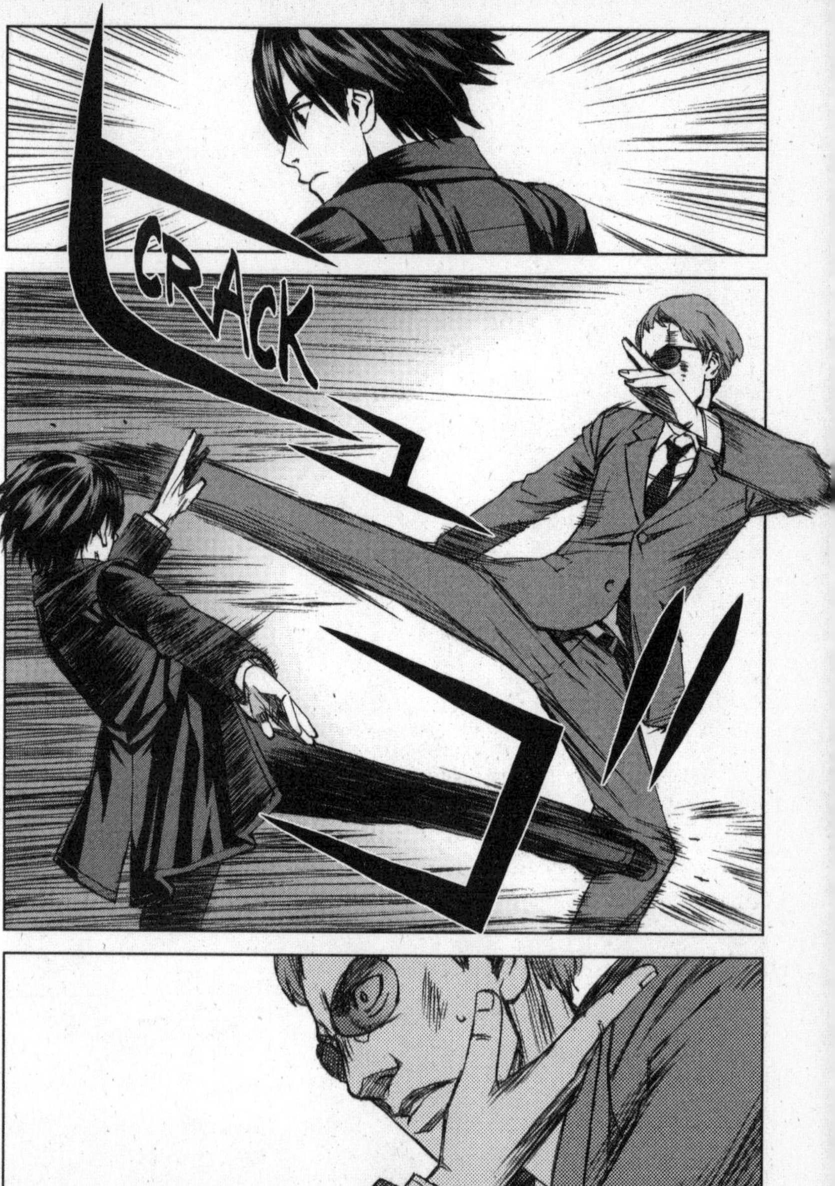
CRACK

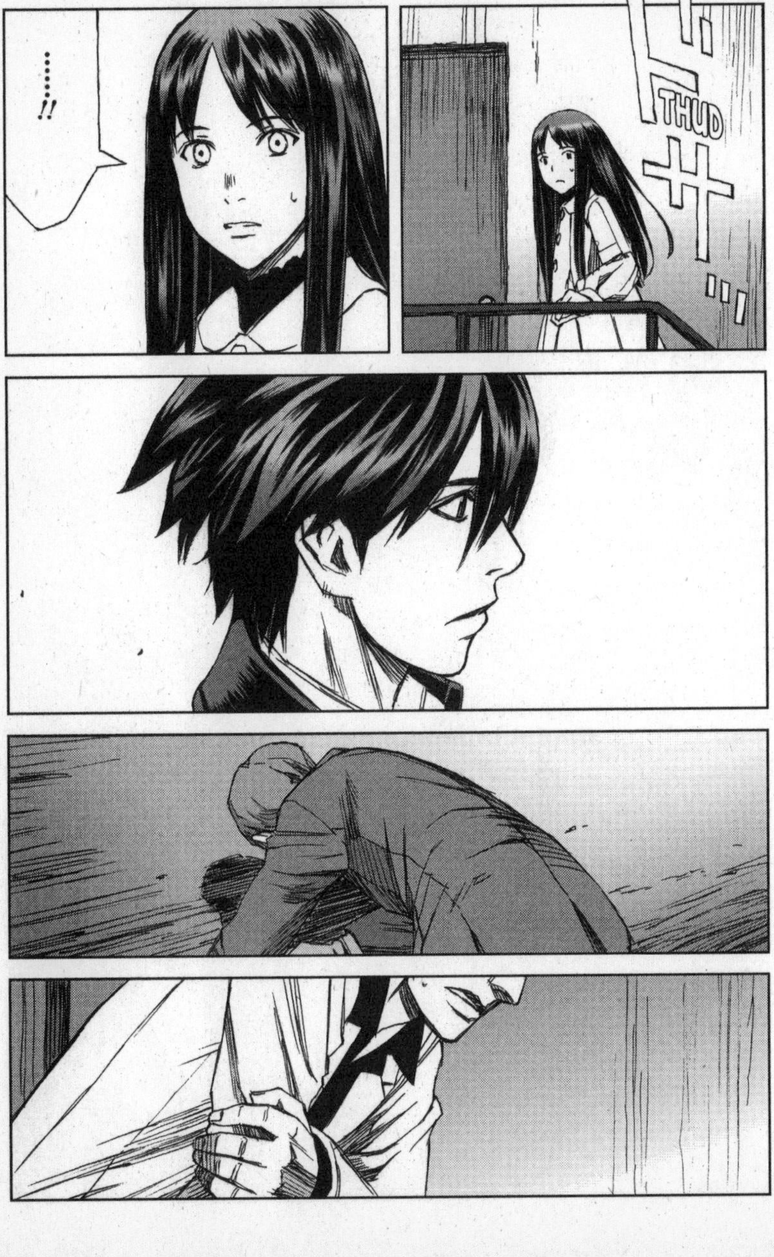
THUD
......!!

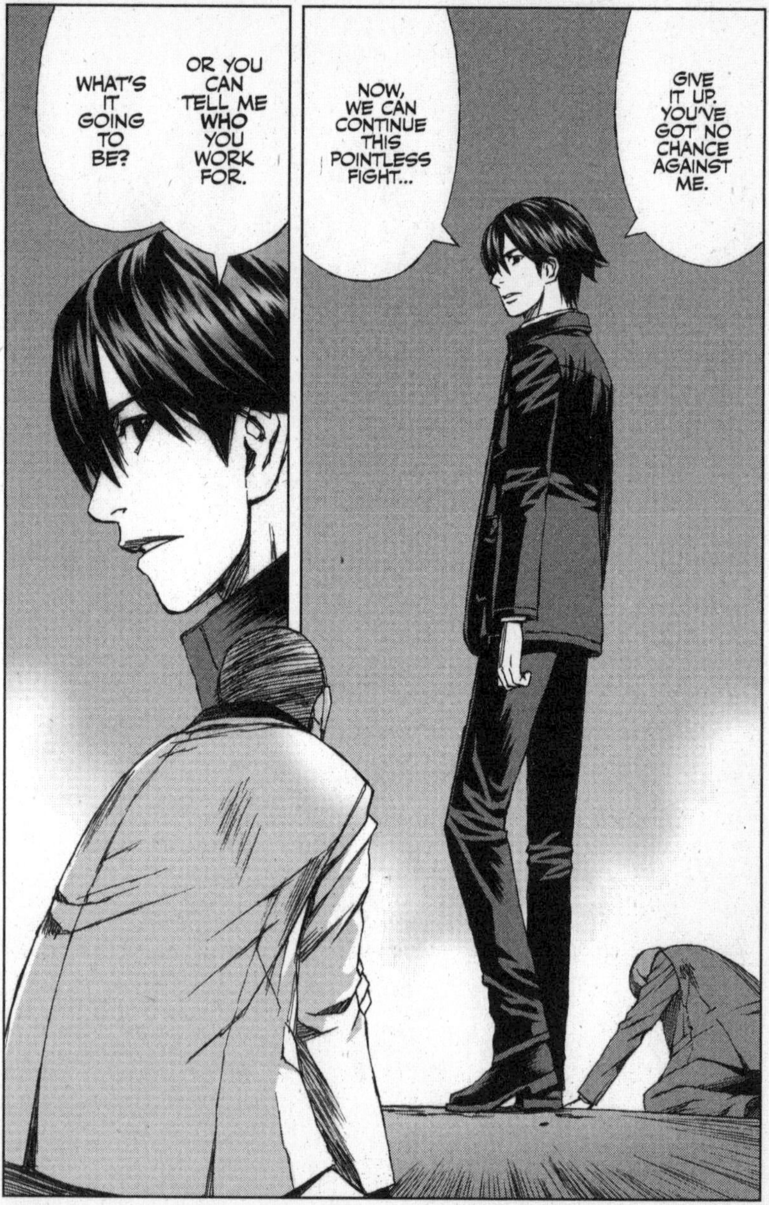
GIVE IT UP. YOU'VE GOT NO CHANCE AGAINST ME.
NOW, WE CAN CONTINUE THIS POINTLESS FIGHT...
OR YOU CAN TELL ME WHO YOU WORK FOR.
WHAT'S IT GOING TO BE?

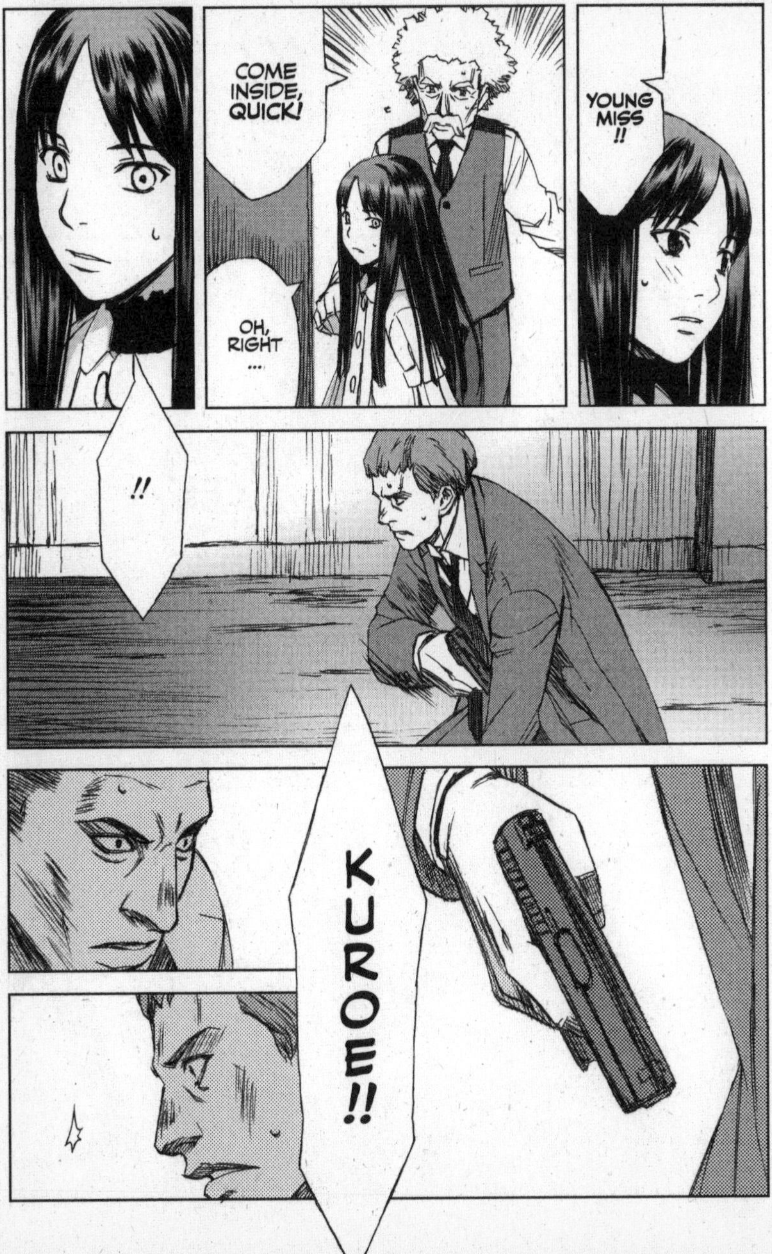
YOUNG MISS !!
COME INSIDE, QUICK!
OH, RIGHT ...
!!
KUROE!!

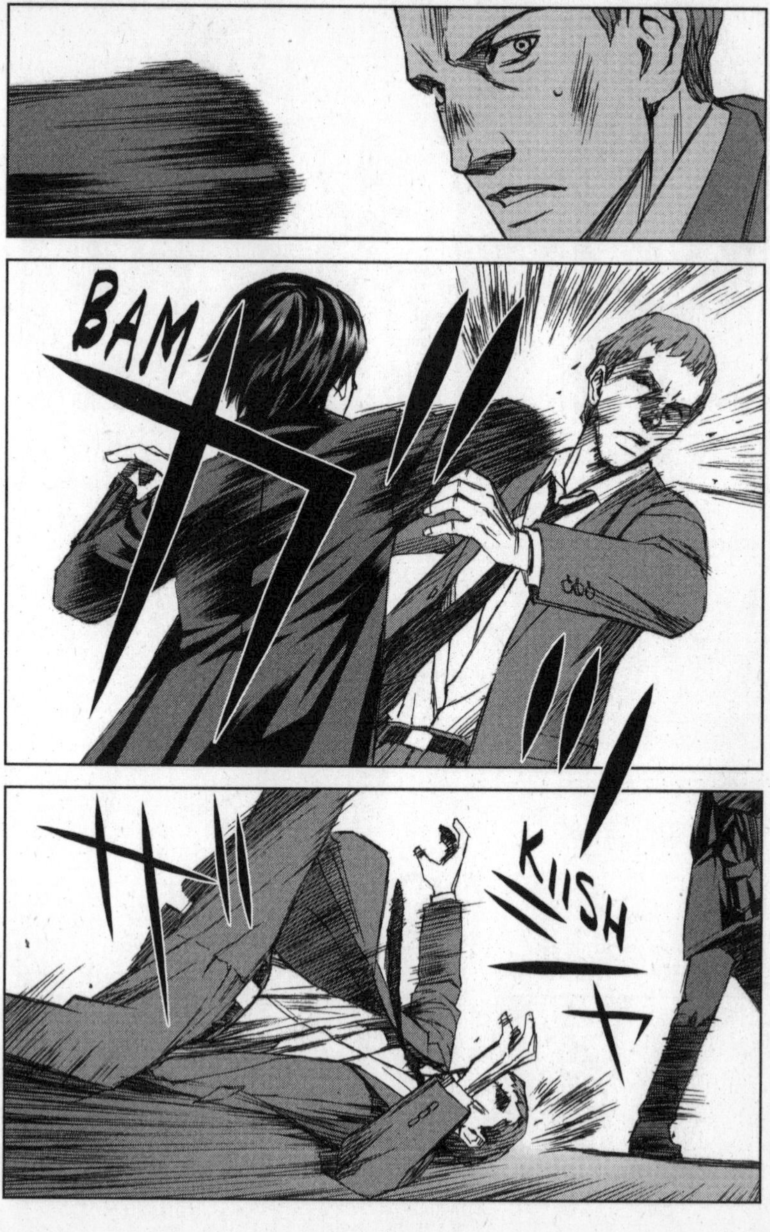
BAM
KIISH

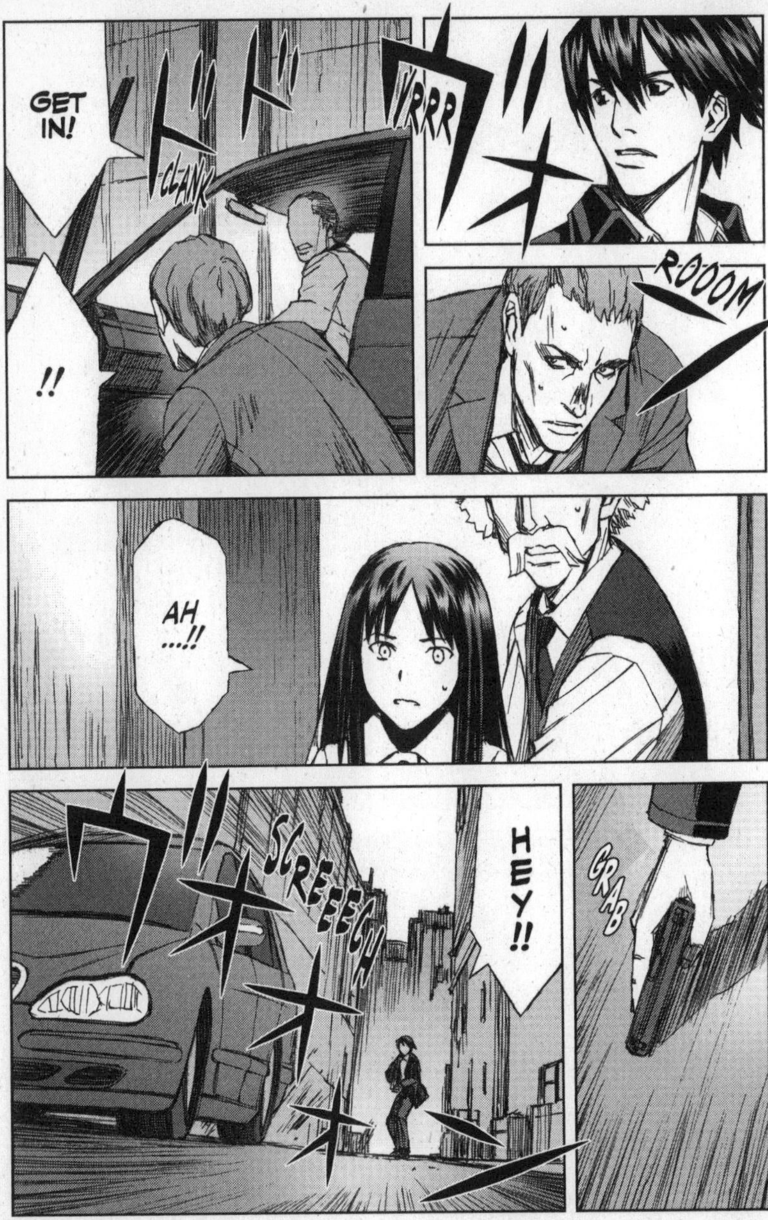
VRRR
ROOOM
GET IN!
CLANK
!!
AH ...!!
GRAB
HEY!!
SCREEEECH

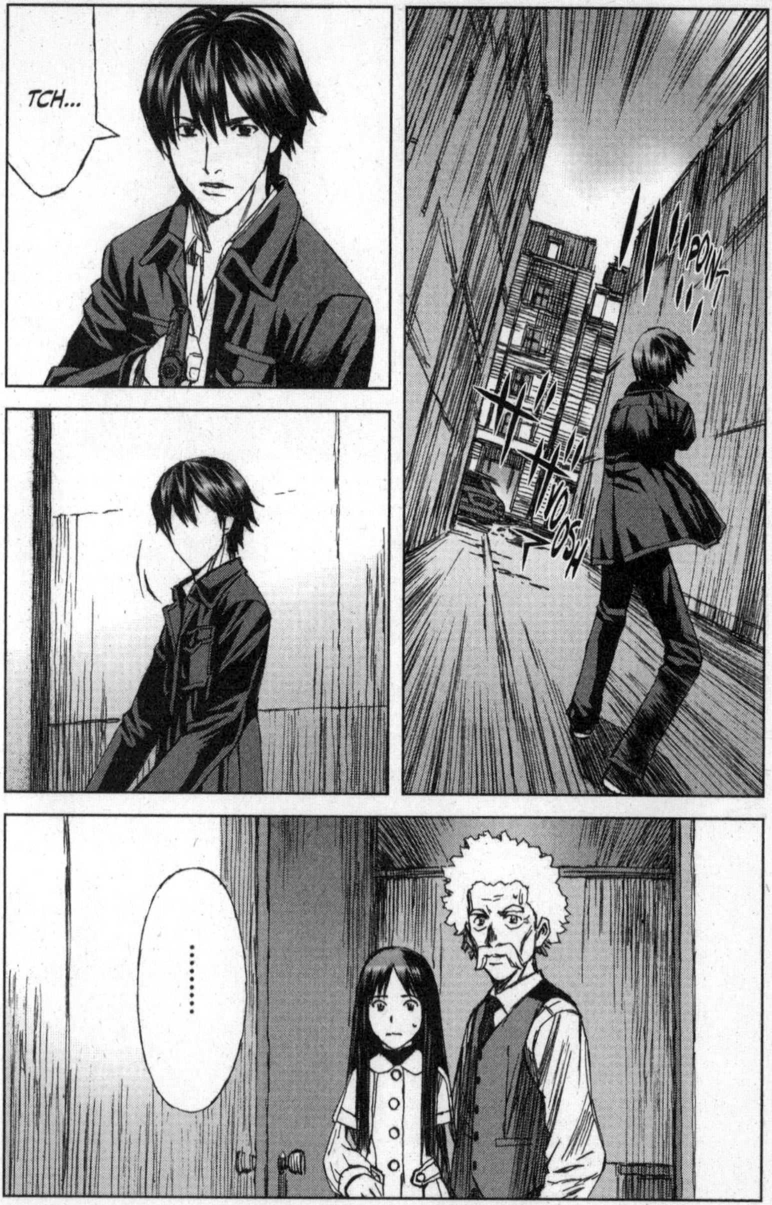
POINT
VOOSH
TCH...
......

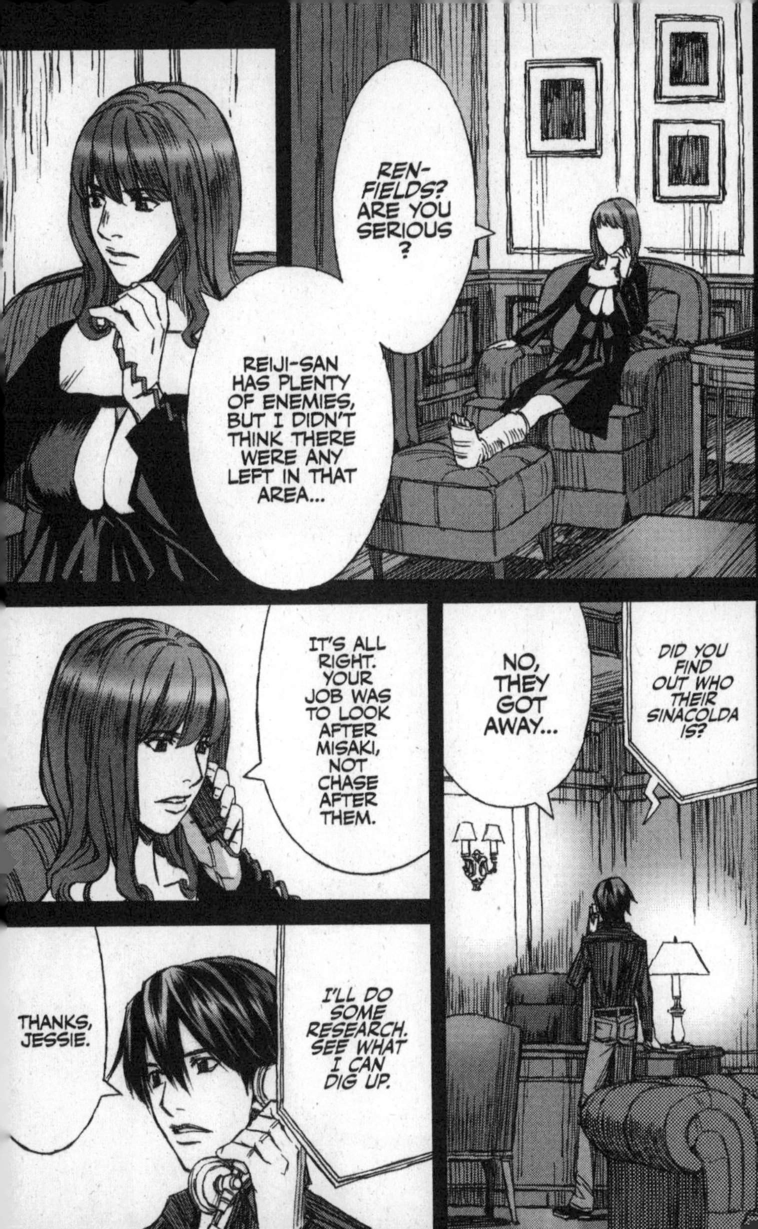
REN-FIELDS? ARE YOU SERIOUS?
REIJI-SAN HAS PLENTY OF ENEMIES, BUT I DIDN'T THINK THERE WERE ANY LEFT IN THAT AREA...
DID YOU FIND OUT WHO THEIR SINACOLDA IS?
NO, THEY GOT AWAY...
IT'S ALL RIGHT. YOUR JOB WAS TO LOOK AFTER MISAKI, NOT CHASE AFTER THEM.
I'LL DO SOME RESEARCH. SEE WHAT I CAN DIG UP.
THANKS, JESSIE.

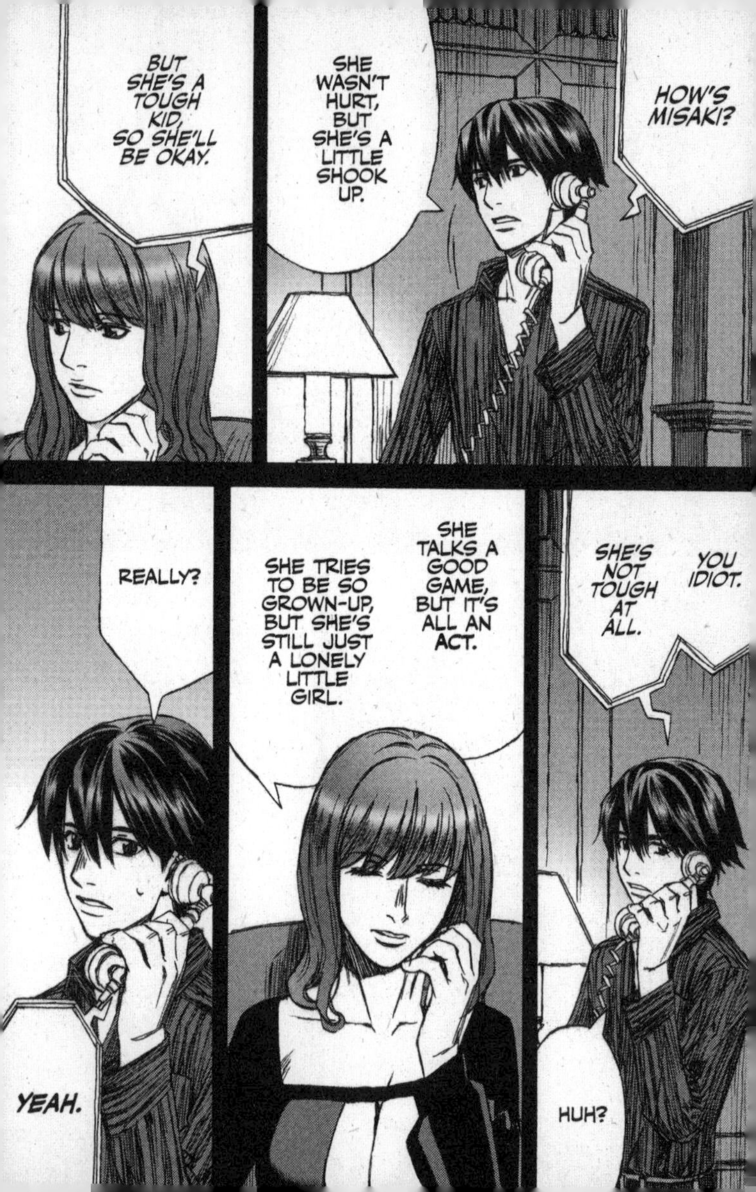
HOW'S MISAKI?
SHE WASN'T HURT, BUT SHE'S A LITTLE SHOOK UP.
BUT SHE'S A TOUGH KID, SO SHE'LL BE OKAY.
YOU IDIOT.
SHE'S NOT TOUGH AT ALL.
HUH?
SHE TALKS A GOOD GAME, BUT IT'S ALL AN ACT.
SHE TRIES TO BE SO GROWN-UP, BUT SHE'S STILL JUST A LONELY LITTLE GIRL.
REALLY?
YEAH.

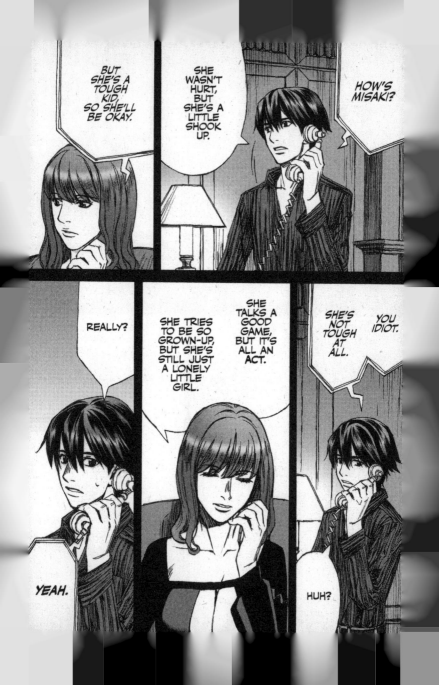

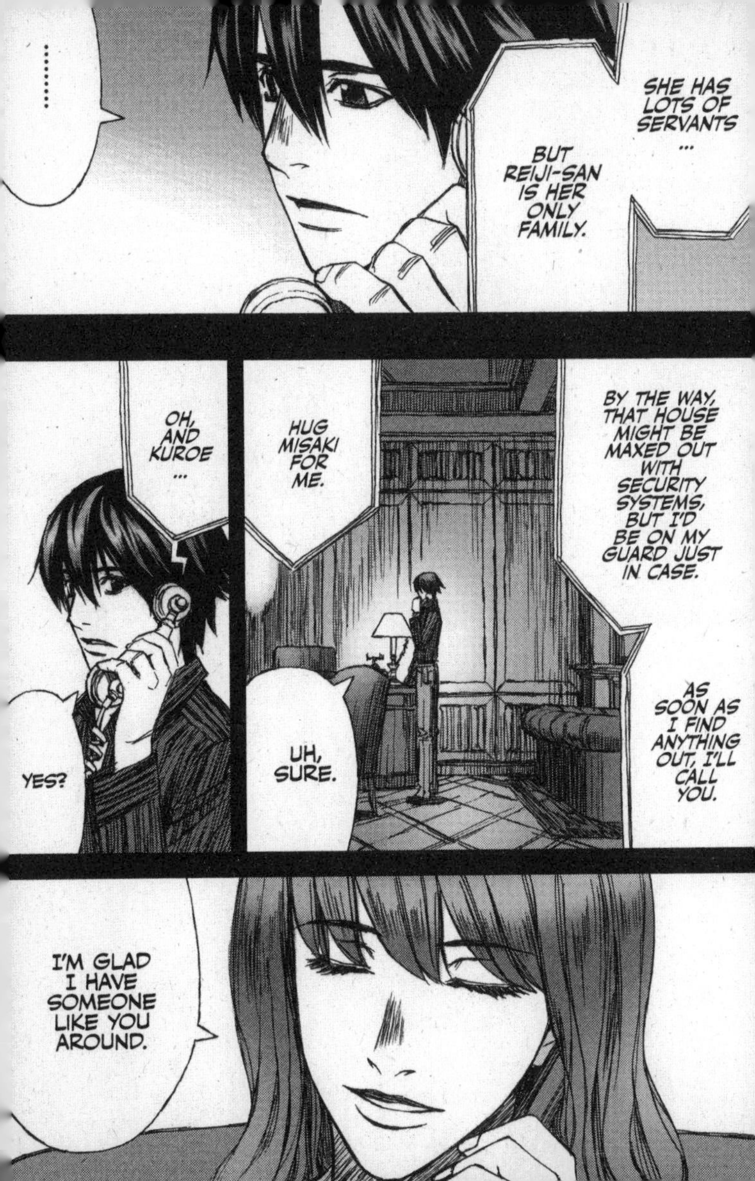
SHE HAS LOTS OF SERVANTS ...
BUT REIJI-SAN IS HER ONLY FAMILY.
......
BY THE WAY, THAT HOUSE MIGHT BE MAXED OUT WITH SECURITY SYSTEMS, BUT I'D BE ON MY GUARD JUST IN CASE.
AS SOON AS I FIND ANYTHING OUT, I'LL CALL YOU.
HUG MISAKI FOR ME.
UH, SURE.
OH, AND KUROE ...
YES?
I'M GLAD I HAVE SOMEONE LIKE YOU AROUND.

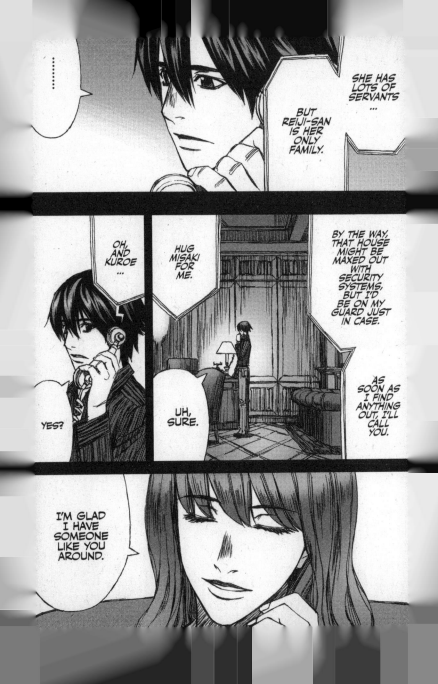

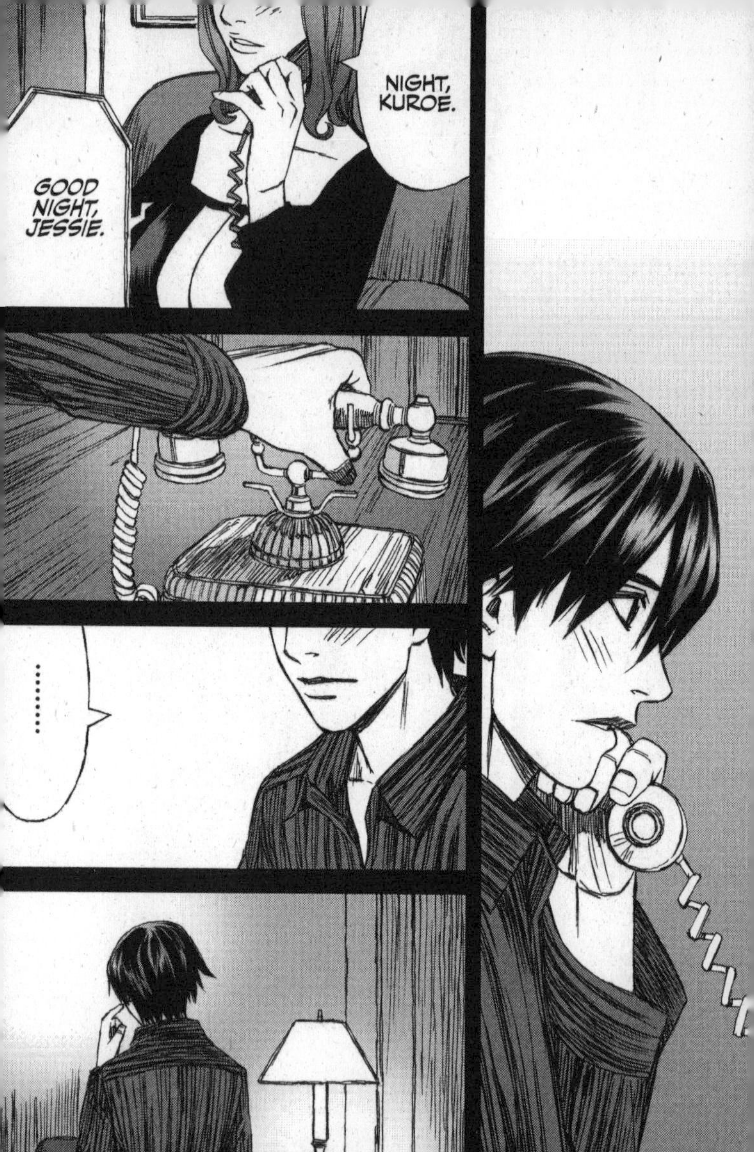
NIGHT, KUROE.
GOOD NIGHT, JESSIE.
....

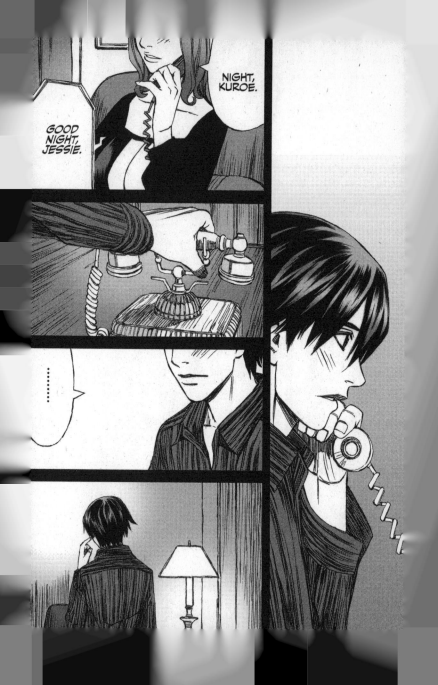

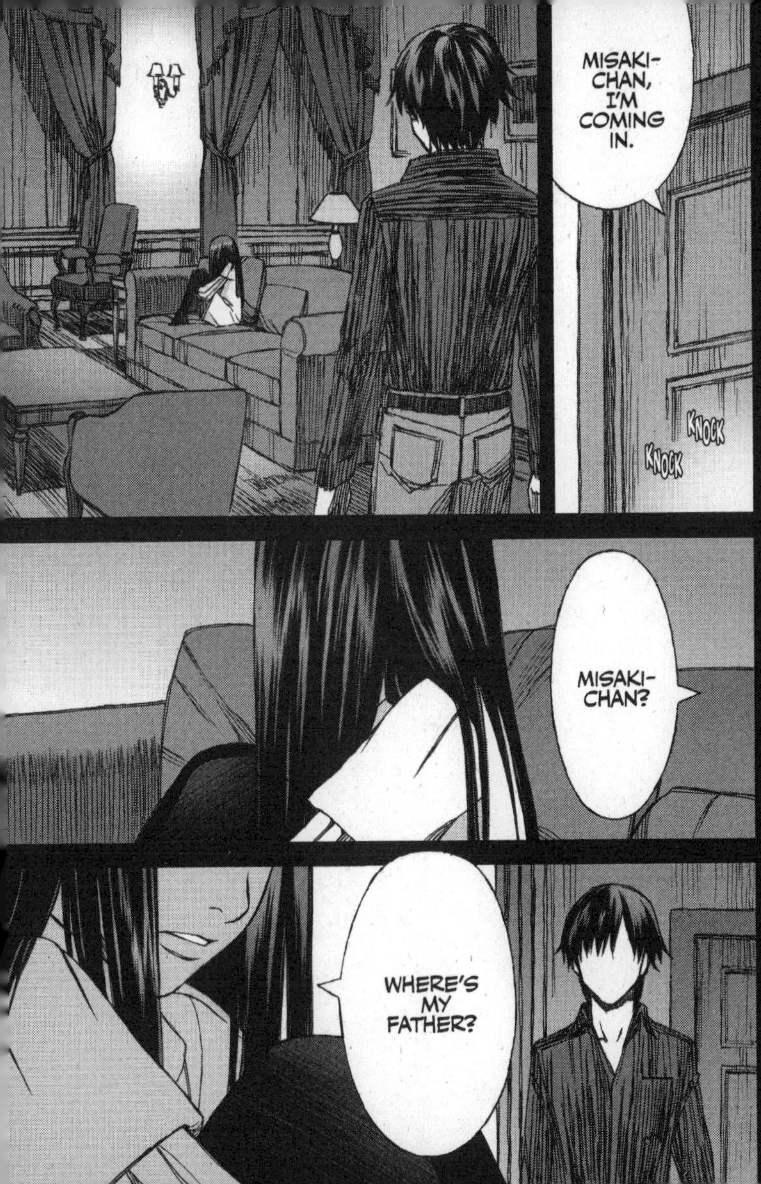
MISAKI-CHAN, I'M COMING IN.
KNOCK
KNOCK
MISAKI-CHAN?
WHERE'S MY FATHER?

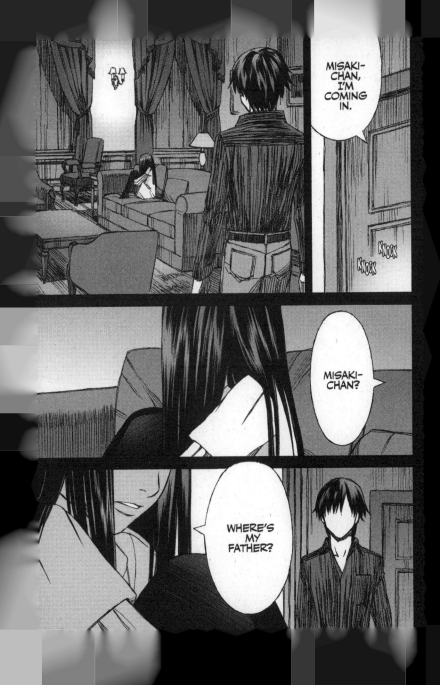

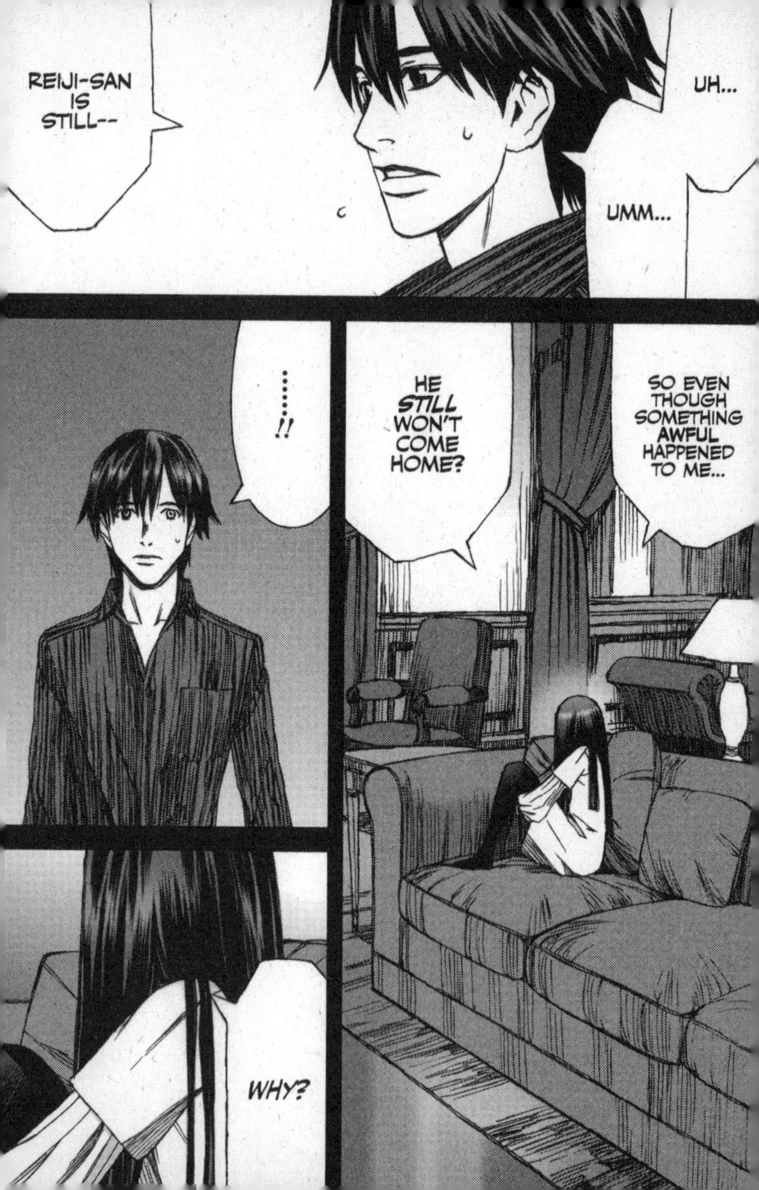
UH...
UMM...
REIJI-SAN IS STILL--
SO EVEN THOUGH SOMETHING AWFUL HAPPENED TO ME...
HE STILL WON'T COME HOME?
......!!
WHY?

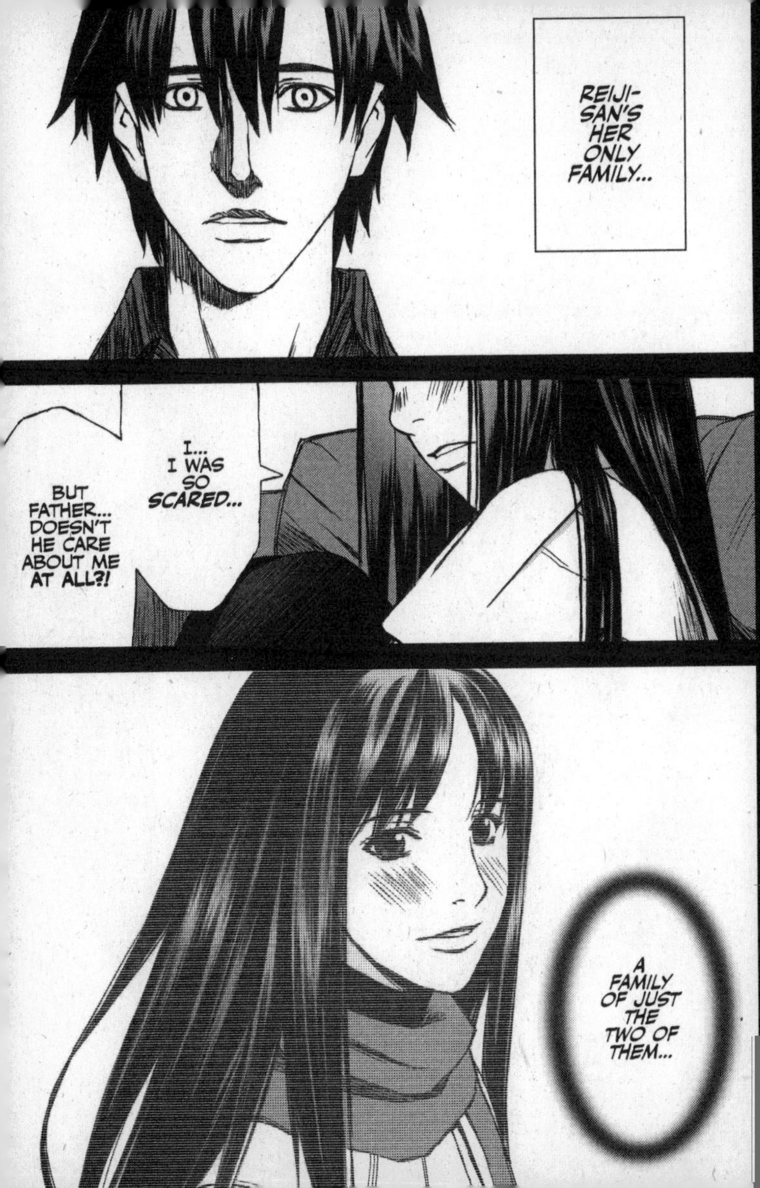
REIJI-SAN'S HER ONLY FAMILY...
I... I WAS SO SCARED...
BUT FATHER... DOESN'T HE CARE ABOUT ME AT ALL?!
A FAMILY OF JUST THE TWO OF THEM...

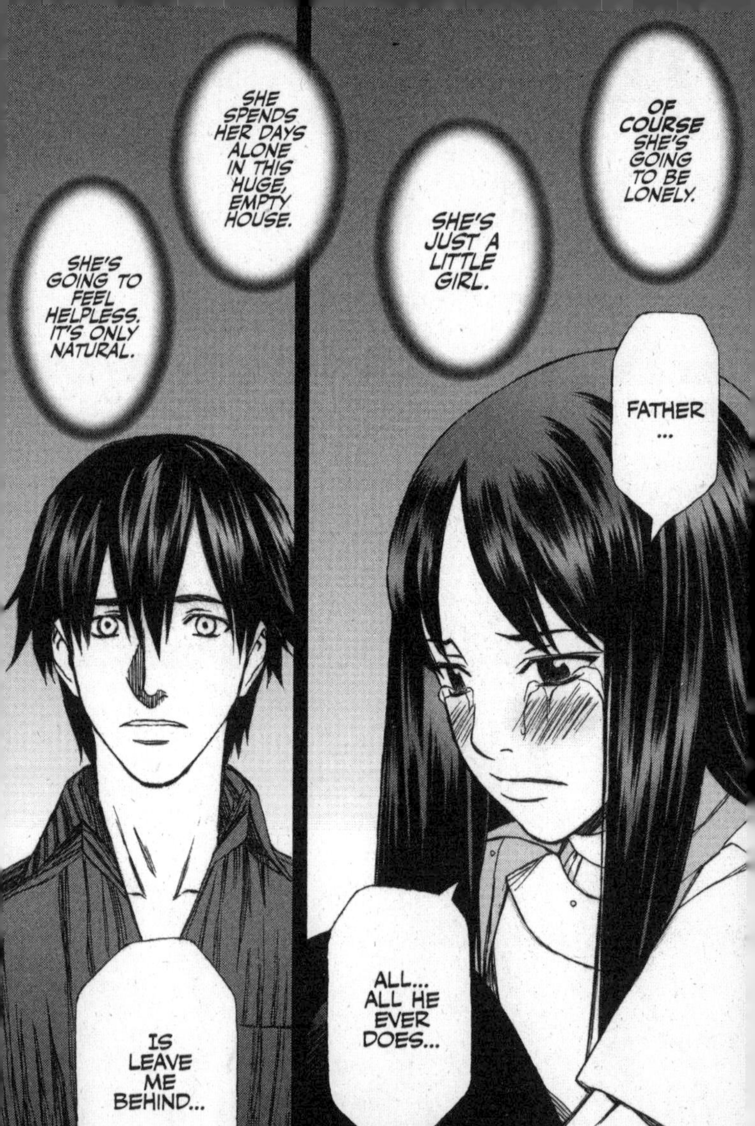
OF COURSE SHE'S GOING TO BE LONELY.
SHE'S JUST A LITTLE GIRL.
FATHER...
ALL... ALL HE EVER DOES...
SHE SPENDS HER DAYS ALONE IN THIS HUGE, EMPTY HOUSE.
SHE'S GOING TO FEEL HELPLESS. IT'S ONLY NATURAL.
IS LEAVE ME BEHIND...

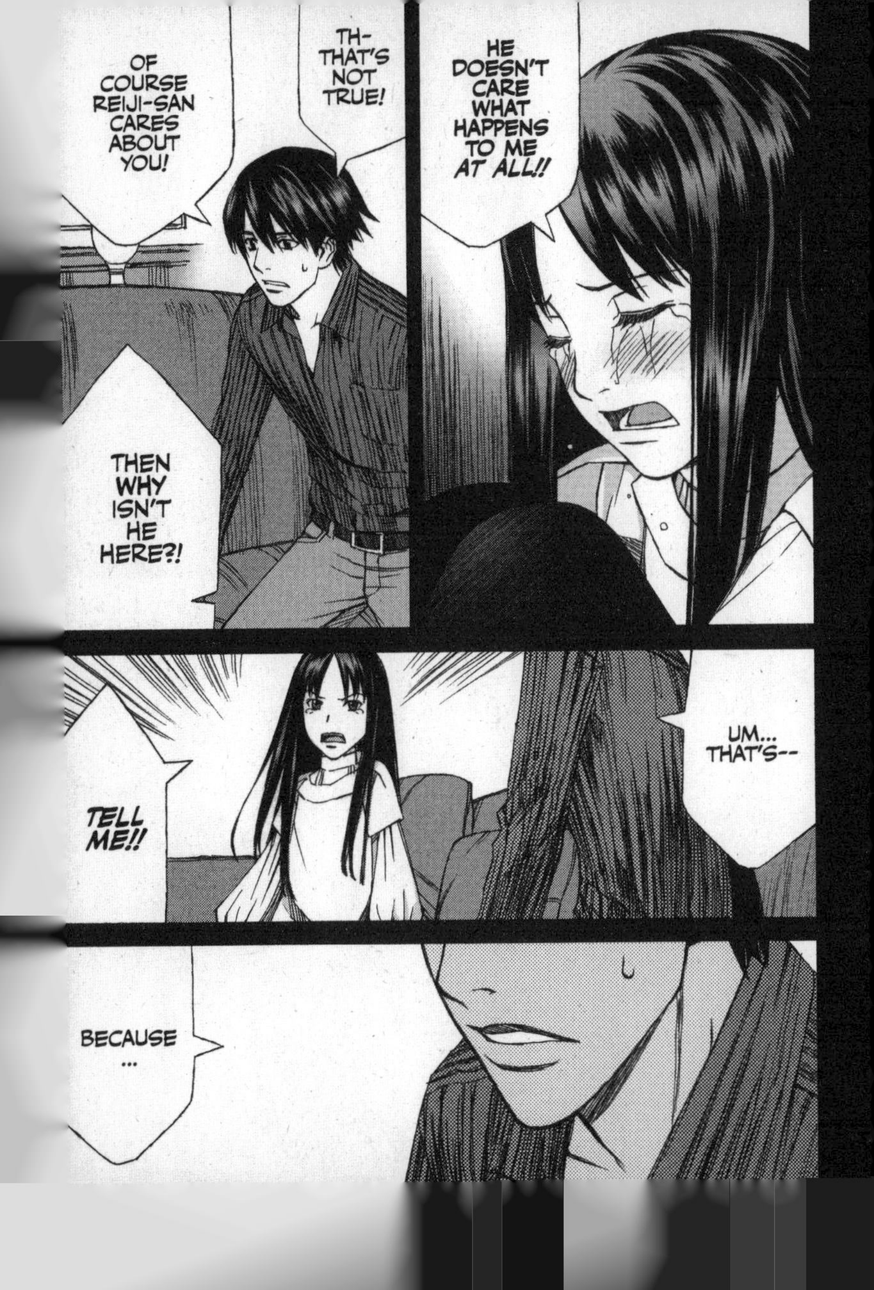
HE DOESN'T CARE WHAT HAPPENS TO ME AT ALL!!
TH-THAT'S NOT TRUE!
OF COURSE REIJI-SAN CARES ABOUT YOU!
THEN WHY ISN'T HE HERE?!
UM... THAT'S--
TELL ME!!
BECAUSE ...

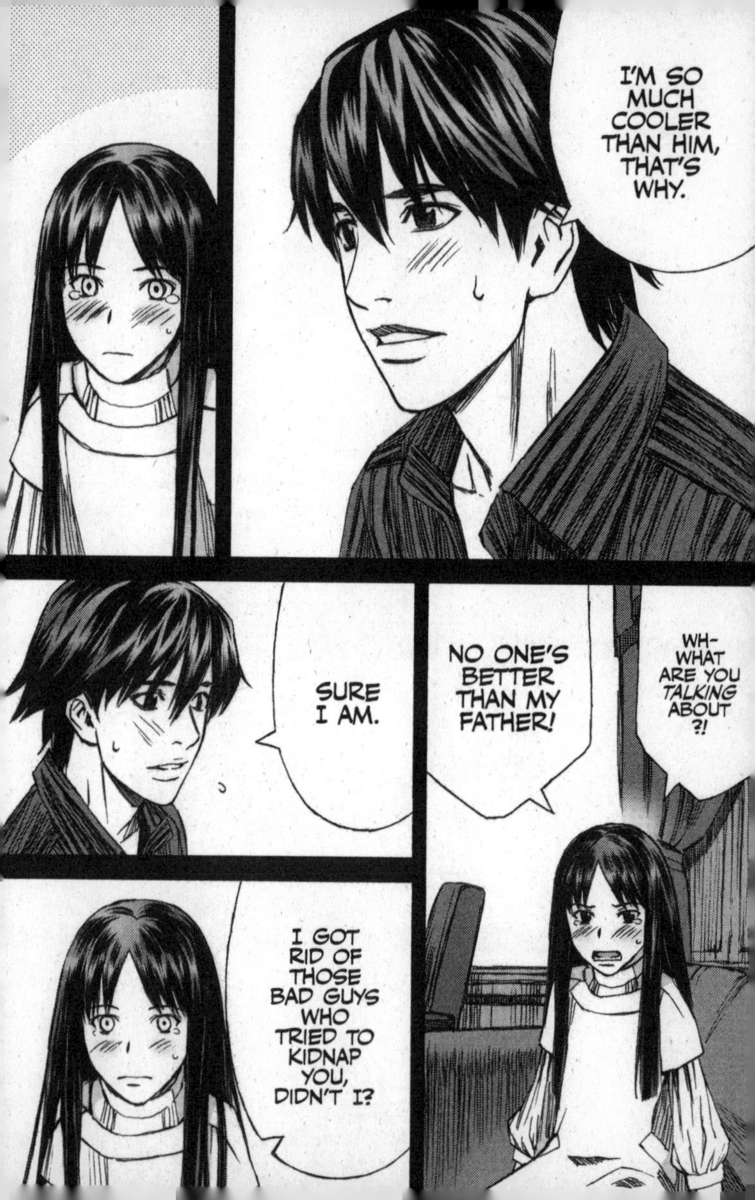
I'M SO MUCH COOLER THAN HIM, THAT'S WHY.
WH- WHAT ARE YOU *TALKING* ABOUT ?!
NO ONE'S BETTER THAN MY FATHER!
SURE I AM.
I GOT RID OF THOSE BAD GUYS WHO TRIED TO KIDNAP YOU, DIDN'T I?

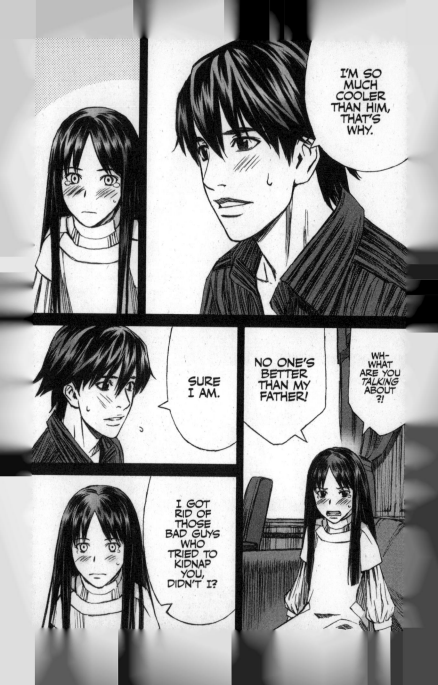

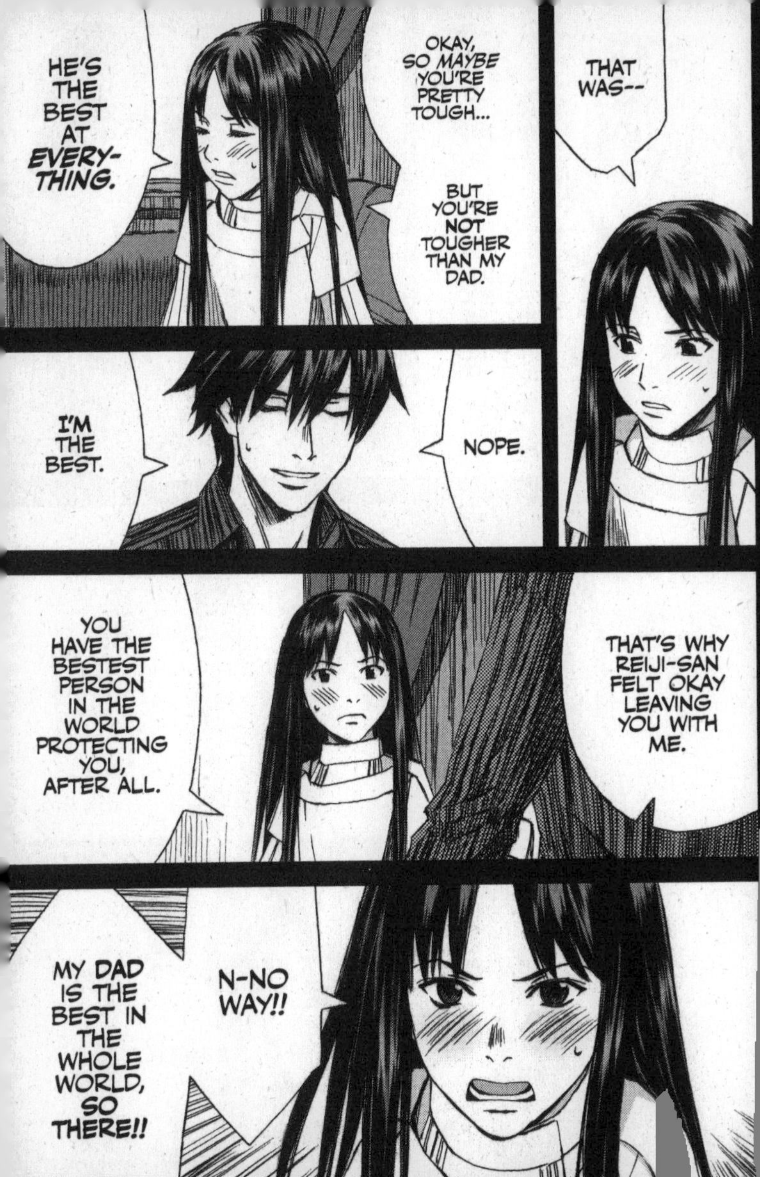
THAT WAS--
OKAY, SO *MAYBE* YOU'RE PRETTY TOUGH...
BUT YOU'RE **NOT** TOUGHER THAN MY DAD.
HE'S THE BEST AT ***EVERYTHING.***
NOPE.
I'M THE BEST.
THAT'S WHY REIJI-SAN FELT OKAY LEAVING YOU WITH ME.
YOU HAVE THE BESTEST PERSON IN THE WORLD PROTECTING YOU, AFTER ALL.
N-NO WAY!!
MY DAD IS THE BEST IN THE WHOLE WORLD, SO THERE!!

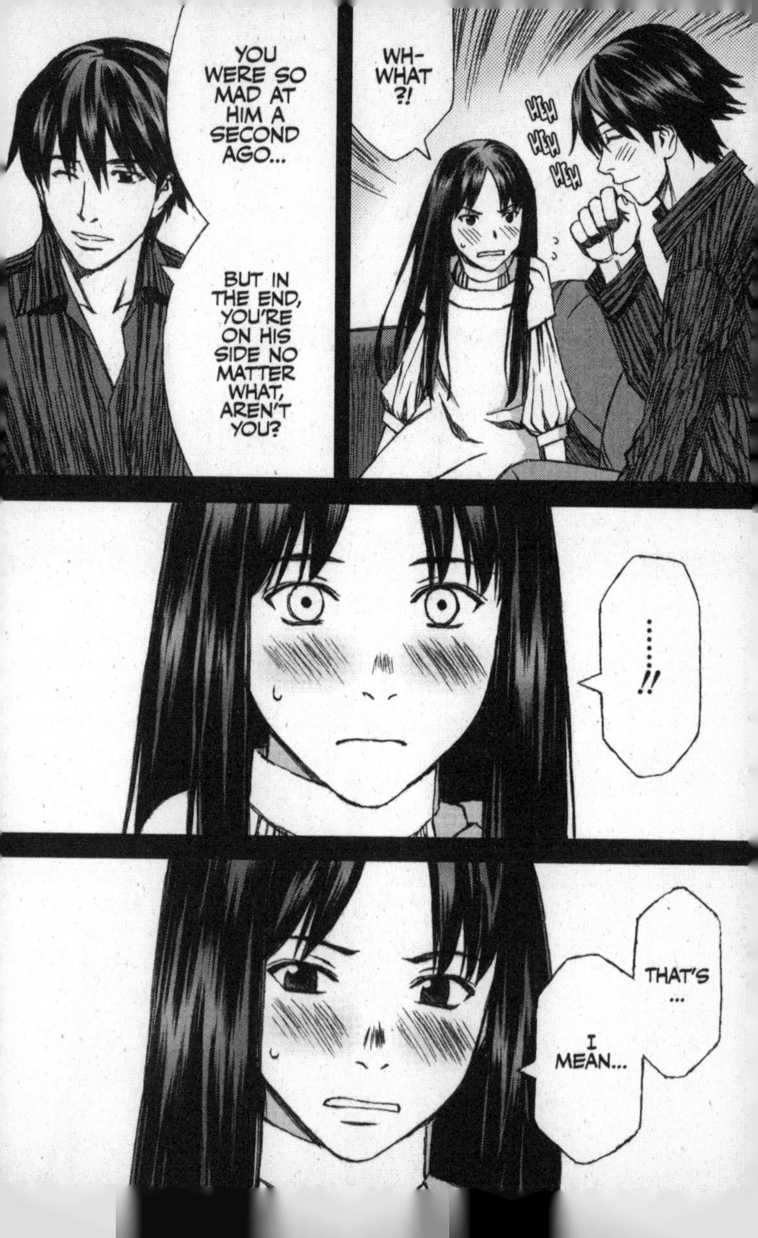
WH-WHAT?!
HEH HEH HEH
YOU WERE SO MAD AT HIM A SECOND AGO...
BUT IN THE END, YOU'RE ON HIS SIDE NO MATTER WHAT, AREN'T YOU?
......!!
THAT'S...
I MEAN...

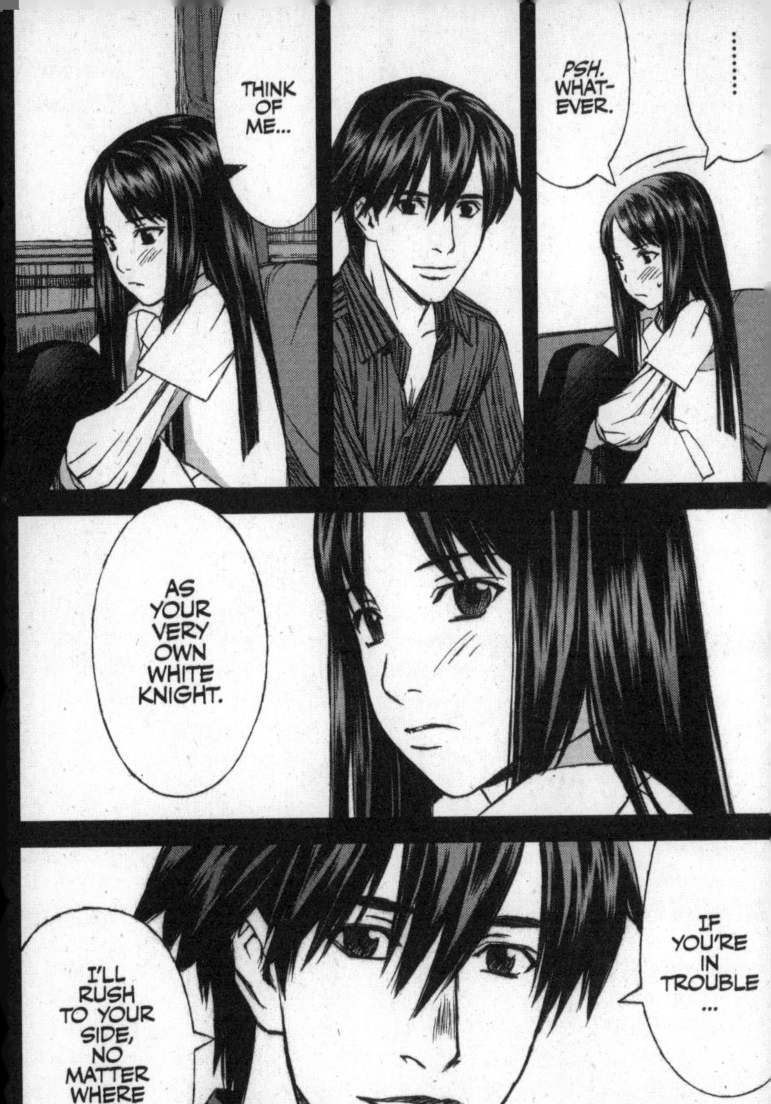
......
PSH. WHAT-EVER.
THINK OF ME...
AS YOUR VERY OWN WHITE KNIGHT.
IF YOU'RE IN TROUBLE...
I'LL RUSH TO YOUR SIDE, NO MATTER WHERE OR WHEN.

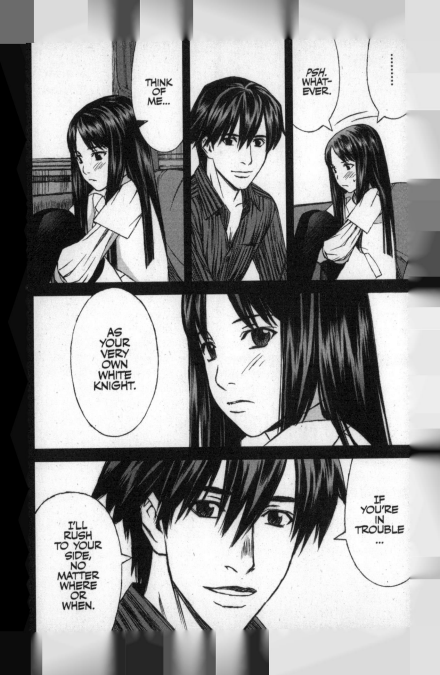

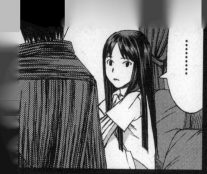

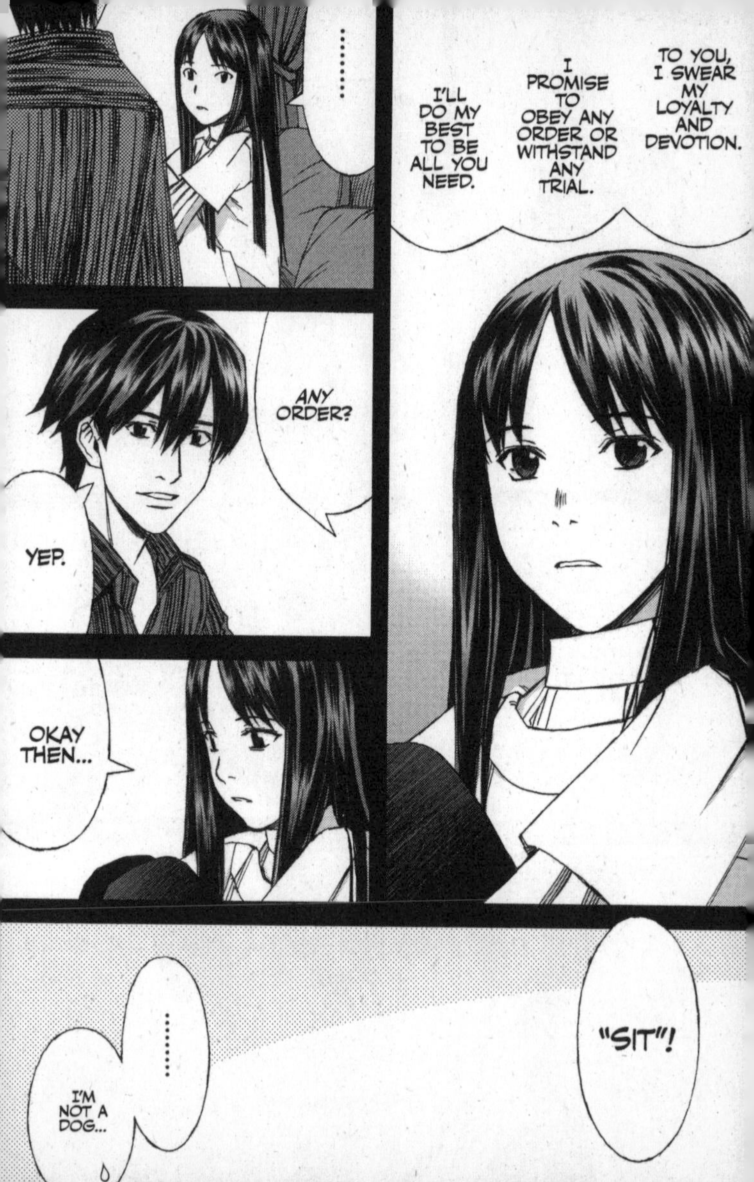
TO YOU, I SWEAR MY LOYALTY AND DEVOTION.
I PROMISE TO OBEY ANY ORDER OR WITHSTAND ANY TRIAL.
I'LL DO MY BEST TO BE ALL YOU NEED.
......
ANY ORDER?
YEP.
OKAY THEN...
"SIT"!
......
I'M NOT A DOG...

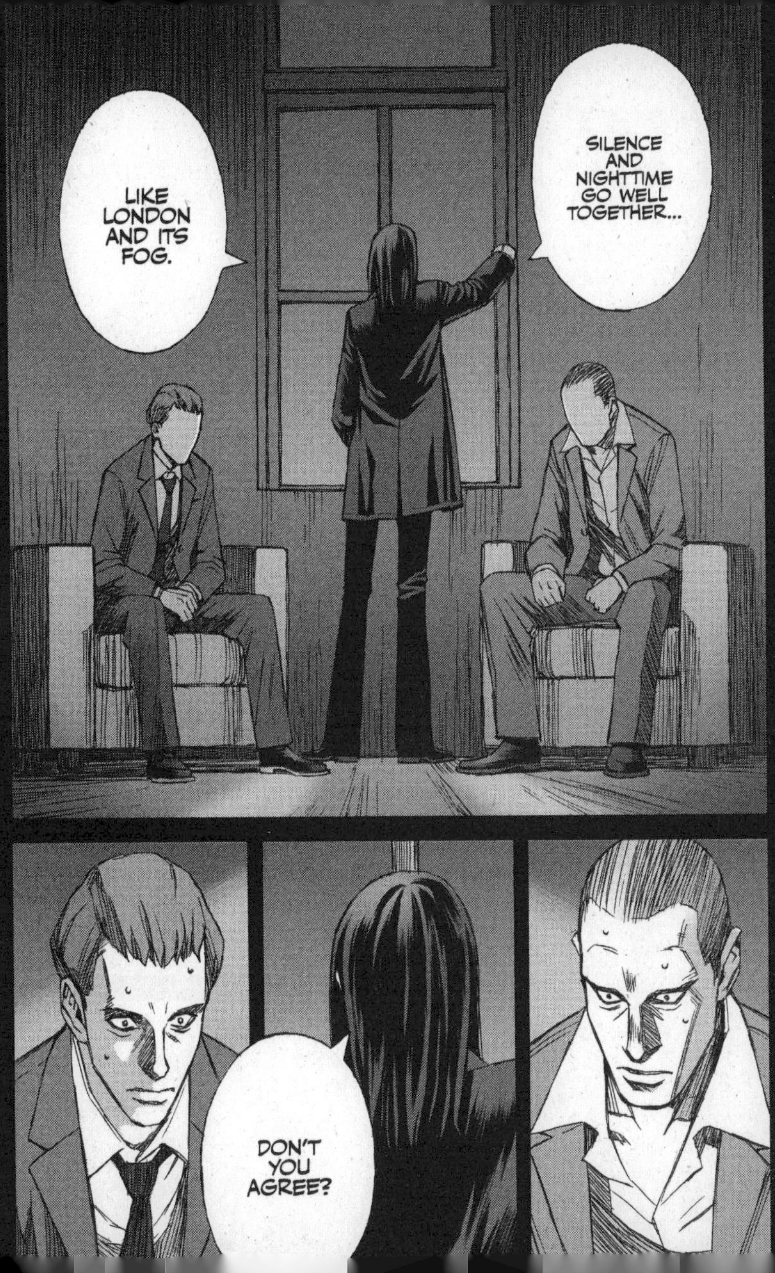
SILENCE AND NIGHTTIME GO WELL TOGETHER...
LIKE LONDON AND ITS FOG.
DON'T YOU AGREE?

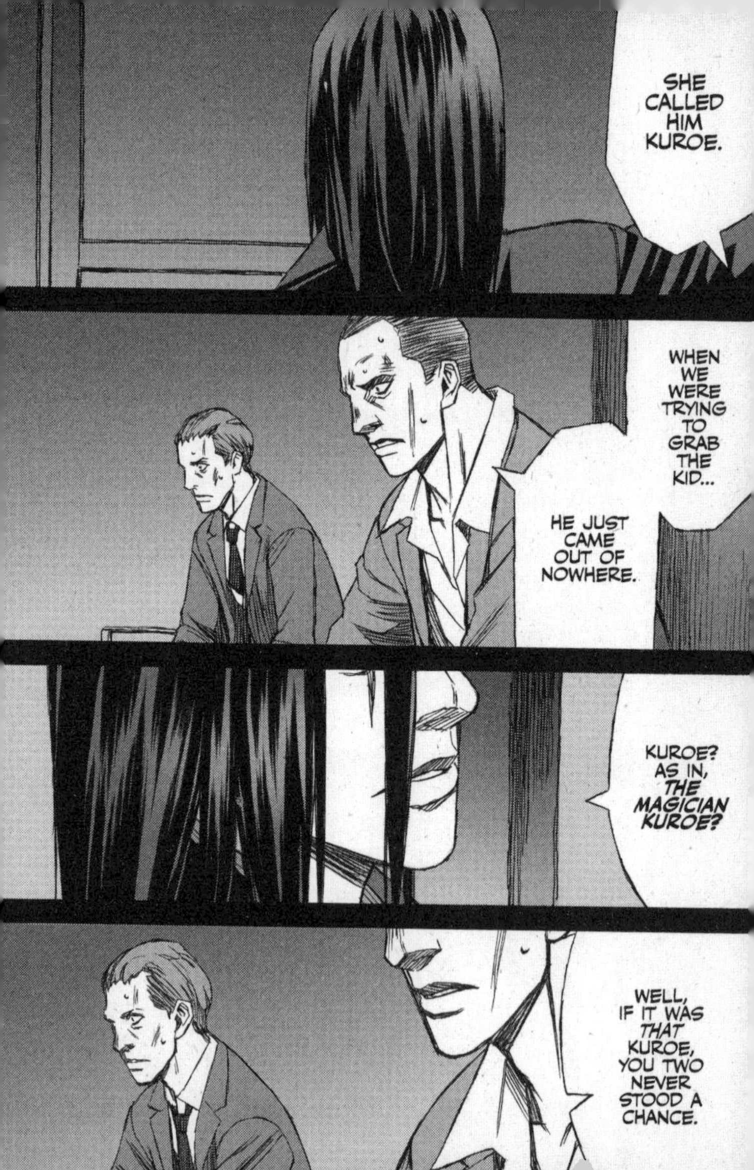
SHE CALLED HIM KUROE.
WHEN WE WERE TRYING TO GRAB THE KID...
HE JUST CAME OUT OF NOWHERE.
KUROE? AS IN, *THE MAGICIAN KUROE?*
WELL, IF IT WAS *THAT* KUROE, YOU TWO NEVER STOOD A CHANCE.

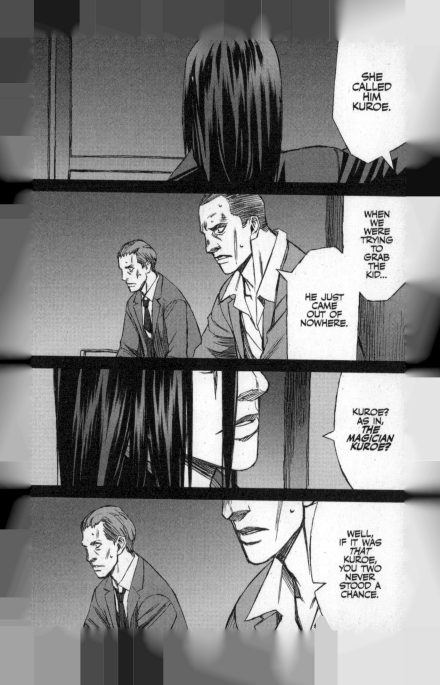

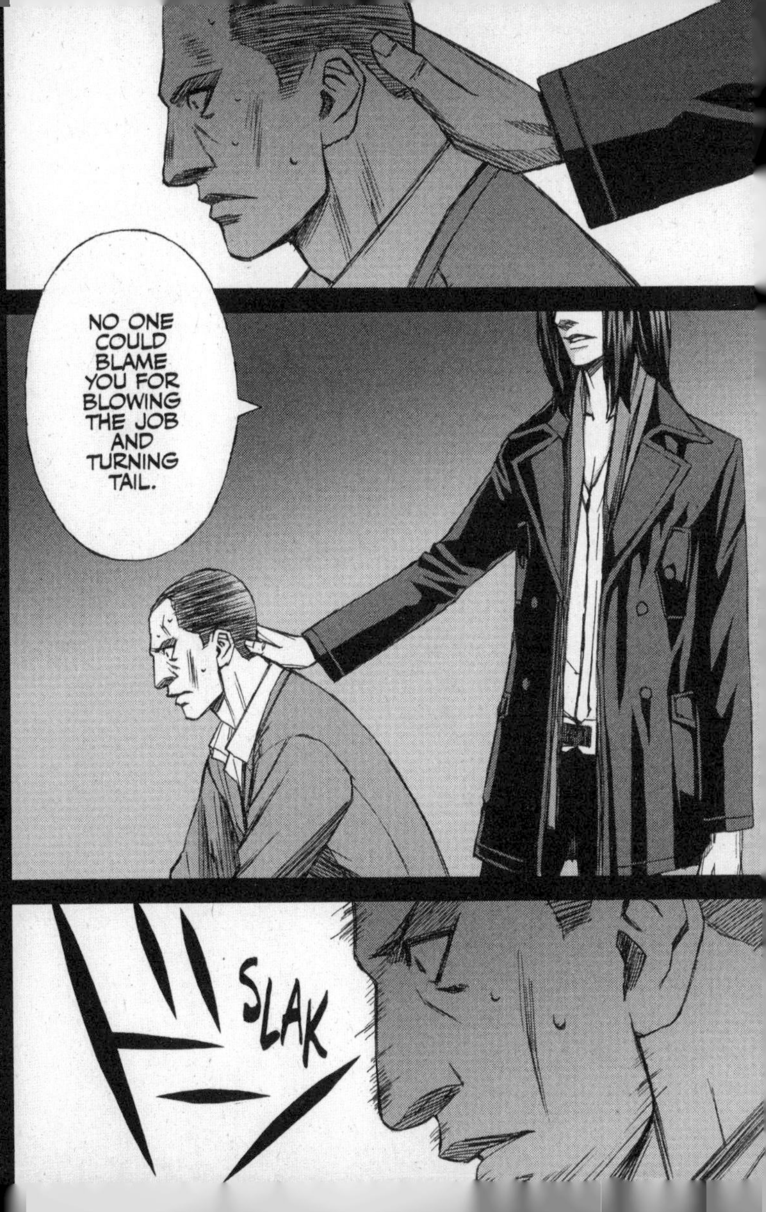
NO ONE COULD BLAME YOU FOR BLOWING THE JOB AND TURNING TAIL.
SLAK

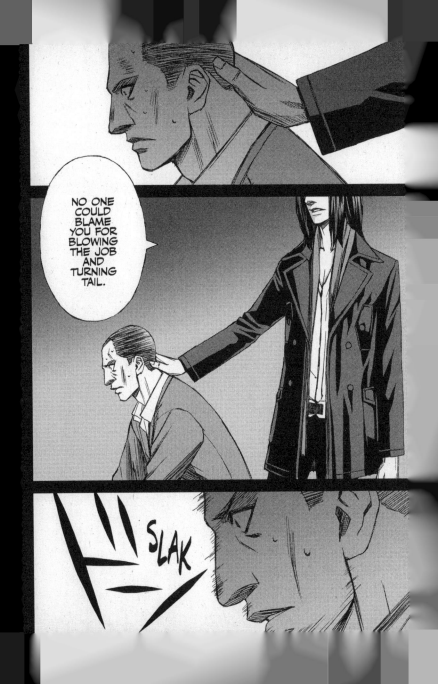

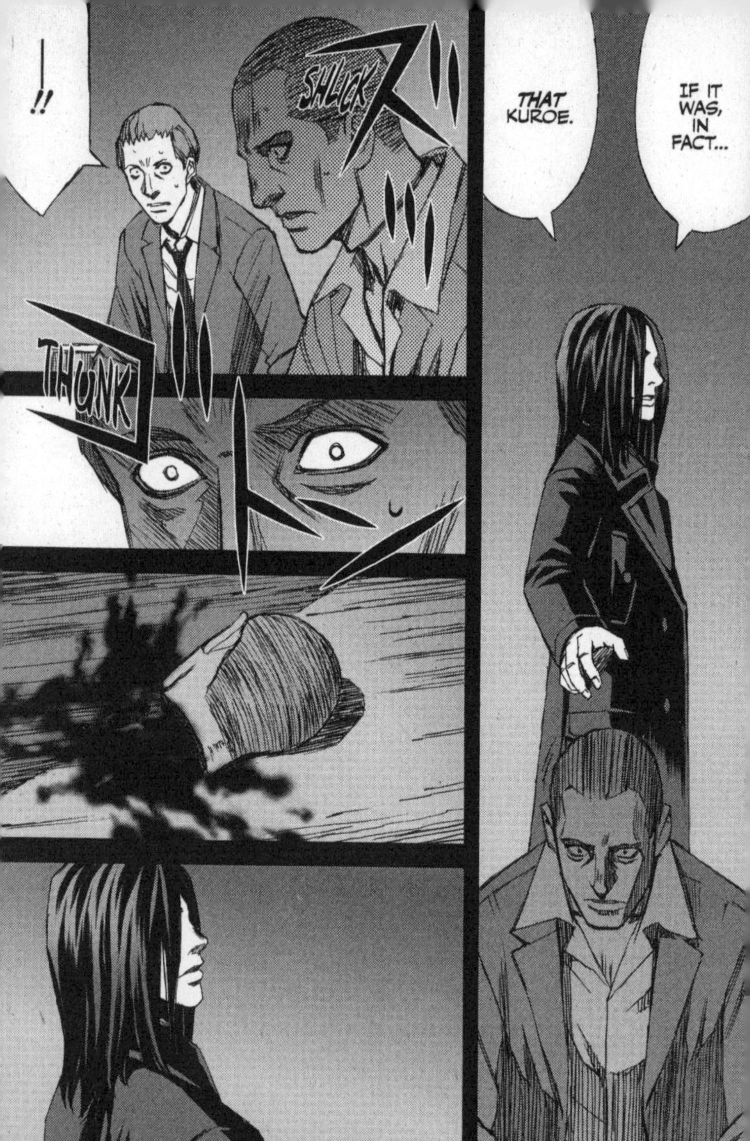
IF IT WAS, IN FACT...
THAT KUROE.
SHLICK
—!!
THUNK

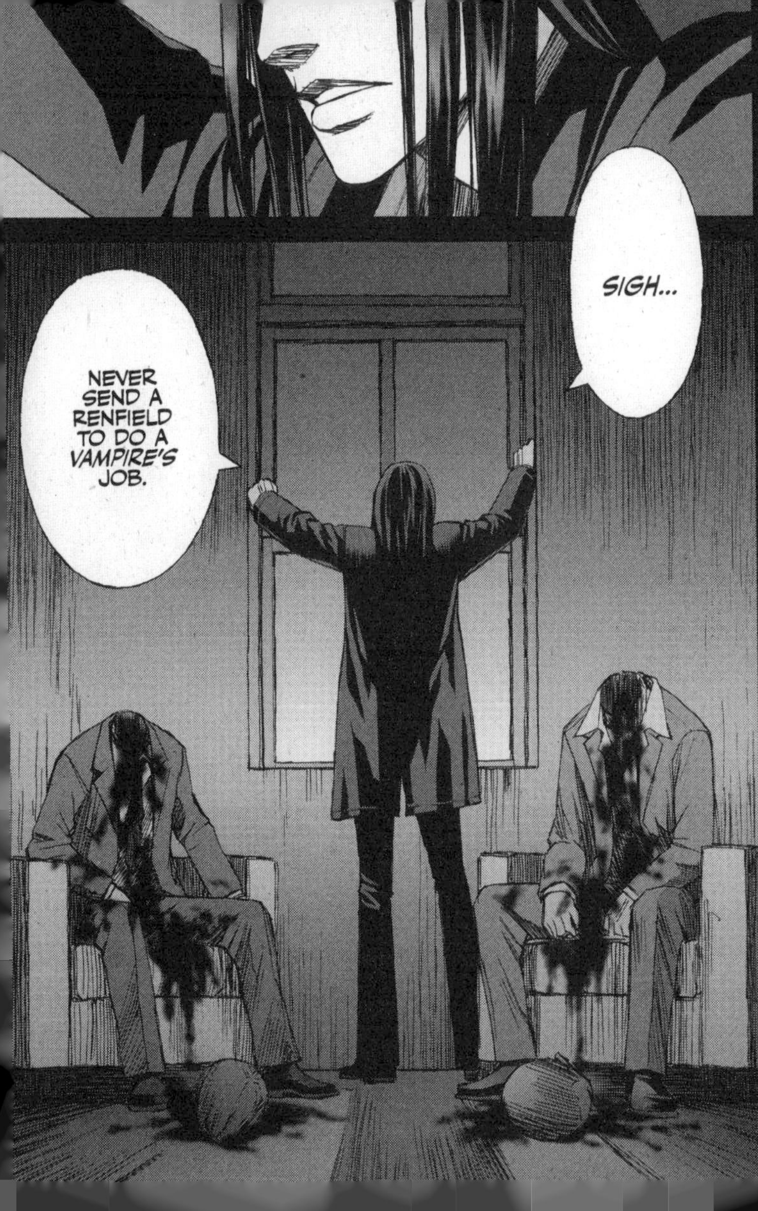
SIGH...
NEVER SEND A RENFIELD TO DO A VAMPIRE'S JOB.

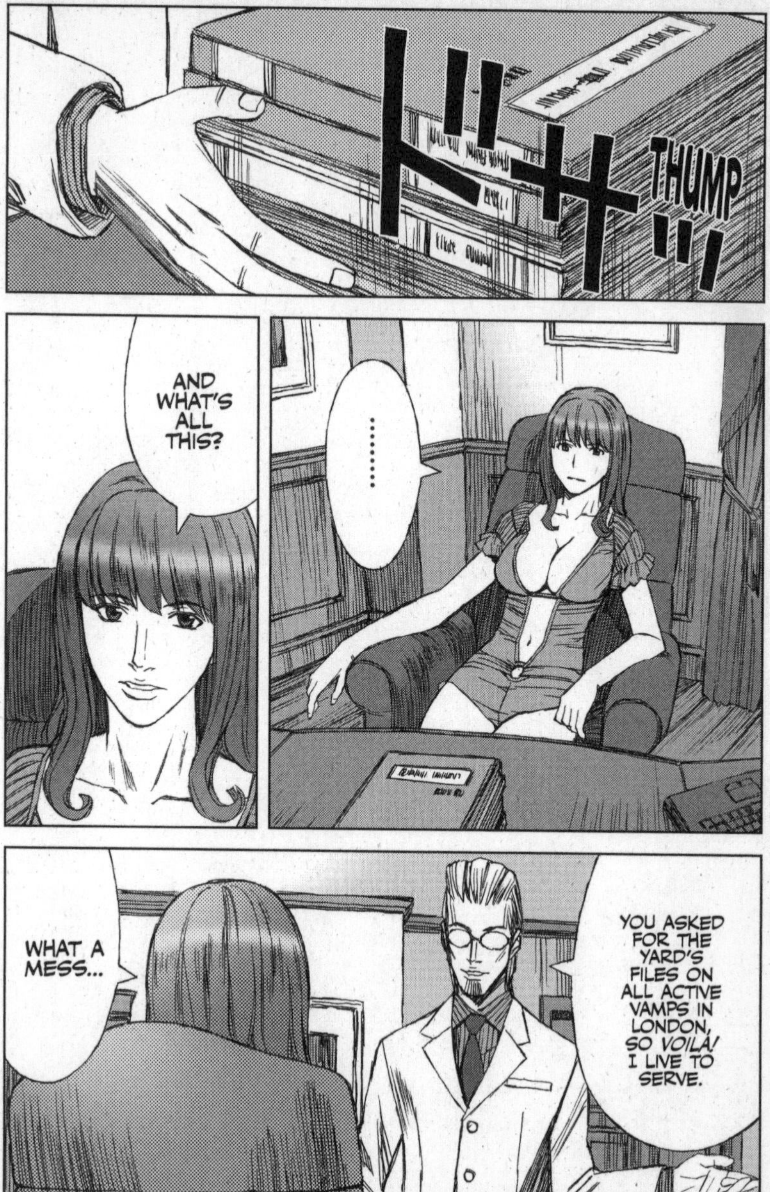
THUMP
......
AND WHAT'S ALL THIS?
YOU ASKED FOR THE YARD'S FILES ON ALL ACTIVE VAMPS IN LONDON, SO *VOILÀ!* I LIVE TO SERVE.
WHAT A MESS...

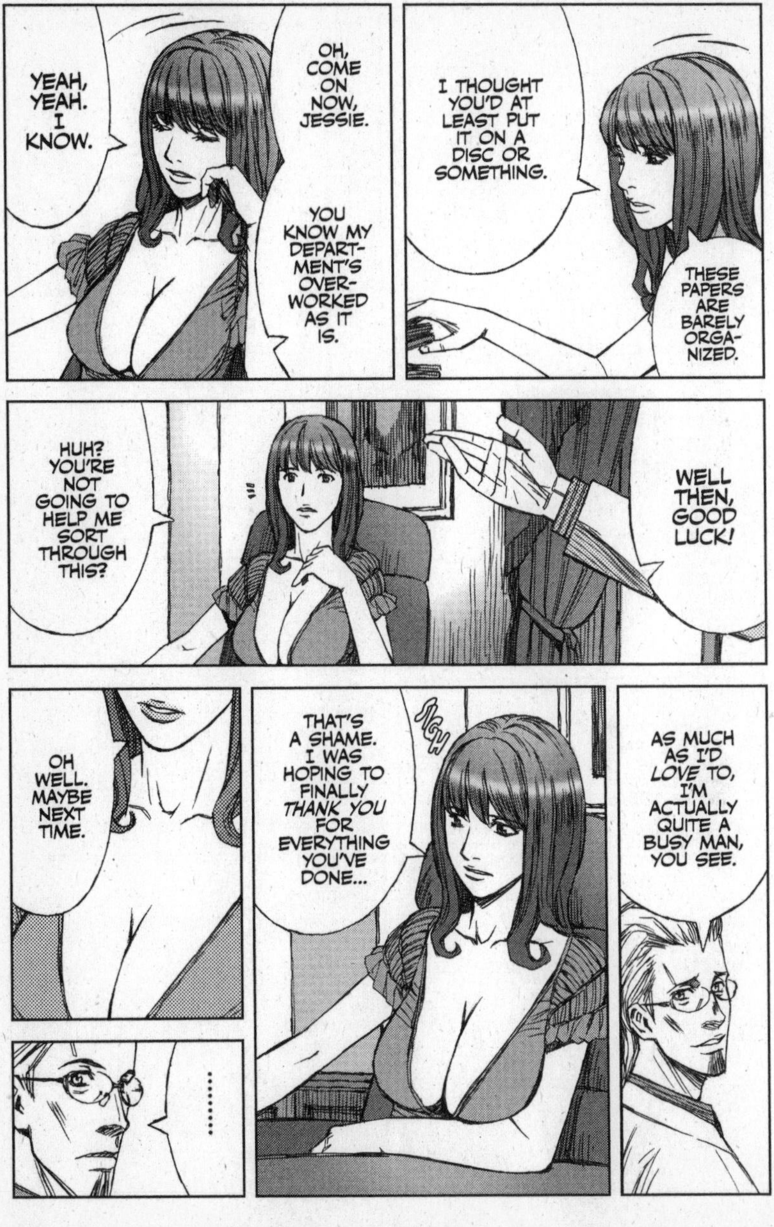
I THOUGHT YOU'D AT LEAST PUT IT ON A DISC OR SOMETHING.
THESE PAPERS ARE BARELY ORGANIZED.
OH, COME ON NOW, JESSIE.
YEAH, YEAH. I KNOW.
YOU KNOW MY DEPART-MENT'S OVER-WORKED AS IT IS.
WELL THEN, GOOD LUCK!
HUH? YOU'RE NOT GOING TO HELP ME SORT THROUGH THIS?
AS MUCH AS I'D *LOVE* TO, I'M ACTUALLY QUITE A BUSY MAN, YOU SEE.
SIGH
THAT'S A SHAME. I WAS HOPING TO FINALLY *THANK YOU* FOR EVERYTHING YOU'VE DONE...
OH WELL. MAYBE NEXT TIME.
......

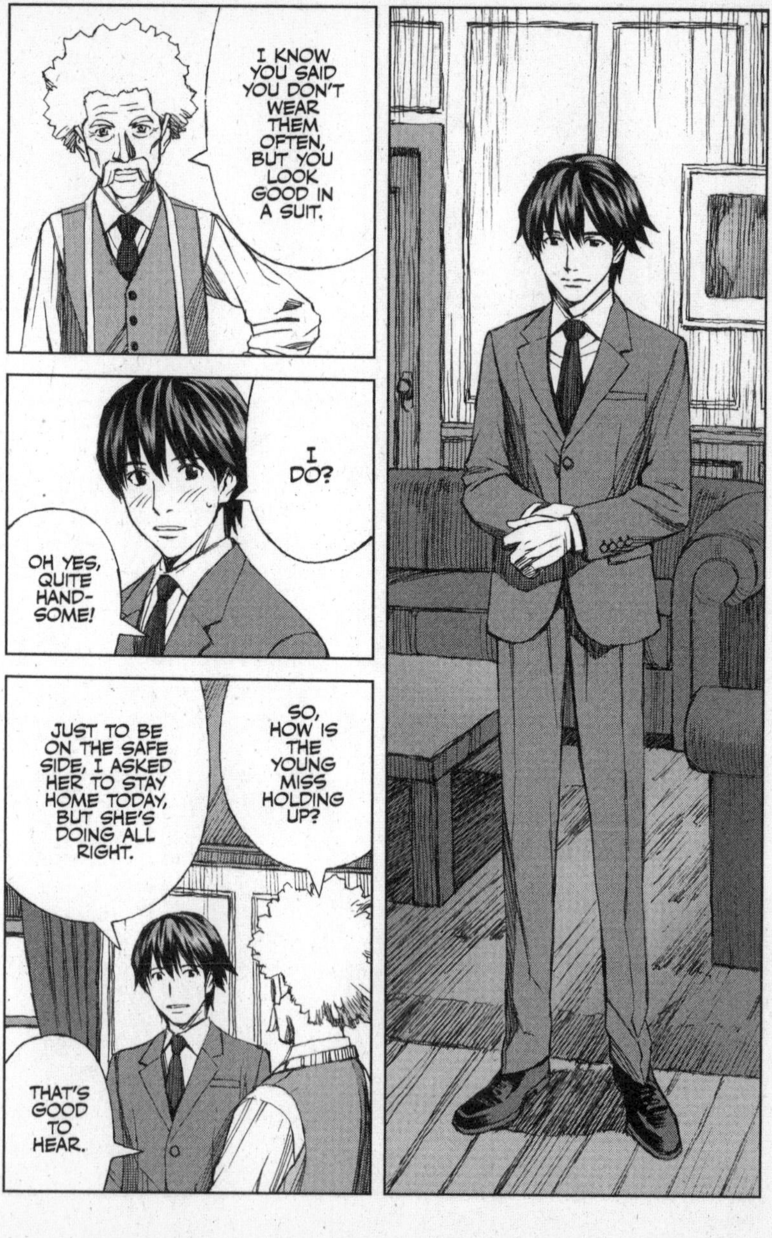
I KNOW YOU SAID YOU DON'T WEAR THEM OFTEN, BUT YOU LOOK GOOD IN A SUIT.
I DO?
OH YES, QUITE HAND-SOME!
SO, HOW IS THE YOUNG MISS HOLDING UP?
JUST TO BE ON THE SAFE SIDE, I ASKED HER TO STAY HOME TODAY, BUT SHE'S DOING ALL RIGHT.
THAT'S GOOD TO HEAR.

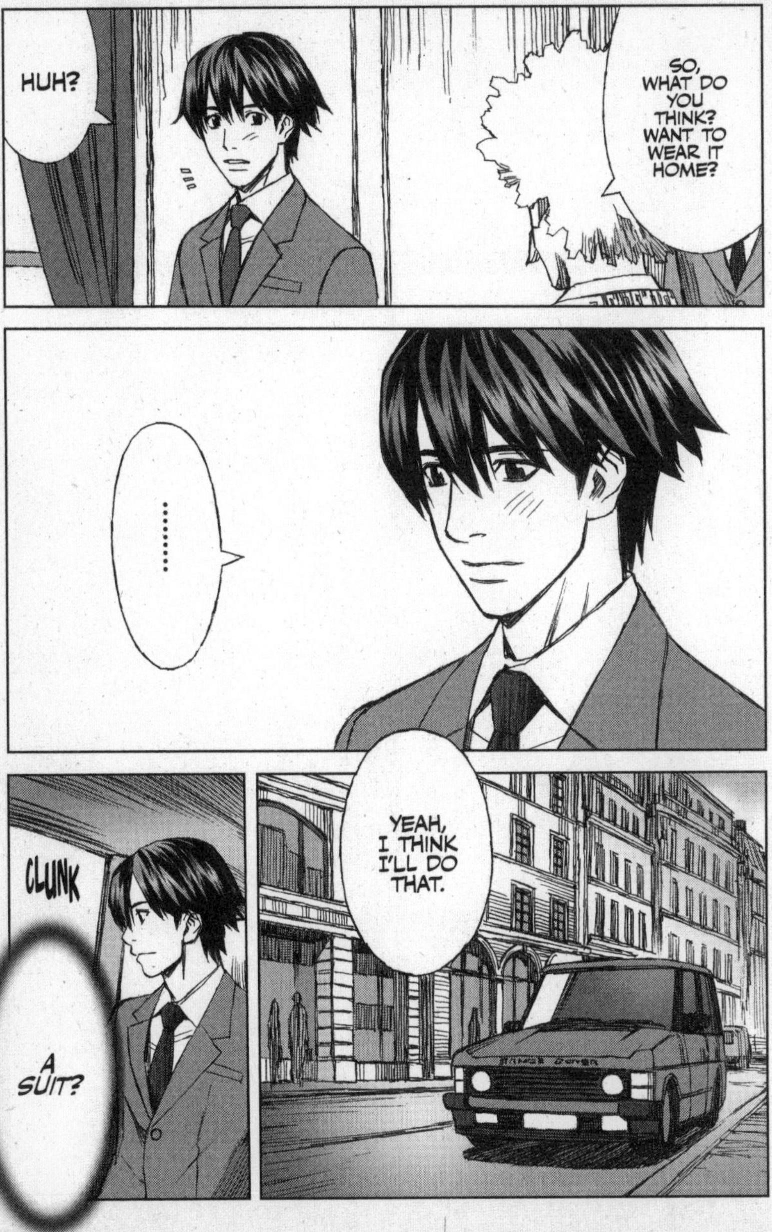
SO, WHAT DO YOU THINK? WANT TO WEAR IT HOME?
HUH?
....
YEAH, I THINK I'LL DO THAT.
CLUNK
A SUIT?

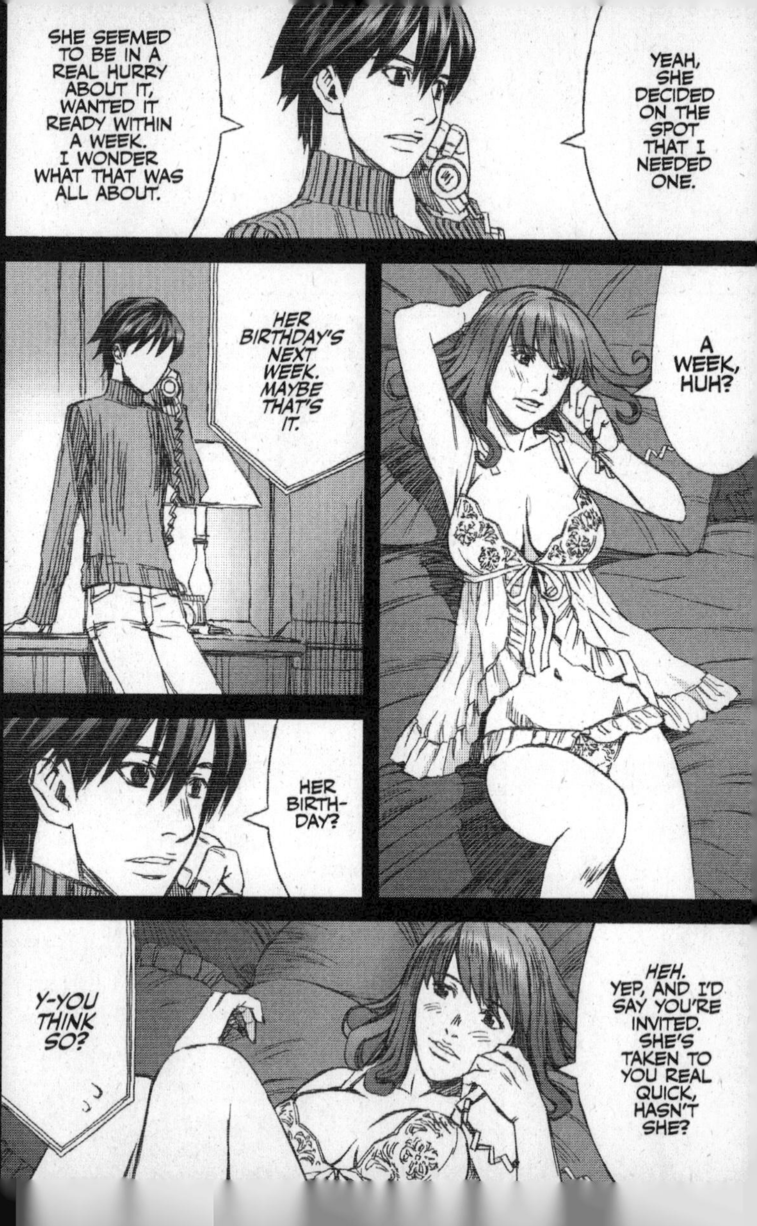
YEAH, SHE DECIDED ON THE SPOT THAT I NEEDED ONE.
SHE SEEMED TO BE IN A REAL HURRY ABOUT IT, WANTED IT READY WITHIN A WEEK. I WONDER WHAT THAT WAS ALL ABOUT.
A WEEK, HUH?
HER BIRTHDAY'S NEXT WEEK. MAYBE THAT'S IT.
HER BIRTH-DAY?
HEH. YEP, AND I'D SAY YOU'RE INVITED. SHE'S TAKEN TO YOU REAL QUICK, HASN'T SHE?
Y-YOU THINK SO?

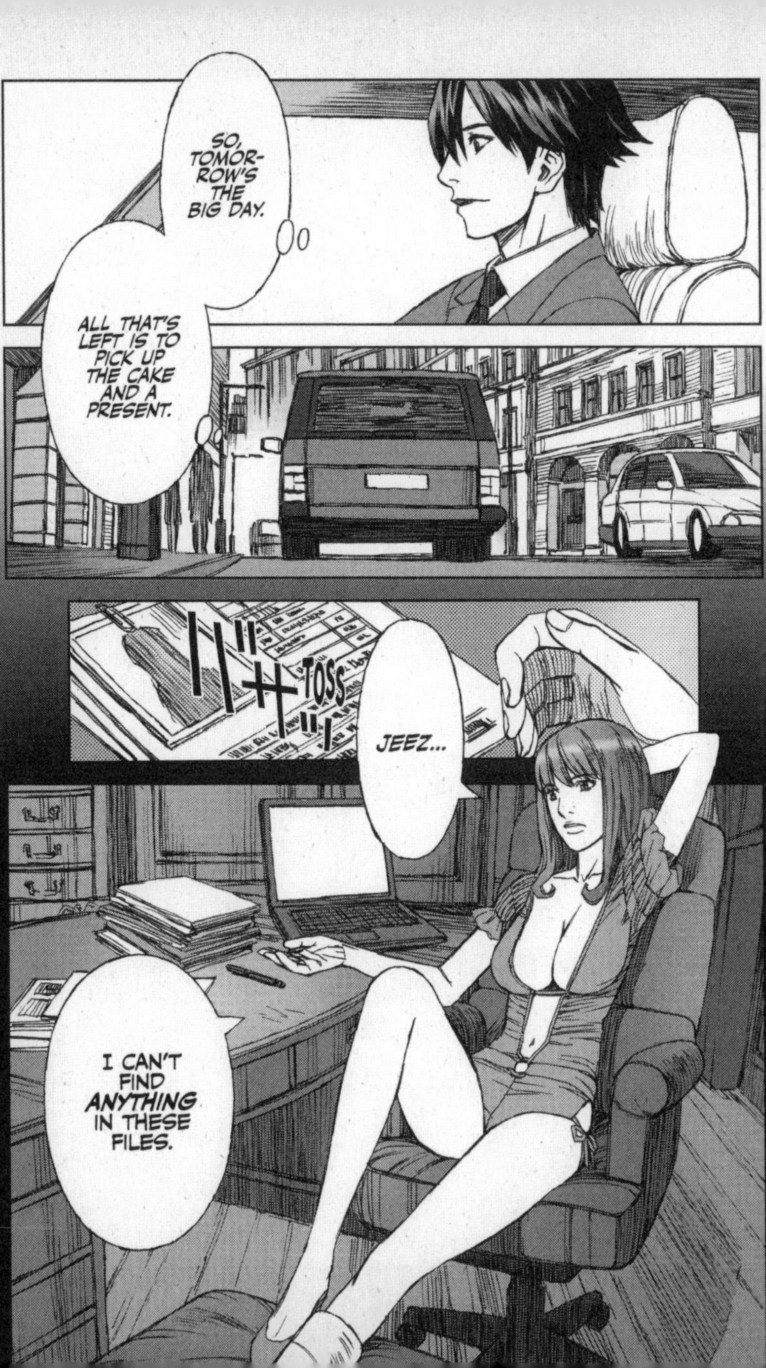
SO, TOMORROW'S THE BIG DAY.
ALL THAT'S LEFT IS TO PICK UP THE CAKE AND A PRESENT.
TOSS
JEEZ...
I CAN'T FIND ANYTHING IN THESE FILES.

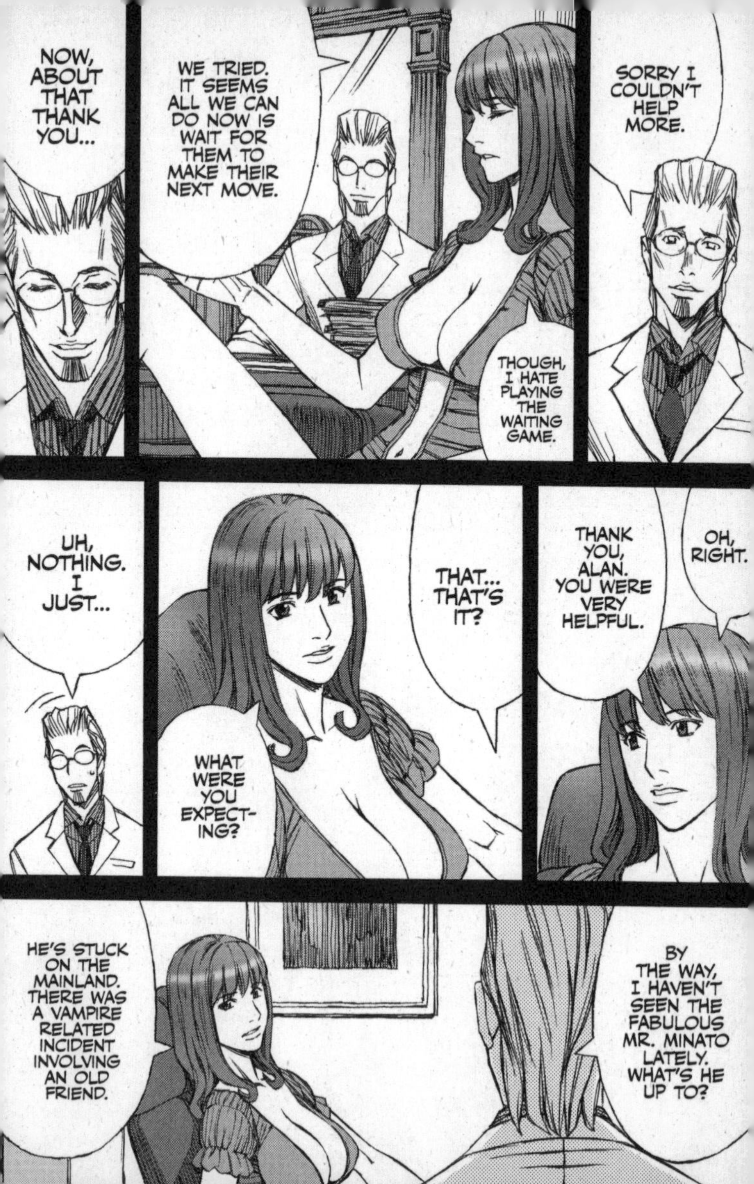
SORRY I COULDN'T HELP MORE.
WE TRIED. IT SEEMS ALL WE CAN DO NOW IS WAIT FOR THEM TO MAKE THEIR NEXT MOVE.
THOUGH, I HATE PLAYING THE WAITING GAME.
NOW, ABOUT THAT THANK YOU...
OH, RIGHT.
THANK YOU, ALAN. YOU WERE VERY HELPFUL.
THAT... THAT'S IT?
WHAT WERE YOU EXPECT-ING?
UH, NOTHING. I JUST...
BY THE WAY, I HAVEN'T SEEN THE FABULOUS MR. MINATO LATELY. WHAT'S HE UP TO?
HE'S STUCK ON THE MAINLAND. THERE WAS A VAMPIRE RELATED INCIDENT INVOLVING AN OLD FRIEND.

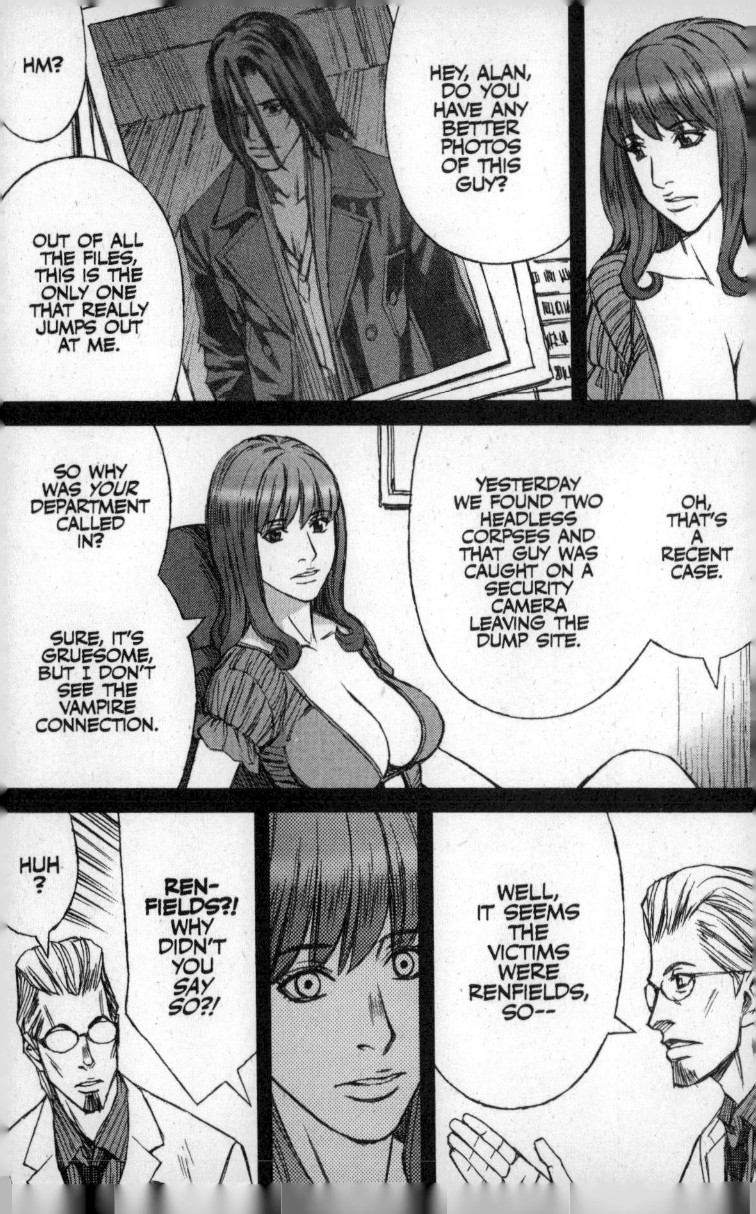
HEY, ALAN, DO YOU HAVE ANY BETTER PHOTOS OF THIS GUY?
HM?
OUT OF ALL THE FILES, THIS IS THE ONLY ONE THAT REALLY JUMPS OUT AT ME.
OH, THAT'S A RECENT CASE.
YESTERDAY WE FOUND TWO HEADLESS CORPSES AND THAT GUY WAS CAUGHT ON A SECURITY CAMERA LEAVING THE DUMP SITE.
SO WHY WAS *YOUR* DEPARTMENT CALLED IN?
SURE, IT'S GRUESOME, BUT I DON'T SEE THE VAMPIRE CONNECTION.
WELL, IT SEEMS THE VICTIMS WERE RENFIELDS, SO--
REN-FIELDS?! WHY DIDN'T YOU SAY SO?!
HUH?

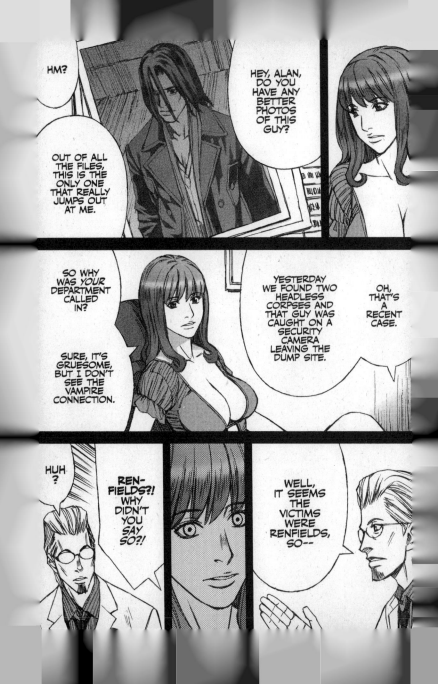

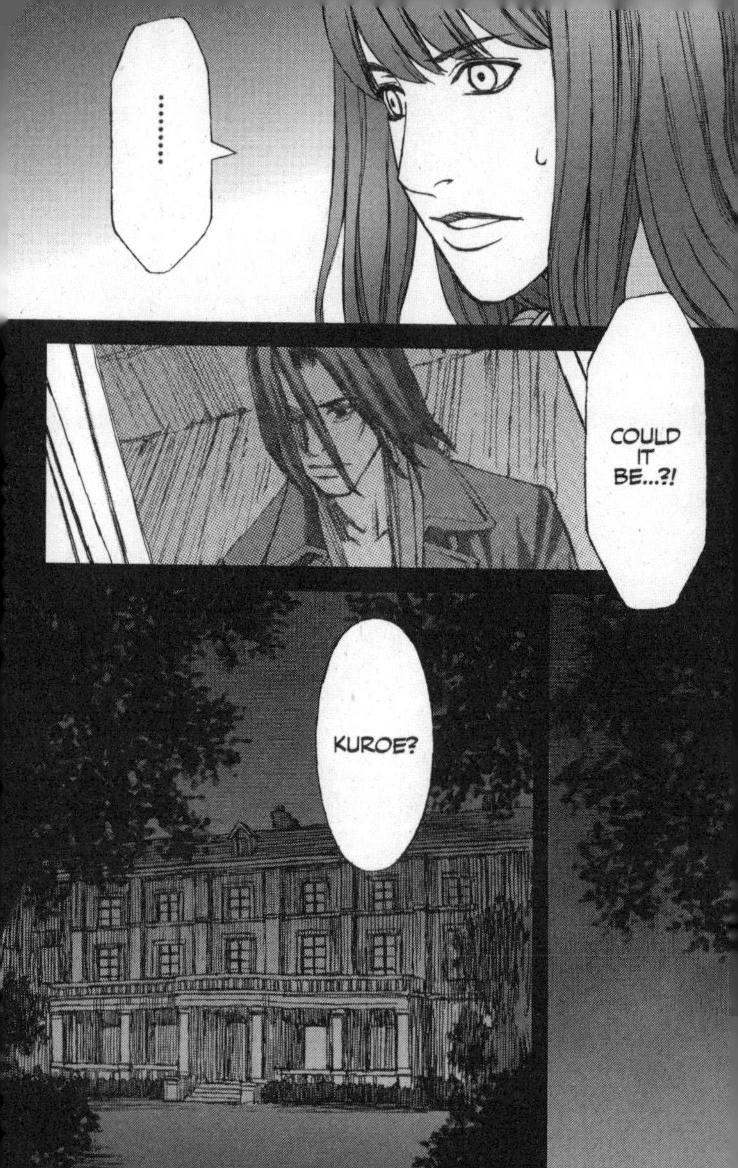
....
COULD IT BE...?!
KUROE?

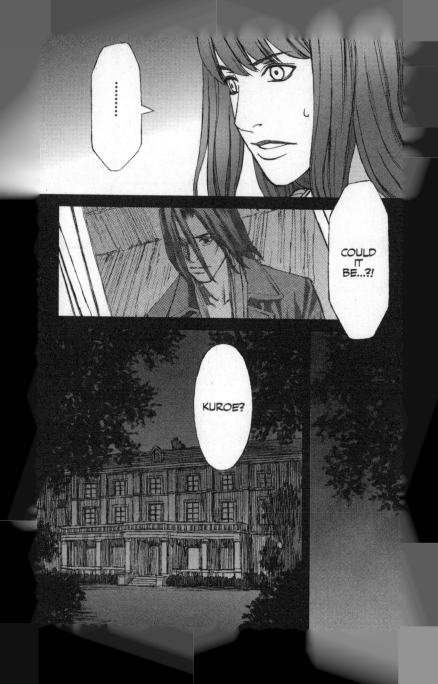

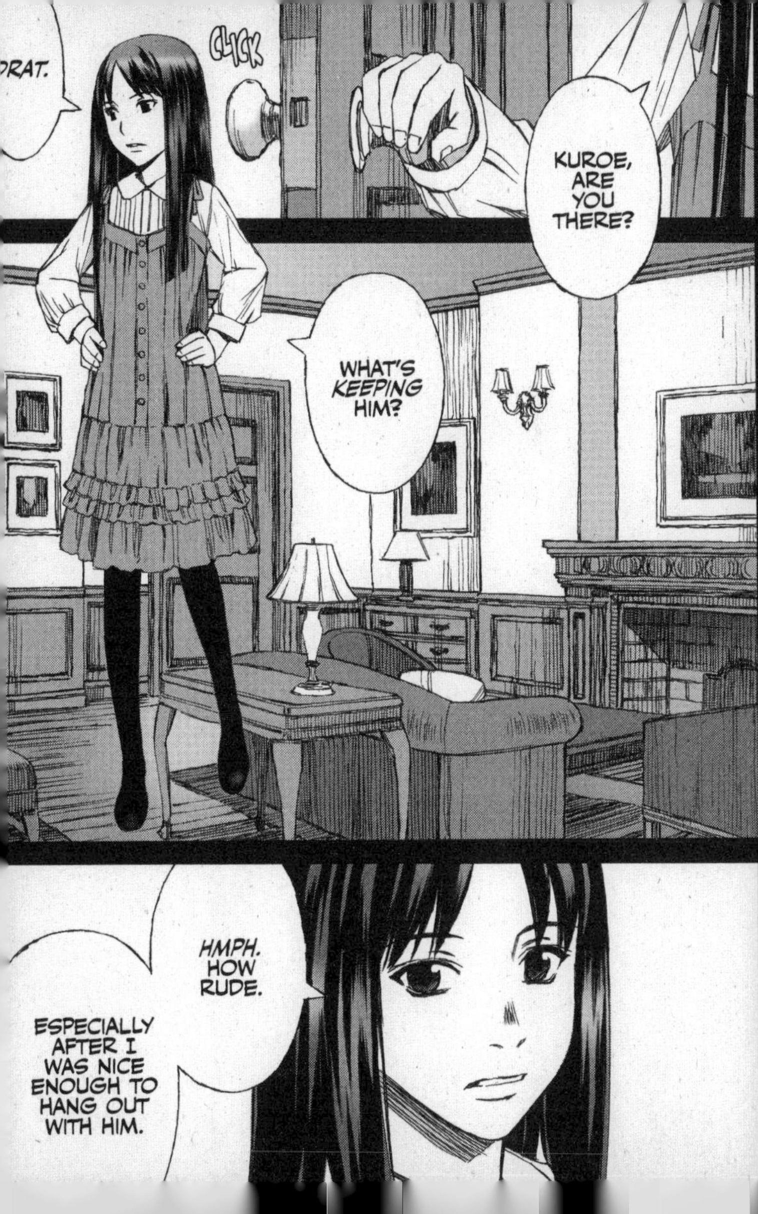
KUROE, ARE YOU THERE?
CLICK
RAT.
WHAT'S KEEPING HIM?
HMPH. HOW RUDE.
ESPECIALLY AFTER I WAS NICE ENOUGH TO HANG OUT WITH HIM.

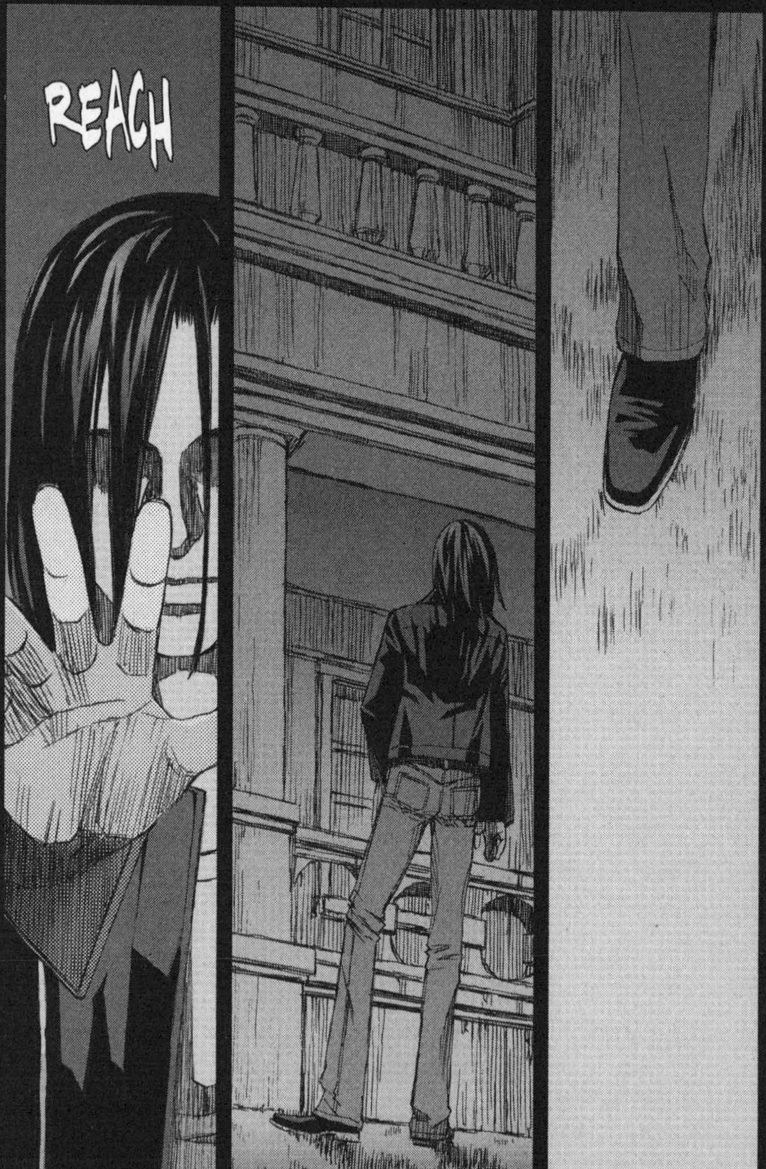
REACH

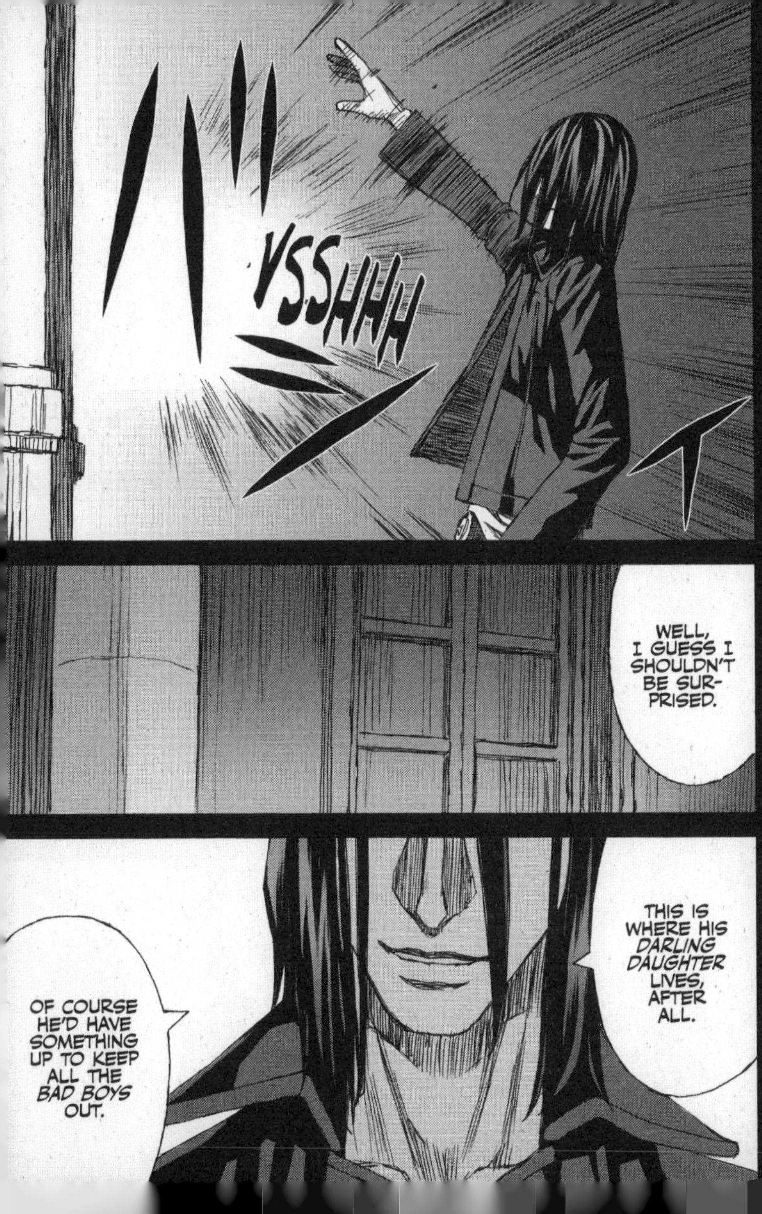
VSSHHH
WELL, I GUESS I SHOULDN'T BE SUR-PRISED.
THIS IS WHERE HIS DARLING DAUGHTER LIVES, AFTER ALL.
OF COURSE HE'D HAVE SOMETHING UP TO KEEP ALL THE BAD BOYS OUT.

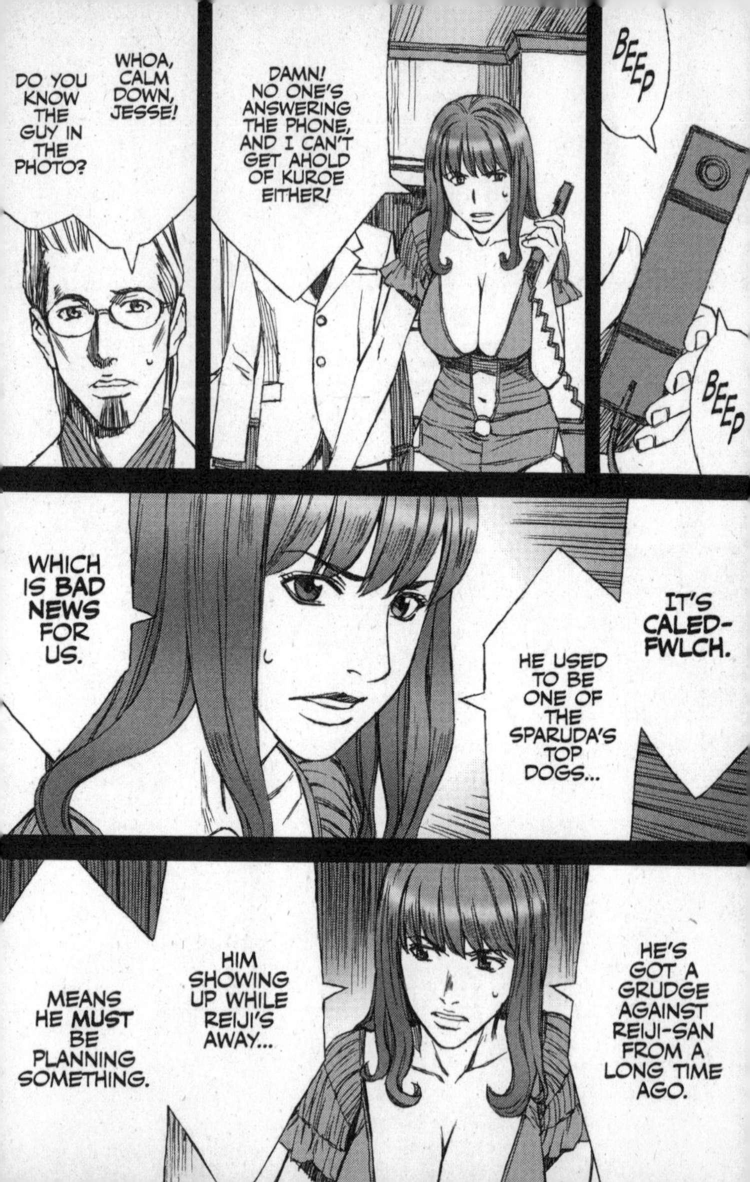
BEEP
BEEP
DAMN! NO ONE'S ANSWERING THE PHONE, AND I CAN'T GET AHOLD OF KUROE EITHER!
WHOA, CALM DOWN, JESSE!
DO YOU KNOW THE GUY IN THE PHOTO?
IT'S CALED-FWLCH.
HE USED TO BE ONE OF THE SPARUDA'S TOP DOGS...
WHICH IS **BAD NEWS** FOR US.
HE'S GOT A GRUDGE AGAINST REIJI-SAN FROM A LONG TIME AGO.
HIM SHOWING UP WHILE REIJI'S AWAY...
MEANS HE **MUST** BE PLANNING SOMETHING.

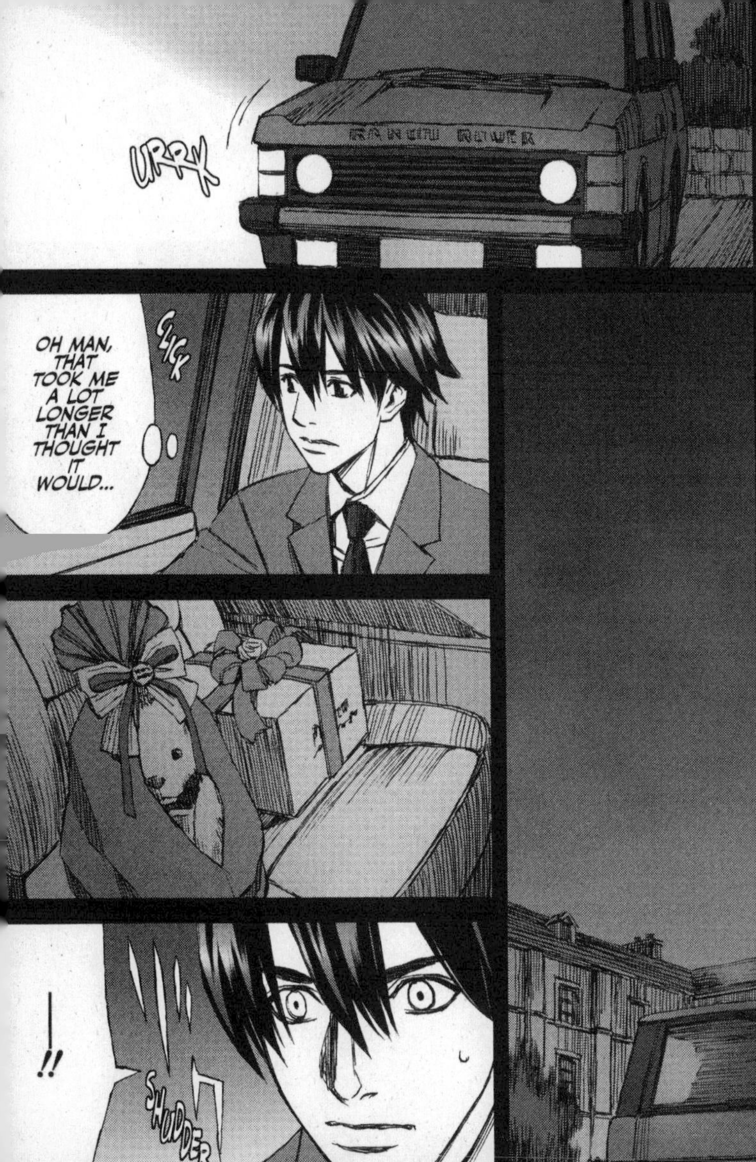
URRK
CLICK
OH MAN, THAT TOOK ME A LOT LONGER THAN I THOUGHT IT WOULD...
—!!
SHUDDER

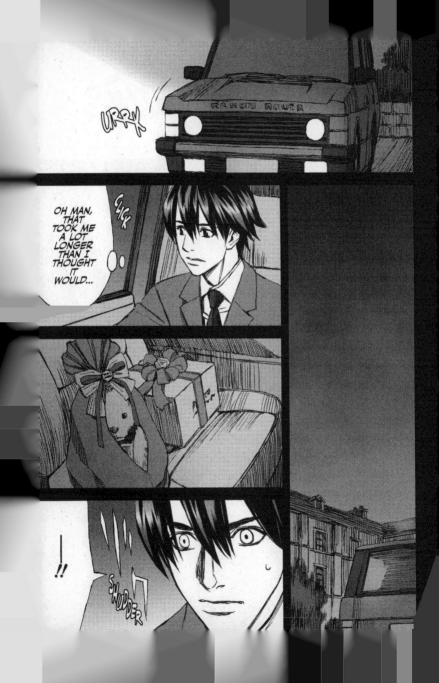

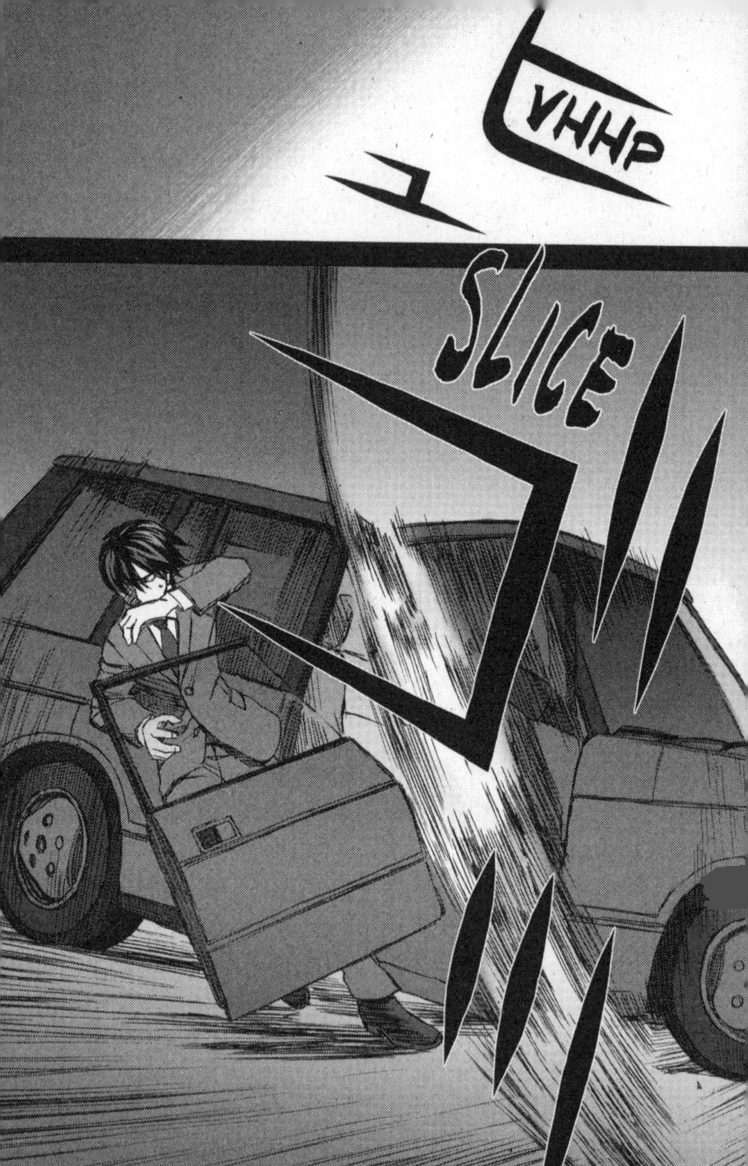
VHHP
SLICE

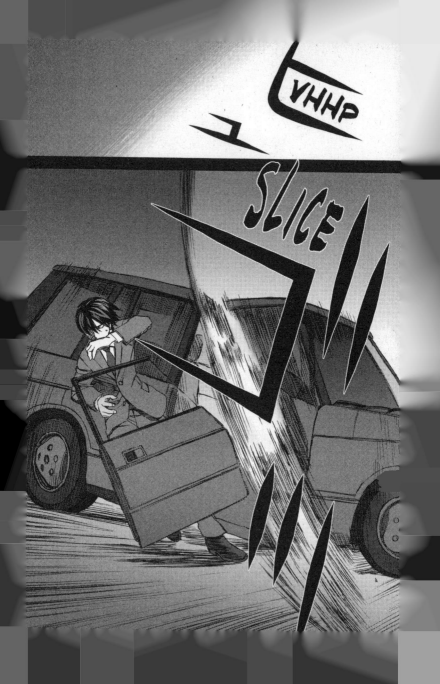

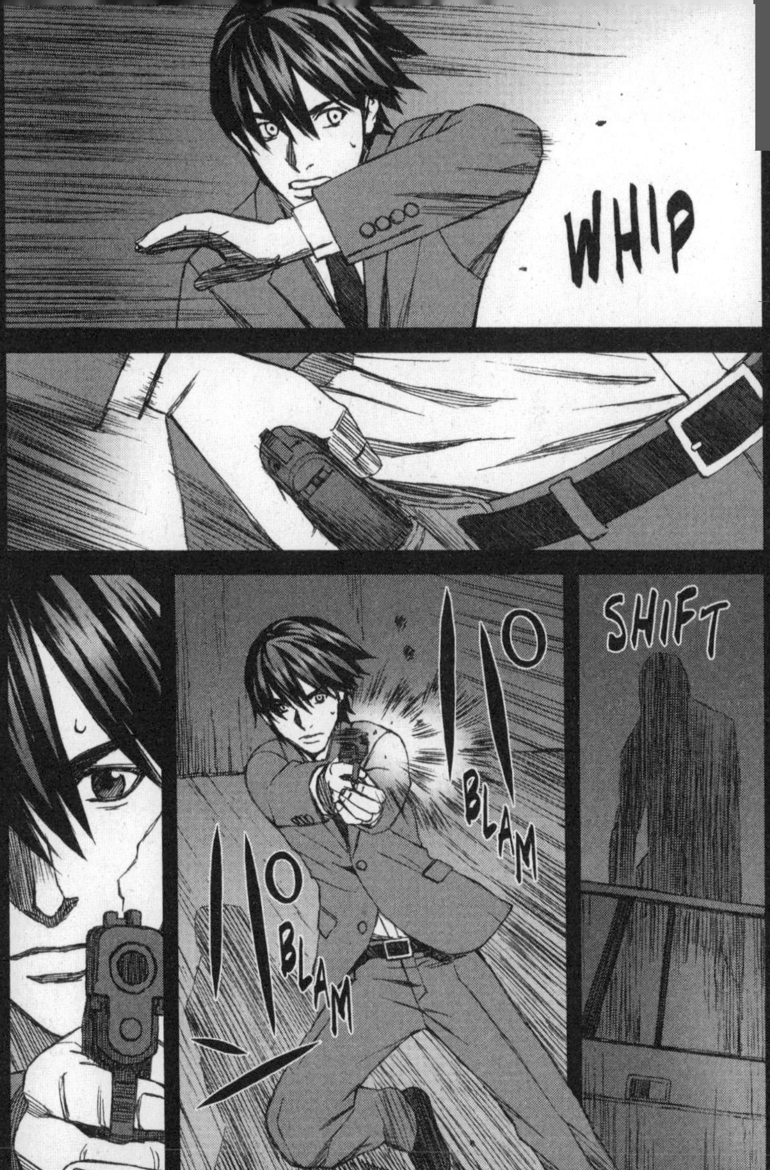
WHIP
SHIFT
BLAM
BLAM

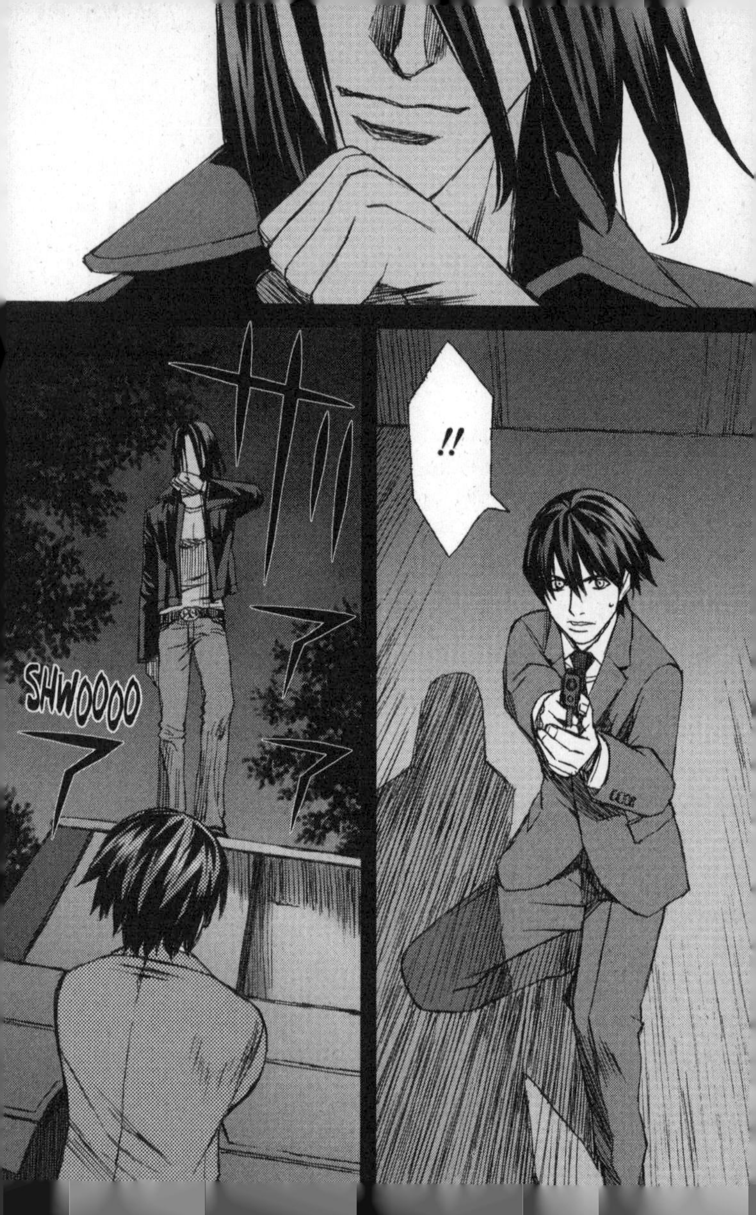
!!
SHWOOOO

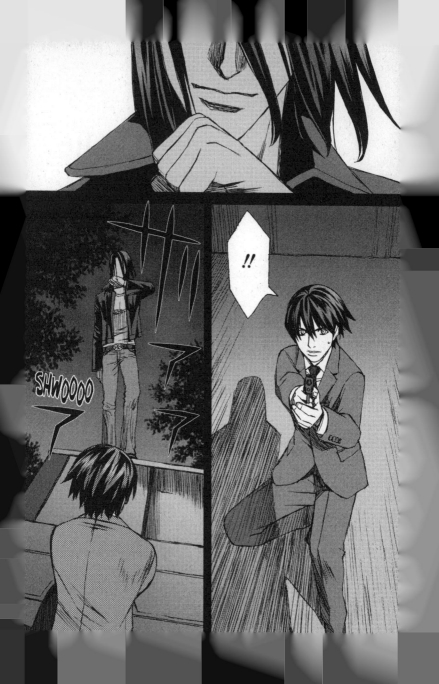

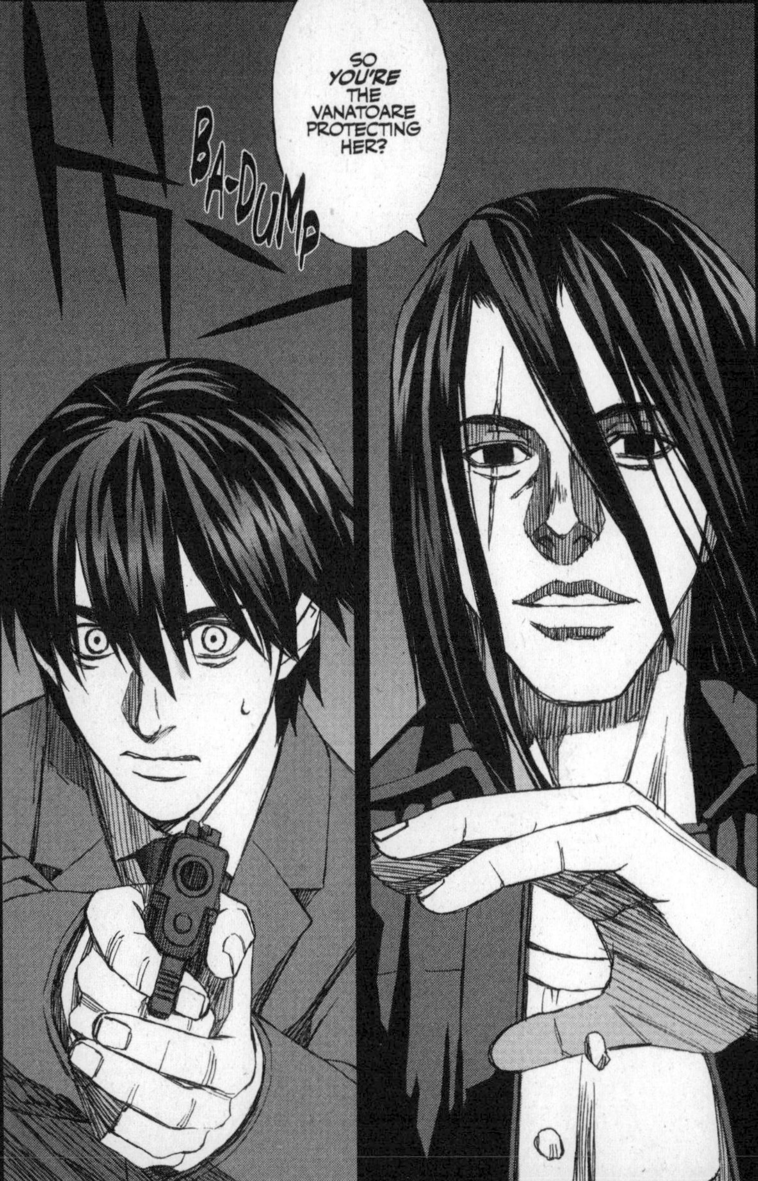
SO *YOU'RE* THE VANATOARE PROTECTING HER?
BA-DUMP

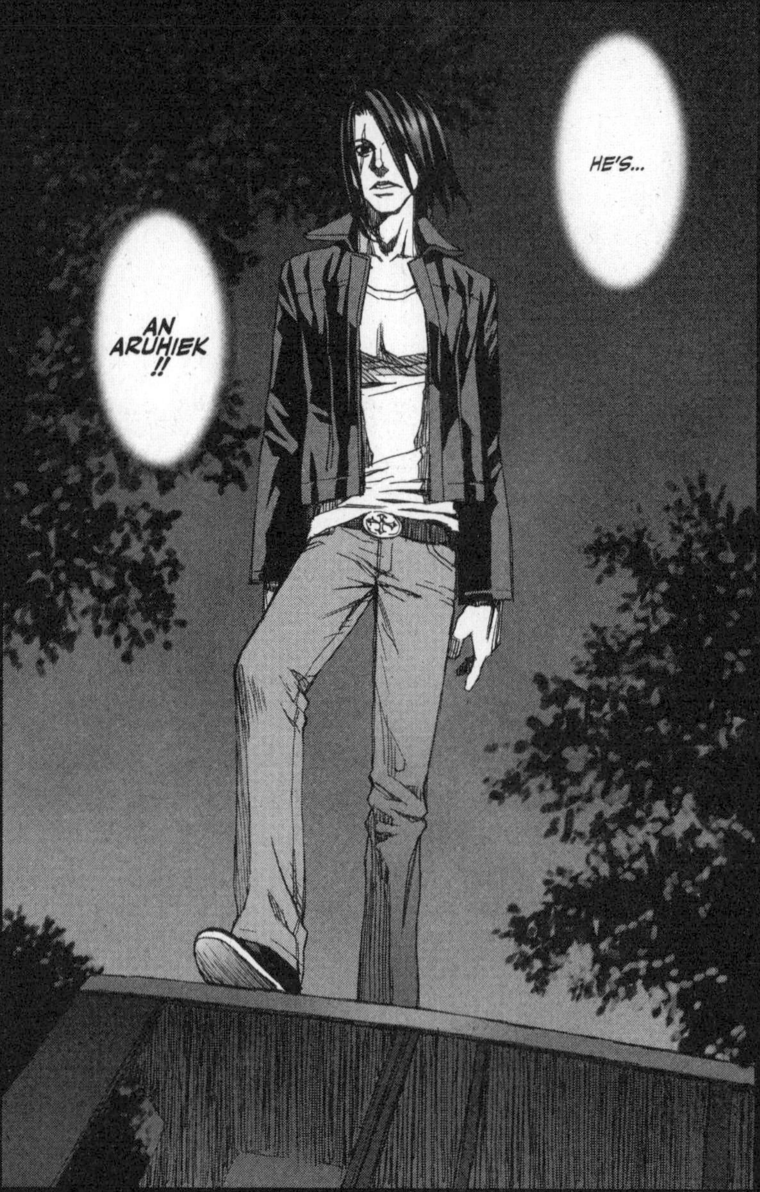
HE'S...
AN ARUHIEK !!

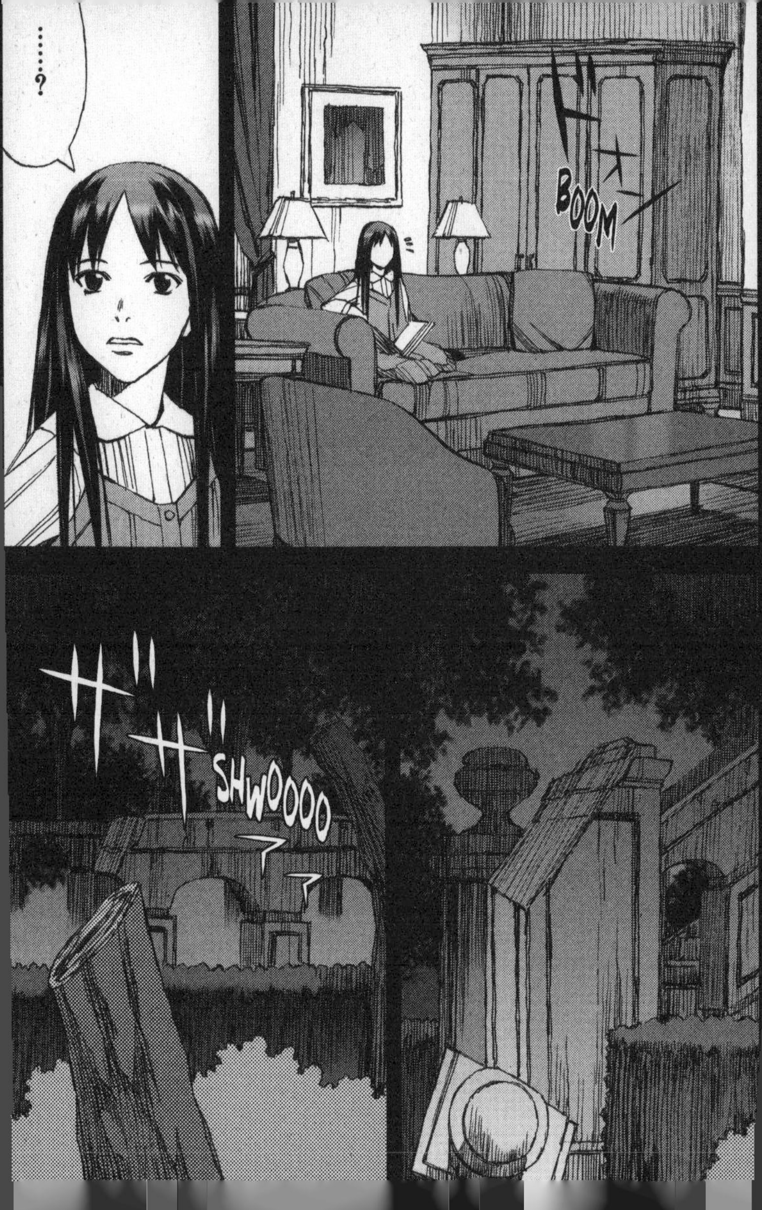
BOOM
......?
SHWOOOO

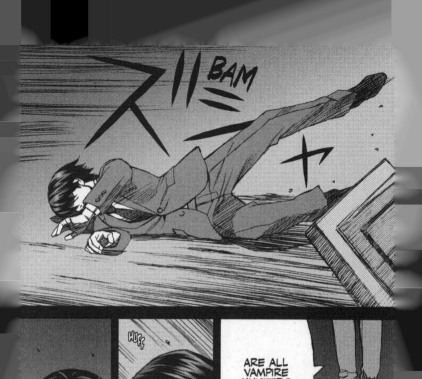

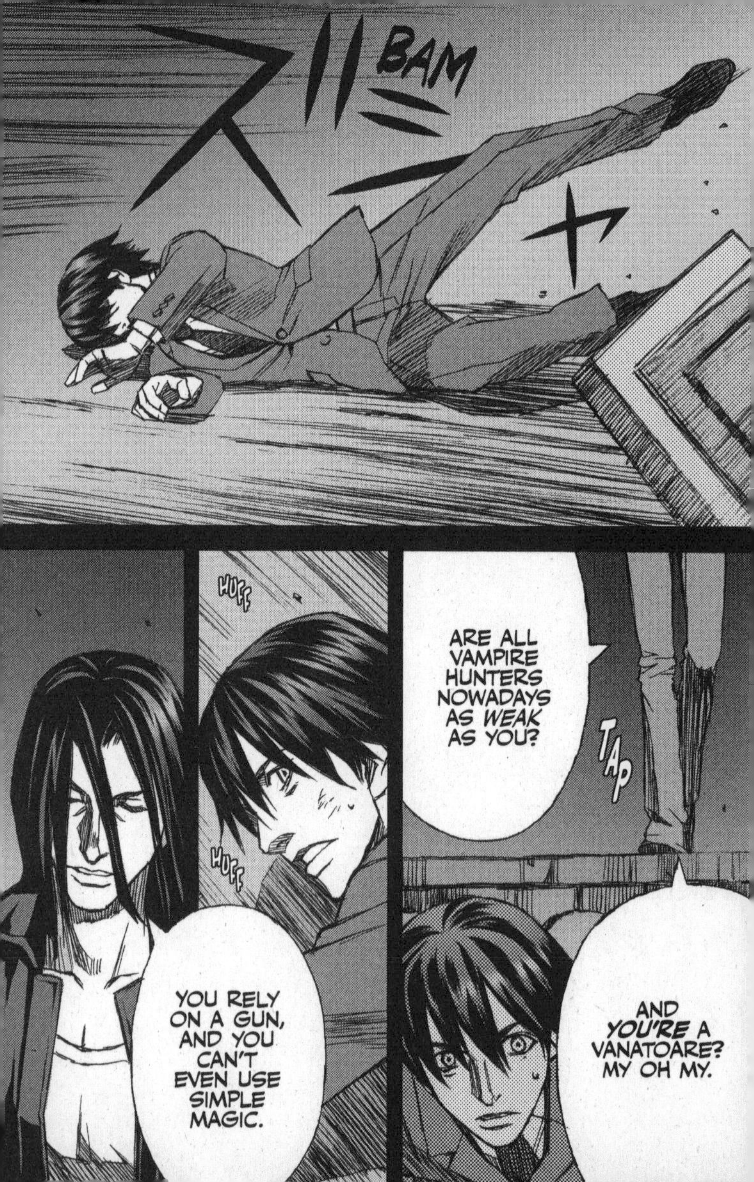
BAM
ARE ALL VAMPIRE HUNTERS NOWADAYS AS *WEAK* AS YOU?
TAP
AND *YOU'RE* A VANATOARE? MY OH MY.
HUFF
HUFF
YOU RELY ON A GUN, AND YOU CAN'T EVEN USE SIMPLE MAGIC.

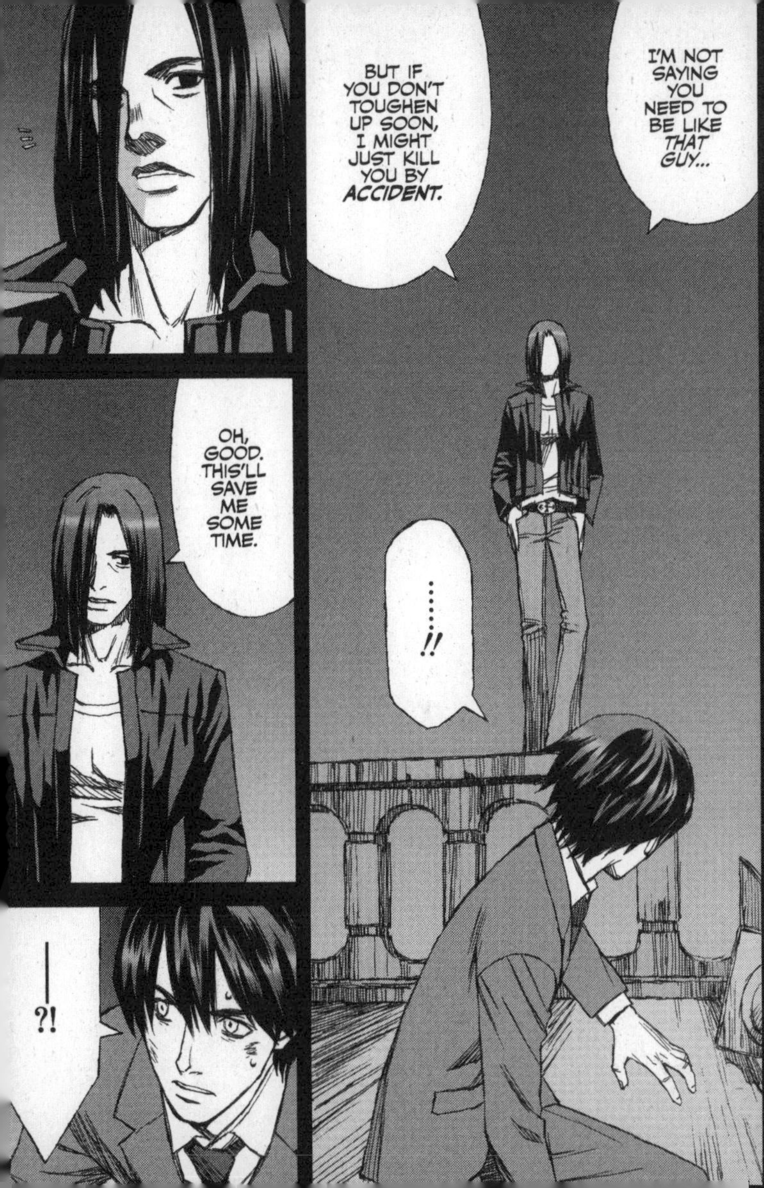
I'M NOT SAYING YOU NEED TO BE LIKE *THAT GUY*...
BUT IF YOU DON'T TOUGHEN UP SOON, I MIGHT JUST KILL YOU BY *ACCIDENT.*
......!!
OH, GOOD. THIS'LL SAVE ME SOME TIME.
—?!

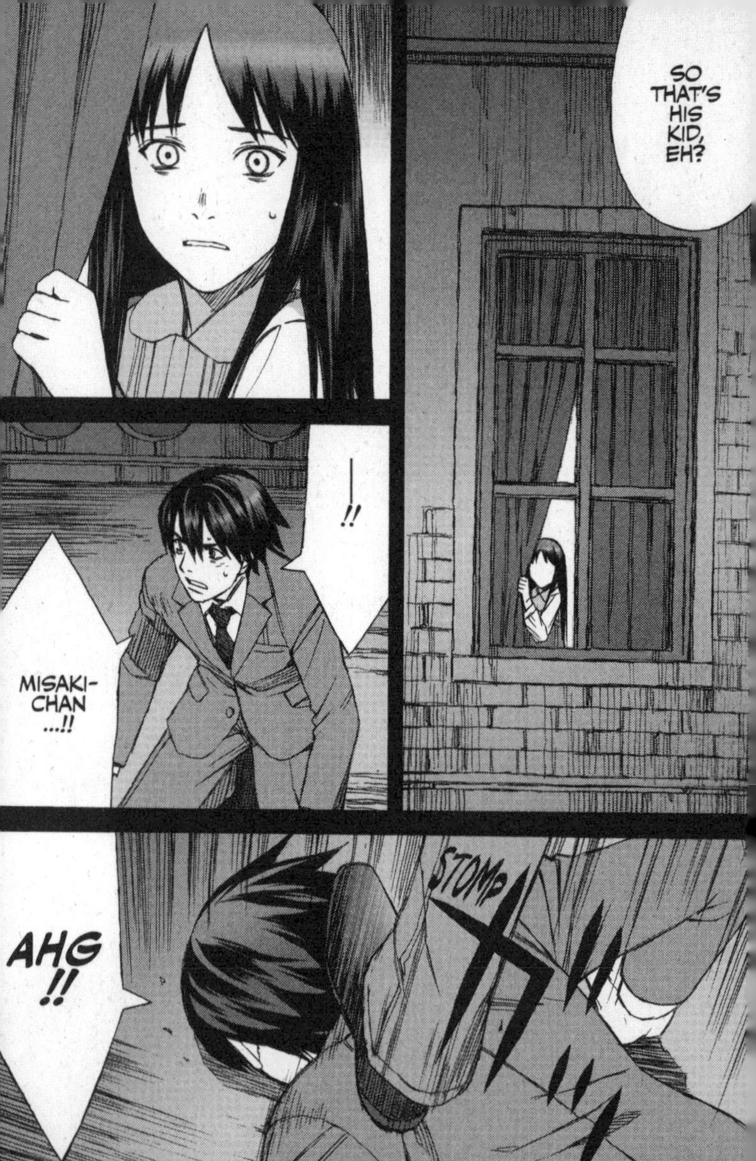
SO THAT'S HIS KID, EH?
—!!
MISAKI-CHAN ...!!
STOMP
AHG!!

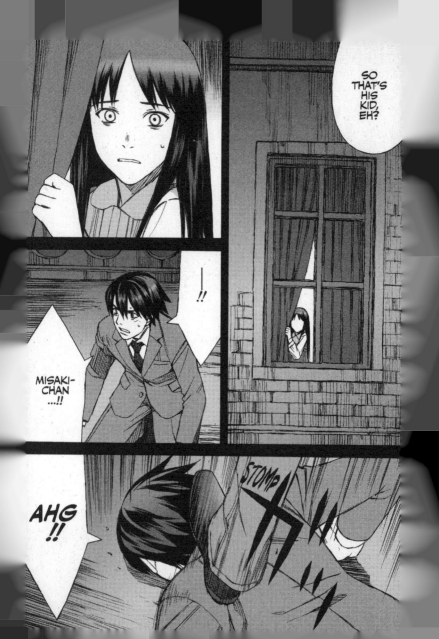

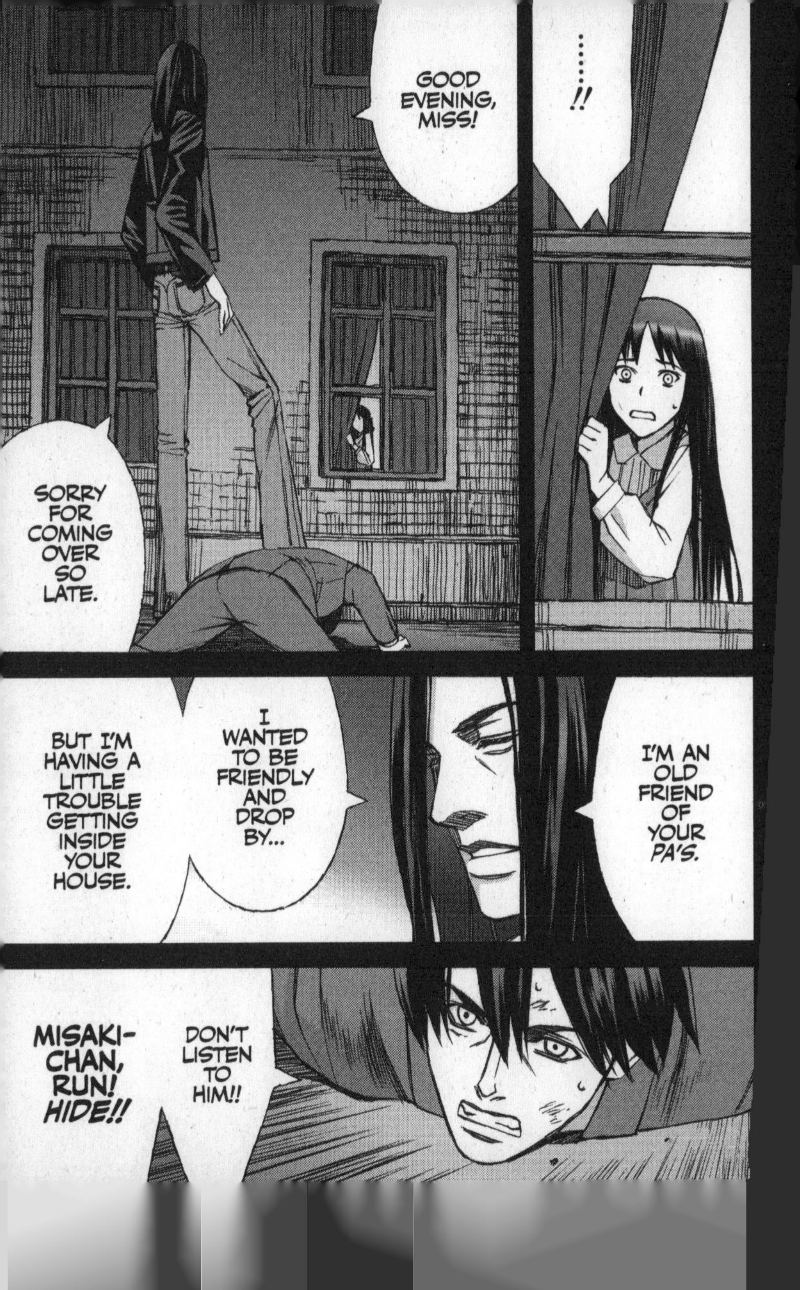
……!!
GOOD EVENING, MISS!
SORRY FOR COMING OVER SO LATE.
I'M AN OLD FRIEND OF YOUR *PA'S.*
I WANTED TO BE FRIENDLY AND DROP BY...
BUT I'M HAVING A LITTLE TROUBLE GETTING INSIDE YOUR HOUSE.
DON'T LISTEN TO HIM!!
MISAKI-CHAN, RUN! *HIDE!!*

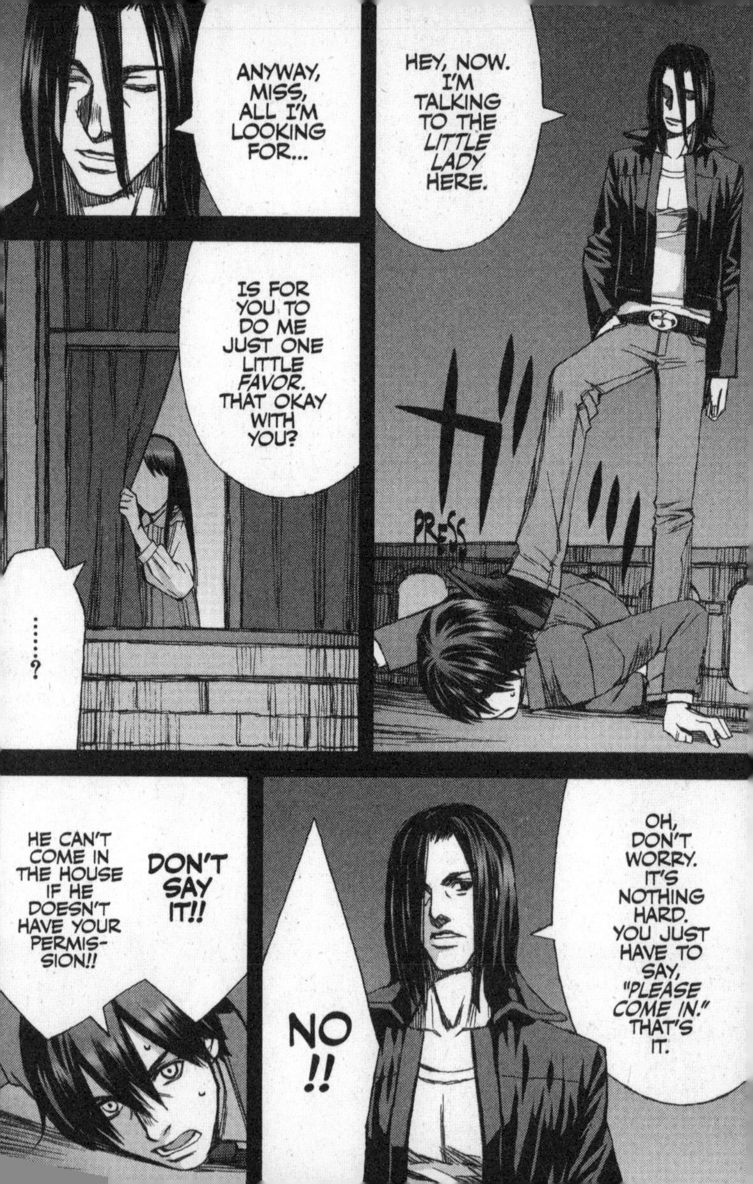
HEY, NOW. I'M TALKING TO THE *LITTLE LADY* HERE.
PRESS
ANYWAY, MISS, ALL I'M LOOKING FOR...
IS FOR YOU TO DO ME JUST ONE LITTLE *FAVOR.* THAT OKAY WITH YOU?
......?
OH, DON'T WORRY. IT'S NOTHING HARD. YOU JUST HAVE TO SAY, "*PLEASE COME IN.*" THAT'S IT.
NO!!
DON'T SAY IT!!
HE CAN'T COME IN THE HOUSE IF HE DOESN'T HAVE YOUR PERMIS-SION!!

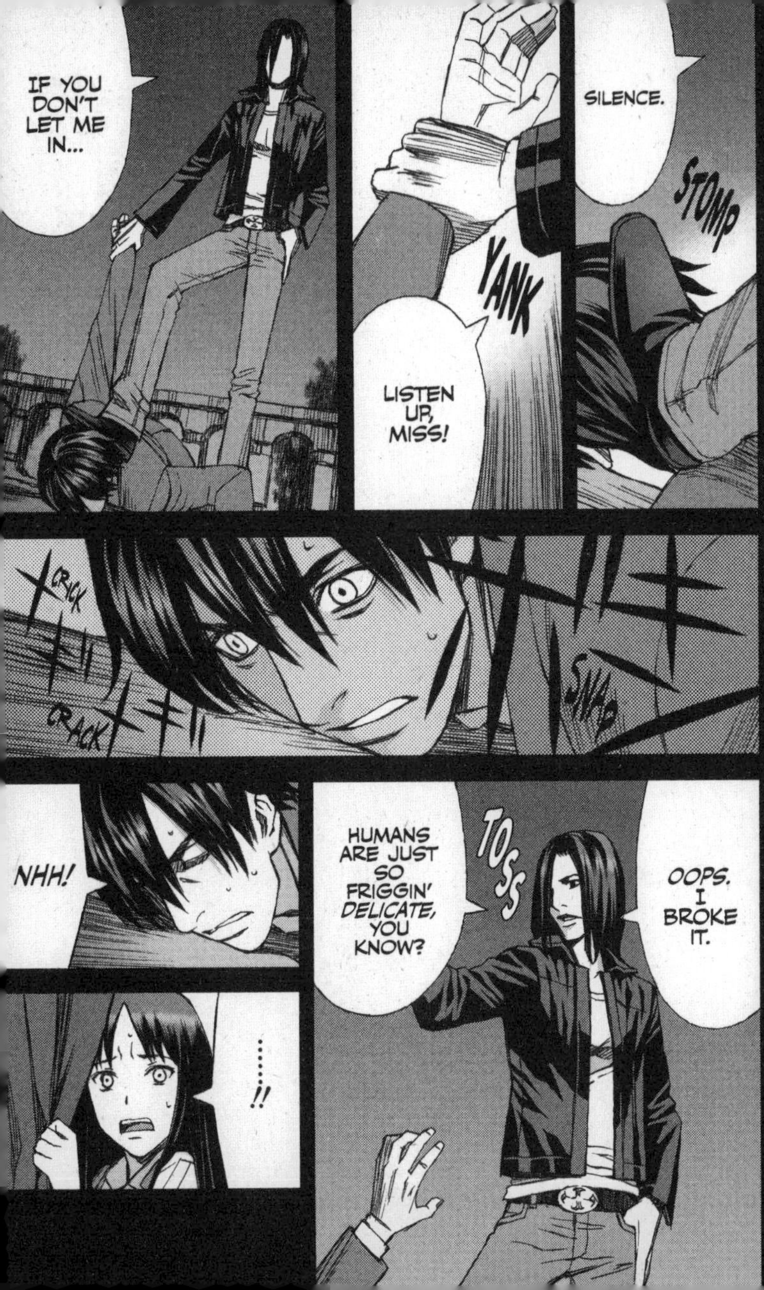
SILENCE.
STOMP
YANK
LISTEN UP, MISS!
IF YOU DON'T LET ME IN...
SNAP
CRICK
CRACK
OOPS. I BROKE IT.
TOSS
HUMANS ARE JUST SO FRIGGIN' *DELICATE,* YOU KNOW?
NHH!
......!!

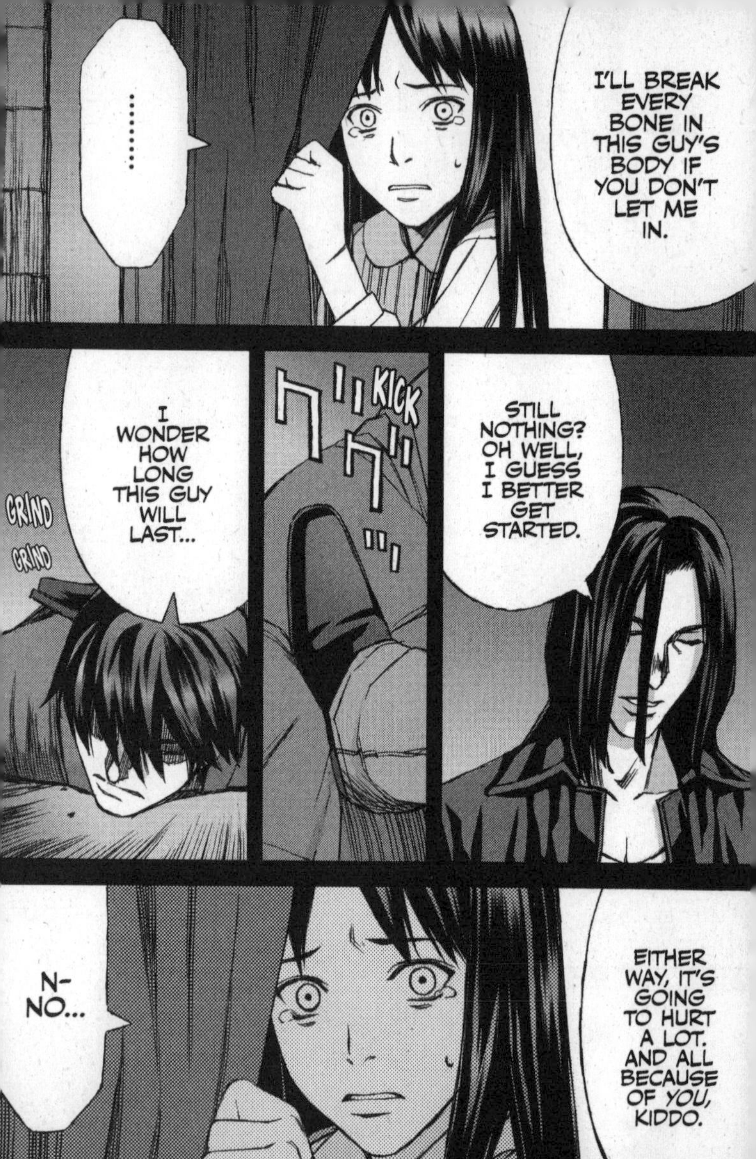
I'LL BREAK EVERY BONE IN THIS GUY'S BODY IF YOU DON'T LET ME IN.
......
STILL NOTHING? OH WELL, I GUESS I BETTER GET STARTED.
KICK
I WONDER HOW LONG THIS GUY WILL LAST...
GRIND
GRIND
EITHER WAY, IT'S GOING TO HURT A LOT. AND ALL BECAUSE OF *YOU*, KIDDO.
N-NO...

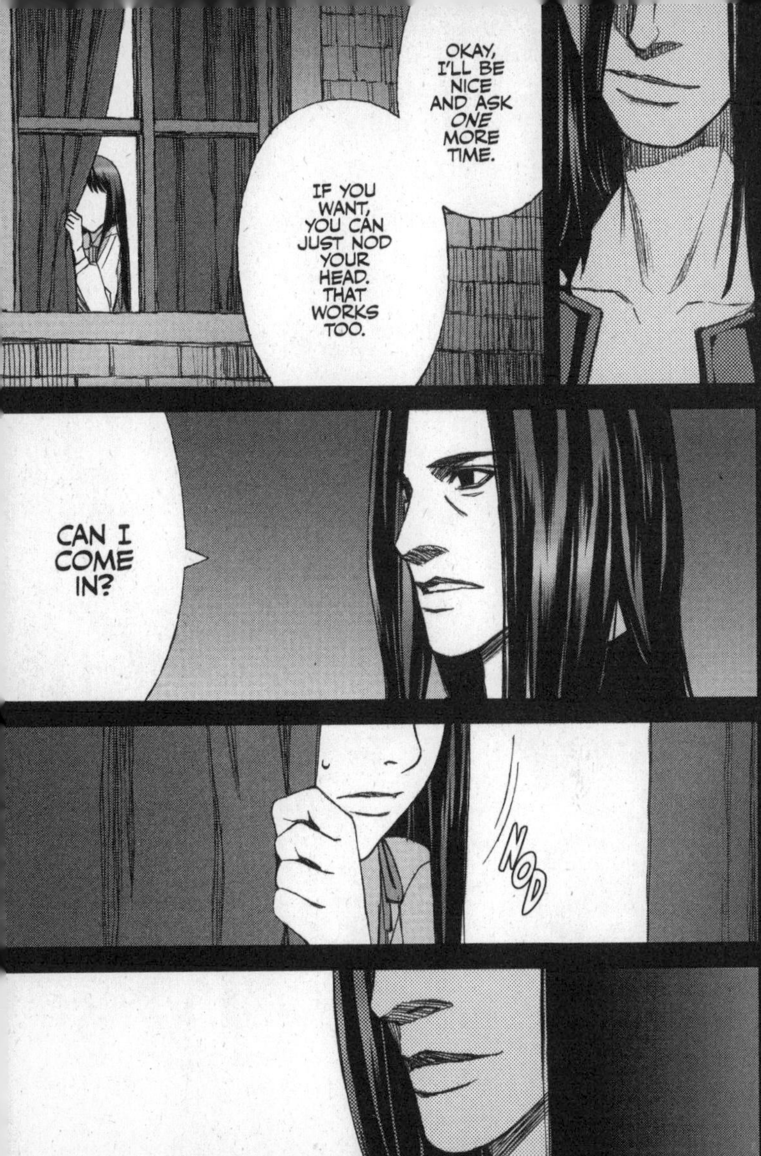
OKAY, I'LL BE NICE AND ASK ONE MORE TIME.
IF YOU WANT, YOU CAN JUST NOD YOUR HEAD. THAT WORKS TOO.
CAN I COME IN?
NOD

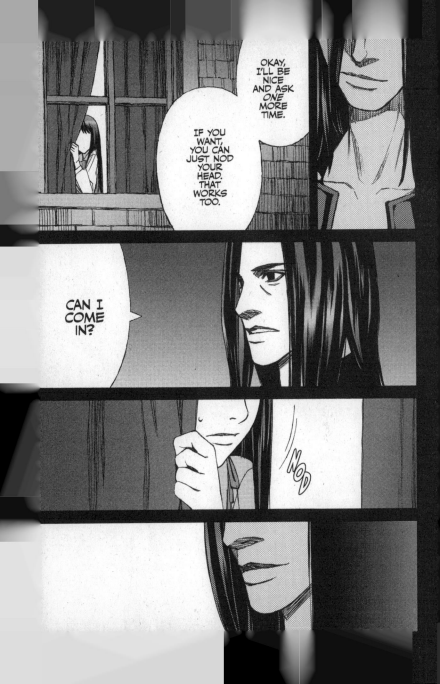

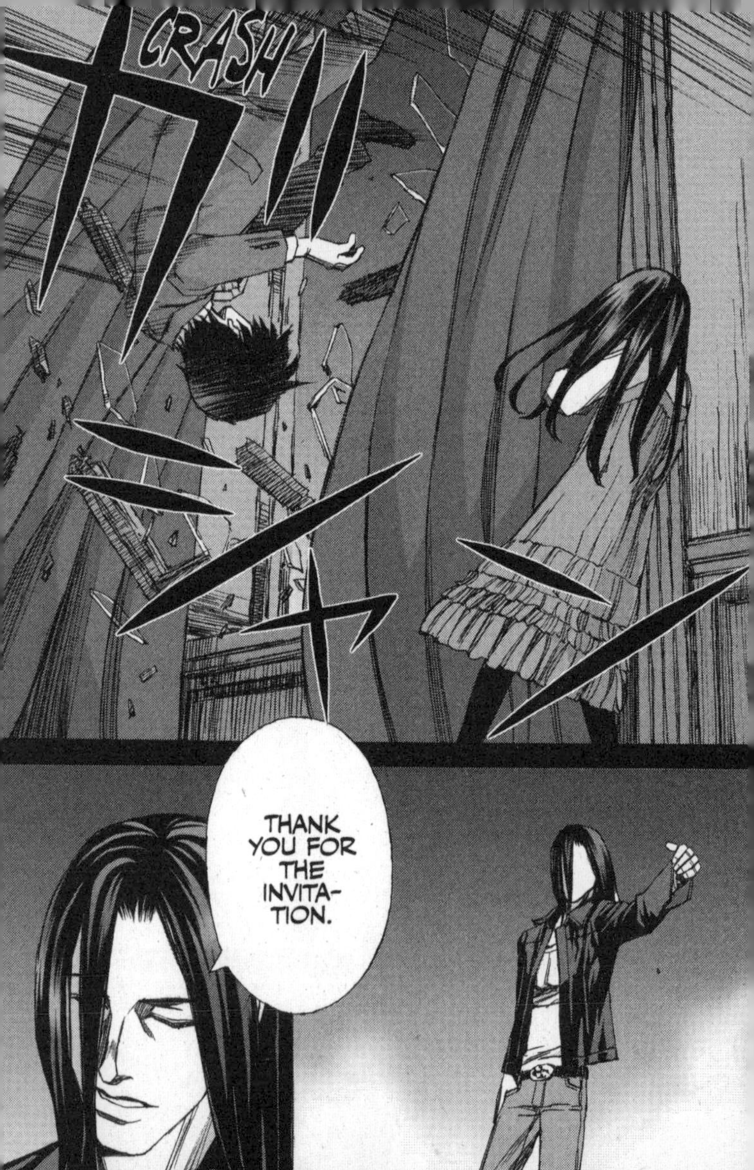
CRASH
THANK YOU FOR THE INVITATION.

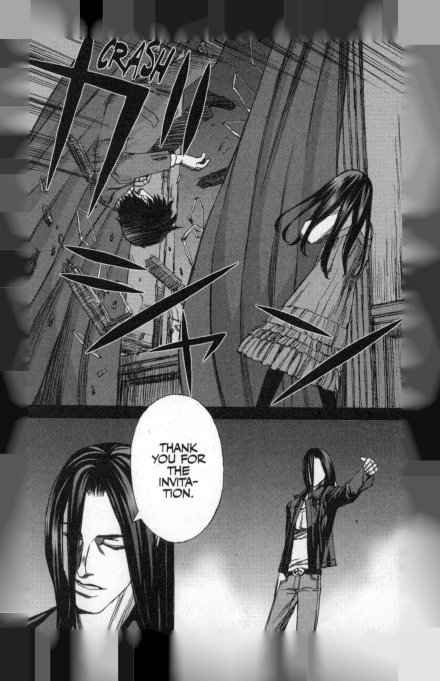

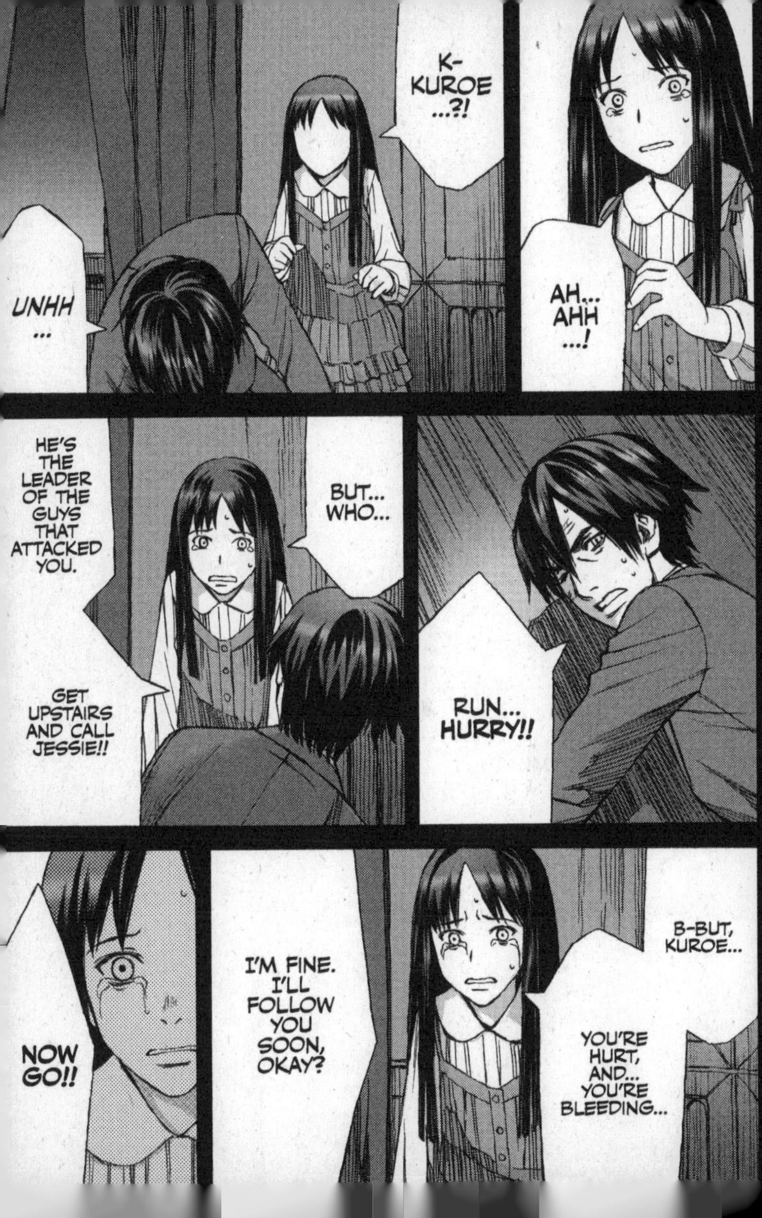
AH... AHH ...!
K-KUROE ...?!
UNHH ...
RUN... HURRY!!
BUT... WHO...
HE'S THE LEADER OF THE GUYS THAT ATTACKED YOU.
GET UPSTAIRS AND CALL JESSIE!!
B-BUT, KUROE...
YOU'RE HURT, AND... YOU'RE BLEEDING...
I'M FINE. I'LL FOLLOW YOU SOON, OKAY?
NOW GO!!

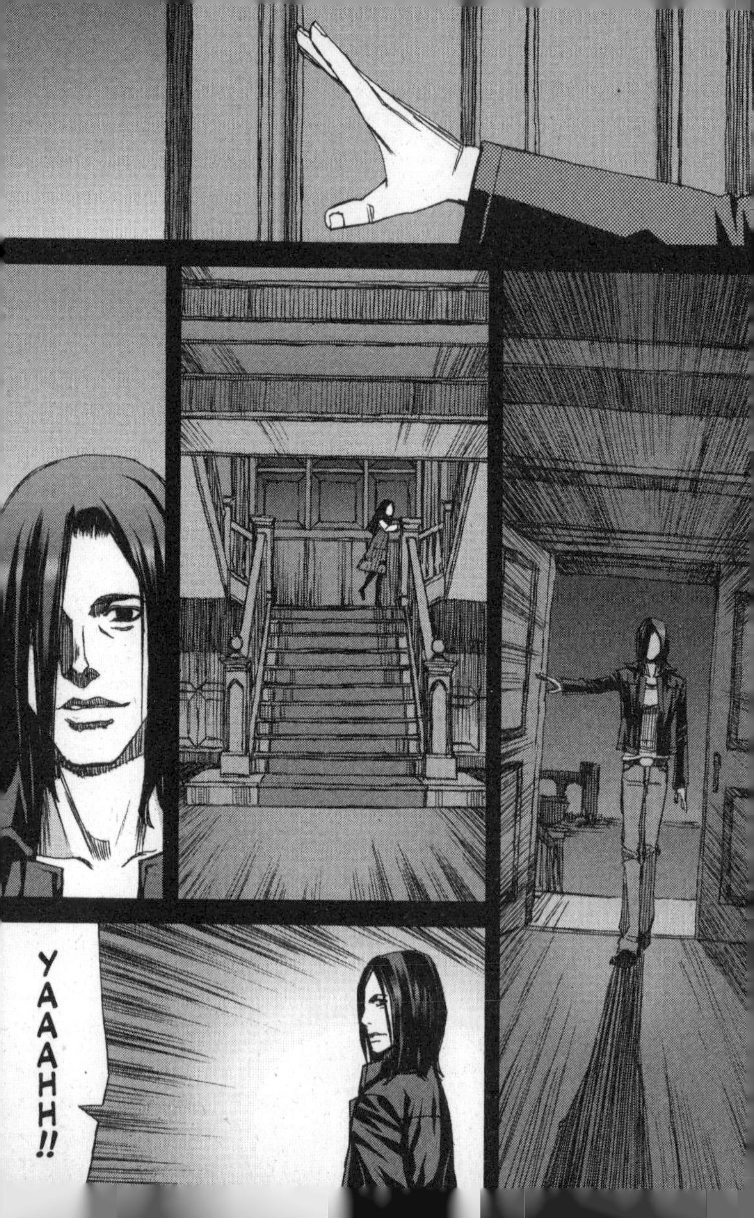
YAAAAHH!!

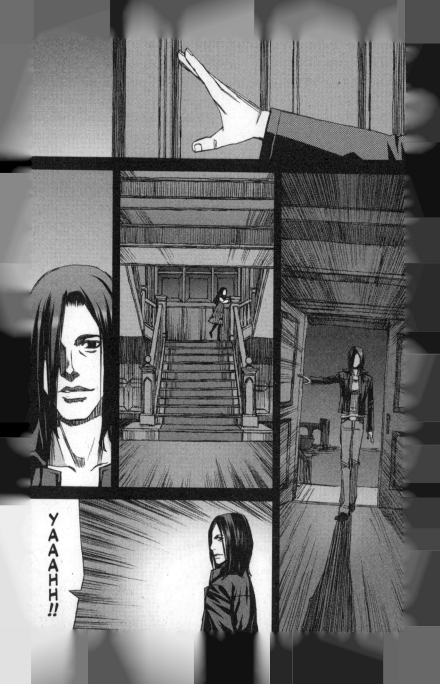

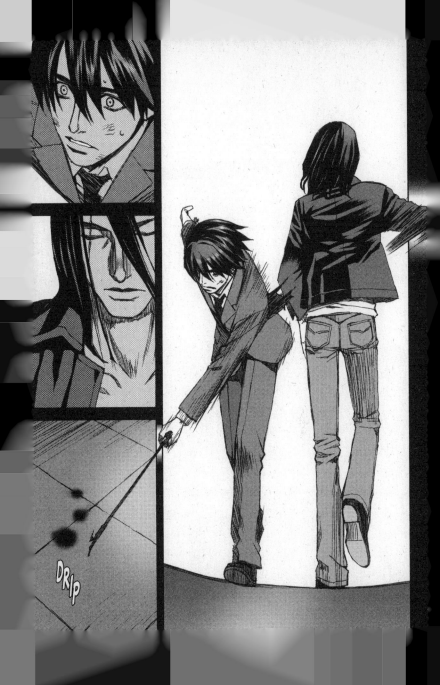

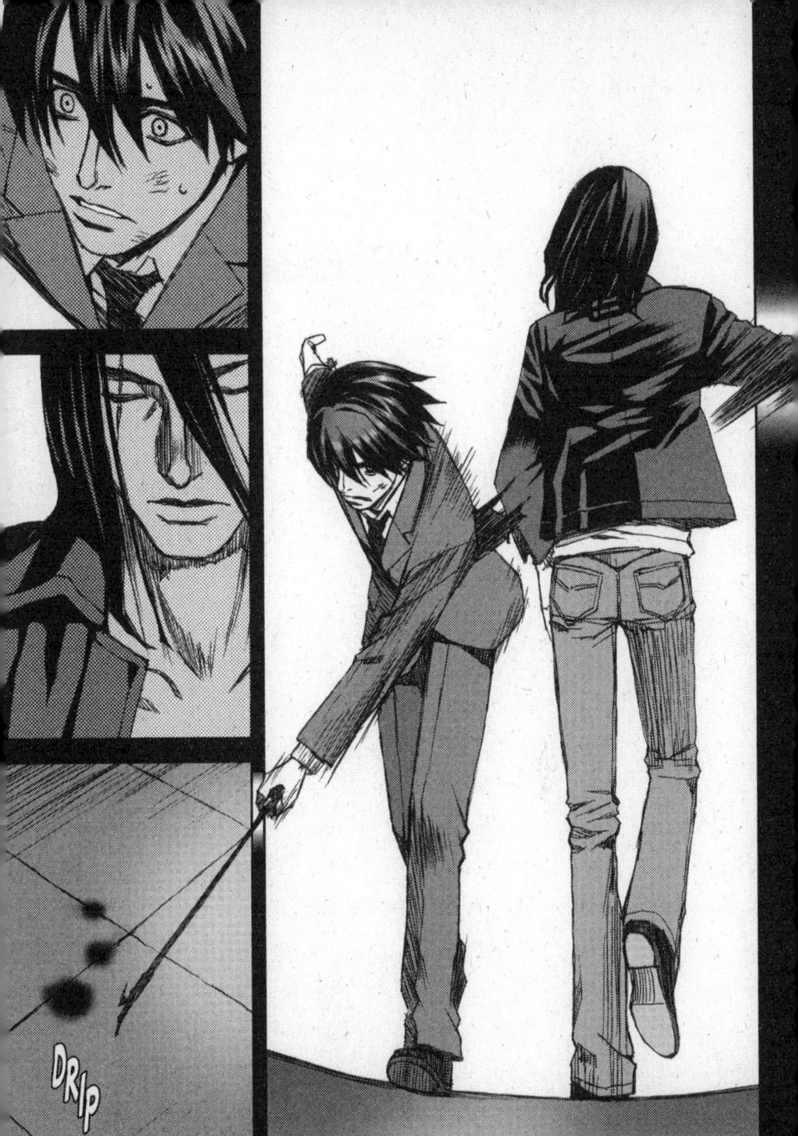
DRIP

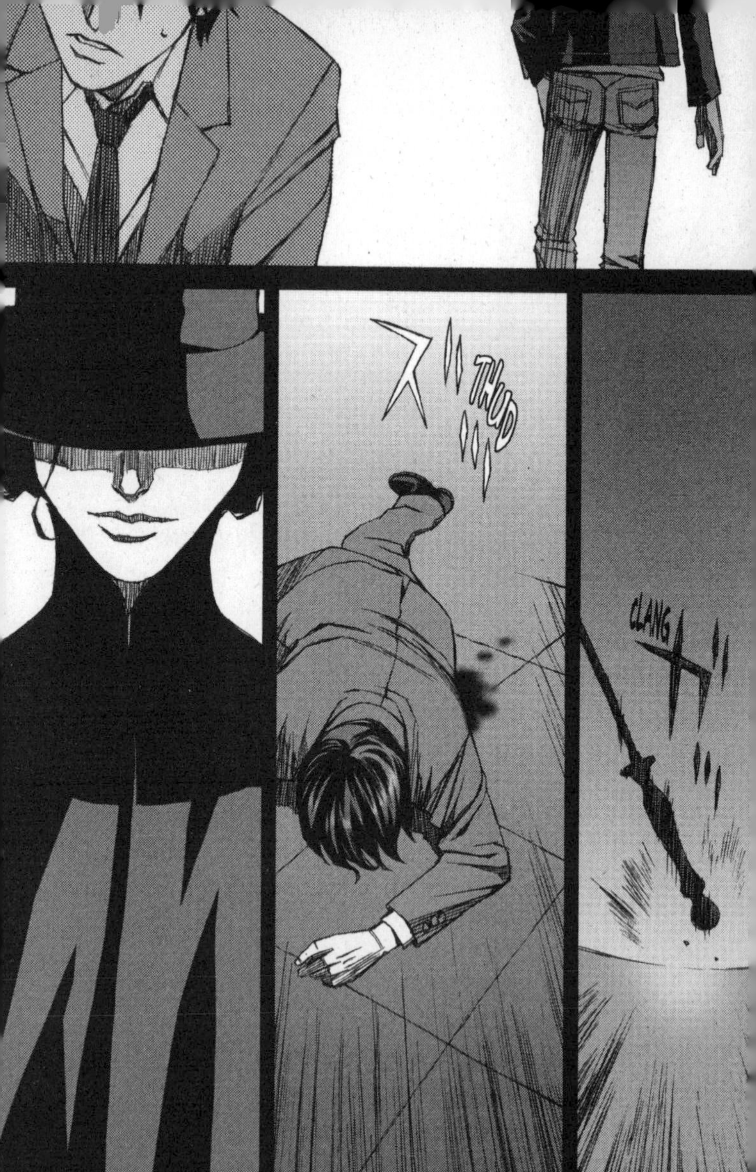
CLANG
THUD

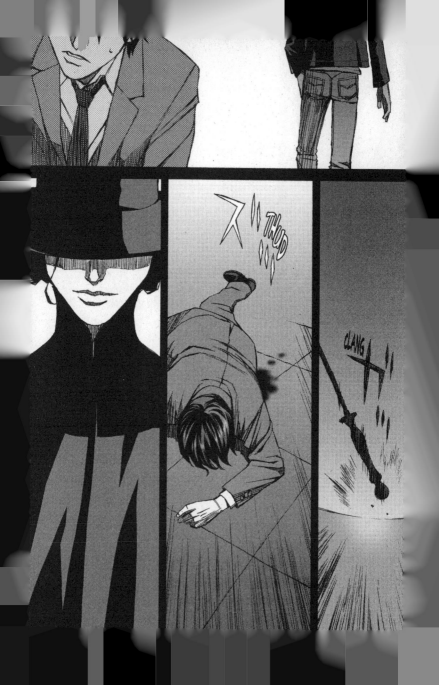

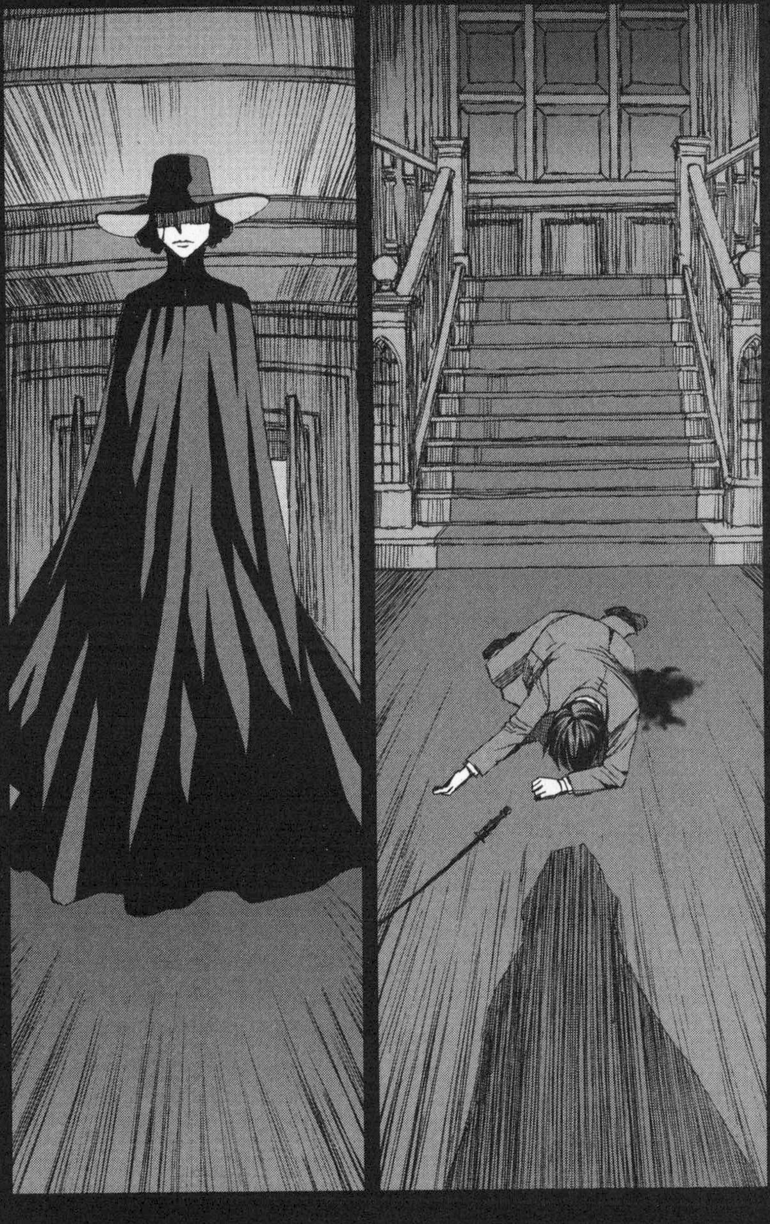

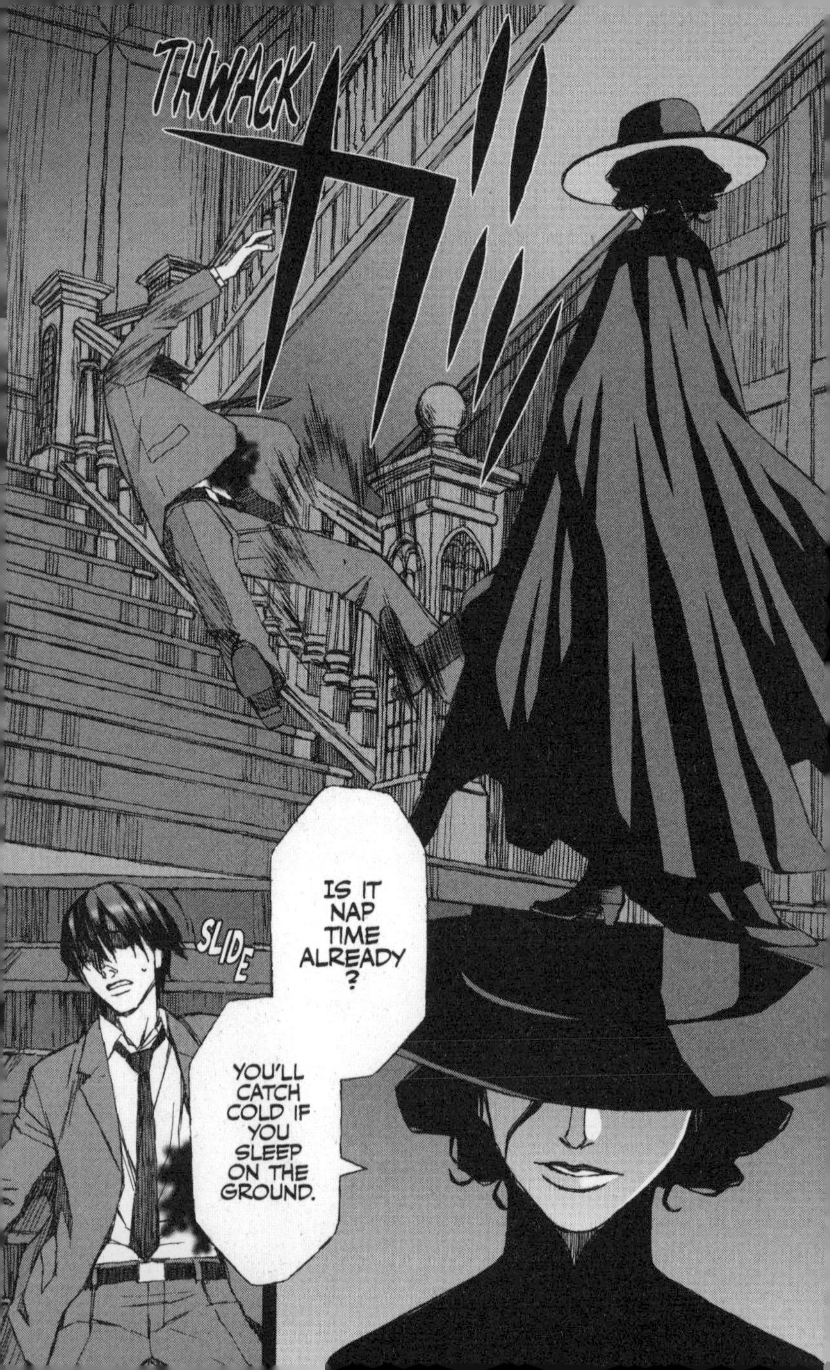
THWACK
IS IT NAP TIME ALREADY?
SLIDE
YOU'LL CATCH COLD IF YOU SLEEP ON THE GROUND.

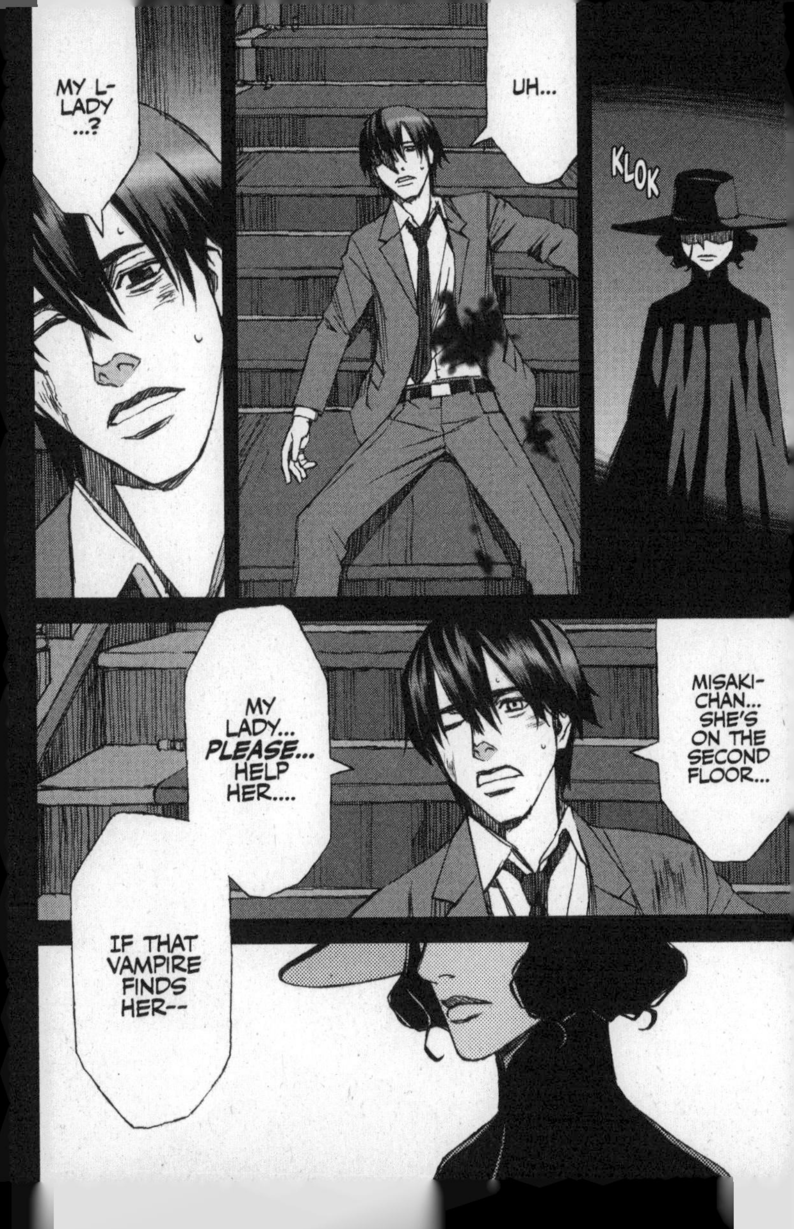
KLOK
UH...
MY L-LADY ...?
MISAKI-CHAN... SHE'S ON THE SECOND FLOOR...
MY LADY... PLEASE... HELP HER....
IF THAT VAMPIRE FINDS HER--

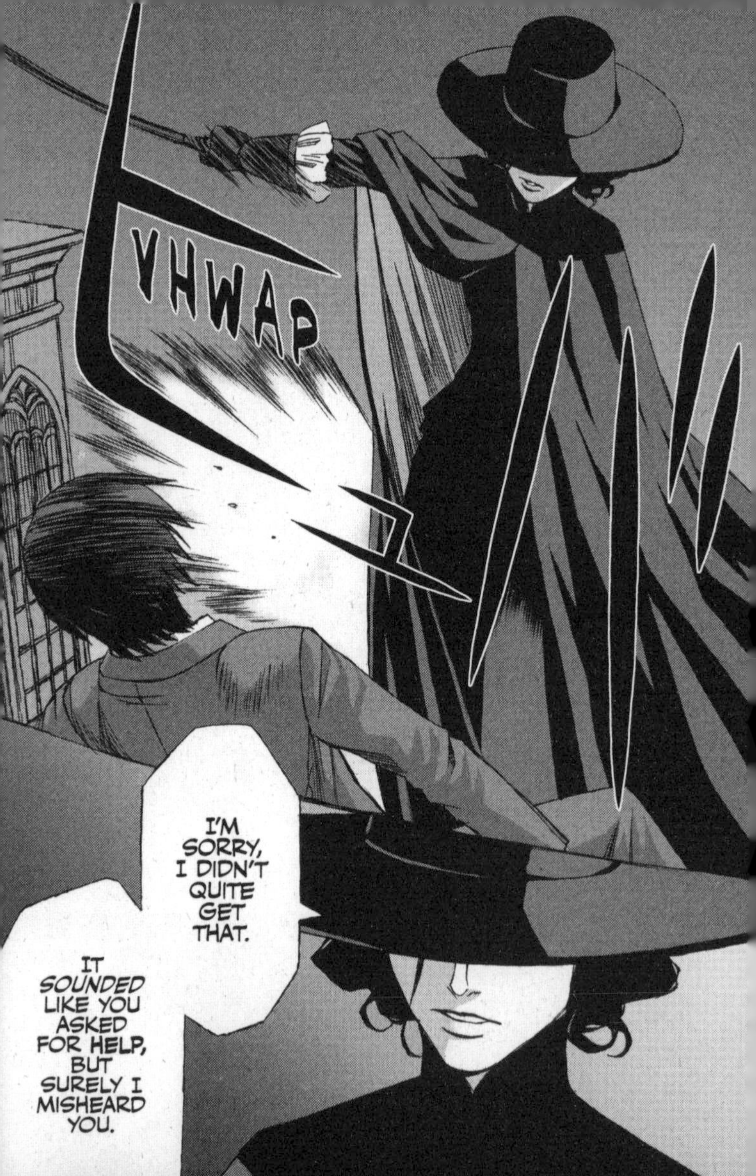
VHWAP
I'M SORRY, I DIDN'T QUITE GET THAT.
IT SOUNDED LIKE YOU ASKED FOR HELP, BUT SURELY I MISHEARD YOU.

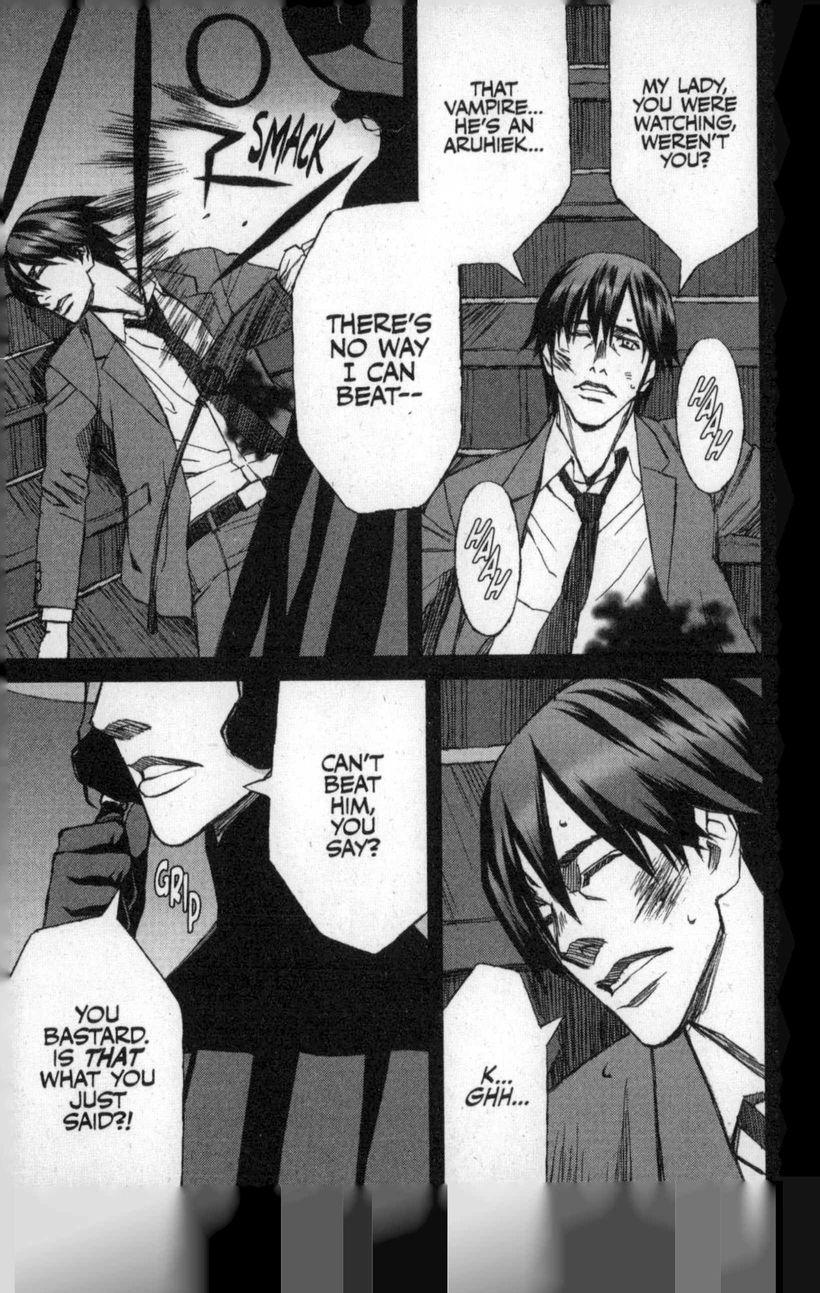
MY LADY, YOU WERE WATCHING, WEREN'T YOU?
THAT VAMPIRE... HE'S AN ARUHIEK...
HAAH
HAAH
SMACK
THERE'S NO WAY I CAN BEAT--
K... GHH...
CAN'T BEAT HIM, YOU SAY?
GRIP
YOU BASTARD. IS *THAT* WHAT YOU JUST SAID?!

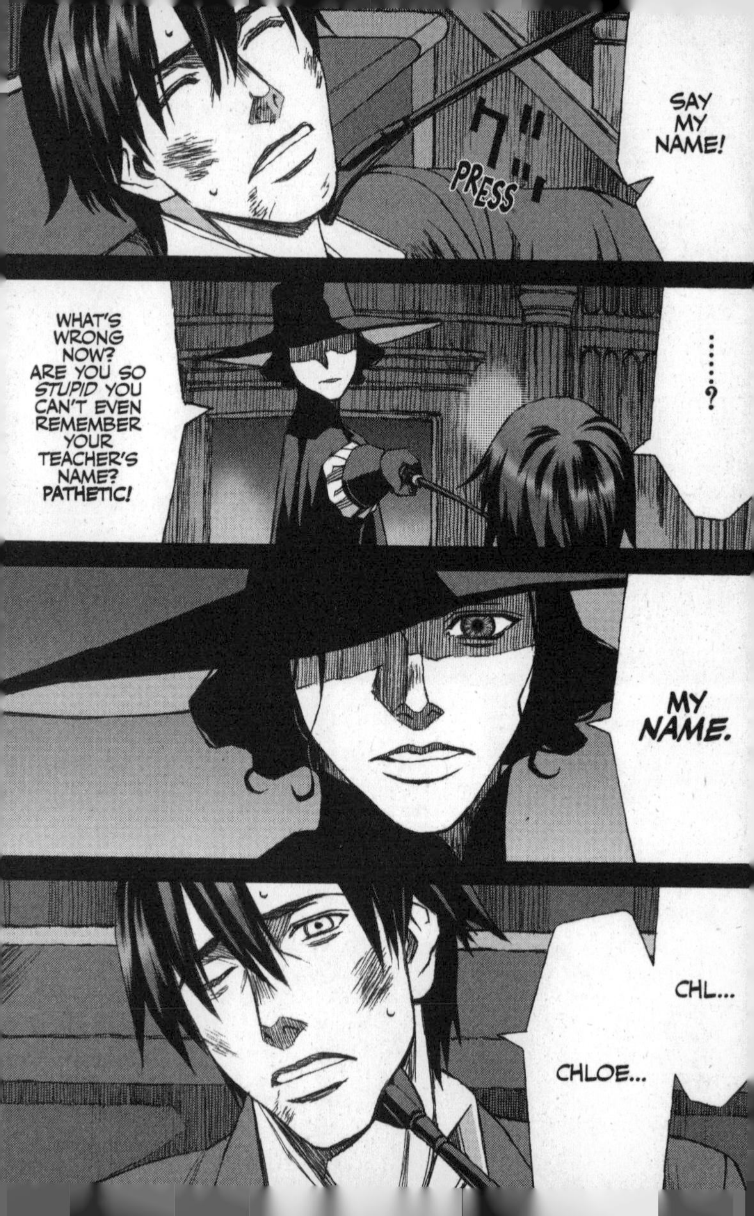
SAY MY NAME!
ク゛ッ
PRESS
...?
WHAT'S WRONG NOW? ARE YOU SO *STUPID* YOU CAN'T EVEN REMEMBER YOUR TEACHER'S NAME? PATHETIC!
MY *NAME.*
CHL...
CHLOE...

THAT'S RIGHT!
CHLOE!!
VHHHPP
THE NAME OF ONE WHO HAS PRODUCED A THOUSAND MIRACLES!
THE NAME OF THE GREATEST MAGICIAN TO EVER EXIST IN ALL OF ETERNITY!!
THAT'S MY NAME!!

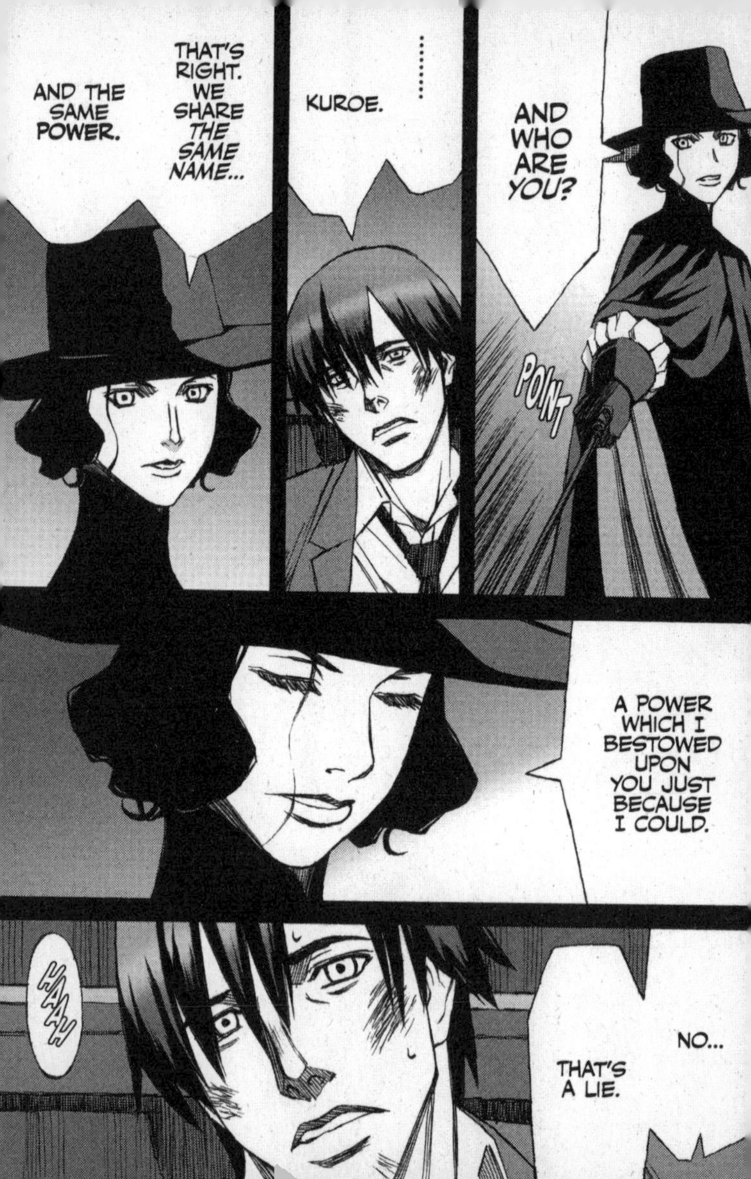
AND WHO ARE YOU?
POINT
KUROE.
THAT'S RIGHT. WE SHARE THE SAME NAME...
AND THE SAME POWER.
A POWER WHICH I BESTOWED UPON YOU JUST BECAUSE I COULD.
NO...
THAT'S A LIE.
HAAH

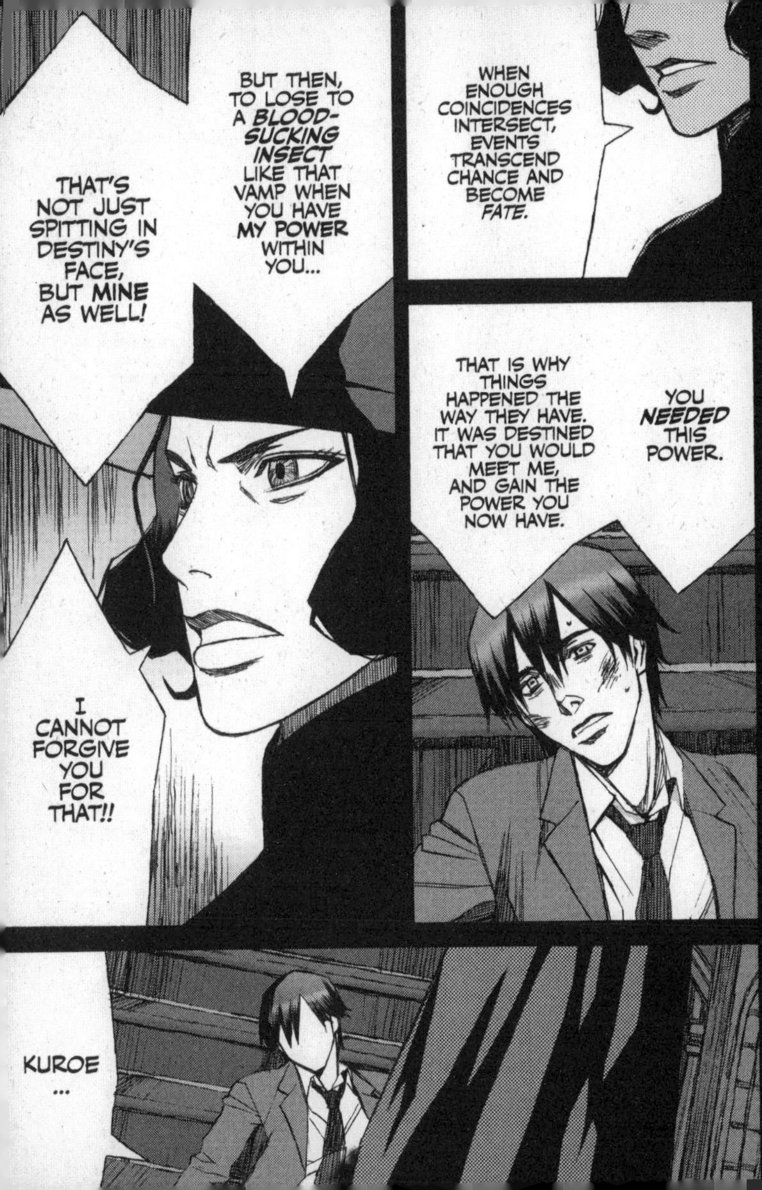
WHEN ENOUGH COINCIDENCES INTERSECT, EVENTS TRANSCEND CHANCE AND BECOME *FATE.*
THAT IS WHY THINGS HAPPENED THE WAY THEY HAVE. IT WAS DESTINED THAT YOU WOULD MEET ME, AND GAIN THE POWER YOU NOW HAVE.
YOU ***NEEDED*** THIS POWER.
BUT THEN, TO LOSE TO A ***BLOOD-SUCKING INSECT*** LIKE THAT VAMP WHEN YOU HAVE **MY POWER** WITHIN YOU...
THAT'S NOT JUST SPITTING IN DESTINY'S FACE, BUT **MINE** AS WELL!
I CANNOT FORGIVE YOU FOR THAT!!
KUROE ...

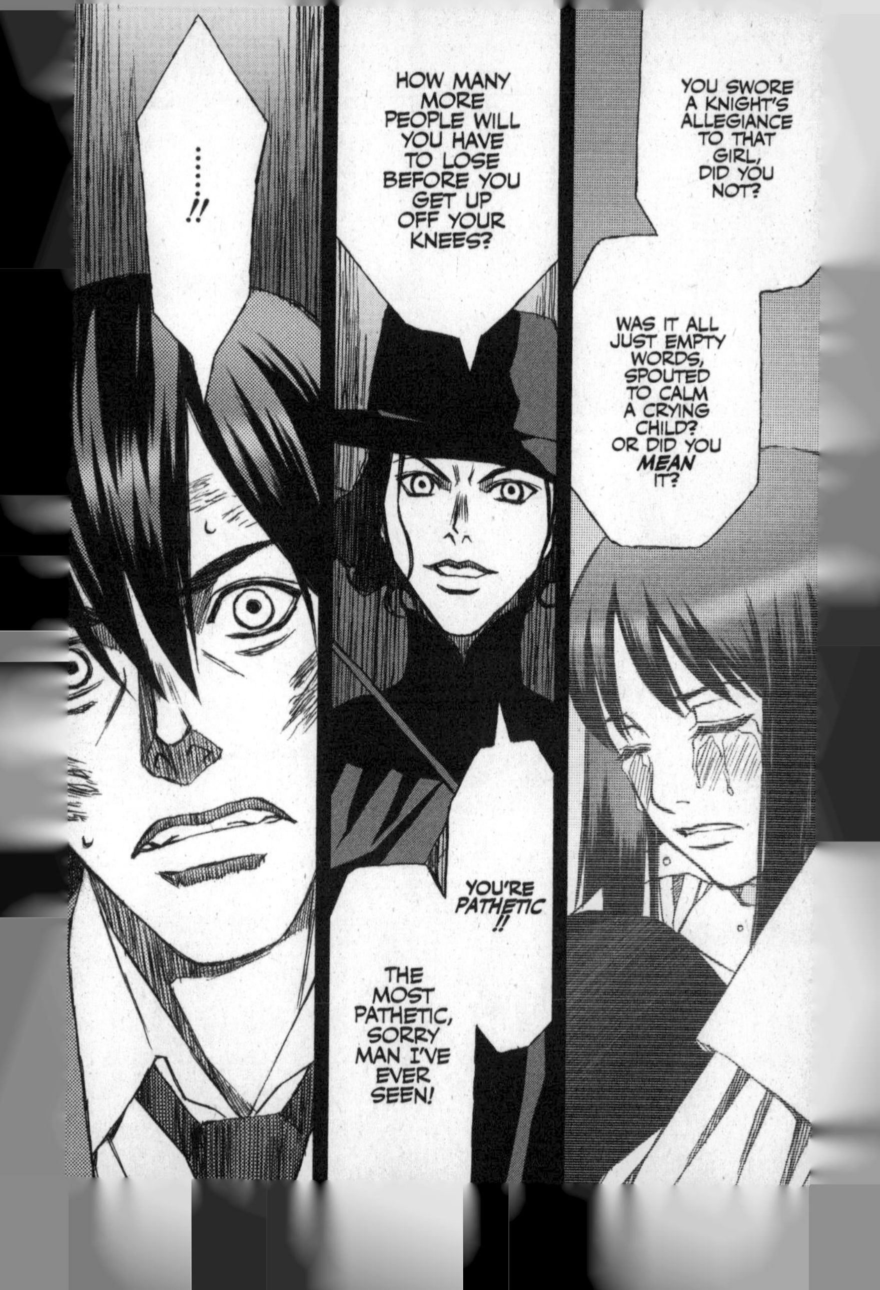
YOU SWORE A KNIGHT'S ALLEGIANCE TO THAT GIRL, DID YOU NOT?
WAS IT ALL JUST EMPTY WORDS, SPOUTED TO CALM A CRYING CHILD? OR DID YOU *MEAN* IT?
HOW MANY MORE PEOPLE WILL YOU HAVE TO LOSE BEFORE YOU GET UP OFF YOUR KNEES?
YOU'RE *PATHETIC*!!
THE MOST PATHETIC, SORRY MAN I'VE EVER SEEN!
......!!

to be continued

Honorifics

To ensure that all character relationships appear as they were originally intended, all character names have been kept in their original Japanese name order with family name first and given name second. For copyright reasons, creator names appear in standard English name order.

In addition to preserving the original Japanese name order, Seven Seas is committed to ensuring that honorifics—polite speech that indicates a person's status or relationship towards another individual—are retained within this book. Politeness is an integral facet of Japanese culture and we believe that maintaining honorifics in our translations helps bring out the same character nuances as seen in the original work.

The following are some of the more common honorifics you may come across while reading this and other books:

-san – The most common of all honorifics, it is an all-purpose suffix that can be used in any situation where politeness is expected. Generally seen as the equivalent to Mr., Miss, Ms., Mrs., etc.

-sama – This suffix is one level higher than "-san" and is used to confer great respect upon an individual.

-kun – This suffix is commonly used at the end of boys' names to express either familiarity or endearment. It can also be used when addressing someone younger than oneself or of a lower status.

-chan – Another common honorific. This suffix is mainly used to express endearment towards girls, but can also be used when referring to little boys or even pets. Couples are also known to use the term amongst each other to convey a sense of cuteness and intimacy.

Sempai – This title is used towards one's senior or "superior" in a particular group or organization. "Sempai" is most often used in a school setting, where underclassmen refer to upperclassmen as "sempai," though it is also commonly said by employees when addressing fellow employees who hold seniority in the workplace.

Sensei – Literally meaning "one who has come before," this title is used for teachers, doctors, or masters of any profession or art.

Kouhai – This is the exact opposite of "sempai," and used to refer to underclassmen in school, junior employees at a workplace. etc.

Oniisan – The title literally means "big brother." First and foremost, it is used by younger siblings, towards older male siblings. It can be used by itself or attached to a person's name as a suffix (niisan). It is often used by a younger person toward an older person unrelated by blood as a sign of respect. Other forms include the informal "oniichan" and the more respectful "oniisama."

Oneesan – This title is the opposite of "oniisan" and means "big sister." Other forms include the informal "oneechan" and the more respectful "oneesama."

Translation Notes

Chapter 2

Ojousama – An honorific used for young woman from wealthy families, it definitely suits a "little princess" like Misaki.

Chapter 6

Chloe/Kuroe – Chloe's comment about how she and Kuroe share the same name makes sense when you keep in mind how their names would sound with a Japanese accent (*Ku-ro-eh* or *Kroh-eh*). When said by a native Japanese speaker like Kuroe, both names would sound alike phonetically, because of the interchangeable nature of Japanese 'l' and 'r' sounds.

Blood Alone

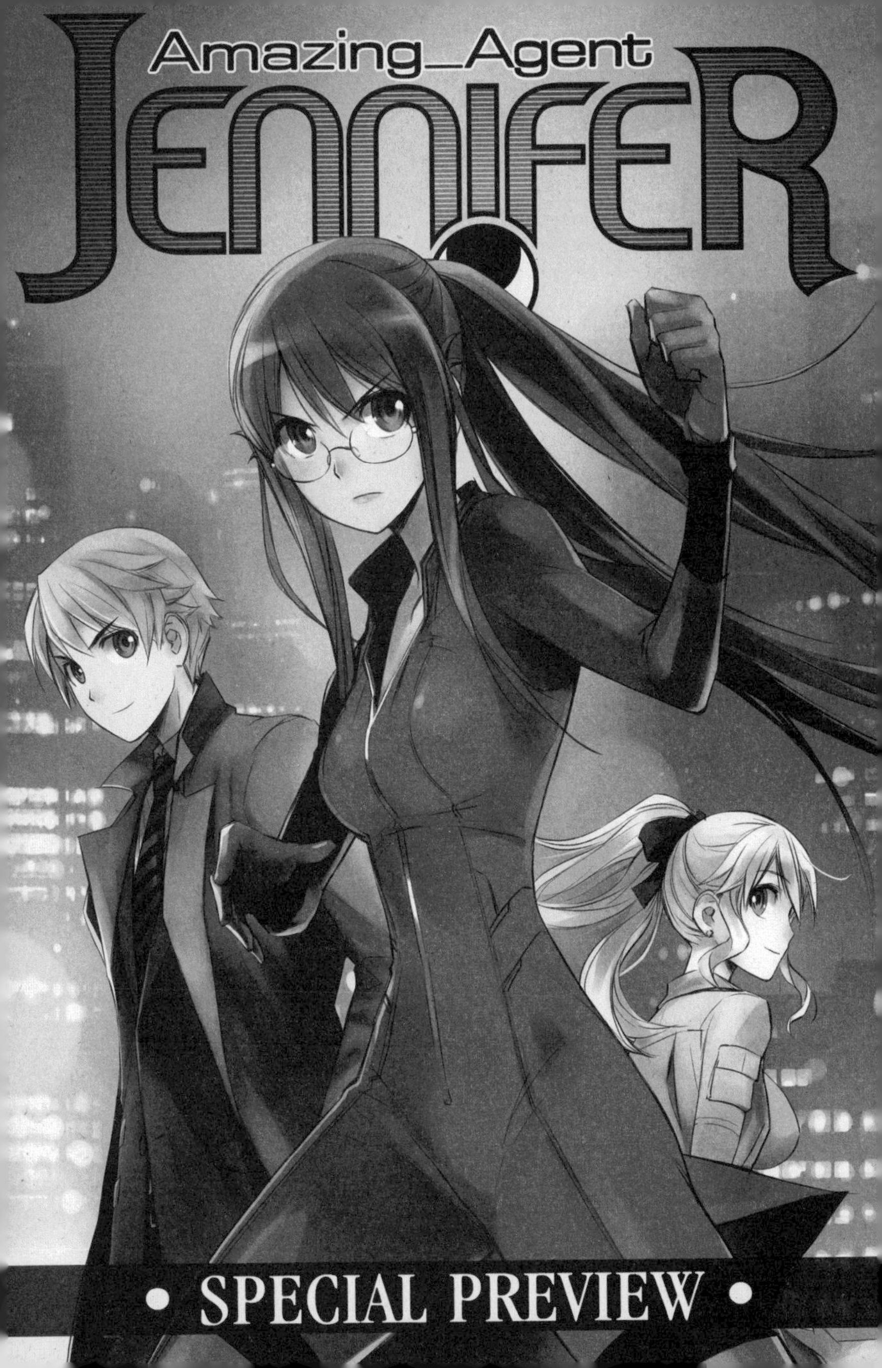
Amazing Agent
JENNIFER
• SPECIAL PREVIEW •

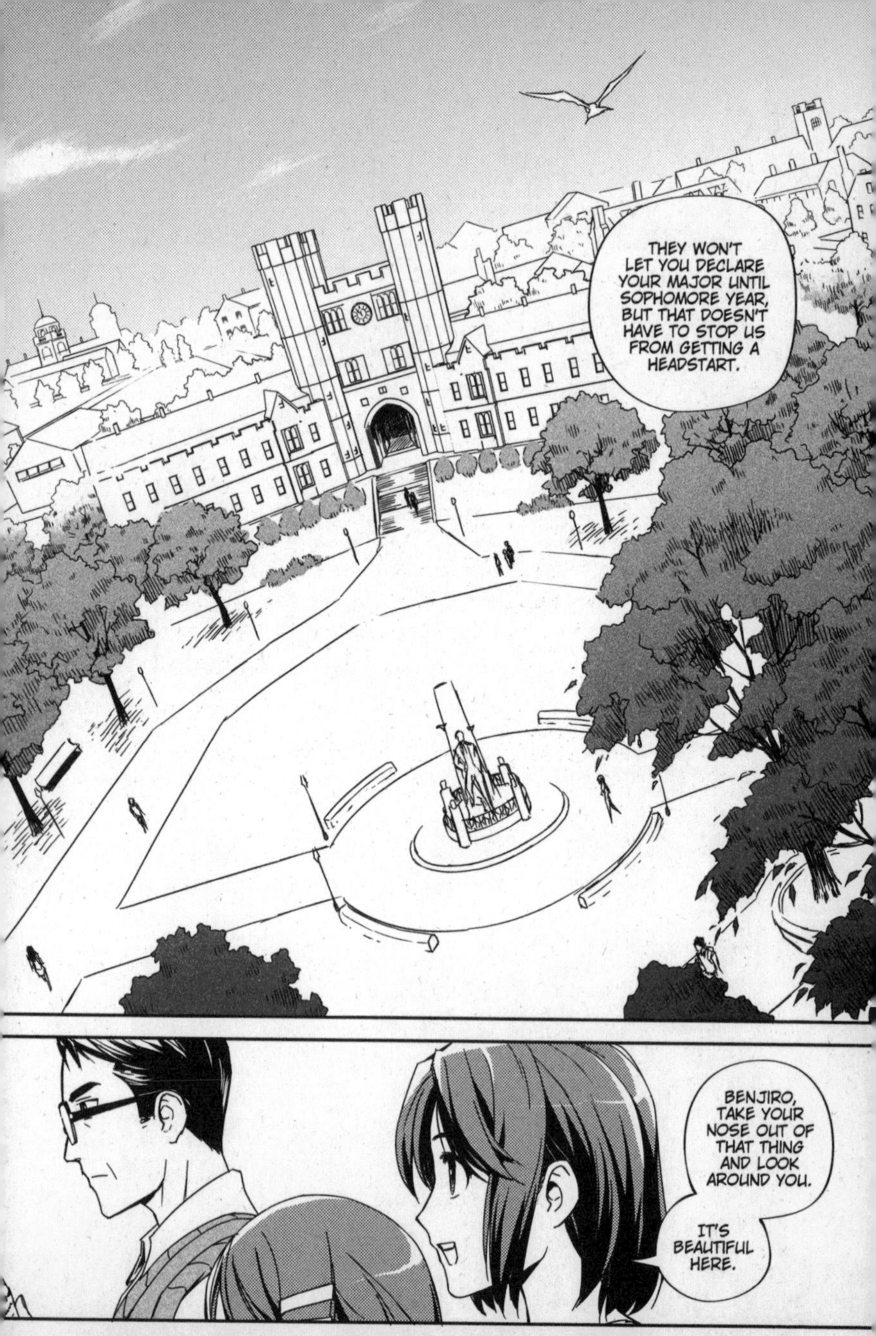
THEY WON'T LET YOU DECLARE YOUR MAJOR UNTIL SOPHOMORE YEAR, BUT THAT DOESN'T HAVE TO STOP US FROM GETTING A HEADSTART.
BENJIRO, TAKE YOUR NOSE OUT OF THAT THING AND LOOK AROUND YOU.
IT'S BEAUTIFUL HERE.

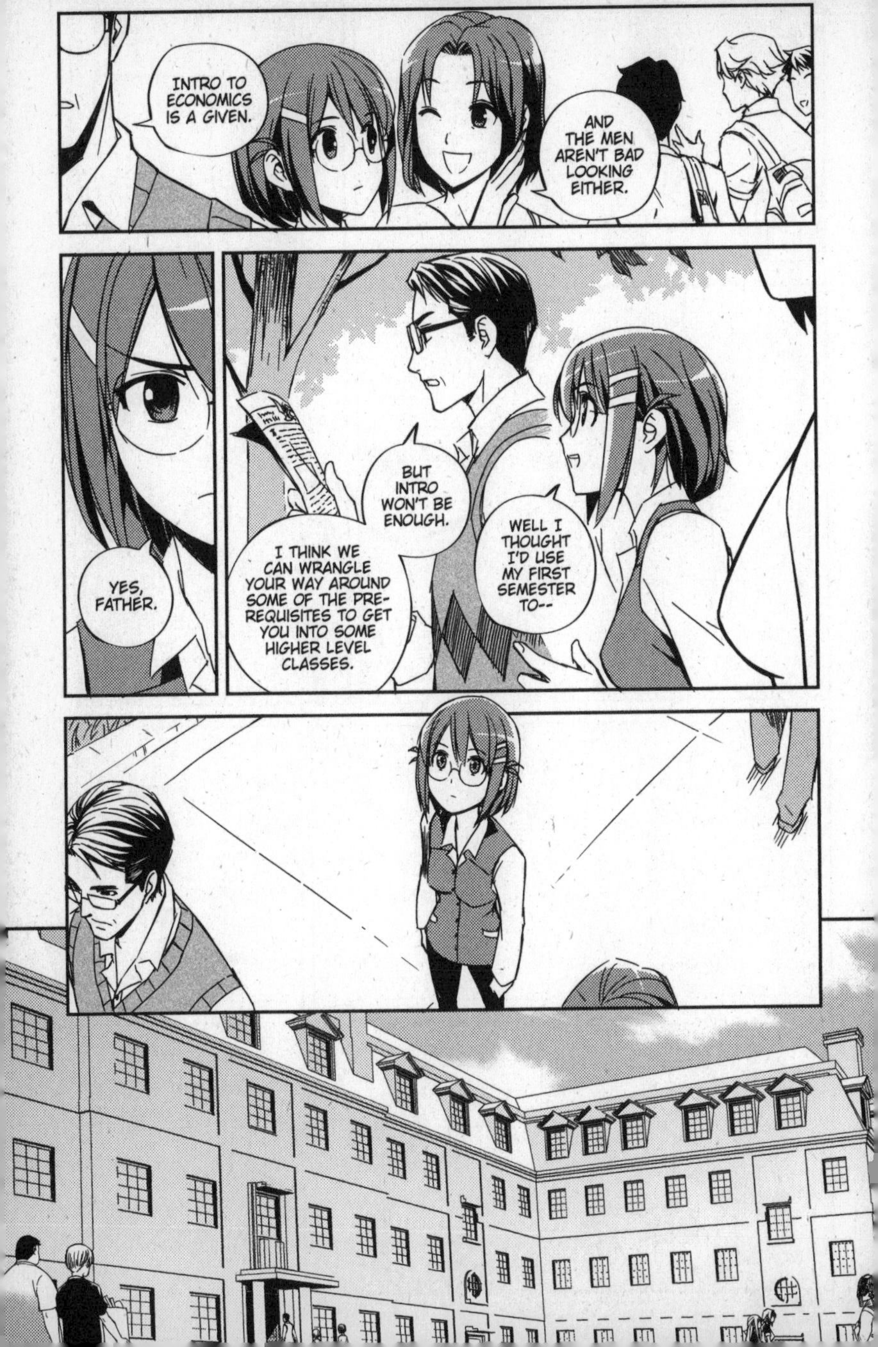
INTRO TO ECONOMICS IS A GIVEN.
AND THE MEN AREN'T BAD LOOKING EITHER.
WELL I THOUGHT I'D USE MY FIRST SEMESTER TO--
BUT INTRO WON'T BE ENOUGH.
I THINK WE CAN WRANGLE YOUR WAY AROUND SOME OF THE PRE-REQUISITES TO GET YOU INTO SOME HIGHER LEVEL CLASSES.
YES, FATHER.

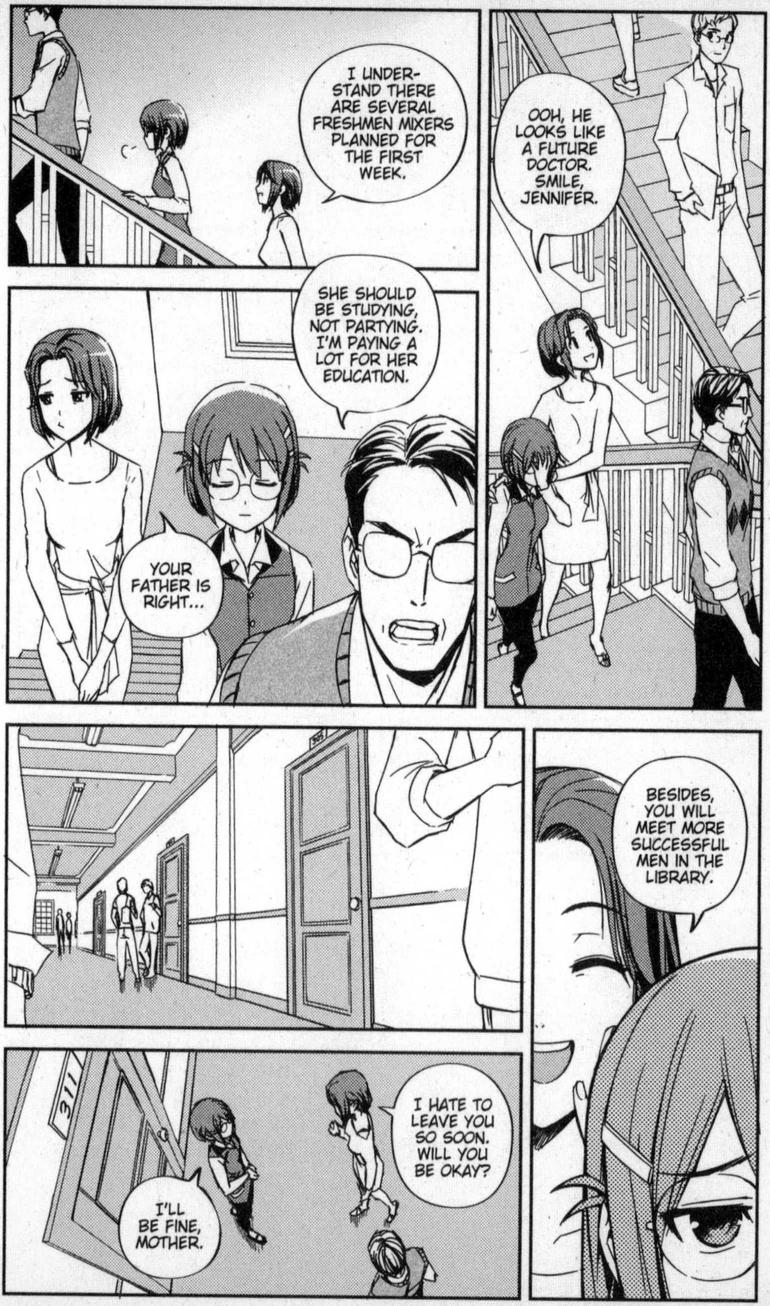
OOH, HE LOOKS LIKE A FUTURE DOCTOR. SMILE, JENNIFER.
I UNDER-STAND THERE ARE SEVERAL FRESHMEN MIXERS PLANNED FOR THE FIRST WEEK.
SHE SHOULD BE STUDYING, NOT PARTYING. I'M PAYING A LOT FOR HER EDUCATION.
YOUR FATHER IS RIGHT...
BESIDES, YOU WILL MEET MORE SUCCESSFUL MEN IN THE LIBRARY.
311
I HATE TO LEAVE YOU SO SOON. WILL YOU BE OKAY?
I'LL BE FINE, MOTHER.

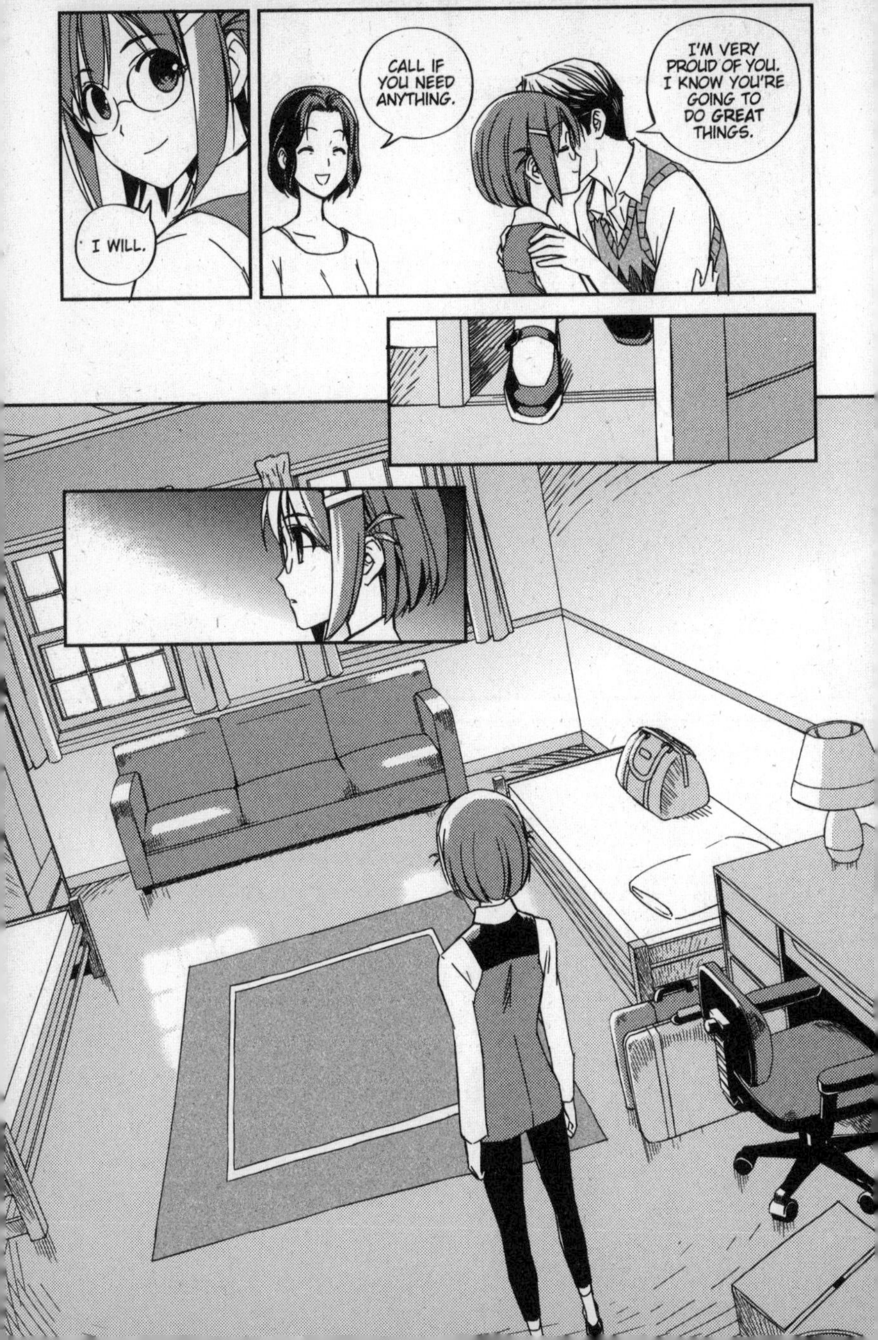
I'M VERY PROUD OF YOU. I KNOW YOU'RE GOING TO DO GREAT THINGS.
CALL IF YOU NEED ANYTHING.
I WILL.

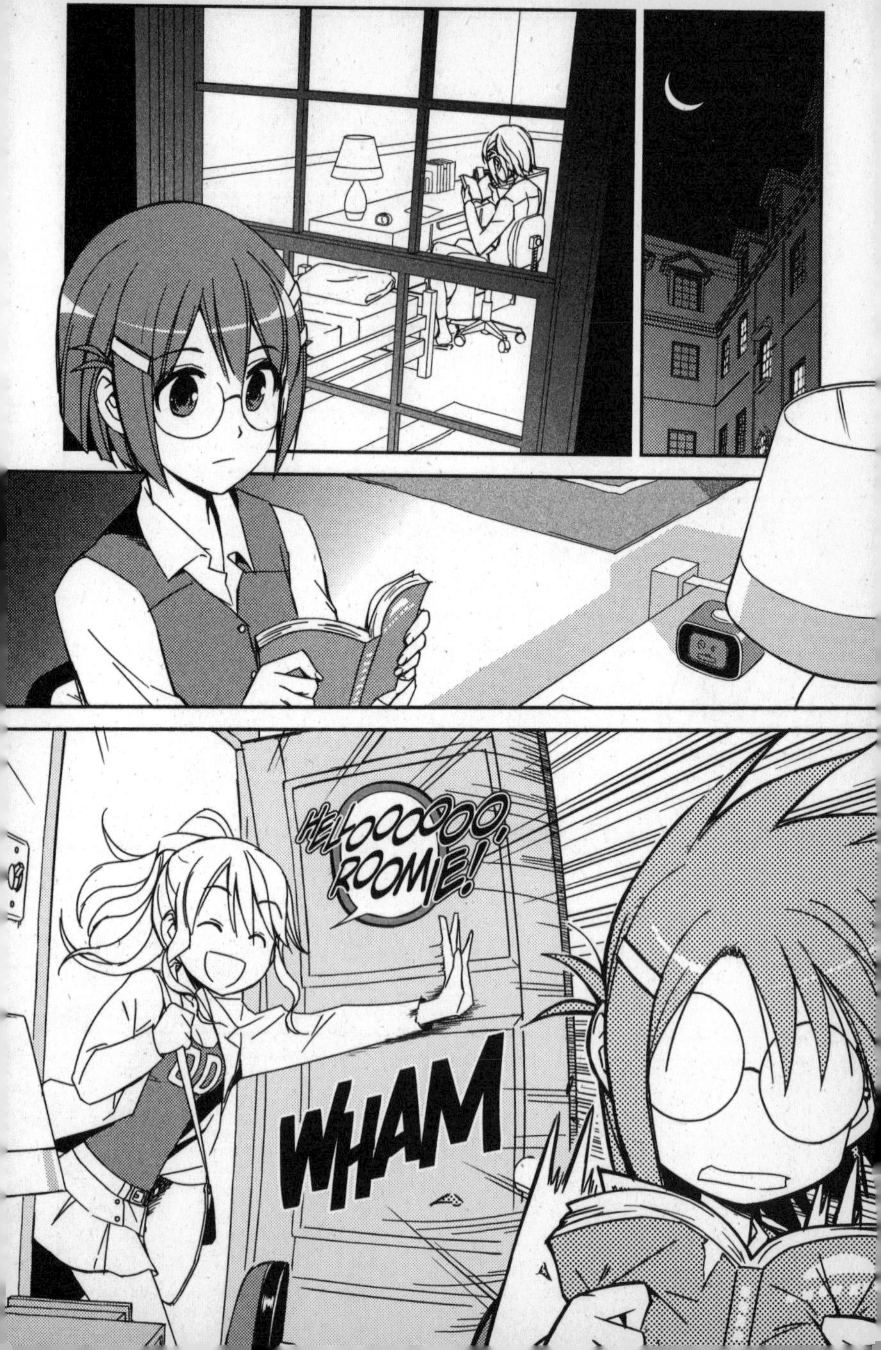
HELLOOOOOO, ROOMIE!
WHAM

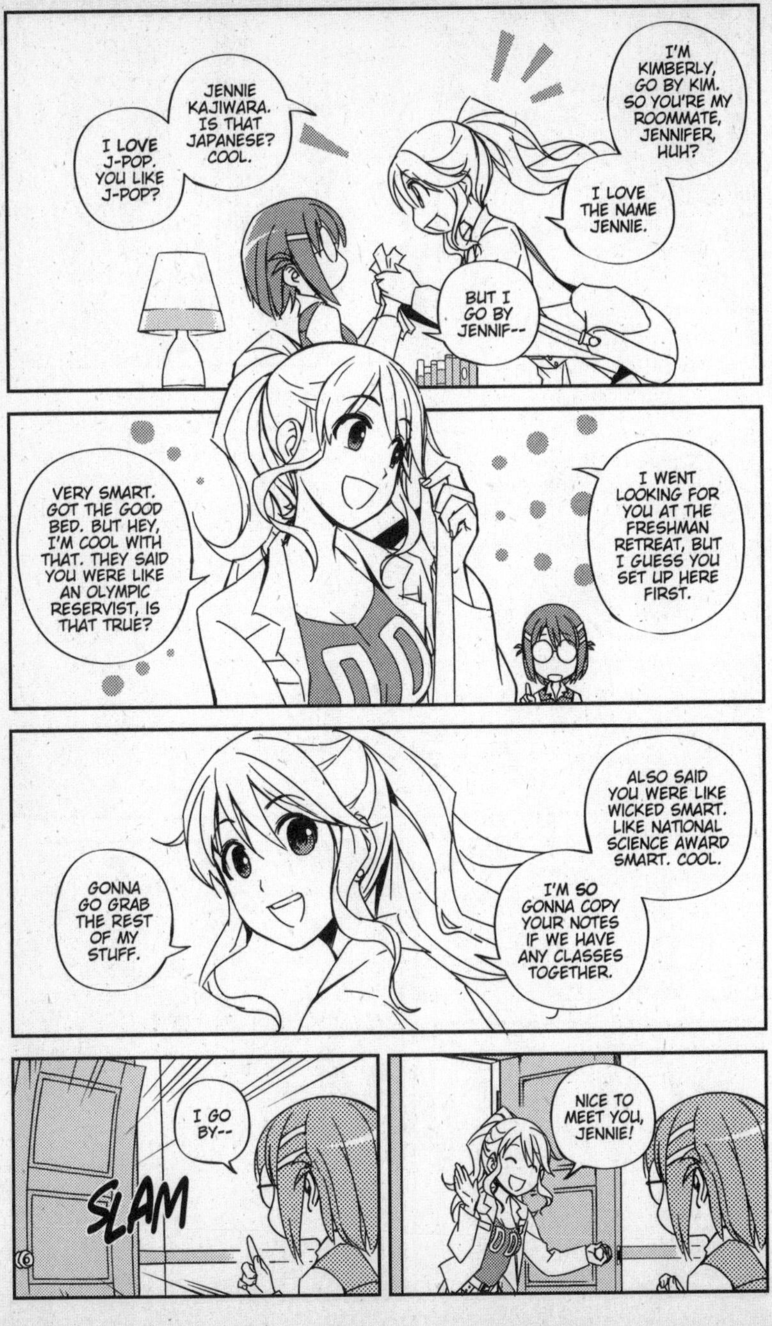
I'M KIMBERLY, GO BY KIM. SO YOU'RE MY ROOMMATE, JENNIFER, HUH?
I LOVE THE NAME JENNIE.
BUT I GO BY JENNIF--
JENNIE KAJIWARA. IS THAT JAPANESE? COOL.
I LOVE J-POP. YOU LIKE J-POP?
I WENT LOOKING FOR YOU AT THE FRESHMAN RETREAT, BUT I GUESS YOU SET UP HERE FIRST.
VERY SMART. GOT THE GOOD BED. BUT HEY, I'M COOL WITH THAT. THEY SAID YOU WERE LIKE AN OLYMPIC RESERVIST, IS THAT TRUE?
ALSO SAID YOU WERE LIKE WICKED SMART. LIKE NATIONAL SCIENCE AWARD SMART. COOL.
I'M SO GONNA COPY YOUR NOTES IF WE HAVE ANY CLASSES TOGETHER.
GONNA GO GRAB THE REST OF MY STUFF.
NICE TO MEET YOU, JENNIE!
I GO BY--
SLAM

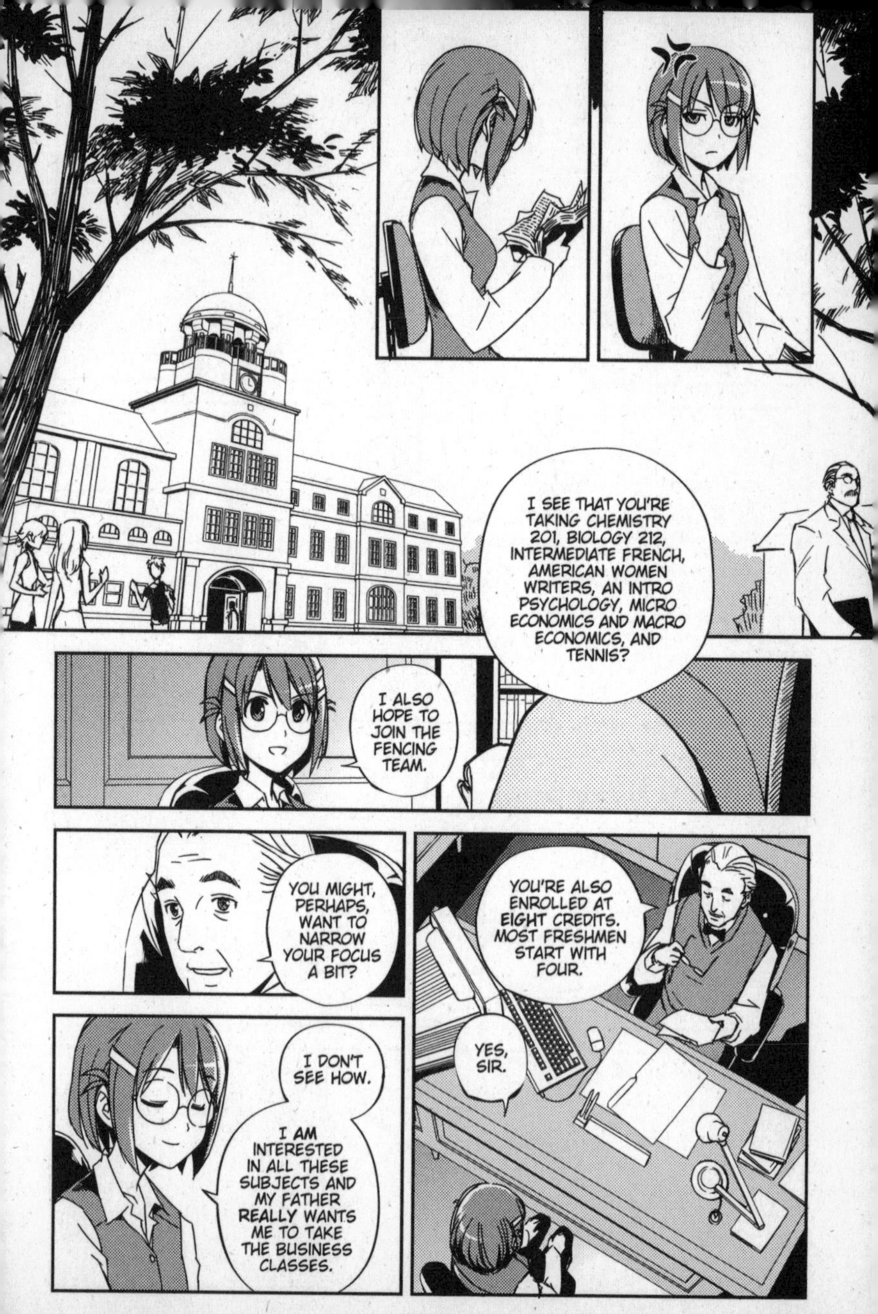
I SEE THAT YOU'RE TAKING CHEMISTRY 201, BIOLOGY 212, INTERMEDIATE FRENCH, AMERICAN WOMEN WRITERS, AN INTRO PSYCHOLOGY, MICRO ECONOMICS AND MACRO ECONOMICS, AND TENNIS?
I ALSO HOPE TO JOIN THE FENCING TEAM.
YOU'RE ALSO ENROLLED AT EIGHT CREDITS. MOST FRESHMEN START WITH FOUR.
YES, SIR.
YOU MIGHT, PERHAPS, WANT TO NARROW YOUR FOCUS A BIT?
I DON'T SEE HOW.
I AM INTERESTED IN ALL THESE SUBJECTS AND MY FATHER REALLY WANTS ME TO TAKE THE BUSINESS CLASSES.

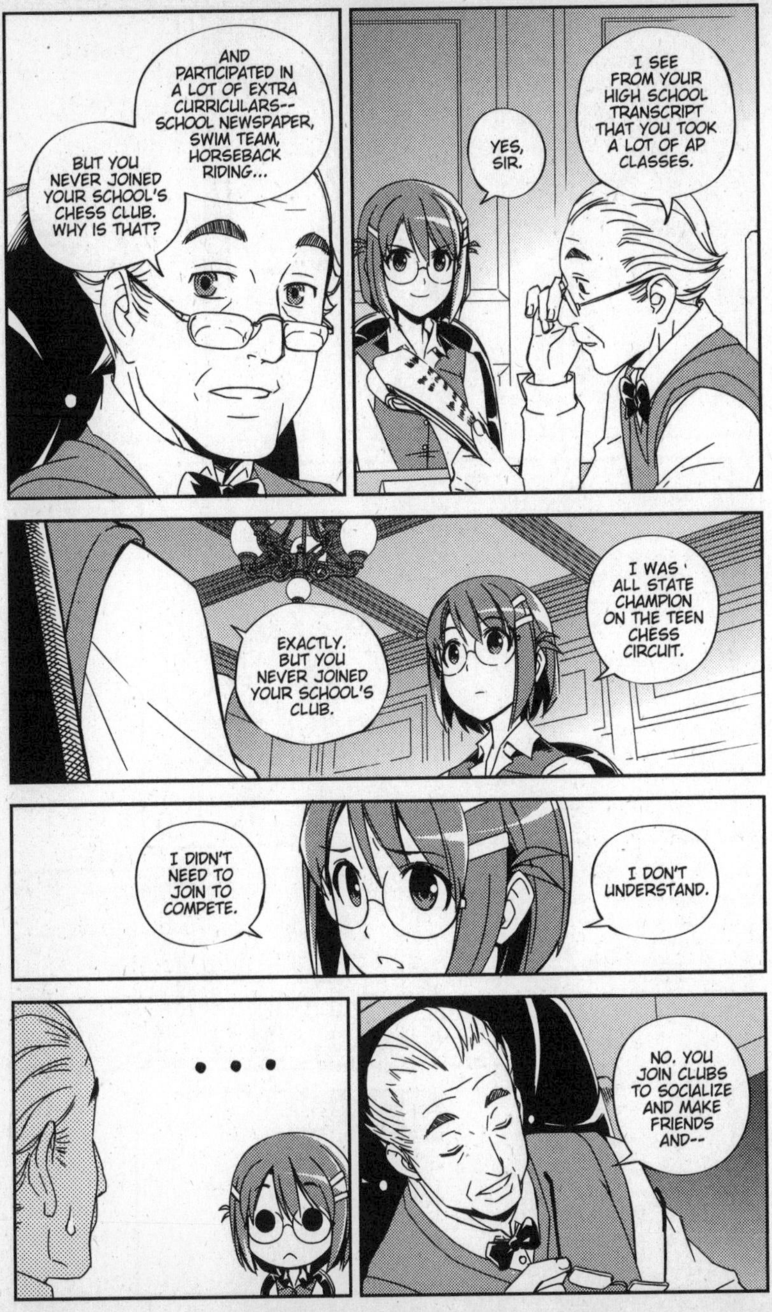
I SEE FROM YOUR HIGH SCHOOL TRANSCRIPT THAT YOU TOOK A LOT OF AP CLASSES.
YES, SIR.
AND PARTICIPATED IN A LOT OF EXTRA CURRICULARS--SCHOOL NEWSPAPER, SWIM TEAM, HORSEBACK RIDING...
BUT YOU NEVER JOINED YOUR SCHOOL'S CHESS CLUB. WHY IS THAT?
I WAS ALL STATE CHAMPION ON THE TEEN CHESS CIRCUIT.
EXACTLY. BUT YOU NEVER JOINED YOUR SCHOOL'S CLUB.
I DON'T UNDERSTAND.
I DIDN'T NEED TO JOIN TO COMPETE.
NO. YOU JOIN CLUBS TO SOCIALIZE AND MAKE FRIENDS AND--
• • •

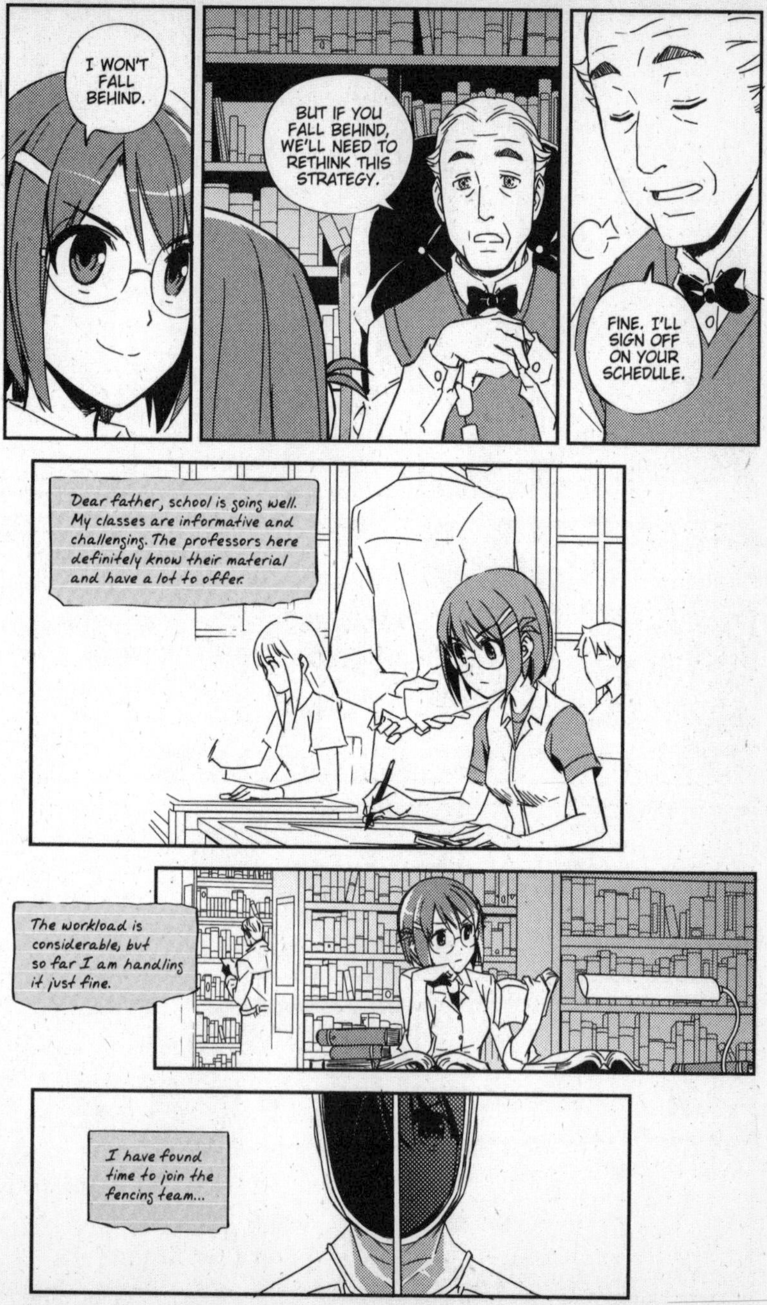
FINE. I'LL SIGN OFF ON YOUR SCHEDULE.
BUT IF YOU FALL BEHIND, WE'LL NEED TO RETHINK THIS STRATEGY.
I WON'T FALL BEHIND.
Dear father, school is going well. My classes are informative and challenging. The professors here definitely know their material and have a lot to offer.
The workload is considerable, but so far I am handling it just fine.
I have found time to join the fencing team...

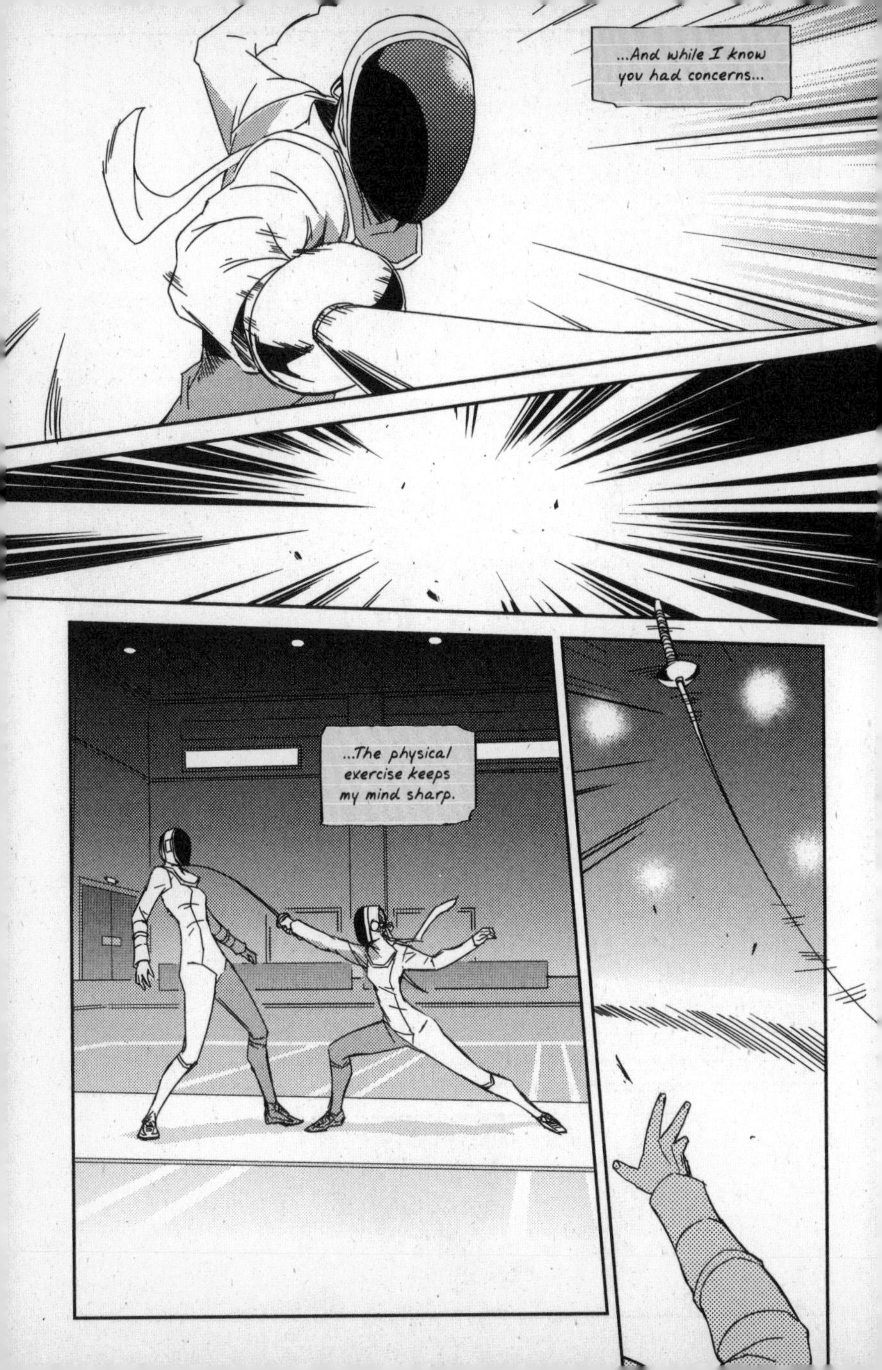
...And while I know you had concerns...
...The physical exercise keeps my mind sharp.

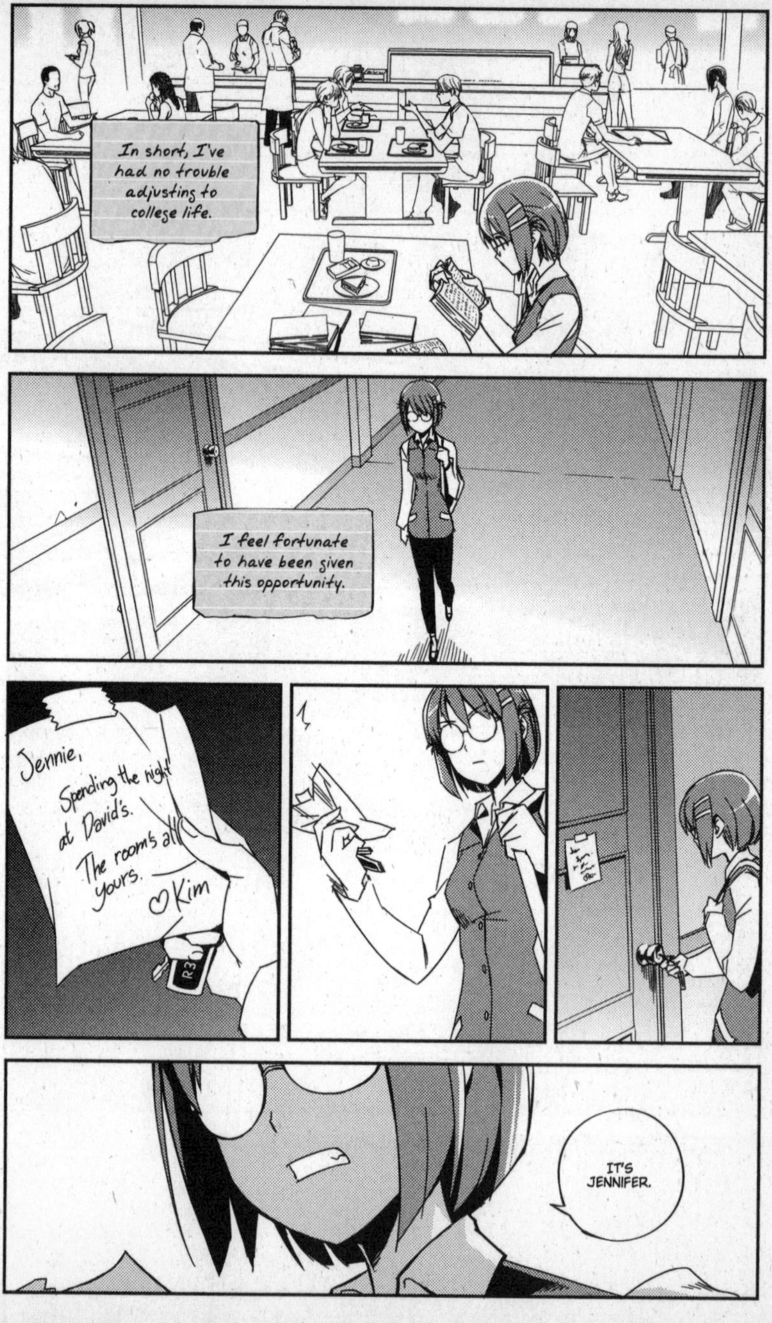
In short, I've had no trouble adjusting to college life.
I feel fortunate to have been given this opportunity.
Jennie,
Spending the night at David's.
The room's all yours.
♡Kim
IT'S JENNIFER.

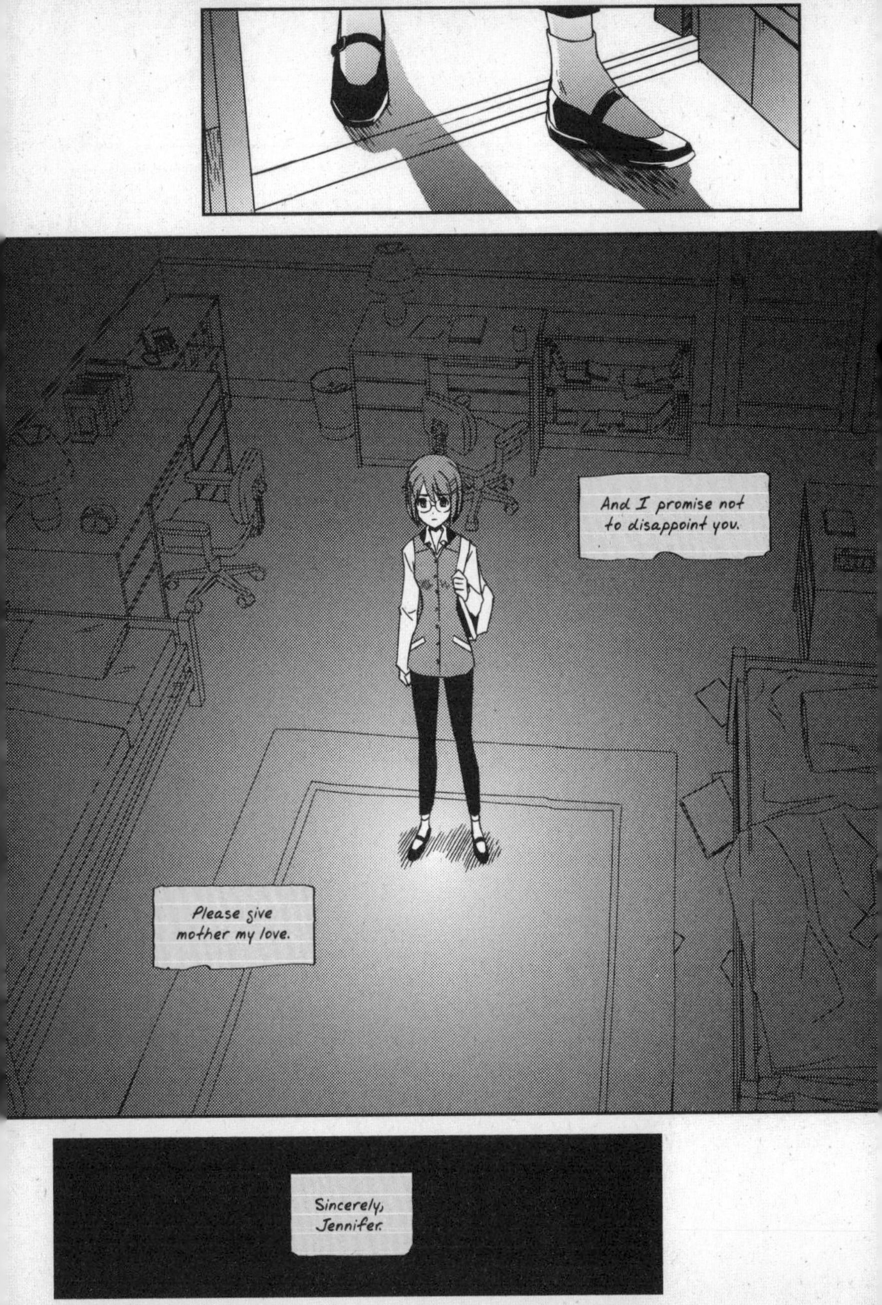
And I promise not to disappoint you.
Please give mother my love.
Sincerely, Jennifer.

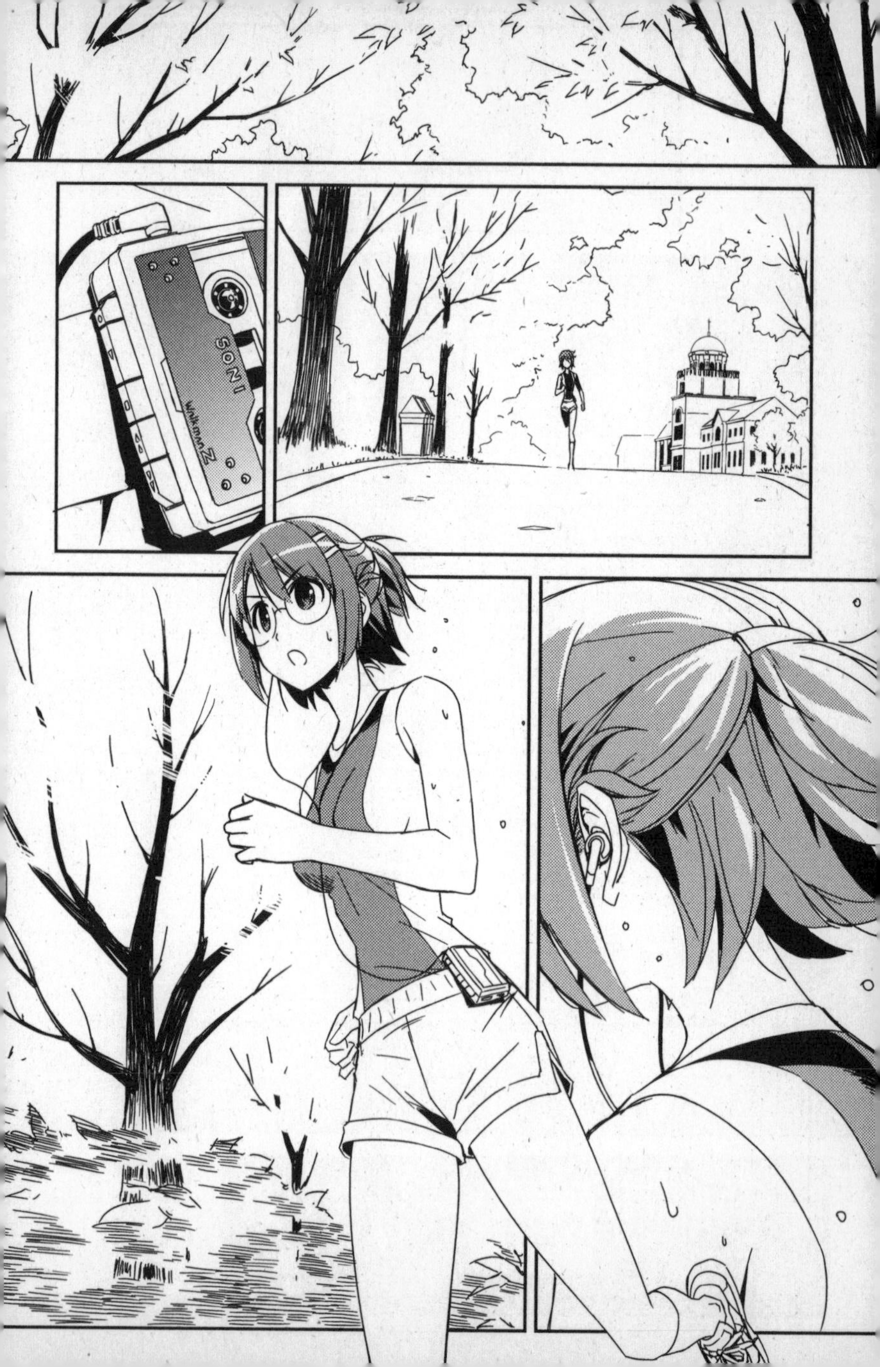
SONI
Walkman Z

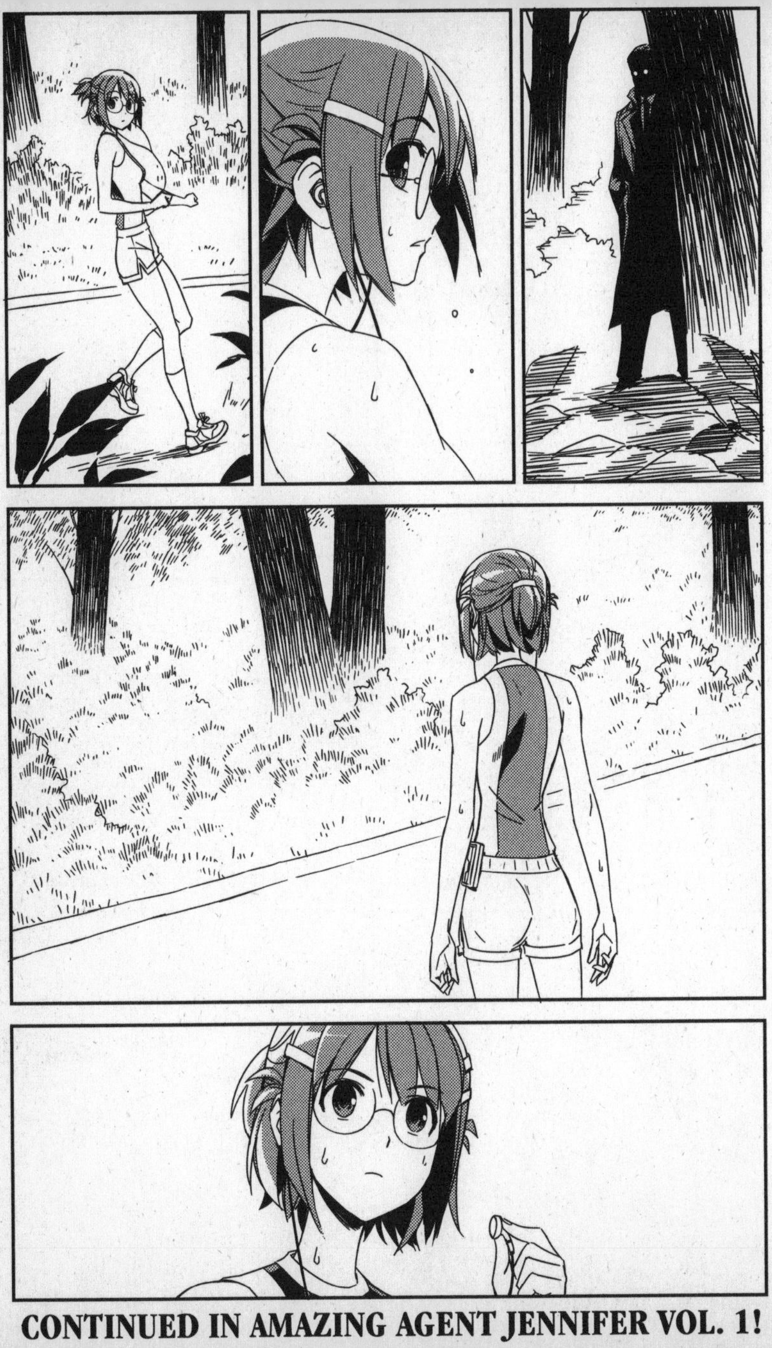

CONTINUED IN AMAZING AGENT JENNIFER VOL. 1!

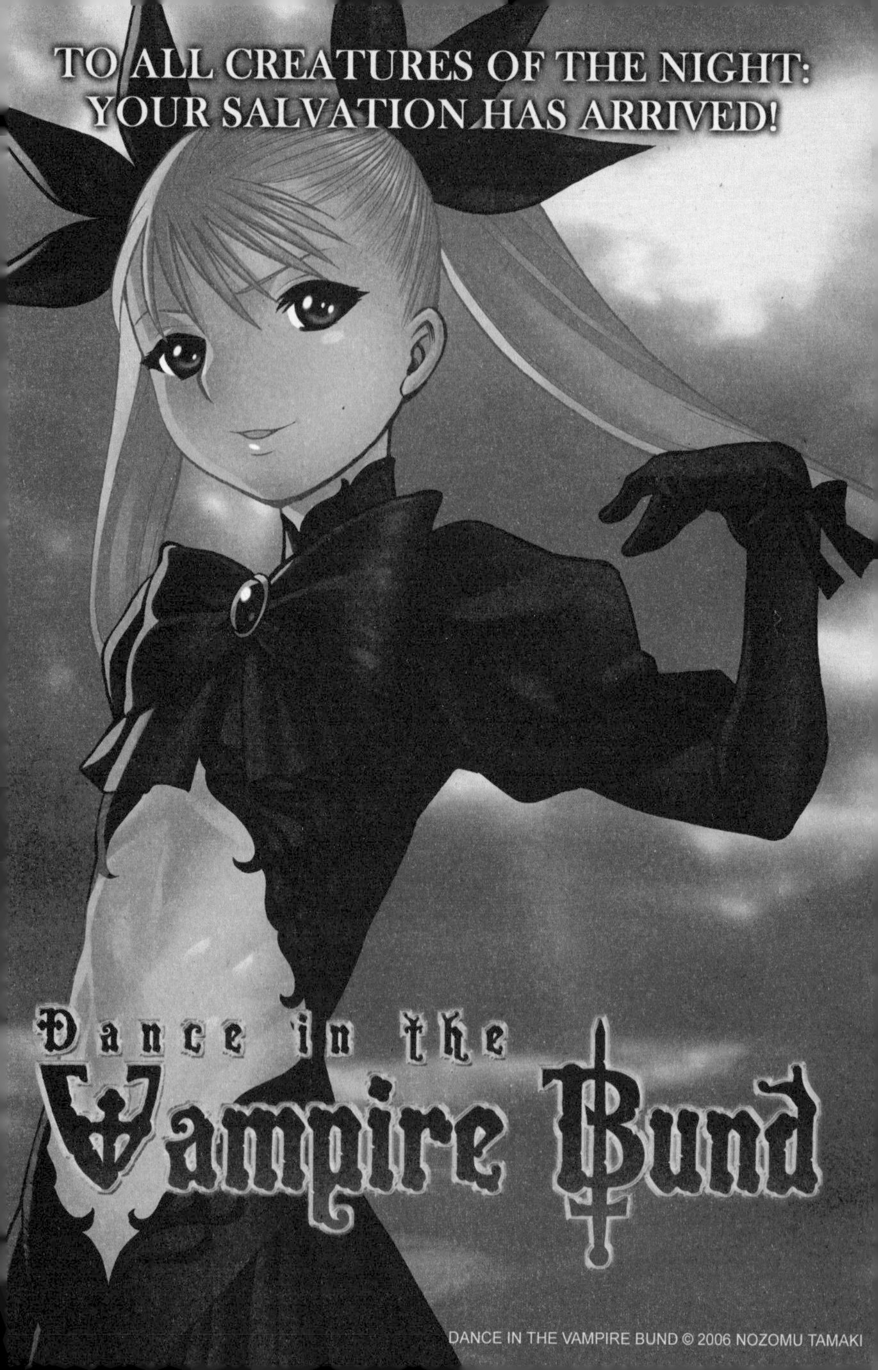
TO ALL CREATURES OF THE NIGHT:
YOUR SALVATION HAS ARRIVED!
Dance in the
Vampire Bund
DANCE IN THE VAMPIRE BUND © 2006 NOZOMU TAMAKI

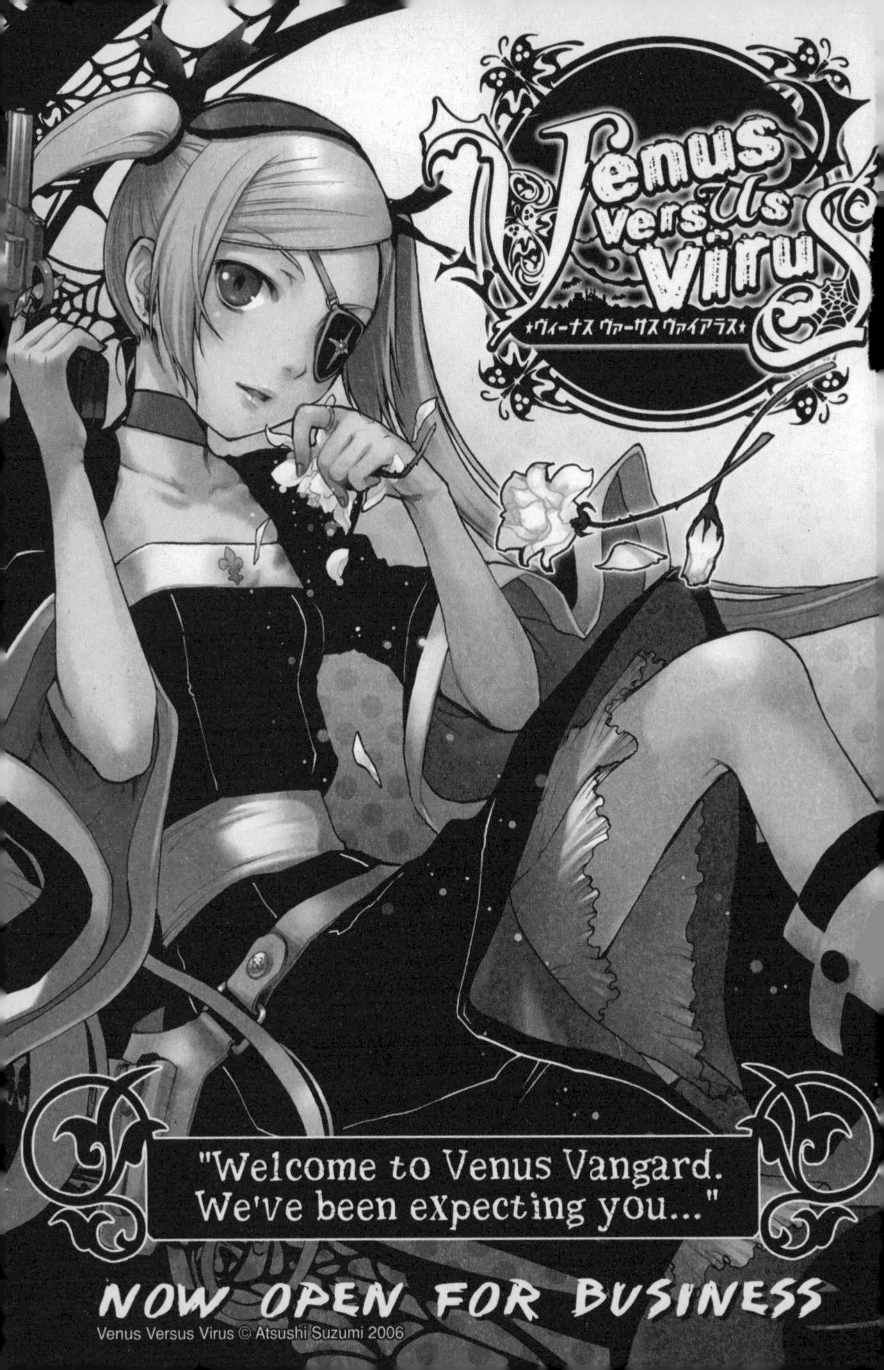
Venus Versus Virus
★ヴィーナス ヴァーサス ヴァイアラス★
"Welcome to Venus Vangard.
We've been expecting you..."
NOW OPEN FOR BUSINESS
Venus Versus Virus © Atsushi Suzumi 2006